Children in Conflict

Children in Conflict

Educational Strategies
for the Emotionally Disturbed
and Behaviorally Disordered

Third Edition

Henry R. Reinert

Allen Huang

University of Northern Colorado

Merrill, an imprint of
Macmillan Publishing Company
New York

Maxwell Macmillan Canada, Inc.
Toronto

Maxwell Macmillan International Publishing Group
New York   Oxford   Singapore   Sydney

To   *Mary Ann, Brennan, Bernadette, Kennan, Kimberly, Becky, and Kristy.*

H.R.R.

Lily Wenli, Leesa, and Janice.

A.M.H.

Cover Photo: Jim Whitmer

Photo Credits: All photos copyrighted by individuals or companies listed. Merrill Publishing/photographs by Lloyd Lemmerman, p. 101; Jean Greenwald, p. 139; and Ben Chandler, p. 213; p. 237. Marjorie McEachron/Cuyahoga County Board of Mental Retardation, p. 39. Gale Zucker, p. 181. All other photographs by Èric W. Blackhurst.

This book was set in Caledonia and Univers.

Administrative Editor: Vicki Knight
Production Coordinator: Carol Sykes
Cover Designer: Cathy Watterson

Library of Congress Catalog Card Number: 87-60451
International Standard Book Number: 0-675-20740-1
Printed in the United States of America
  2 3 4 5 6 7 8 9—92 93 94 95

Macmillan Publishing Company
866 Third Avenue, New York, New York 10022

Macmillan Publishing Company is part of
the Maxwell Communication Group of Companies.

Maxwell Macmillan Canada, Inc.
1200 Eglinton Avenue East, Suite 200
Don Mills, Ontario M3C 3N1

Preface

This book, like the two previous editions, is about children and youth with emotional and behavioral disorders. It is teacher and education directed, designed to translate psychological information into useful educational strategies for the classroom practitioner. A major highlight of this edition is that no single strategy is emphasized. Rather, all of the major educational interventions for the emotionally disturbed are reviewed and their strengths and weaknesses identified. This allows the teacher to understand the various theoretical approaches and to select the most viable alternative(s) to meet the educational needs of each student. As such, this text allows the student to develop a broad perspective of emotional disturbance from a single, easily read text.

The book opens with a review of the field of emotional disturbance and develops the rationale for the use of the concept of *children in conflict*. The succeeding five chapters review different theoretical approaches to understanding and teaching children in conflict. These chapters highlight the definition of emotional disturbance according to each approach, the basic theory, screening and evaluation procedures, classroom application, current status of the approach, and vignettes of applications.

Chapter 7 presents a synthesis of approaches and classroom application. Chapter 8 is a new component of this edition, featuring the emotionally disturbed adolescent. Chapter 9 outlines the various roles of change agents in the schools, and chapter 10 expands the previous coverage of materials for use with emotionally disturbed children. The future of teaching the emotionally disturbed is covered in chapter 11.

Three major changes have been made in the third edition of this text, in addition to updating research: (1) a unique section on computer use in the classroom, (2) significant additions to the chapter on adolescents, and (3) embellishment of the chapter on test instruments and materials.

Several of these changes were made in response to users of the text. We thank those who responded to our inquiries or who volunteered suggestions. We are indebted to William R. Rhodes and Michael Tracy, whose seminar on the Conceptual Project for Child Variance stimulated our conceptualization and organization of this text. We are also grateful to our colleagues, who have helped us grow in the understanding of children in conflict. Special thanks go to Ron Steward and Eric Blackhurst, who did some of the photography for this edition.

Our warmest gratitude goes to our wives, Mary Ann and Lily, who gave freely of their time and tolerated long absences in the library to enable us to complete this edition.

Special thanks to Lorae Blum, who typed and reviewed this edition, and to Kathy L. Ruhl, Pennsylvania State University, Marion S. Boss, University of Toledo, and Melvyn Reich, Central Connecticut University, who reviewed the manuscript and provided us with constructive suggestions for improving it.

Contents

1

Emotional Disturbance: An Overview

INTRODUCTION

The education of emotionally disturbed children and youth continues to be in a state of change. This change is not the rapid, programmatic growth experienced in the 1970s, but a consolidation of that growth into efficient and effective programs. Although this consolidation is taking place in all programs for the handicapped, programs for the emotionally disturbed are under particular stress since there are so many diverse groups interested in their eventual configuration of service. A few of these interested groups include social services, medicine, mental health, and the legal system. This scrutiny should help our programs become better able to meet the diverse needs emotionally disturbed children exhibit.

Our charge for the 1990s is quality. New studies point to the need for qualitative change in education, and educational programs for the disturbed are included in this challenge. In order to meet these demands, we must become better prepared academically and able to accept closer scrutiny from those who evaluate public education.

This chapter will (a) familiarize you with the concept of emotional disturbance and its many definitions; (b) help you establish a personal construct for deviance that is tolerant of the various perceptions of the term *emotional disturbance;* (c) identify historical landmarks and their effects on the education of children in conflict; and (d) interpret the legal implication of legislative and court actions as they relate to children, parents, teachers, and school administrative responsibility.

Special programs for the emotionally disturbed became a reality in public schools because of an interesting combination of forces. These include the social unrest of the 1960s, the testing of individual rights in the judicial system, the rise in concern for individual rights, an emphasis on the "whole" child, and, most dramatically, the concern of influential political figures.

The first politician to speak out publicly on the problems facing the handicapped was John F. Kennedy. On February 5, 1963, he announced:

I have sent to the Congress today a series of proposals to help fight mental illness and mental retardation. These two afflictions have long been neglected. They occur more frequently, affect more people, require more prolonged treatment, and cause more individual and family suffering than any other condition in American life.

It has been tolerated too long. It has troubled our national conscience, but only as a problem unpleasant to mention, easy to postpone, and despairing of solution. The time has come for a great national effort. New medical, scientific, and social tools and insights are now available. (*Public Papers of the President of the United States*, 1963, p. 137)

The president was successful in securing a bill, Public Law 88–164, that included broad benefits for the handicapped. In addition to other provisions, this law was aimed at increasing the number of professional persons available to work with the handicapped, seriously emotionally disturbed, crippled, and other health-impaired individuals (Martin, 1968). Kennedy, who had done so much to awaken America's conscience to the educational needs of handicapped children, died tragically at the hand of an assassin who, as a child, was labeled "an emotionally, quite disturbed youngster" (President's Commission on the Assassination of President Kennedy, 1964, p. 10).

The signing of Public Law 88–164 climaxed the efforts of dedicated professional and political leaders of the previous decade; additional legislative breakthroughs would follow. Kennedy's bill was the catalyst for future growth, a foundation on which subsequent educational programs were built. In

1975 President Gerald Ford signed Public Law 94–142 (Education for All Handicapped Children Act of 1975), which mandated a free, appropriate public education for all handicapped children. This law (to be reviewed later) has provided a continuing emphasis on programs for emotionally disturbed children.

Educators have come a long way in building programs that were only dreams in the late 1950s and early 1960s, but many problems remain unsolved. How do educators best address themselves to problems concerning emotionally disturbed children? What is the correct position for the school to take? Where do educators go from here in their efforts to support mental health and a more productive future for all children? And, finally, how will specialized programs survive in an era of extreme pressure for academic efficiency? These and other issues will be discussed in this text beginning with the problem of defining *emotional disturbance*.

DEFINING EMOTIONAL DISTURBANCE

The term *emotionally disturbed* crept into the literature some eighty years ago without being defined (Reinert, 1972). Since then, it has served a variety of needs for teachers, physicians, psychologists, and others interested in children's emotional problems but has no universally accepted definition.

Over the past two decades numerous definitions have been proposed to describe the emotionally disturbed. These have varied according to the purpose for which the definition was offered. As Rhodes and Paul (1978) state so precisely:

Each time a group of special children gain social and professional attention, a plethora of definitions of the problems of those children follow. The inconstancy is not, as is typically thought, simply in the definitions, but rather in the primary view of the world from which the definition is derived. (p. 137)

Public school programs are currently affected by the definition originally proposed by Bower (1969), as outlined by Public Law 94–142. This definition proposed that serious emotional disturbance is a condition that occurs over a long period of time, to a marked degree, and that adversely affects the educational performance of the child. This definition does not include socially maladjusted children who are not emotionally disturbed. One or more of the following characteristics is needed for the child to be labeled *emotionally disturbed:*

1. An inability to learn that cannot be explained by intellectual, sensory, or health factors.
2. An inability to build or maintain satisfactory interpersonal relationships with peers and teachers.
3. Inappropriate behaviors or feelings under normal conditions.
4. A pervasive mood of unhappiness or depression.
5. A tendency to develop physical symptoms, pains, or fears associated with personal or school problems.

Notice that this holistic interpretation does not support any one approach to the education of disturbed children. Its specifics, purposely vague, suggest that a scientific and measureable definition, appropriate to all situations, does not exist. On the other hand, Bower's definition does offer guidance to the practitioner and structure from which to identify children experiencing severe emotional conflict.

No wonder a precise definition of emotional disturbance is difficult to develop. The term has become the property of the public forum and is discussed widely in popular magazines, films, and television documentaries. Newsstand articles proclaim every imaginable point of view—from the claim that our whole society is sick to the belief that mental illness is nonexistent; from the suggestion that psychiatry is a hoax to the possibility that dramatic psychiatric breakthroughs are imminent (Rhodes & Paul, 1978).

In addition to Bower's definition as expressed in Public Law 94–142, there are several contrasting definitions of emotional disturbance and behavioral disorders, which include the following:

1. Emotionally disturbed children may exhibit a multitude of deviant behaviors. Some children are overly aggressive, others are withdrawn. Whatever the behavior, it tends to create discomfort in the people around them, particularly adults. Emotionally disturbed children tend to have difficulty getting along with others. They often exhibit behavior that does not match the situation they find themselves in. The problem appears to be multifaceted. It may involve (a) the inability to identify quickly and correctly the environmental expectations being placed on the child; (b) not knowing what behaviors are appropriate to respond successfully to a situation and to people's expectations; (c) a timing problem in which the child's response is delayed to the extent that when it is given, the situation has changed to the degree that the response is no longer appropriate; (d) knowing the appropriate response to an expectation, but deliberately choosing an inappropriate response to elicit a desired positive or negative response from the environment; and (e) having learned or been taught an inappropriate response to a given situation. Regardless of how the disturbed behavior manifests itself, it reflects the stress felt be the emotionally disturbed child, which is generally felt by everyone around him or her (McDowell, 1982, p. 2).
2. *Behavioral disabilities* are defined as a variety of excessive, chronic, deviant behaviors ranging from impulsive and aggressive to depressive and withdrawal acts which (a) violate the perceiver's expectations of appropriateness and (b) the perceiver wishes to be stopped (Graubard, 1973, p. 246).
3. A behavior deviation is that behavior of a child which (a) has a detrimental effect on his development and adjustment, and/or (b) interferes with the lives of other people (Kirk, 1972, p. 330).
4. One, who because of organic and/or environmental influences, chronically displays (a) inability to learn at a rate commensurate with his intellectual, sensory-motor and physical development; (b) inability to establish and maintain adequate social relationships; (c) inability to respond appropriately in day-to-day life situations; and (d) a variety of excessive behavior ranging from hyperactive, impulsive responses to depression and withdrawal (Haring, 1963, p. 291).
5. The child who cannot or will not adjust to the socially acceptable norms for behavior and, consequently, disrupts his own academic progress, the learning efforts of his classmates, and interpersonal relations (Woody, 1969, p. 7).

These five definitions demonstrate how broad the concept has become. As so defined, what is the likelihood of the occurrence of emotional problems? While most states typically use incidence figures between 1 and 2 percent, there are studies that indicate a much wider disparity. Hobbs (1982) studied the incidence figures of the emotionally disturbed and found estimates that range from 2 to 15 percent.

As if this weren't enough confusion, various terms are used to describe deviance. A partial listing representing a variety of viewpoints, follows.

asocial—Without apparent social values.
autistic—Exhibiting severe withdrawal from reality.
behavior problem—Any of the more severe behavior deviations.
character disorder—Suffering from flaws in personal behavior.

crazy—Acting in a very unusual fashion.

delinquent—A youth exhibiting behavior that is in violation of the law.

disruptive—Causing disorder, usually aggressively, that interferes with others.

emotionally disturbed—Deviating from or interfering with normal emotional processes.

learning problem—Any one of many behaviors that interferes with acquisition of knowledge.

nervous—Excessively anxious.

neurotic—Suffering from anxiety, fears, obsessions, and unusual behavior.

personality disorder—Personality trait that interferes with social adjustment.

psychopathic—Exhibiting lack of feeling that allows social deviance without guilt.

psychotic—Exhibiting extreme denial of reality through behavior.

schizophrenic—Suffering from severely disorganized behavior.

sick—Mentally ill.

socially maladjusted—Deviating from accepted norms of behavior.

sociopathic—Badly adjusted in regard to social relationships.

spoiled—Excessively indulged.

uninhibited—Acting without normal cautions.

unsocialized—Lacking in social skills.

withdrawn or overinhibited—Restricted in behavior.

CHILDREN IN CONFLICT—
A WORKING DEFINITION

Some terms are common to our language and do not represent any serious attempts by professionals to clarify the issue of defining just what is emotional disturbance (e.g., *crazy*, *disruptive*, and *spoiled*). Others (e.g., *autistic*, *psychotic*, and *schizophrenic*) represent thoughtful attempts by professionals to delineate significant types of serious disorders, but ones that are seldom encountered by the regular classroom teacher. Still others are examples of behaviors that occur frequently in the classroom.

Many teachers have begun to disregard the use of labels like *emotional disturbance* when referring to behavior problems in the classroom. The emerging pattern in special education programs is to abandon terms borrowed from other professions in favor of educationally related terms like *behavioral disabilities* (Hobbs, 1982; Graubard, 1973; Kerr & Nelson, 1983). But we believe that *behaviorally disordered* fails to describe these children adequately because it implies deficiency. The truth is that many children have daily problems not because of themselves but because of the situations in which they find themselves. For example, a child whose mother has died recently may experience a serious problem that manifests itself in unusual behaviors that require professional attention. This child, although showing behavior problems, cannot really be labeled *behaviorally disordered*.

Thus throughout this text, labeling children *emotionally disturbed*, *behaviorally disordered*, or *mentally ill* will generally be avoided. We prefer the more general term *children in conflict*, which offers several advantages for children.

1. The sometimes traumatic impact of a term such as *emotional disturbance* can be reduced significantly for both children and their parents.

2. Self-fulfilling prophecy can be minimized.

3. It more accurately describes the broad range of children being served.

4. The mystique surrounding mental illness could be diminished.

For the purposes of this text, then, *children in conflict* are defined as youngsters whose behavior has a deleterious effect on their personal or educational development and/or that of their peers. Negative effects may vary considerably from one child to another in terms of severity and prognosis.

Many writers have tried to specify the deviant emotional behaviors typically found in the classroom (Bower, 1960, 1982; Cullinan, Epstein, & Lloyd, 1983; Dunn, 1973; Hobbs, 1982; Kauffman, 1981; Maes, 1966; McDowell, Adamson, & Wood, 1982; Pate, 1963; Quay, Morse, & Cutler, 1966; Rhodes & Paul, 1978; Walker, 1970; Wood, 1982). From their efforts and our own experiences, a list of four categories of behaviors can be proposed:

1. acting-out (hitting, being aggressive and disruptive)
2. withdrawn (silence, thumb-sucking, acting restricted)
3. defensive (lying, cheating, avoiding tasks)
4. disorganized (out of touch with reality)

A child may exhibit combinations of these behaviors. For example, a child may hit another child. When questioned by the teacher, he may lie or withdraw into a shell of self-pity. The variety of behaviors exhibited is confusing. To be sure, classifying behaviors into meaningful systems simplifies the behavior and increases our understanding and effectiveness in coping with it. But classification will not, in itself, bring about a change in the child's behavior; it will only help the teacher identify the deviance and develop an educational plan.

All of these behaviors should be viewed in terms of severity of the problem. Delineation of severity allows schools to separate children in ways that will facilitate the achievement of the needs of each individual. Kelly, Bullock, and Dykes (1974) outlined three broad programs, or service categories, using the following classifications:

1. *Mild behavioral disorders* Children or youth with behavioral disorders who can be helped adequately by the regular classroom teacher and/or other school resource personnel through periodic counseling and/or short-term individual attention and instruction
2. *Moderate behavioral disorders* Children or youth with behavioral disorders who can remain at their assigned school but require intensive help from one or more specialists (i.e., mental health clinics, diagnostic centers, and resource rooms)
3. *Severe behavioral disorders* Children or youth with behavioral disorders who require assignment to a special class or special school (p. 10).

The impact of these three service categories will be discussed more fully in Chapter 3. For now, we will merely outline the programs and relate them briefly to children in conflict.

Marmor and Pumpian-Mindlin (1950) outline the relationship that exists between the adjustive resources of an individual and the degree of stress under which he or she lives in Figure 1–1.

1. Most children are in the *mental health* portion of the diagram, whereas only a small portion of the total population falls into the *severe* category.
2. Each child's problems are a composite of stress and adjustive resources. For example, a child can have good mental health but be living with moderate to severe stress. Similarly, a child with only mild stress may have a moderate to severe problem because of poor adjustive resources.
3. Our mental health is a living interaction that changes with our adjustive resources and stress.

Prevalence/Incidence

While the concepts of prevalence and incidence are individual and unique, they are sometimes used interchangeably, as they will be in this discussion. **Prevalence** means

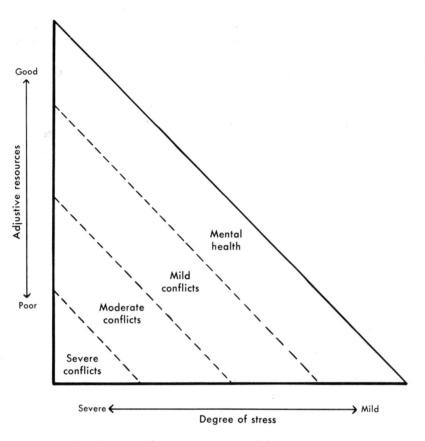

FIGURE 1–1. Relationship between adjustive resources and degree of stress.

the number of occurrences of a behavior, per 100 individuals, during a given period of time. **Incidence** means the number of new cases of a certain problem during a specific period of time. The prevalence of emotional disturbance varies considerably from one study to another, depending on (1) the agency or individual making the prediction; (2) the definition used in the study; (3) the reason for estimating the population; and (4) the instrument used in evaluating deviance.

The U.S. Office of Education estimates that 2% of children of school age are emotionally disturbed (1979). Kirk (1972), in a review of several studies of emotional disturbance, reports estimates ranging from 2% to 22%. Kelly and coworkers (1977) report a mean percentage of 20.4 exhibiting behavior disorders to a mild, moderate, or severe degree. Studies that suggest that up to 20% of the population are emotionally disturbed should be viewed with extreme caution since prevalence figures depend so heavily on the population from which the study was taken (Cullinan, Epstein, & Lloyd, 1983). Even more drastic prevalence figures are reported by Glidewell and Swallow (1968). They report between 2% and 69.3% of children to be maladjusted. Bower (1960) is one of the most frequently cited authors regarding the incidence of emotional handicaps; he suggests that 10% of the school-age population is in need of some measure of professional assistance during the years in school. Bower (1960) says that fewer than 1% of the school population require intensive intervention programs, however. The U.S. Department of Education reports that 362,073 students or approximately 8.4% of the total of 4,341,399 handicapped school-age children on the implementation of Public Law 94–142 are seriously emotionally disturbed (1985).

EMOTIONAL DISTURBANCE: AN OVERVIEW

Although studies of prevalence do not agree as to the specific number of disturbed children, they generally show that the number of children in conflict is high. Boys who are identified as having emotional problems generally outnumber girls with such problems by about 6 or 7 to 1, and sometimes outnumber girls in special class placement by 9 or 10 to 1. This is generally attributed to the aggressive types of behaviors that boys exhibit, whereas girls often exhibit withdrawing behaviors that are more acceptable in classrooms.

Recent studies point to the fact that certain minority populations also exceed expected incidence figures. Kelly and coworkers (1977) report that approximately two black students for every white student were identified as having behavior disorders in kindergarten through grade 7. Between grades 7 and 12, differences between black and white youngsters were minimal.

Regardless of which studies of prevalence are reported, it is obvious that more children need service than is currently being supplied. It is also apparent that the task of judging human behaviors for appropriateness and inappropriateness is a complicated and difficult one.

Background Information

It is important for teachers of children in conflict to know the history of educational practices with such children. Such knowledge offers three advantages. First, it should put today's practices into perspective with what has gone before. Second, it should enable educators to avoid many of the errors of the past and capitalize on the positive approaches that have made an impact on children in conflict. Third, understanding will serve as a springboard to provide an impetus for new learning to take place.

HISTORY OF PROGRAM DEVELOPMENT OF THE EMOTIONALLY DISTURBED

Before the 20th Century

Developing a thread that can be followed through a period of history is difficult when that thread is largely undefined, when those who have interacted with the problem are under constant change, and when a variety of labels have been used to describe the problem. For example, youngsters with emotional problems have been labeled as "behavior problems," and a host of other terms including *spoiled, psychotic, immature, hyperactive,* and *insane.* These labels reflect the social and scientific conditions that existed at the time of their development (Lewis, 1941).

Education has not been central to the lives of the emotionally disturbed until relatively recent times. In fact, there were very few meaningful educational interventions available before the mid-20th century. Kanner (1962) reports that before the 18th century there was not so much as an allusion to emotional disorders in children. Table 1–1 includes material from Kauffman (1981, pp. 57, 58) and his excellent review of the development of programs for emotionally disturbed.

Note that the history of treatment for emotionally disturbed certainly has had a

TABLE 1–1. Landmarks in Treatment of Emotional Problems

Date	Treatment
400 B.C.	Hippocrates proposed that emotional disturbance was the result of natural causes, rather than supernatural powers.
375 B.C.	Plato postulated that mentally disturbed persons who committed criminal acts should not be held responsible for their deeds in the same manner as "normal persons."
330 B.C.	Alexander the Great built temples dedicated to Saturn that were excellent sanatoriums for the mentally ill patients and made the first attempts at psychiatric classification of mental illness.
90 B.C.	Asclepiades advocated humane treatment of mentally ill patients and made the first attempts at psychiatric classification of mental illness.
100	Aretaeus described phases of mania and melancholia as expressions of the same illness.
200	Death of Galen started the "Dark Ages" of psychiatry.
1450–1700	Most difficult period in history for the mentally ill; saw their persecution; society reverted to demonology and superstition.
1750	Anecdotal writings concerning deviant children began to appear.
1799	Itard publishes his report of the wild boy of Aveyron.
1825	House of Refuge, first institution for juvenile delinquents in the United States, founded in New York; similar institutions founded in Boston (1826) and Philadelphia (1928).
1841	Dorothea Dix begins crusade for better care of the insane.
1847	State Reform School for Boys established in Westborough, Massachusetts, the first state institution for juvenile delinquents.
1850	Massachusetts incorporates school for idiotic and feebleminded youth at urging of Samuel Gridley Howe; Edward Seguin moves to the United States.
1866	Edward Seguin publishes *Idiocy and Its Treatment by the Physiological Method in America*.
1871	Ungraded class for truant, disobedient, and insubordinate children opened in New Haven, Connecticut.
1898	New York City Board of Education assumes responsibility for two schools for truant children.
1899	First U.S. juvenile court established in Chicago.
1908	Clifford Beers publishes *A Mind that Found Itself*.
1909	National Committee for Mental Hygiene founded; Ellen Key publishes *The Century of the Child*; William Healy begins the Juvenile Psychopathic Institute in Chicago.
1911	Arnold Gesell starts the Clinic for Child Development at Yale University.
1912	Congress create the U.S. Children's Bureau.
1919	Ohio passes law for state-wide education of the handicapped.
1922	Council for Exceptional Children founded.
1924	American Orthopsychiatric Association founded.
1931	First psychiatric hospital for children in the United States is founded in Rhode Island.
1935	Leo Kanner publishes *Child Psychiatry*; Loretta Bender and others begin school for psychotic children at Bellevue Psychiatric Hospital in New York City.
1943	Leo Kanner describes early infantile autism.
1944	Bruno Bettelheim opens the Orthogenic School at the University of Chicago.
1946	New York City Board of Education designates 600 schools for disturbed and maladjusted pupils; Fritz Redl and David Wineman open Pioneer House in Detroit.

TABLE 1–1 (continued)

Date	Treatment
1947	Alfred Strauss and Laura Lehtinen publish *Psychopathology and Education of the Brain-Injured Child,* based on work at Wayne County Training School in Northville, Michigan.
1953	Carl Fenichel founds the League School in Brooklyn, first private day school for severely emotionally disturbed children.
1955	Leonard Kornberg publishes *A Class for Disturbed Children,* the first book describing classroom teaching of disturbed children.
1960	Pearl Berkowitz and Esther Rothman publish *The Disturbed Child,* describing a permissive, psychoanalytic educational approach.
1961	William Cruickshank, et al., publish *A Teaching Method for Brain-Injured and Hyperactive Children,* reporting results of a structured educational program in Montgomery County, Maryland; Nicholas Hobbs and associates begin "Project Re-Ed" in Tennessee and North Carolina.
1962	Norris Haring and Lakin Phillips publish *Educating Emotionally Disturbed Children,* reporting results of a structured program in Arlington, Virginia; Eli Bower and Nadine Lambert publish *An In-School Process for Screening Emotionally Handicapped Children,* based on research in California.
1963	PL 88–164 provides federal money for support of personnel preparation in the area of emotionally disturbed.
1964	William Morse, Richard Cutler, and Albert Fink publish *Public School Classes for the Emotionally Handicapped: A Research Analysis;* Council for Children with Behavioral Disorders established as a division of Council for Exceptional Children.
1965	Nicholas Long, William Morse, and Ruth Newman publish *Conflict in the Classroom;* National Society for Autistic Children founded; First Annual Conference on the Education of Emotionally Disturbed Children held at Syracuse University.
1968	Frank Hewett publishes *The Emotionally Disturbed Child in the Classroom,* reporting the use of an engineered classroom in Santa Monica, California.
1970	William Rhodes begins Conceptual Project in Emotional Disturbance, summarizing theory, research, and intervention in the field.
1974	Association for the Severely Handicapped founded.
1975	Nicholas Hobbs publishes *Issues in the Classification of Children* and *The Futures of Children,* reporting the work of the Project on the Classification of Exceptional Children.
1978	PL 94–142 (enacted in 1975) requires free, appropriate education for all handicapped children, including the seriously emotionally disturbed.

Note. Some data from Kauffman, 1981, pp. 57, 58.

varied development. Leadership within the area has been shared at various times by philosophers, medical doctors, psychiatrists, sociologists, teachers, and, more recently, legislators.

These landmarks represent *the advances* in treatment for emotionally disturbed. Dur-

ing some periods these advances were commonplace; at other times, they are the exception, and the disturbed were treated badly. Such was the case in eras B.C.; treatment did not, generally, exist, or was negative, although there are some noteworthy examples of humanistic treatment that had positive effects on the lives of the disturbed. For example, Plato postulated that the mentally disturbed who committed crimes should not be held as accountable as "normal persons."

It appears that opinion setters before the l8th century were preoccupied with matters other than children's emotional problems. Whether this lack of attention represented a gross indifference to children with emotional problems (stemming from a lack of humanistic attitudes) or a simple setting of priorities for survival, is not known. A plausible explanation might be that children in conflict were less of a problem in agrarian society than in the more complex world after the 19th century.

Probably the worst period for the disturbed was a time known as the "Dark Ages of Psychiatry," following the death of the philosopher Galen. Not only was there a return to the practice of demonology (Despert, 1965), but also there were instances of children and youth being punished as adults for behavior disorders that were morally or socially unacceptable. The punishment sometimes included bleeding (to get rid of "bad spirits") as well as other forms of abuse and neglect (such as leaving the child exposed to the weather).

After the French and American Revolutions, the rights of the individual were seen as very important, so it naturally followed that people began to think about the needs and rights of the handicapped. Techniques and materials, however, were not immediately available to those interested in helping children in need; but the idea took shape, and people began to care and to speak up for those who would otherwise not be heard.

During the 1700s and 1800s, anecdotal writings indicated that progress was being made in the understanding of emotional problems. An example of this progress was the work of Jean Itard's *The Wild Boy of Aveyron* (1801). Also, there were writings by Benjamin Rush and William James, and a classification system developed by Emil Kraepelin.

During the eighteenth century various accounts, or case reports, of deviant children began to be published. These were generally in diary form rather than scientific studies and were written more for general informational value than for any other purpose. Kanner (l962) has translated a paragraph from a clergyman's diary that tells the story of Emerentia. The excerpt was taken from an autobiographical novel, *Der grüne Heinrich*, by Gottfried Keller, in whose village the incident took place in 1713.

This 7-year-old girl, the offspring of an aristocratic family, whose father remarried after an unhappy first matrimony, offended her "noble and god-fearing" stepmother by her peculiar behavior. Worst of all, she would not join in the prayers and was panic-stricken when taken to the black-robed preacher in the dark and gloomy chapel. She avoided contact with people by hiding in closets or running away from home. The local physician had nothing to offer beyond declaring that she might be insane. She was placed in the custody of a minister known for his rigid orthodoxy. The minister, who saw in her ways the machinations of a "baneful and infernal" power, used a number of would-be therapeutic devices. He laid her on a bench and beat her with a cat-o'nine-tails. He locked her in a dark pantry. He subjected her to a period of starvation. He clothed her in a frock of burlap. Under these circumstances, the child did not last long. She died after a few months, and everybody felt relieved. The minister was amply rewarded for his efforts by Emerentia's parents.

The late 1800s and early 1900s ushered in a new era for the emotionally disturbed. This era featured continued writings that benefited the disturbed population, such as Clifford Beers's book *A Mind That Found Itself* and social reform initiated by Dorothea Dix. This was also the era of the first juvenile court, established in the United States in Chicago.

By the middle of the 19th century, a few mental health professionals were not satisfied with simply reporting the accounts of deviant behavior—they wanted to study this behavior. In 1867 Maudsley wrote a chapter on "Insanity of Early Life," which he included in his text *Physiology and Pathology of Mind.* This work encouraged interest in children and the mental disorders that affected their lives.

In the final decades of the 19th century, several texts were written concerning various mental and psychic disorders. These texts leaned toward fatalism. The authors described the disorders as the result of heredity, degeneracy, masturbation, overwork, preoccupation with religion, intestinal parasites, or sudden changes in temperature (Kanner, 1962).

Some of the ideas held by theorists of the l9th century were preliminary attempts at the much more sophisticated science of medicine that exists today. The lack of medical technology, however, prevented these early attempts from reaching their goals.

Mental illness as a sickness based on organic brain pathology is called the *organic viewpoint* (established by Kraepelin, 1856); it represented the first great advance of modern science in the understanding and treatment of mental illness. Several theorists, including Albrecht von Haller (1708–1777) and William Griesinger (1817–1868), advocated the study of the brain as a basis of mental illness. However, Emil Kraepelin, whose textbook *Lehrbuch der Psychiatrie (Theories of Psychology)* was published in 1883, is generally credited with establishing the basis for the present psychiatric classification system, with the subsequent period in psychiatry often referred to as the "descriptive era." One of the finest hours of the organic approach came with the discovery of the syphilitic basis of general paresis (syphilis of the brain). This discovery was not accom-

plished as a shot in the dark, but became a reality only after many years of research by the most able medical scientists in the world. The medical model also achieved significant success in uncovering the organic pathological basis of toxic psychosis and certain types of mental retardation.

Early efforts to study the individual child were being made in education toward the end of the 19th century. These early writers were undoubtedly influenced by such giants as Rousseau and Pestalozzi and by the teachings of William James and John Dewey. The change from looking at the individual as one who should fit into the mold of society to one who should grow as an individual was revolutionary at the turn of the century.

Two of the earliest writings that deal with the descriptive aspects of mental diseases in children were published in Paris in the latter part of the nineteenth century. One by Paul Moreau, *La Folie chez les enfants (Madness in Children,* 1888), indicates that little was done before the 19th century to understand either mentally ill children or the phenomena that caused the mental illness (Crutcher, l943). A second early work was Marcel Manheimer's *Les Troubles mentaux de l'enfance (Childhood Mental Problems,* 1899). This text was similar to Moreau's work but was more complete. Both Moreau and Manheimer emphasized the importance of treatment. Preventive treatment was stressed for parents and teachers; for example, setting a good example, and loving and showing affection to the child.

The 20th Century

Although there were many theorists who paved the road for child psychiatry, formal attempts to study children and their unique psychiatric problems really did not begin until 1900 (Kanner, 1957). This era saw dramatic changes for the child in need of special help for emotional problems. In 1900 Ellen

Key, a Swedish sociologist, made her often-quoted announcement that the 20th century would become "the century of the child." The diaries written by Darwin, Pestalozzi, and others cleared the way for a new science called "developmental" psychology.

Biogenetic theorists believed that the pathological bases of mental illness would soon be as easily defined and the course of such illness as predictable as measles. The basis for their optimistic predictions originated during the 18th century when medical science was slowly discovering some of the causes of problems in physical health. It was only natural that proponents of this system would quickly develop confidence that medical science was about to solve many of the questions related to mental illness. Unfortunately, this has not proved to be true, since more than one half of the patients studied during this period failed to show any organic pathology (Coleman, 1964).

Early in the 20th century the organic viewpoint lost some of its earlier popularity as a new psychological viewpoint began to take hold. Some advocating the medical model, however, were not ready to capitulate. The discovery of phenylketonuria (PKU) in 1934 did show that there were organic causes; this metabolic disorder is found in infants who are void of an enzyme that is needed, and is directly related to mental retardation, (Coleman, 1964). New life was breathed into the organic movement.

The development of testing instruments for children paralleled medical advances of the 20th century. Among these advances were formalized psychological testing, including the initial work done by Alfred Binet and Theodore Simon on intelligence scales. Their test first appeared in print in 1905 and was later revised into what is now called the Stanford-Binet Individual Intelligence Test. The Stanford-Binet Test (1973) and, later, the Wechsler Intelligence Scale for Children (WISC) (1949, revised 1974) were to have a dramatic impact on the evaluation of children in conflict. These two instruments continue to provide valuable information to clinicians who must differentiate between children who are mentally retarded and those who are mentally ill.

After the development of individual intelligence tests came tests to measure certain personality variables. The study of a person's "inner life" has become known as *projective testing*. The best known of the projective techniques is undoubtedly the Rorschach, developed by the Swiss psychiatrist Hermann Rorschach. This test, first described in 1921, attempts to predict from the subject's associations to inkblots how he or she will react to others in the environment in specific and more complex situations (Anastasi, 1968).

Sociological thought was a part of both medical theory and test development at the turn of the 20th century. Through vigorous research of professionals in sociology and anthropology, evidence began to accumulate that suggested a relationship between sociocultural factors and mental illness (Becker, 1963; Benedict, 1934). Crucial factors included the importance of the child's home and community, the values of society, and the technology of the world in which a child lives. These sociocultural findings began to permeate psychology and psychiatry, giving these two disciplines a more socially oriented appearance, as illustrated in the work of psychiatrists Alfred Adler, Karen Horney, Harry Stack Sullivan, and Erich Fromm. It was a great step forward for children in conflict that parents, siblings, peers, and significant others were now included in the study of childhood deviance. Organic, psychological, and sociological viewpoints became fused into a holistic approach (Rhodes & Sagor, 1974).

An outgrowth of biological science is

today's emphasis on ecological theory. Proponents of this theory point out that children are not only affected by their environment, as suggested in sociological theory, but they in turn modify the environment into which they enter.

Twentieth century educational thought was molded, to a great extent, by psychodynamic thought. When special education programs were initiated, they often followed an analytical or introspective bent. In 1907 the Public Education Association in New York City employed several workers, called "visiting teachers," who had a combined knowledge of social work and classroom teaching (Krugman, 1948). This concept began with little recognition or success. But with the growth of the mental hygiene movement of the 1920s, the program began to develop some stature in educational and psychological circles. In 1921 there were approximately 90 visiting teachers in 13 states; by 1927 there were more than 200. After World War II the increase in visiting teachers paralleled other educational growth; almost every community of any size had one or more visiting teachers employed. This program stimulated interest in special education techniques, individual diagnostics, and prescriptive educational programming. The two have become mutually supportive, since many teachers working as visiting teachers received some or all of their training in special education. Working with psychologists and psychiatrists (either through direct consultation or as a referring agent), the visiting teacher promoted trust and cooperation between professional mental health workers and the school (Nudd, 1925).

In a discussion such as this is cannot be overlooked that Sigmund Freud (1856–1939) has made a dramatic impact on the study of the human personality. The study of the emotions of children in conflict would be considerably different if it were not for his pioneer work.

Middle 20th Century

During the 1940s, two antithetical trends began to develop. One group of theorists favored the preKraepelinian period of "indefiniteness" in labeling. For example, Rank (1949) introduced the idea of the *atypical* child with determined disregard for a precise meaning of *atypical*. Rank's system allowed no difference between childhood psychosis, mental retardation, or any other form of childhood disturbance. As Szurek (1956) adequately states:

We are beginning to consider it clinically fruitless, and even unnecessary . . . to draw any sharp dividing lines between a condition that one could consider psychoneurotic and another that one could call psychosis, autism, atypical development, or schizophrenia. (p. 522)

In contrast, some theorists who thought differences in etiology did exist maintained that these differences had direct implications for treatment. Kanner (1949) graphically outlines early infantile autism; Mahler (1952) describes symbiotic infantile psychosis; and Bergman and Escalona (1949) discuss children with unusual sensitivity to sensory stimulation. About this same time Bender (1955) was observing children with retarded and otherwise irregular development. Seeing that schizophrenic children exhibited specific behaviors, she began to classify the condition into specific clinical types.

As Kanner (1962) effectively points out, the field had occupied itself almost exclusively with psychosis in early childhood or, more specifically, with schizophrenia. While that is true in regards to the fields of medical and psychodynamic thought, one must also realize that behavioral theory was getting a strong hold in education during the late

1950s. Behaviorism was really not new, but that is when it impacted on schools. Prior to that time data concerning mental processes was obtained by the introspective, or *projective*, method.

In contrast, by applying to human subjects, the conditioning techniques developed by Pavlov, Watson (Watson & Raynor, 1920) showed that children's behavior could be conditioned. Importantly, Raynor's work advanced a radically new idea in opposition to the German tradition of psychoanalysis (Hill, 1963). His first formal statement was *Psychology—From the standpoint of a behaviorist* (Watson, 1929). The American psychological revolution was on.

Watson's theory had greater impact on programming for children in conflict than any other idea of our time (Woody, 1969). Professionals were stimulated by his pioneer work and came to new levels of understanding. The principles of contingency and reinforcement eventually led to classroom application, often with children in conflict.

Much recent criticism has been aimed at various policies, many of which have their background in the history just discussed: labeling, grading, "special" segregation, categorization by grades, leadership of schools, use of intelligence as a descriptive tool, and role of teacher training institutions in the educational system (Tracy, 1972).

Obviously, then, the study of children in conflict has been anything but a logical, uninterrupted, well-directed attack on childhood deviance. Clearly at no time has the term *emotional disturbance*, although intended to be a specific, descriptive term, been used with any measure of precision.

In the 1970s we focused our attention on the wholeness of children more than at any time in our history. This concept, along with children's rights, an advanced knowledge base for education and psychology, and co-operative programming between health care professionals has brought a new era in educational programming.

Rhodes and Paul (1978) point out that our concern for the "least restrictive" alternative has allowed new methodological and philosophical directions to be discovered. In order to teach the disturbed child with his or her peers we have had to look closely at the theoretical constructs that are effective with wide ranges of behavior.

We are in a time of new awareness of the value of all people, no matter color or handicap. Schools now strive to educate all those who are exceptional, not just those who are exceptionally capable.

What of the trends for the future? Undoubtedly Public Law 94–142 will be continually challenged by administrators and legislators who would prefer a less forceful law. On the positive side, computerized education may have considerable impact on how children in conflict are helped. Also, teachers of disturbed children are becoming considerably more sophisticated. They are more wary of the panaceas that are continually offered and are beginning to select more prudently from the many techniques available.

In this century, mental illness is a concern of everyone who comes into contact with the problems it generates. As a result, there is an explosion of information and subsequent confusion about treatment. Interest not only has spread across disciplines, but also has grown within professions. Theories have been developed that include a wide array of possible interventions. As the theories proliferate, the confusion grows.

The concepts of emotional disturbance, behavior disorders, and children in conflict, then, are products of the 20th century. While these concepts have broadened the idea of mental illness, they have clouded the issue of what mental illness really is.

THE LAW AND THE EDUCATION OF CHILDREN IN CONFLICT

Not all of the reforms of education have been generated by educational institutions. Much reform has been due to social changes and subsequent legal actions. Today, handicapped people are seeking and obtaining jobs, advanced education, and personal mobility; professionals are being held accountable by them and their advocates. In a sense, special education has become a focal point for conflicts between various minority groups and a bureaucracy that often seeks to segregate, to institutionalize, and to oppress those who are different.

The civil rights marches of the 1960s and 1970s made many people aware of the rights of the individual. Gradually, the issue of individual rights moved from the streets to the legislative chambers and courts of law. This section will review those legal actions that have affected children in conflict and their teachers.

Court Cases

During recent years the courts have set the direction for the treatment of handicapped persons. The legal treatment of the maladjusted child has slowly unfolded in the school through cases involving diagnostic techniques, due process, tracking systems, and busing.

The first case of note was *Brown v. Board of Education of Topeka* (1954), in which the Supreme Court ruled it a violation of the 14th Amendment for states to require or permit segregation. Although all of the cases about children that followed were important, our discussion will concentrate on these recent decisions concerning the disturbed child:

Pennsylvania Association of Retarded Children (PARC) v. Commonwealth of Pennsylvania (1971). Due process procedures must be followed. Parents of the retarded must be notified before any changes are made in the child's educational status. Included in the parents' rights, in accordance with the 14th Amendment, are the rights to counsel, cross-examination, presentation of evidence, and the right to appeal.

Wyatt v. Stickney (1971). Institutions must provide educational programs.

Mills v. Board of Education of the District of Columbia (1971). All children previously excluded from receiving an education have a right to an education.

Lebanks v. Spears (1973). No child can be excluded from free public education by reason of a handicapping condition.

Halderman v. Pennhurst (1977). Retarded individuals have a right to an adequate habilitation, in the least restrictive conditions consistent with commitment, to be free from harm, and to have equal protection of the laws. This decision, which has many implications for institutional placements, could lead to drastic changes in institutional care.

Hendrick Hudson School District v. Rowley (Flygere, 1982). School districts are not required to provide a sign-language interpreter for the hearing impaired.

Additional recent court cases associated with legal rights of handicapped children and youth include Board v. Katherine D. (1983), Larry v. Riles (1984), and Burlington School Committee v. Commonwealth (1985). As one can readily see from the cases reviewed, handicapped persons are in many cases seeking and achieving their individual rights. Although court decisions alone cannot guarantee that all individuals will receive fair treatment, the effects will certainly help to make the lives of handicapped children more wholesome.

Federal Legislation

Following is a brief review of recent laws of profound educational impact (references for these laws are found in Table 1–2.

TABLE 1–2. Federal Laws for the Handicapped

Public Law	Title & References
83–531	Cooperative Resource Act of 1954, 20 U.S.C. 311 (1982 edition)
85–905	Deaf, Loan Service of Films Act of 1958, 42 U.S.C. 2495 (1982 edition)
85–926	Education of Mentally Retarded Children Act of 1958, 20 U.S.C. 611-617
88–164	Mental Retardation Facilities and Community Mental Health Centers Construction Act of 1963, 42 U.S.C. 292-292i
89–10	Elementary & Secondary Education Act of 1965, 20 U.S.C. 239
89–105	Mental Retardation Facilities and Community Mental Health Centers Construction Act Amendments of 1965, 20 U.S.C. 2661-2691
89–750	Elementary and Secondary Education Amendments of 1966, 20 U.S.C. 881-885
90–538	Handicapped Children's Early Education Assistance Act of 1968, 43 U.S.C. 372
91–61	National Center on Educational Media and Materials for the Handicapped, establishment. 42 U.S.C. 1396b (1969).
91–230	Elementary and Secondary Education Assistance Programs and Extension Act of 1970, 42 U.S.C. 2000d.
92–424	Economic Opportunity Amendments of 1972, 42 U.S.C. 2771
93–112	The Rehabilitation Act of 1973, 504, 29 U.S.C. 794.
93–380	Education Amendments of 1974, 20 U.S.C. 821
94–142	Education for All Handicapped Children Act of 1975, 20 U.S.C. 1401
98–199	Education of the Handicapped Act Amendments of 1983, 20 U.S.C. 1400-1433.

Public Law 83–531, The Cooperative Research Act (1954), was approved by Congress and President Eisenhower. It was designed to assist cooperative research in education. Funding for the bill began in 1957. Of the $1 million appropriated, $675,000 was earmarked for research with the mentally retarded. This law was the first Congressional recognition of a need for aid to handicapped children since the beginning of support to Gallaudet College in 1864 and the American Printing House for the Blind in 1879 (Martin, 1968).

Public Law 85–926, Training of Professional Personnel (1958), encouraged expansion of teaching of the mentally retarded. It provided grants to state agencies and institutions of higher learning, establishing a model for support to teacher trainees in special education.

Public Law 88–164, The Mental Retarda-tion Facilities and Community Mental Health Center's Construction Act (1963), was a cornerstone legislative act for handicapped children. It brought together into one unit the "captioned film" program of Public Law 85–905 (1958), an expanded teacher training program from Public Law 85–926, and a new research program in the education of handicapped children.

Public Law 88–164, Section 301, Training Professional Personnel, amended Public Law 85–926 to include a number of other handicapping conditions. Included in this legislation was funding of personnel training to teach the emotionally disturbed.

Public Law 88–164, Section 302, Research and Demonstration Projects in Education of Handicapped Children, authorized the Commissioner of Education to make grants to various state and local agencies for projects on the education of the handicapped. Public

Law 89–105 later supplemented Public Law 88–164, Section 302, by allowing funds to be used for construction, equipping, and operation of facilities for research and training research personnel.

Public Law 89–10, Assistance to Children in Disadvantaged Areas (including the handicapped) (1965), established strong federal support to education, especially for handicapped children in low-income families.

Public Law 89–105, The Community Mental Health Centers Act Amendments (1965), provided additional traineeships and fellowships from original legislation developed by the 88th Congress. Public Law 89–105 also provided additional funds for research and demonstration projects in the education of handicapped children and for construction of at least one research facility.

Public Law 89–750, Title VI, Education for Handicapped Children (1966), allowed grants to states through the Elementary and Secondary Education Act (ESEA) for handicapped children. P.L. 89–750 was particularly important because the Division of Handicapped Children and Youth had been disbanded in 1965.

Public Law 90–538, The Handicapped Children's Early Education Assistance Act (1968), was signed by President Johnson. Developed *exclusively* for the handicapped, it authorizes the Commissioner of Education, acting through the Bureau of Education for the Handicapped, to negotiate grants and contracts with both private and public agencies to establish experimental preschool and early education programs for the handicapped. Emphasis is on innovative programs, of a comprehensive nature, with potential for the young.

Public Law 91–61, National Center of Educational Media and Materials for the Handicapped (1969), was signed by President Nixon. It authorizes the Secretary of Health, Education, and Welfare to contract a university to develop, construct, and operate a national center of educational media and materials for handicapped persons.

Public Law 91–230, The Elementary and Secondary Education Act Amendments of 1969, *Title VI*, The Education of the Handicapped Act (1970), brings together current and new legislation to ensure efficient administration of the law by the Bureau of Education for the Handicapped.

Public Law 92–424, The Economic Opportunity Amendments of 1972, established that a minimum of 10% of the nation's places in Head Start programs be made available to handicapped children.

Public Law 93–380, The Education Amendments of 1974, was signed by President Ford. Its focus is on elementary and secondary programs in education. It also adds significant legislation, some of which affects handicapped children. Title VI extends and revises the Adult Education Act, The Education of the Handicapped Act, The Indian Education Act, and The Emergency School Aid Act. It requires that states locate and serve all handicapped children. The state must protect the rights of handicapped children and their parents in making educational changes; it assures an education with one's peers, as possible; and it asks that evaluation materials are racially and culturally fair.

Public Law 94–142, The Education of All Handicapped Children Act of 1975, extends Public Law 93–380 (1974). After many years of efforts by the courts and legislators, this law is very important; its scope is broad and its guidelines are specific. You are encouraged to not only read the law but also examine some enlightened reviews of what the law does and does not say. Several excellent articles have appeared in *Exceptional Children* since the passage of the legislation, such as Abeson and Zettel (1977) and Ballard and Zettel (1977 and 1978). These articles survey the law from three perspectives: (1) the rights and protections of handicapped (Ballard & Zettel, 1977), (2) the fiscal arrangements of the law (Ballard & Zettel, 1978), and (3) the managerial aspects of the law (Ballard & Zettel, 1978).

The law's major implication's for teachers include

1. Development and use of individualized education programs (IEPs) for each handicapped child.
2. Policies that guarantee confidentiality of data and other information about the child.
3. Provisions for nondiscriminatory evaluation procedures.
4. Assurance that each handicapped child is placed in the least restrictive environment where maximum growth can also be achieved.
5. Requires ongoing consultation with parents or the parent surrogate.
6. Requires due process.
7. Mandates ongoing inservice programs.
8. Requires that "child-find" activities be undertaken to identify those in need of special assistance.

Accountability

Accountability means that persons are responsible and must answer for that for which he or she is responsible. That seems simple, but it is not so easy to determine who is accountable, for which actions, under which conditions, according to what standards, and by whose interpretation!

Turnbull (1978) points out that two major themes underlie the complex judicial response: (1) Human rights are not divisible and cannot be legally parceled out according to emotional, mental, or physical abilities of a person; and (2) The unequal person in mental, physical, or emotional development requires equal treatment under the law. The judicial concept, then, is one of responsibility

to one another in society. The "prudent man" concept requires that the caretaker of another's property be responsible to the owner for his or her actions. Turnbull (1975) also points out that in the law of torts the "reasonable man" rule requires that a person answer in damages for acting in an unreasonable way toward another person. The implications of the "prudent man" and "reasonable man" concepts are evident for handicapped persons and their treatment by professional caretakers. They must be treated in a prudent and reasonable fashion in light of the information and techniques available to professionals.

The court decisions cited earlier establish the right to treatment; professionals are held accountable for the manner in which that treatment is carried out. Three legal theories hold professionals accountable:

1. *Procedural due process.* A person has the right to be heard and to protest if a government agency is about to take action affecting that person.
2. *Substantive due process.* Certain rights are inviolate, that is, cannot be taken away by any state agency. For example, the state cannot arbitrarily institutionalize a disturbed child.
3. *Equal protection.* The state must provide the same rights and benefits to handicapped as to nonhandicapped persons. Any variance must be justified by the court.

Abeson and Zettel (1977) outline the minimum requirements for due process:

1. Parents must be notified, in writing, before evaluation of their child is made. This written notification should be in the primary language of the parents.
2. Parents must receive written notice before a change in educational placement is made.

3. A periodic review of educational placement is required. For classes of emotionally disturbed, this would generally be a yearly evaluation.
4. Parents must have the opportunity for an impartial hearing; this includes the right to (a) receive timely notice of such a hearing; (b) review all records pertaining to the child; (c) obtain an independent evaluation from an outside agency; (d) be represented by counsel, cross-examine, call witnesses, present evidence, and appeal decisions; (e) receive an accurate record of all proceedings.
5. A surrogate parent is assigned if (a) the child's parent is not known or available; (b) the child has been designated a ward of the state. (p. 71)

Teachers are legally required to keep adequate records regarding individual student evaluation, progress, and placement; who has access to these records is also mandated. For the teacher in charge of records, this means that disclosure of records must be carefully monitored so that unwarranted disclosure is not made.

The concept of personal liability should be foremost in the teacher's mind. Today personal liability suits against medical doctors, directors of institutions, and nursing home proprietors are common. Teachers should constantly apply the "prudent man" and "reasonable man" concepts to what they are doing. Is my behavior what a "reasonable man" would do in this situation? Is my professional treatment of the children in my care within acceptable professional guidelines?

What is the teacher's liability? What happens in cases involving student injury by another child, truancy, and in many other situations that may arise in teaching children who are out of control or out of touch with reality. Recall that government employees are personally liable in cases where negligence (either misfeasance or nonfeasance) can be shown. The teacher acts *in loco parentis* to pupils and must conduct himself or herself so as not to injure or subject children to injury. Generally, the law requires that teachers exercise the care and prudence that any reasonable person would use in a similar situation.

In cases where correct action is unclear, the teacher should seek advice from the immediate supervisor or program director. When this is not possible because of time constraints and the seriousness of the situation, the teacher must act in a reasonable manner to alleviate the problem at hand. For example, if a child is seriously injured, the teacher should seek assistance if possible and also do what is necessary, as far as the teacher's skills permit, to help the child.

Teachers of disturbed children, obviously should be aware of their rights and responsibility. There has been more legal and legislative action on behalf of students, teachers, and parents in the past 10 years than in any time in history! This fact should not be viewed with alarm but with diligence, since children are the benefactors of our concern.

SUMMARY

The history of the development of concern for emotionally disturbed has been both varied and complex. The term *emotionally disturbed* has been used to label children with a variety of behavioral problems in schools. It first appeared in the literature over 75 years ago, without being defined. Emotionally disturbed children have not been a homogeneous group in incidence, causation, or remediation. Labeling children emotionally disturbed, therefore, should be avoided whenever possible to avoid the stigma of labeling and the self-fulfilling prophecy that goes with labeling. As an alternative to the label *emotional disturbance*, the term *children in conflict* is more comprehensive and educationally practical.

Children in conflict can be defined as those whose manifest behavior has a deleterious effect on their personal or educational development and/or the personal or educational development of their peers. Deviant behaviors are divided into four basic types, which can be delineated through observation: these are acting-out behaviors, withdrawing behaviors, defensive behaviors, and disorganized behaviors.

The history of children in conflict outlines several significant features of the treatment of children. The historical development indicates that progression in treatment has been anything but logical, sequential, or predictable.

Background information for teachers of children in conflict is important for three basic reasons: (1) it puts today's practices into perspective; (2) it helps educators avoid many of the errors of the past and capitalize on positive approaches; and (3) it provides a springboard for future knowledge.

The status of programs for emotionally disturbed before the twentieth century was uncertain because opinion setters were preoccupied with other matters. As society became more complex, children in conflict presented a more serious problem for parents. With the Industrial Revolution came a new awareness of children and the role they were to play in society. As the rights of individuals of this society became more pronounced, it was inevitable that the problems of handicapped children would come into sharper focus. The fact that little seemed to be done for emotionally disturbed children before the twentieth century is an indication that people's attention was not focused on the needs of children, not that they believed children's problems to be nonexistent.

The work of Kraepelin at the turn of the twentieth century stimulated the development of psychiatric classification. The discovery of the syphilitic basis of general paresis is generally considered a milestone in the "descriptive era."

Early in the twentieth century, the Stanford-Binet test and later the Wechsler Intelligence Scale for Children were developed. Individual projective tests designed to pinpoint various forms of mental illness constituted a major breakthrough during the twentieth century. A parallel movement at this time was the dramatic work of Sigmund Freud and his associates. Freud established the analytical approach to child study.

In sharp contrast to the analytical approach was the behavioral approach put forth by John Watson. Just as Freud has been such a dynamic force in the realm of the subconscious, Watson became the torchbearer for those who were seeking a theoretical construct based on conscious thought.

During the twentieth century, social and ecological thought brought new perspectives to those interested in the development of children with emotional problems.

A major recent development has been the setting of educational direction through court cases and federal legislation. The treatment of emotionally disturbed children has undergone dramatic changes in the last several years because of this development.

BIBLIOGRAPHY

Abeson, A., & Zettel, J. (1977) The end of the quiet revolution: The Education for All Handicapped Act of 1975. *Exceptional Children 44*, 114–128.

Adler, A. (1964). *Social interest: A challenge to mankind.* New York: Capricorn.

Anastasi, A. (1968). *Psychological testing.* New York: Macmillan.

Ballard, J., & Zettel, J. (1977). Public Law 94–142 and Section 504: What they say about rights and protections. *Exceptional Children, 44*, 177–184.

Ballard, J., & Zettel, J. (1978). Fiscal arrangements of Public Law 94–142. *Exceptional Children, 44*, 333–337.

Ballard, J., & Zettel, J. (1978). The managerial aspects of Public Law 94–142. *Exceptional Children, 44*, 457–462.

Bandura, A. (1963). *Principles of behavior modification.* New York: Holt, Rinehart & Winston.

Becker, H. (1963). *Outsiders: Studies in the sociology of deviance.* New York: The Free Press.

Beers, C. (1953). *A mind that found itself: An autobiography.* Garden City, N,Y.: Doubleday.

Bender, L. (1955). Twenty years of clinical research on schizophrenic children, with special reference to those under six years of age. In G. Capian (Ed.), *Emotional problems of early childhood.* New York: Basic Books.

Benedict, R. (1934). Anthropology and the abnormal. *Journal of General Psychology, 10,* 59–80.

Bergman, P., & Escalona, S. (1949). Unusual sensitivities in very young children. In R. S. Eissler et al. (Eds.), *Psychoanalytic study of the child* (Vols. 3 and 4). New York: International Universities Press.

Bower, E. (1969). *Early identification of emotionally handicapped children in school.* Springfield, IL: Charles C Thomas.

Bower, E. (1982). *Early identification of emotionally handicapped children in school.* Springfield, IL: Charles C Thomas.

Bower, E., & Lambert, N. (1971). In-school screening of children with emotional handicaps. In N. Long, W. Morse, & R. Newman (Eds.), *Conflict in the classroom* (2nd ed.). Belmont, CA: Wadsworth.

Bron, A. (1972). Some strands of counter psychology. In W. C. Rhodes, *A study of child variance.* Ann Arbor: University of Michigan Press.

Brown v. Board of Education, 347 U.S. 483 (1954).

Buckley, N., & Walker, H. (1970). *Modifying classroom behavior.* Champaign, IL: Research Press.

Burlington School Committee v. Department of Education of the Commonwealth of Massachusetts, 105 s. ct. 1996 (1985).

Cleaver, E. (1970). *Soul on ice.* New York: Dell.

Coleman, J. C. (1964). *Abnormal psychology and modern life.* Glenview, IL: Scott, Foresman.

Crutcher, R. (1943). Child psychiatry: A history of its development. *Psychiatry, 6,* 191–201.

Cullinan, D., Epstein, M., & Lloyd, J. (1983). *Behavior disorders of children and adolescents.* Englewood Cliffs, NJ: Prentice-Hall.

Cumming, J., & Cumming, E. (1968). On the stigma of mental illness. In S. P. Spitzer & N. K. Denzin (Eds.), *The mental patient: Studies in the sociology of deviance.* New York: McGraw-Hill.

DesJarlais, D. (1972). Mental illness as social deviance. In W. C. Rhodes, *A study of child variance.* Ann Arbor: University of Michigan Press.

Despert, L. (1965). *The emotionally disturbed child: An inquiry into family patterns.* Garden City, NY: Anchor Books.

Dunn, L. M. (1973). *Exceptional children in the schools.* New York: Holt, Rinehart & Winston.

Erickson, E. (1968). *Identity, youth, and crisis.* New York: W. W. Norton.

Erikson, K. (1957). Patient role and social uncertainty. *Psychiatry, 20,* 263–268.

Erikson, K. (1964). Notes on the sociology of deviance. *Social Problems, 1,* 307–314.

Farber, J. (1970). *The student as nigger.* New York: Pocket Books.

Faris, R. E. L., & Dunham, H. W. (1939). *Mental disorders in urban areas.* Chicago: University of Chicago Press.

Feagans, L. (1972) Ecological theory as a model for constructing a theory of emotional disturbance. In W. C. Rhodes, *A study of child variance.* Ann Arbor, MI: University of Michigan Press.

Felix, R. (1967). *Mental illness: Progress and prospects.* New York: Columbia University Press.

Gagne, R. M. (1965) *The conditions of learning.* New York: Holt, Rinehart & Winston.

Glasser, W. (1969). *Schools without failure.* New York: Harper & Row.

Glidewell, J., & Swallow, C. (1968). *The prevalence of maladjustment in elementary schools.* Chicago: University of Chicago Press.

Goffman, E. (1963). *Stigma: Notes on the management of spoiled identity.* Englewood Cliffs, NJ: Prentice-Hall.

Goodman, P (1970, October). High school is too much. *Psychology Today, 25.*

Graubard, P. S. (1973). Children with behavioral disabilities. In L. Dunn (Ed.), *Exceptional children in the schools.* New York: Holt, Rinehart & Winston.

Halderman v. Pennhurst, 446 Ft. supp. 1295 (E.D. Pa. 1977).

Hall, C. S. (1954). *A primer of Freudian psychology.* New York: The New American Library.

Hall, R., Lund, D., & Jackson, D. (1968). Effects of teacher attention on study behavior. *Journal of Applied Behavioral Analysis, 1,* 1–12.

Haring, N. (1963). The emotionally disturbed. In S. Kirk & B. Weiner (Eds.), *Behavioral research on exceptional children.* Washington, DC: The Council for Exceptional Children.

Haring, N., & Phillips, E. (1962). *Educating emotionally disturbed children.* New York: McGraw-Hill.

Hawaii Department of Education v. Katherine D., No. 82: 4096 (9th Cir. No. 7, 1983).

Hersch, C. C. (1968). The discontent explosion in mental health. *American Psychologist, 23(7),* 497–506.

Hewett, F. (1968). *The emotionally disturbed child in the classroom.* Boston: Allyn & Bacon.

Hill, W. (1963). *Learning: A survey of psychological interpretations.* San Francisco: Chandler Publishing.

Hobbs, N. (1982). *Troubled and troubling children.* San Francisco: Jossey-Bass.

Hoffer, W. (1945). Psychoanalytic education. *Psychoanalytic Study of the Child, 1,* 293–306.

Itard, J. M. G. (1932, 1962). *The wild boy of Aveyron.* In G. Humphrey & M. Humphrey (Eds. and trans.). New York: Appleton-Century-Crofts (Prentice-Hall). (Originally published in Paris by Gouyon, 1801.)

Kanner, L. (1949). Problems of nosology and psychodynamics of early infantile autism. *American Journal of Orthopsychiatry, 19,* 416–426.

Kanner, L. (1957). *Child psychiatry* (3rd ed.). Springfield, IL: Charles C Thomas.

Kanner, L. (1962). Emotionally disturbed children: A historical review. *Child Development, 33,* 97–102.

Kauffman, J. (1981). *Characteristics of children's behavior disorders.* Columbus, OH: Merrill.

Kelly, T., Bullock, L., & Dykes, M. (1974). *Teacher's perceptions of behavioral disorders in children.* Gainesville: Florida Educational Research and Development Council.

Kelly, T., et al. (1977). Behavioral disorders: Teacher's perceptions. *Exceptional Children, 43,* 316–318.

Kennedy, J. F. (1964). *Public papers of the President of the United States* (January 1 to November 22, 1963). Washington, DC: U.S. Government Printing Office.

Kerr, M., & Nelson, C. M. (1983). *Strategies for managing behavior problems in the classroom.* Columbus, OH: Merrill.

Kirk, S. A. (1972). *Educating exceptional children* (2nd ed.). Boston: Houghton Mifflin.

Krasner, L., & Ullmann, L. (1965). *Research in behavior modification: New developments and implications.* New York: Holt, Rinehart & Winston.

Krugman, M. (1948). Orthopsychiatry and education. In L. G. Lowrey & V. Sloan (Eds.), *Orthopsychiatry, 1923–1948.* New York: American Orthopsychiatric Association.

Larry P. v. Riles, 495 F. Supp. 96 (N. D. Cal. 1979) Aff'r (9th Cir. 1984), 1983–84. EHLR DEC. 555:304.

Lebank v. Spears, Civil Action No. 71-2897, (E.D. La. 1973).

Lewis, N. (1941). *A short history of psychiatric achievement.* New York: W. W. Norton.

Long, N., Morse, W., & Newman, R. (1971). *Conflict in the classroom: The education of children with problems* (2nd ed.). Belmont, CA: Wadsworth.

Lovaas, O., Schaeffer, B., & Simmons, J. (1965). Building social behavior in autistic children by use of electric shock. *Journal of Experimental Research in Personality, 1,* 99–109.

Lyman, F. (1963). *Phenylketonuria.* Springfield, IL: Charles C Thomas.

McDowell, R. (1982). Prologue. In R. McDowell, G. Adamson, & F. Wood, *Teaching the emotionally disturbed.* Boston: Little, Brown.

MacMillan, D. (1973). *Behavior modification in education.* New York: Macmillan.

Maes, W. (1966). The identification of emotionally disturbed elementary school children. *Exceptional Children, 32,* 607–609.

Mahler, M. (1952). On child psychosis and schizophrenia. *Psychoanalytic Study of the Child, 7,* 286–305.

Marmor, J., & Pumpian-Mindlin, E. (1950). Toward an integrative conception of mental disorder. *Journal of Nervous Mental Disorders, 3,* 19–29.

Martin, E. (1968). Breakthrough for the handicapped, legislative history. *Exceptional Children, 34,* 493–503.

McCarthy, J., & Paraskevopoulos, J. (1969). Behavior patterns of learning disabled, emotionally disturbed, and average children. *Exceptional Children, 36,* 69–74.

Menninger, R. (1944). The history of psychiatry. *Disabilities of the Nervous System, 5,* 52–55.

Merton, R. (1957). *Social structure and social theory.* New York: The Free Press.

Meyer, A. (1957). *Psychobiology.* Springfield, IL: Charles C Thomas.

Mills v. D.C. Board of Education, 348 F. Supp. 366 (D.D.C. 1972).

Nudd, H. (1925). The purpose and scope of visiting teacher work. In M. B. Sayles, *The problem child in school.* New York: Joint Committee on Methods of Preventing Delinquency.

O'Leary, K., & Drabman, R. (1971). Token reinforcement programs in the classroom: A review. *Psychology Bulletin, 75,* 379–398.

Orme, M., & Purnell, R. (1970). Behavior modification and transfer in an out-of-control classroom. In G. Fargo et al., *Behavior modification in the classroom.* Belmont, CA: Wadsworth.

Parsons, T. (1951). *The social system.* Glencoe, IL: The Free Press.

Pate, J. (1963). Emotionally disturbed and socially maladjusted children. In L. Dunn, *Exceptional children in the schools.* New York: Holt, Rinehart & Winston.

Pennsylvania Association for Retarded Children v. Commonwealth of Pennsylvania, 334 F. Supp. 1257 (E.D. Pa. 1971), and 343 F. Supp. 279 (E.D. Pa. 1972).

President's Commission on the Assassination of President Kennedy. (1964). Washington, DC: U.S. Government Printing Office.

Quay, H., Morse, W., & Cutler, R. (1966). Personality patterns of pupils in special classes for the emotionally disturbed. *Exceptional Children, 32,* 297–301.

Rank, B. (1949). Adaptation of the psychoanalytic techniques for the treatment of young children with atypical development. *American Journal of Orthopsychiatry, 19,* 130–139.

Reimer, E. (1972). Unusual ideas in education. In W. C. Rhodes, *A study of child variance.* Ann Arbor: University of Michigan Press.

Reinert, H. (1972). The emotionally disturbed. In B. R. Gearheart (Ed.), *Education of the exceptional child.* San Francisco: Intext Education Publishers.

Rezmierski, V., & Kotre, J. (1972). A limited literature review of theory of psychodynamic model. In W. C. Rhodes, *A study of child variance.* Ann Arbor: University of Michigan Press.

Rhodes, W. C. (1967). The disturbing child: A problem in ecological management. *Exceptional Children, 33,* 449–455.

Rhodes, W. C., & Paul, J. (1978). *Emotionally disturbed and deviant children: New ideas and approaches.* Englewood Cliffs, NJ: Prentice-Hall.

Rhodes, W. C., & Sagor, M. (1974). *A study of child variance: The future.* Ann Arbor: University of Michigan Press.

Rhodes, W. C., & Tracy, M. (1972). *A study of child variance.* Ann Arbor: University of Michigan Press.

Rimland, B. (1969). Psychogenesis versus biogenesis: The issues and evidence. In S. C. Plog & R. B. Edgerton (Eds.), *Changing perspectives in mental illness.* New York: Holt, Rinehart & Winston.

Rogers, C. (1939). *The clinical treatment of the problem child.* New York: Houghton Mifflin.

Rogers, C. (1959). A theory of therapy, personality and interpersonal relationships, as developed in the client-centered framework. In S. Kock (Ed.), *Psychology: A study of a science* (Vol 3). New York: McGraw-Hill.

Rosenthal, D. (Ed.). (1963). *The Genain quadruplets: A case study and theoretical analysis of heredity and environment in schizophrenia.* New York: Basic Books.

Sagor, M. (1972). Biological bases of childhood behavior disorders. In W. C. Rhodes, *A study of child variance.* Ann Arbor: University of Michigan Press.

Silberman, C. (1970). *Crisis in the classroom.* New York: Random House.

Skinner, B. (1953). *Science and human behavior.* New York: Macmillan.

Szasz, T. (1961). *The myth of mental illness.* New York: Dell.

Szasz, T. (1970). *Ideology and insanity.* Garden City, NY: Doubleday.

Szurek, S. (1956). Psychotic episodes and psychic maldevelopment. *American Journal of Orthopsychiatry, 16,* 519–543.

Terman, L. M., & Merrill, M. A. (1973). *The Stanford-Binet Intelligence Scale* (3rd rev.). Boston: Houghton-Mifflin.

Tracy, M. (1972). Conceptual models of emotional disturbance: Some other thoughts. In W. C. Rhodes, *A study of child variance.* Ann Arbor: University of Michigan Press.

Turnbull, H. R. (1975). *Legal aspects of educating the developmentally disabled.* National Organization on Legal Problems in Education.

Turnbull, H. R. (1976). *Special education and law: Implications for the schools.* Paper presented at the International Council for Exceptional Children. Chicago, April 4–7.

Turnbull, H., & Turnbull, A. (1978). *Free appropriate public education, law and implementation.* Denver: Love Publishing Co.

Ulman, C. (1952). Identification of maladjusted school children. *Public Health Monograph No. 7.* Washington, DC: Federal Security Agency, United States Public Health Service.

Ulmann, L., & Krasner, L. (Eds.). (1965). *Case studies in behavior modification.* New York: Holt, Rinehart & Winston.

U.S. Department of Education (1985). *Seventh annual report to Congress on the implementation of the Handicapped Act.* Washington, DC: U.S. Government Printing Office.

U.S. Office of Education (1982). In R. McDowell, *Teaching emotionally disturbed.* Boston: Little, Brown.

Walker, H. (1970). *Walker problem behavior identification checklist.* Los Angeles: Western Psychological Services.

Watson, J. (1929). *Psychology: From the standpoint of a behaviorist.* Philadelphia: J. B. Lippincott.

Watson, J. B., & Rayner, R. (1920). Conditioned emotional reactions. *Journal of Experimental Psychology, 3,* 1–14.

Wechsler, D. (1949, rev. 1974). *Wechsler Intelligence Scale for Children: Manual.* New York: Psychological Corporation.

Weinberg, S., Costello, M., & Rotchford, J. (1962). Inborn errors of amino acid metabolism. *New York State Journal of Medicine, 62,* 43–52.

Whelan, R. J., & Haring, N. G. (1966). Modification and maintenance of behavior through systematic application of consequences. *Exceptional Children, 32,* 281–289.

Wood, F. (1982). In F. Wood & K. C. Lakin, *Disturbing, disordered or distrubed.* Reston, VA: Council for Exceptional Children.

Wood, F., & Lakin, K. C. (1982). *Disturbing, disordered, or disturbed.* Reston, VA: Council for Exceptional Children.

Woody, R. H. (1969). *Behavioral problem children in the schools.* New York: Appleton-Century-Crofts.

Wyatt v. Stickey 325 F. Supp. 788, 784 (M.D. Ala. 1971)

2

The Biophysical Approach

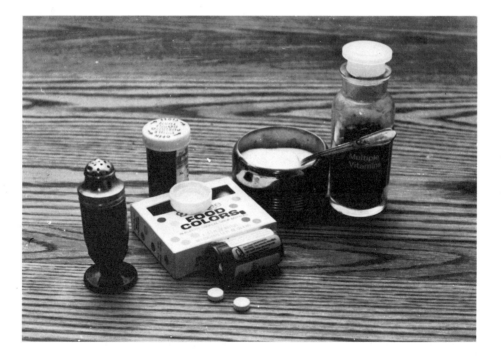

INTRODUCTION AND OBJECTIVES

Chapter 2 is the first of six chapters that will focus on theory and practice with children in conflict. Biophysical theory is presented first for historical and practical reasons. In recent history we have assumed the medical aspects of development to be important to psychological growth. This assumption has led to major emphasis on biophysical assessment (Rhodes & Sagor, 1974), which is a valued component of psychoeducational evaluation.

In this chapter you will (a) become familiar with biophysical theory; (b) identify biophysical causes of deviance; (c) describe screening and evaluation procedures; and (d) explain procedures for treating biophysical problems and develop classroom approaches for intervention.

DEFINING EMOTIONAL DISTURBANCE

Biophysical theorists suggest that emotional traits have their origin in nature. The components that affect the psychological development of youngsters include genetic, biochemical, developmental, neurological, and arousal factors (Sagor, 1972). Any biophysical factor can affect our emotions; some experts believe they can cause emotional disturbance. Rimland, an eminent spokesperson for the biophysical position, defines a biogenic disorder as "a severe behavior disorder that results solely from the effects of the physical/chemical environment." Biophysical factors may exert their effects prenatally, during labor and birth, and at any subsequent time" (1969, p. 706).

Rosenthal (1963), however, has supported the diathesis-stress theory—that is, the idea of inherited, predisposition/environmental stimulation. This theory postulates that an overactive thyroid, for example, would be necessary for emotional outbreaks to occur; however, the hyperactive thyroid would not be sufficient to cause biting and hitting behavior. An environmental catalyst such as being overly tired would be needed to complete the circuit.

An example of a biophysical deviation is the child with a rare biochemical disorder, such as phenylketonuria (PKU). A child with PKU will begin to act in ways different from a normal child if treatment for the disease is not initiated. However, with dietary controls the child can grow to be relatively the same as peers.

BASIC THEORY

Those who advocate the biophysical construct of emotional disturbance believe that a positive relationship exists between biological and emotional development. They also believe that this relationship can be altered to the benefit of the child.

In the past, behavioral problems were seen as having their genesis in either environment or genetic makeup of the person in question (Rhodes & Sagor, 1974). Our current view of deviance has grown from one of limited concerns to a more global view, which includes not only the environment and biological factors, but also subtle components of these and other theories discussed in Chapter 1. Algozzine (1980) identified several areas of biophysical concern including genetic predisposition, biochemical inconsistencies, and nutritional inadequacies.

Many theorists support the concept of an inherited predisposition and biogenetic "triggering" system that together result in emotional conflict (Pollin, 1972). Other studies point to the role of the environment in deviance. For example, poor nutrition, injury, or stress that affects diet or sleep habits have all been studied as possible causal factors (Knapczyk, 1979; Rimland, 1969; Walton, 1979).

Recent theorists are very interested in the relationships between emotions and behavior. This extremely diverse interest covers everything from infant bonding (Stell & Alexander, 1982) to the relationship of personality and immunity to cancer (Elsa, 1982). This interest, coupled with computer use and the resurgence of the case study approach of research, promises to broaden the study of intrapersonal relationships.

Rimland has long advocated the importance of biophysical factors in the determination of emotional stability: "I predict that research will ultimately show psycho-social factors to have minor if any relevance in causing a severe disorder known as *psychosis*" (1969, p. 704). But we seem to be no nearer to fulfilling this prediction today than we were then. What has happened? Cowen and Shaywitz et al., (1982) suggest that change has been slow in coming for three reasons. First, there are probably multiple determinants of biophysical deviance. This fact means researchers are studying issues in multiple rather than singular fashion. Second, medical research has generally been fragmented and episodic. Finally, economic and institutional resources have been meager when compared to the resources available to other disorders under study.

Biogenetic theorists have become increasingly concerned with the apparent weaknesses of psychotherapy as demonstrated in research, the tendency to blame parents for the psychopathology of their children, and sweeping generalizations of a theory that tries to explain everything with one model (Sagor, 1972). In an effort to demonstrate the tunnel vision of psychoanalytical interpretation, Rimland discussed a case formerly reviewed by Bettelheim (1959). In his review, Bettelheim attributed the pathological condition of a psychotic Jewish girl to a lack of maternal affection. The girl was conceived and raised in a small, cramped, dark hole beneath a farm building in Poland during World War II. German soldiers were nearby and had even fired shots into the building. Bettelheim emphasized psychological factors such as the mother's dislike for the father and the "unplanned" nature of the pregnancy. Rimland suggested that four possible causes of the deviance had been overlooked in the analytical evaluation: (1) faulty endocrine development due to maternal stress during pregnancy; (2) an absence of adequate sanitary facilities, both prenatally and postnatally; (3) poor prenatal and postnatal nutrition; and (4) postnatal sensory deprivation.

Most individuals who have experienced anxiety in their lives know well its effect on bodily functions. Sleeping, eating, and emotional stability can all be adversely affected as a result of internal anxiety. One can easily believe that the fear of captivity and death for a pregnant mother could have a negative impact on the unborn child. When this deprivation and fear continue after birth, the problems are compounded.

The study of genetic problems in children presents three major drawbacks for the researcher. First, genetic study is a time-consuming task, often taking the entire lifetime of the researcher to complete. Second, there is the inability of the researcher to control future relationships in the child's life. Lifestyles change—and with them, research implications. Genetic counseling is tenuous, and the results are questionable. Third, permission to research the genetic components of a child's life is often not available. A lack of research permission can prove discouraging in an area where subjects are limited. In spite of these difficulties, several productive efforts have been made.

Studies in genetics of schizophrenia, infantile autism, and related mental problems have generally been made through the study of twins. By comparing the agreement between the behavior of monozygotic (identical) and dizygotic (fraternal) twins, researchers have tried to establish a relationship between mental illness in children and factors of heredity. The assumption is that if all factors are controlled except the twin relationship, the results will show the contribution of genetics to mental illness.

Although the evidence is not conclusive, various studies indicate that a genetic relationship between certain severe mental disorders and genetic factors does exist. Meehl (1969) describes the ability to diagnose schizophrenia without having any behavioral data from the patient or those who may observe the patient's behaviors. His belief is based on studies that show that identical twins are likely to exhibit an affliction similar to schizophrenia. If one identical twin is schizophrenic, the other is also likely to be schizophrenic. This relationship is not absolute but various studies suggest this relationship in as many as 85% of patients (Karlson, 1966).

Buss (1966) presents a summary of studies outlined in Table 2–1. It can be seen that, in general, the closer the genetic relationship of a child to someone who has schizophrenia, the more likely it is that the child will also be sick. For example, a child whose fraternal twin has schizophrenia will be 3 to 17 times as likely to be affected as a child who has no history of schizophrenia in the family. Based on such data, Buss concludes (a) an inherited component of schizophrenia does exist, and (b) environmental factors are necessary for schizophrenia to develop.

Note in Table 2–1 the dramatic difference between the rates of occurrence in identical and fraternal twins, (4 to 1) which suggests that biological factors outweigh environmental factors in the transmission of schizophrenia. If the environmental factors were primary, twins would show similar prevalence, whether identical or fraternal. Note that the rate of occurrence in fraternal twins is much the same as that between siblings.

TABLE 2–1. Rates of Occurrence of Schizophrenia

Group	Percentage
General population	1
Grandchildren, cousins, nephews, and nieces	3–4
Half-siblings	7
Siblings	5–14
Children with 1 schizophrenic parent	16
Children with 2 schizophrenic parents	39–68
Dizygotic twins (fraternal)	3–17
Monozygotic twins (identical)	67–86

Note: Data from Buss, 1966.

Sometimes only one identical twin is afflicted with schizophrenia. There is no conclusive evidence why this is so.

Pollin's review (1972) of studies on twins indicates a lower concordance than reported by Buss. A summary of his findings appears in Table 2–2.

The results of studies on twins raises several questions. Is the concordance genetic? Does the intrauterine position play a role? Is the life space of the identical twin different from that of the fraternal twin? Pollin suggests that concordance cannot be assumed to be only genetic. As indicated by Table 2–2, the more recent studies show monozygotic concordance of less than 50%. Further, that the report findings are not in total agreement raises some doubts concerning the genetic causation of schizophrenia. In his discussion of genetics and schizophrenia, Sagor (1972) postulates that prenatal and postnatal physical environment and psychosocial interpretation may both be responsible in cases where schizophrenia exists.

Rimland (1969) also points out:

TABLE 2–2. Concordance Rates of Schizophrenia in Twins

Investigator	Number of MZ* Pairs	Percent of MZ Concordance	Number of DZ* Pairs	Percent of DZ Concordance
Luxenberger (1928)	17	60–76	33	0
Luxenberger (1930)	21	67	37	
Luxenberger (1934)	27	33		
Rosanoff (1934)	41	61	101	10
Moller (1941)	11	55–64	27	15
Kallmann (1946)	174	69–86	517	10–15
Slater (1953)	41	68–76	115	11–14
Inouye (1961)	55	36–60	17	22
Tienari (1963)	16	6	21	5
Harvald & Hauge (1965)	9	44	62	10
Gottesman & Shields (1966)	24	42–65	33	9–17
Kringlen (1967)	55	25–38	172	4–10
Pollin & co-workers (1969)	80	14–16	146	4–4

Data from Pollin, 1972.
*MZ, monozygotic (identical twins); DZ, dizygotic (fraternal twins).

Actually, genetic familiar data on known physical disorders, such as tuberculosis and diabetes, give results very similar to those reported above for schizophrenia. . . . Some critics claim the data do not show genetic causation. By this they mean that the percentages do not follow the simple Mendelian model for dominant and recessive genes. (p. 731)

A few studies appear to separate environmental factors in schizophrenia from genetic factors by studying specific target groups that were freed of the environmental factors that might contribute to the illness. In these studies it was found that children with one schizophrenic parent who were reared apart from the sick parent experienced substantial schizophrenic problems (Wender, 1969). Higgins (1966) compared the development of 25 children raised by their schizophrenic mothers with a control group of children raised apart from their schizophrenic moth-

ers. The study indicated that no significant differences in maladjustments were noted between these two groups.

In a complex and interesting study of children with schizophrenic mothers, Mednick (1971) found a solid relationship between heredity and environment. Bender (1968) also has made significant research contributions on schizophrenia in children. She has summarized her concept of childhood schizophrenia as follows:

It is a total organismic disorder of the organism as a whole. It is inherited, according to Kallman's dictates, as a vulnerability and an inability to compensate. It is characterized by a lag in maturation at the embryonic level and, therefore, carries with it embryonic plasticity in all areas of bodily function, particularly that which is integrated by the central nervous system. This plasticity means both a lack of differentiation into patterns and boundaries of every function, and a failure of determination. The individual can accelerate, maturate, regress, stand still, or move in almost any direction as he gets older because this plasticity is retained throughout the individual's lifetime.

The maturational lag Bender suggests has been indicated in a number of studies on schizophrenic and autistic children (Fowle, 1968; Kennard, 1965; Ritvo et al., 1970). In these studies the deviant child is more like a normal infant than a child of his or her own mental age in such developmental factors as sleep patterns, white blood cell development, and blood and platelet studies.

In studying the concordance of identical twins for schizophrenia, one must use caution before assigning causation totally to developmental factors. In the studies cited, little has been done to separate biogenetic factors from prenatal factors that influence the psychological development of the child. Research is complicated further by a lack of a common objective tool for diagnosis of schizophrenia. Each study relies on one or more definitions of this disease, none of which is totally in agreement with the others. Often, studies have been done with patients with chronic schizophrenia in psychiatric hospitals, which tends to raise concordance figures. In addition, many studies have been done with female subjects; these studies tend to show a higher concordance than do studies of male twins. As Buss (1966) indicates, a lowering of the concordance rate with twin studies does not raise the probability that the environmental factors are the key to schizophrenia.

Pollin (1972) lists five major conclusions that have emerged from studies of the pathogenesis of schizophrenia:

1. A genetic predisposition to schizophrenia exists that may be nonspecific for this particular psychosis.
2. Genetic predisposition does not take the form of a single, dominant gene, as in Mendel's law.
3. The genetic predisposition may be expressed, in part, as an abnormality in one or both of two interrelated systems of biogenic amines.
4. Additional pathogenic determinants include familiar experiences and constitutional factors; for example, interuterine experience of the unborn child.
5. One cannot validate empirically conceptual integration of biogenetic and experiential factors through the use of a construct that emphasizes weak ego boundaries.

Obviously there is no conclusive pathological determinant of schizophrenia. Genetic weakness for schizophrenia is a key but cannot be specifically predicted. Possibly environmental factors determine the eventual outcome of the illness.

Theorists support a variety of biogenetic causal factors in describing mental illness. Some lean toward perceptual causation (McGhie & Chapman, 1961), others take an arousal approach (Deslauriers & Carlson, 1969), some indicate neurological impairment (Strauss and Kephart, 1955), while others suggest biochemical factors (Thompson, 1967). Other theorists group biophysical problems into two broad categories: genetic and environmental (Rhodes & Sagor, 1974). For those who relate to the biophysical orientation only on a superficial level, this grouping appears useful. The genetic component provides a base of general understanding for issues such as genetic counseling in family living or health courses, whereas environmental explanations should underscore the importance of nutrition, stress, accidents, classroom noise levels, and the quality of air that children breathe. Some caution is needed in the environmental area, however. Although it is logical to assume that noise level, the quality of air in the classroom, and diet are variables that make a difference in classroom performance of children, research evidence is still equivocal. Rimland (1969) has predicted that most neurotic behaviors will eventually be determined to have a biophysical basis, but presently this interpretation is not possible.

Meehl (1969) sets limits on the inferences often drawn by those who oppose a medical interpretation of schizophrenia.

1. The etiological factor does not always, or even usually, produce clinical illness.
2. If illness occurs, the particular form and content of symptoms are not derivable by reference to the specific etiology alone.
3. The course of the illness can be materially influenced by procedures directed against factors other than the specific causes.
4. All persons who share the specific etiology will not have closely similar histories, symptoms, and course of illness.
5. The largest single contributor to symptom variance is generally not the specific etiology (cause).

Meehl makes it clear that education has a place in the process of changing the behaviors of children in conflict. If his limits could be accepted and employed by the various professionals working with children, many of the defensive barriers that now persist between theorists could be lowered.

Ritvo and coworkers (1970) make a strong case for biophysical interpretation of deviance by pointing out that these children are found all over the world, at all levels of socioeconomic background, with a variety of ethnic backgrounds, and living in homes with a variety of psychological types of parents. The biophysical, or medical, model is one of the oldest theoretical systems being applied to children in conflict. Its followers are among the most positive and energetic in their belief that mental illness is caused by one of several biophysical factors. This enthusiasm is healthy for professional growth. It is an attitude that can lead to a new cooperation between professional groups that strive to answer difficult questions from a medical point of view.

SCREENING AND EVALUATION PROCEDURES

Biophysical screening and evaluation are important to individuals who work with children in conflict. Screening is the process of selecting a small number of children who need further evaluation from the total population of a class, school, district, or other unit. Generally, biophysical screening is done prior to the beginning of school. This strategy often consists of a general physical examination and the required immunizations. Medical screening continues once the child is enrolled in school in the form of physical examinations for extracurricular activities, camps, and athletic competition. Other physical evaluations include periodic examinations for sight, hearing, and even dental health. In addition to these more formal screening procedures, the youngsters are continually evaluated for signs of physical problems, e.g., undue tiredness, eye-strain, poor attention span, low vitality, or failure to thrive. If any problems appear or if progress in school suggests that biophysical problems may exist, the teacher or school nurse might suggest additional evaluation by the family pediatrician or general practitioner.

A positive relationship exists between a child's physical health and his or her emotional well-being. Although many children have regular medical evaluations, there are some who have never received adequate medical care and others who have medical problems that go undetected during routine medical evaluation. In an age of sophisticated medical practice, there is still a place for biophysical screening and evaluation within the school.

Role of the Teacher

The classroom teacher is an excellent person to observe or aid in screening the child and to recommend further evaluation. The teacher observes the child in a variety of unique situations throughout the school day. These observations include large- and small-group activities requiring strenuous and quiet participation over varying time periods. In addition, the teacher has the unique opportunity to observe individual children in the presence of many others of the same age and sex, which allows a backdrop that is ideal for screening, evaluation, and placement recommendations.

Selected Screening Instruments

Screening instruments provide the opportunity to evaluate large numbers of children in a school setting. Very general and somewhat superficial, these instruments are designed to gather information that is useful in making decisions regarding the feasibility and necessity of additional evaluation.

The screening instrument on pp. 33 and 34 is similar to ones being used in classrooms in Greeley, Colorado. It may serve as an example for those developing biophysical components to educational programs. It was designed for use by the school nurse; however, the classroom teacher might also administer the form if no school nurse is available.

Evaluation

Biophysical evaluation can take many directions depending on the results of initial screening. This evaluation would usually include a complete physical examination. It might include an assessment of vision, hearing, body chemistry, and neurology.

Following biophysical evaluation, it is critical that communication take place between school personnel and the physicians. During this communication the teacher and nurse should be alert to any information that may have educational implications.

CLASSROOM APPLICATION OF BIOPHYSICAL THEORY

The biophysical system is an area where the teacher's role is supportive of medical intervention. A knowledge of and interest in the work being carried on in the biophysical disciplines could help promote an understanding and cooperative spirit that will benefit children.

Growing medical involvement is a positive step toward solving the health problems that often manifest themselves in schools. This involvement should not be viewed as a new panacea for children's behavior problems, nor should it threaten the role of the teacher. Medical intervention centers on three areas:

1. Physical examination or medical evaluation is generally specified to determine the role of physiological problems in deviant behavior. Although the medical evaluation itself does not entail intervention, it does help outline the next step if a medical problem is discovered.

2. Manipulation of physiological functions is sometimes indicated. Examples include surgery to correct physical defects that may have a direct effect on behavior. Special diets for phenylketonuria, diabetes, and weight problems, and prosthetic devices such as glasses and hearing aids are all examples of biophysical intervention. Also Knapazyk (1979) suggests that although there are many critics of diet control measures to ease emotional problems, there is sufficient evidence to warrant further study.

PARENT INTERVIEW FORM

Pupil's name _____ Sex _____ Date of birth _____

Length of pregnancy _____ Birthplace _____

I. Prenatal

Mother's health during pregnancy?

Medication used during pregnancy? _____

Length of labor _____ Birth weight _____

Instruments used? _____ Onset of respiration _____

Describe any problems or complications at birth _____

_____

Type of anesthetic? _____ Child's days in hospital? _____

Feeding—breast? _____

II. Physical development

How was solid food accepted? _____

Constipation or diarrhea? _____

Age: Sat _____ Crawled _____ Walked _____ Buttoned and unbuttoned _____

Tied shoes _____ Bladder trained _____ Bowel trained _____ Talked words _____

Sentences _____ Speak clearly? _____ Bed-wetting? _____

Right-handed—Left-handed _____

III. Behavioral development

Plays with other children? _____ Has close friends? _____

Retained in school? _____ Grade _____

Cooperates when asked to do simple household tasks? _____

Has temper tantrums? _____ Type discipline that works best _____

_____

Sucks thumb? _____ Enjoys listening to stories? _____

Cries easily? _____ Likes to remain with an activity? _____

Previous school experience? _____

IV. Family history

Father's age _____ Occupation _____ Work hours _____

Last grade in school _____ Glasses? _____

Right-handed—Left-handed _____

Mother's age _____ Occupation _____ Work hours _____

Last grade in school _____ Glasses? _____

Right-handed—Left-handed _____

Language(s) spoken in home _____

Health of siblings _____

School experience of siblings _____

_____

V. Significant health problems, illnesses, and complaints

1. Has the child ever had asthma or wheezing? _____

2. Has the child had allergies—either to medications, foods, or other substances? _____
   Explain _____

3. Does the child have any serious health problems or has he or she had any severe
   illnesses? _____ Explain _____

4. Has your child had a convulsion, seizure, or fainting spell? _____

5. How many throat infections or colds does your child have each year? _____

6. Date of last eye examination _____ Results _____

7. Date of last ear examination _____ Results _____

8. Has the child had any ear infections and/or hearing loss? _____ If so, please explain _____

9. Circle any of the following your child has had: 3-day measles (German)—10-day measles (red)—chicken pox—whooping cough—mumps—pneumonia

VI. Information in regard to past and present medications

Has the child been on routine use of any medicine? _____ Is your child presently taking medication? _____ Explain _____

_____

VII. Recommendations for school management, health care, etc. _____

_____

_____

_____

_____

_____

Date _____

R.N./Tchr. _____

3. Treatment of the symptoms of biophysical defects often becomes the most common medical intervention and includes artificial means aimed at remedying behavioral problems. The use of tranquilizers and the use of energizing medications are two recent examples of treatment of symptoms through artificial means.

Wilson and Sherrets (1981) caution, however, against the sweeping claims made on behalf of chemical remedies.

Biofeedback may have potential for use with handicapped children. Strider and Strider (1979) point out that although the technique has been used for the past 10 years, the research is still scarce with most emphasis still on adults.

In another study, Walton (1978) reported the use of a relaxation curriculum and biofeedback training with five severely emotionally disturbed boys. He reports that four of the five boys in the study showed a reduction in inappropriate behavior of over 50%. One youngster showed a slight rise in inappropriate behavior. While this study is only a very small sample, it is obvious that change occurred.

Role of the Teacher

Obviously teachers cannot prescribe treatment with medications, put children on diets, or perform surgery. They can, however, alert medical personnel of problems that might be helped through medical intervention. Referral, therefore, is one of the teacher's major responsibilities. Usually the school has specific guidelines for this referral process. Often the school nurse begins by contacting the physician. Once the medical evaluation is completed and the intervention decided on, the teacher lets the physician know the educational plan, perhaps on an ongoing basis. For example, a child on medication may need continued monitoring in the classroom so that medication levels can be adjusted as needed by the physician. The concerns raised by Beck and coworkers (1978) should receive serious consideration so that relationship problems between the teacher and physician are held to a minimum.

There is much interest in the use of various biophysical interventions in the treatment of emotional difficulties. Parents and teachers are being bombarded with new treatment plans for children. The decade of the '80s will surely shed some light on the validity of many of these current hopes. While quick cures and fixes are not likely to occur, there is reason for some guarded optimism. The teacher must be alert to biophysical advances as they relate to education and become sensitive to the intense interest of parents and their continued search for better treatment for their children.

The following journals are representative of the vast array available:

International Journal of Psychobiology. A technical journal presenting current information on biophysical, biochemical, and neuroendocrine mechanisms and how they relate to psychoenvironmental adaptation. This journal will be of interest to the professional who is concerned with how biophysical problems are linked with emotional difficulties.

Lancet. This medical journal is widely quoted in the lay press. It is designed for professionals as well as lay persons.

Journal of Autism and Childhood Schizophrenia. This technical journal features recent studies in biology and psychology. It has a comprehensive book review section.

Journal of Child Psychology and Psychiatry. One of the most diversified journals available to the teacher of disturbed children, it publishes articles useful to the student, teacher, and helping professional.

The Journal of School Health. This is the

most commonly read journal available to schools and teachers. It is designed for school personnel and the problems they face. If the teacher has time to read only one journal of this type, this one would be appropriate.

Health Education. This is the official journal of the American Alliance for Health, Physical Education, and Recreation. It features many excellent articles that are easily read by the professional and the interested and informed lay person.

Health Education Monograph. The Society for Public Health Education publishes this monograph for those interested in public health education, both professionals and others.

VIGNETTES

Vignette 1: Diet as a Biophysical Interaction
REPORTED BY Hartman, 1981

Sally was removed from her parents at age 3 because of severe abuse. (A younger sibling died from abuse and starvation.) Following a short period of hospitalization, Sally was transferred to a series of foster homes and institutions. She had been diagnosed as hyperactive and possibly retarded. She had been placed on a medical regime of 40 mg of Ritalin (10 mg Q.I.D.) daily and was given between-meal snacks consisting mostly of Kool Aid, which contains large quantities of chemicals suspected to cause hyperkinetic behavior. The Ritalin apparently stunted her physical development and by age 12, when she arrived at Children's Village, she was unable to perform normal exercises, her behavior was without normal controls, and she was suffering from malnutrition.

On the first day of her arrival, the Ritalin was terminated. With dietary intervention, a vegetarian fare consisting of the elimination of additives and all refined foods, Sally began to prosper. The setting was rural, with outdoor activities, horseback riding, and many opportunities for structured, self-image enhancing activities. No television was allowed. Within three months, Sally showed many positive developmental changes, possibly due to diet. Some emotional problems remained.

Vignette 2: Diet Control and Behavior

Donna, 14, attended junior high. During the ninth grade she started getting out of her seat, extremely distractible and restlessness. The staff tried to reinforce attention and sitting still. This failed and medical help was sought. During medical evaluation the doctor discovered a pin lodged in Donna's hip. Once this was surgically removed, her restlessness in school stopped.

How could such a problem have been avoided, the staff wondered. She had sat on the pin while sitting on the stage during a school program. She didn't want to "make a scene" so she remained very still, thinking she would remove it later. Later, it was not there! Donna became frightened and didn't tell her parents. During the following year, she experienced fears of what her parents would say and anxiety about what the pin was doing to her body.

Obviously, the staff's relationship with Donna could have been more open; however, there seemed to be no problem before her accident. The major error was in failing to suggest medical evaluation before behavioral intervention was undertaken. Perhaps individuals could have counseled with Donna regarding her reluctance to sit and gained her confidence—but they didn't and she paid a high price: a long time of discomfort and anxiety.

SUMMARY

The biophysical model is basic to other theoretical positions since it is the foundation on which learning takes shape. This model considers the pathology to be part of the child. Biophysical theorists generally follow one of two positions. The more restricted position is taken by those who believe that deviance can occur solely as a result of biophysical problems. A less structured position is taken by those who believe that a biophysical predisposition is necessary for deviance to occur but must be stimulated by an environmental catalyst before deviance can develop.

Regardless of the position taken by bio-physical theorists, they all believe that a relationship exists between biological growth and emotional development, and that this relationship can be altered to the advantage of the child. In order to affect this relationship, a positive interaction must develop between care givers around the needs of the child.

The teacher of children in conflict has a definite role in screening and evaluation of biophysical problems. This role usually decreases in the evaluation and medical intervention stages of this process. Even though the teacher is not the center of focus in biophysical theory, he or she has a critical function to perform.

BIBLIOGRAPHY

Algozzine, B. (1980). The disturbing child: A matter of opinion. *Behavior Disorders, 5*(2), 112–115.

Beck, G., et al. (1978). The physician-educator team: Let's make it work. *Journal of School Health, 48,* 79–83.

Bender, L. (1955). Twenty years of clinical research on schizophrenic children with special reference to those under six years of age. In G. Capian (Ed.), *Emotional problems of early childhood* New York: Basic Books.

Bender, L. (1968). Childhood schizophrenia: A review. *International Journal of Psychiatry, 5,* 211–300.

Bettelheim, B. (1959). Feral children and autistic children. *American Journal of Sociology, 64,* 155–167.

Bower, E. (1960). *Early identification of emotionally handicapped children in school.* Springfield, IL: Charles C Thomas.

Bower, E., & Lambert, N. (1971). In-school screening of children with emotional handicaps. In N. Long, W. Morse, & R. Newman (Eds.), *Conflict in the classroom.* Belmont, CA: Wadsworth.

Boyce, W. T., Sprunger, L. W., Duncan, B., & Sobolews, S. (1983). A survey of physician consultations in an urban school district. *Journal of School Health, 53*(5), 308–311.

Buss, A. (1966). *Psychopathology.* New York: John Wiley.

Deslauriers, A., & Carlson, C. (1969). *Your child is asleep: Early infantile autism.* Homewood, IL: Dorsey.

Erikson, K. (1964). Notes on the sociology of deviance. *Social Problems, 1,* 307–314.

Fowle, A. (1968). A typical leucocyte pattern of schizophrenic children. *Archives of General Psychiatry, 18,* 666–680.

Hartman, T. C. (1981). A nutritional model for effecting change in behavior disordered and severely emotionally disturbed victims of child abuse—The experiences of the Salem Children's Village. *Journal of Orthopsychology, 10*(1), 35–37.

Higgins, J. (1966). Effects of child rearing by schizophrenic mothers. *Journal of Psychiatric Research, 4,* 153–167.

Karlson, J. (1966). *The biological basis of schizophrenia.* Springfield, IL: Charles C Thomas.

Kennard, M. (1965). Application of EEG to psychiatry. In W. Wilson (Ed.), *Applications of electroneephalography in psychiatry.* Durham, NC: Duke University Press.

Knapczyk, D. R. (1979). Diet control in the management of behavior disorders. *Behavioral Disorders, 5*(1), 2–9.

Lyman, F. (1963). *Phenylketonuria.* Springfield, IL: Charles C Thomas.

McGhie, A., & Chapman, J. (1961). Disorders of attention and perception in early schizophrenia. *British Journal of Medical Psychology, 34,* 105–116.

Mednick, S. (1971). Birth defects and schizophrenia. *Psychology Today, 4,* 48–50, 80–81.

Meehl, P. (1969). Schizotaxia, schizotypy, schizophrenia. In A. H. Buss & E. H. Buss (Eds.), *Theories of schizophrenia.* New York: Atherton.

Pollin, W. (1972). The pathogenesis of schizophrenia. *Archives of General Psychiatry, 27,* 29–37.

Powers, H. (1974). Dietary measures to improve behavior and achievement. *Academic Therapy, 9,* 203–214.

Rhodes, W. C., & Sagor, M. (1974). *A study of child variance: The future.* Ann Arbor: University of Michigan Press.

Rimland, B. (1969). Psychogenesis versus biogenesis. The issues and evidence. In S. C. Plog & R. B. Edgerton (Eds.), *Changing perspectives in mental illness.* New York: Holt, Rinehart & Winston.

Ritvo, E., Yuwiler, A., Geller, E., Ornitz, E., Saeger, K., & Plotkin, S. (1970). Increased blood serotonin and platelets in early infantile autism. *Archives of General Psychiatry, 23,* 566–572.

Rogers, C. (1939). *The clinical treatment of the problem child.* Boston: Houghton Mifflin.

Rosenthal, D. (Ed.). (1963). *The Genain quadruplets: A case study and theoretical analysis of heredity and environment in schizophrenia.* New York: Basic Books.

Sagor, M. (1972). Biological bases of childhood behavior disorders. In W. C. Rhodes (Ed.), *A study of child variance.* Ann Arbor: University of Michigan Press.

Shaywitz, S. E., et al. (1982). Psychopharmacology of attention deficit disorder—Pharmacokinetic, neuroendocrine, and behavioral measures following acute and chronic treatment with methylpkenidate. *Pediatrics, 69*(6), 680–694.

Sinacore, J. S. (1978). Priorities in health education. *The Journal of School Health, 48,* 213–217.

Strauss, A., & Kephart, N. (1955). *Psychopathology and education of brain injured child* (Vol. 2). New York: Grune & Stratton.

Thompson, R. (1967). *Foundations of physiological psychology.* New York: Harper & Row.

Ullman, L., & Krasner, L. (Eds.). (1965). *Case studies in behavior modification.* New York: Holt, Rinehart & Winston.

Walton, M. M. (1978). An analysis of behavior acquisition and maintenance with conditioned reinforcers developed through pairing. *Dissertation Abstracts International* (Purdue University), 39(2–B), 455–456.

Walton, W. T. (1979). The future of biofeedback training in the field of special education. Paper presented at the Annual International Convention, The Council for Exceptional Children, Dallas, Texas, April 22–27.

Wender, P. (1969). The role of genetics in the etiology of schizophrenias. *American Journal of Orthopsychiatry, 39,* 447–458.

3

The Psychodynamic Approach

INTRODUCTION AND OBJECTIVES

Psychodynamic theory has heavily influenced special programs for children in conflict. Programs of the 1950s and early 1960s relied on it almost exclusively. Although in more recent years behavioral theory has predominated, psychodynamic theory has continued in a supportive role.

The psychodynamic approach originated from the analytical, internalized approach to personality, generally attributed to Sigmund Freud (1856–1939). In addition, recent psychodynamic theorists have combined ideas about the internal components of personality development with ideas about environmental influences. The results of this theoretical merger can be seen in current educational thought.

In this chapter, you will (a) become familiar with psychodynamic theory, (b) be able to identify psychodynamic causes of deviance, (c) become familiar with screening and evaluation procedures, and (d) be able to explain various approaches to treatments, including crisis intervention, life space interviewing, intervention with supportive media, and the mental health center approach.

DEFINING EMOTIONAL DISTURBANCE

Psychodynamic theory begins with the analytical, intrapsychic personality theory of Sigmund Freud. From this viewpoint, the child in conflict has not successfully negotiated the various intrapsychic and external complications of maturation. For example, the child whose transition from the oral stage of development (feeding, learning to make appropriate sounds) to the anal stage (toilet training) has been too severe may later show behavior problems. Similarly, a child whose progression through the oedipal phase (sexual identification) has been unsatisfactory may have difficulty in establishing appropriate relationships with those of the opposite sex at a later time in life (Rezmierski & Kotre, 1972).

While Sigmund Freud emphasized the power of the id as the motivating force within the individual, later theorists like Anna Freud and Erik Erikson emphasized the role of the ego and the influence of society and environment on the individual. Psychodynamic thought is, therefore, a maturing theory, not restricted to any one theory or approach.

BASIC THEORY

Psychodynamic theory includes such widely discussed approaches as psychoanalytic thought, psychoeducational programming, psychodynamic treatment, and counseling. All of these approaches include at least three basic components: (a) children's relationships to themselves, or intrapersonal interactions, (b) interactions with others, or interpersonal relationships, and (c) children's ability to involve themselves in educational tasks with emotional vigor.

There is controversy over the validity and usefulness of this theory. There is evidence, however, that the abandonment of psychodynamic theories for more simplistic forms of intervention has not been as productive as it originally appeared.

Psychodynamic theory has its roots in Freudian thought, but it has evolved into much more than analytic thought. Fine (1973) briefly describes nine theoretical systems that he believes have direct relationships to Freudian thought. These include Rogerian client-centered theory (Rogers, 1951), the rational emotive system of Ellis (1970), the encounter movement developed by Schultz (1967) and Burton (1969), the eclectic system of Thorne (1967), the gestalt therapy of Perls, Hefferline, and Goodman (1951), reality therapy of Glasser (1965),

Jungian analysis (Jung, 1959), and Adlerian therapy (Ansbacher & Ansbacher, 1956). According to Fine's thesis, there seems to be little theory that is actually new; it is just put together in different ways and with new emphasis and labels. Therefore, the easiest way to understand the many theoretical constructs being offered would be through study of the Freudian model of psychoanalysis. Freud's theory is the basis of many theoretical constructs and indeed is the heart of most theories that approach behavior from a dynamic point of view. Even Skinner, the avowed behaviorist, suggests that Freud would, if he were alive, support his theoretical position (Skinner, 1972)!

Freud studied medicine and graduated from the University of Vienna in 1881. Finding the salary of a researcher inadequate to support six children and a wife, he began to practice medicine. Then from Jean Charcot he learned the use of hypnosis in treating various mental disorders, particularly hysteria. He also learned the cathartic, or "talking out your problems" form of therapy (Hall, 1954) from Joseph Breuer. As Freud began to probe deeply into the minds of his patients, he gradually put physiology and neurology aside and became a psychological investigator.

Today Freud would be considered a psychiatrist, but by his admitted preference, Freud was a scientist and philosopher. As you read the following sections on Freudian psychoanalysis, recall that Freud believed (1935, 1949, 1953) people resist knowing the truth about themselves and that society reflects this irrationality (Hall, 1954).

Causes of Deviance

Within the psychodynamic theoretical approach there are diverse beliefs regarding the cause of deviance. If we look at the roots of psychodynamic theory, we see an approach deeply entrenched in the analytical tradition. If we look at the more recent development of the theory, we will see a more humanistic approach. In either case, the basic causes of emotional disturbance will be seen somewhat differently.

The strength of psychodynamic thought is its divergence. All of the individual approaches within the theory combine into three themes—that behaviors are meaningful, that behaviors reflect both conscious and unconscious motivation; and that the past continues into the present. As you read each of these related components of psychodynamic theory, you will appreciate their individual yet related contributions to the education of children in conflict.

Analytical Psychology. A child's personality is made up of the *id, ego,* and *superego*. In healthy children these three systems work in harmony, meeting the individual's basic needs and desires. If, however, the three systems are in conflict, the child is said to be maladjusted.

The id is the only system that is present at birth. It is the total inherited system of instinctual energy that supplies the power for the entire personality. The id operates on the pleasure principle (the reduction or elimination of tension from the person). Tension is seen as pain or discomfort, whereas pleasure or satisfaction is achieved when this pain or discomfort is eased. The goal of the id is to avoid pain and achieve pleasure.

The ego is the mediating system between the demands of the id and the constraints of the world in which the child lives. The ego derives its power from the id; however, in the course of interacting with the external world, the ego often must subdue the demands made by the id. When this occurs, a conflict inevitably arises between these two systems of the personality. In procuring objects of gratification for the id, the ego must follow a logical and rational process, which is known as the reality principle.

The third system of personality is the superego, which develops from the ego. The superego represents the norms and values of society that are taught to the child by his or her parents and significant others. The superego can be thought of as punishing or controlling (conscience) or as a positive ego-ideal, which are actually opposite sides of the same moral coin (Hall, 1954). The superego manipulates the ego by use of rewards and punishments. For example, appropriate responses to the demands of the id are rewarded by a satisfied feeling, whereas inappropriate responses might be followed by feelings of guilt.

Psychic energy, which allows the total personality system to function, is supplied by the id and is called the libido. This energy is sexual in nature, fluid, and displaceable. Being fluid and displaceable, it can be invested in any number of objects or activities (cathexis) (Rezmierski & Kotre, 1972). This energy can be invested in a wide variety of objects either singly or together. Object cathexis is the process of investing psychic energy to satisfy an instinct. At times the ego must use its libido (psychic energy) to control the id. This is called anticathexis, an example of which might be a child trying to control his temper. The temper is motivated by the needs of the id, whereas control is apparent in the efforts of the ego to calm the temper. If the anticathexis is not strong enough, the impulsive desires of the id may break through and the child has a temper tantrum.

In addition to the three systems of personality developed by Freud, it seems appropriate to outline his five stages of development. It should be pointed out that Karl Abraham, an associate of Freud, elaborated the psychosexual stages of development that were later accepted by Freud (Hall, 1954). These include the oral, anal, phallic, latency, and genital stages. Each stage will be discussed in terms of children in conflict.

The five stages of development are all centered around the three erogenous zones: the area around the mouth, the anal area, and the genital area. As the child passes through the various developmental stages, one of the three erotic zones becomes the focal point of gratification for the child. There is much overlapping between stages, but normal development does follow a fairly systematized pattern. Even "normal" progression through the psychosexual stages is fraught with problems. The child may have feeding problems with various formulas being tried, difficulty at the time of weaning, difficulty adjusting to toileting routines, or an array of similar conflicts.

The oral stage begins at birth and usually continues until the child is about 2 years of age. During this psychological stage, the mouth is the center of gratification. At this stage the child begins to differentiate between the mother's breast and himself. This is the beginning of ego development, which will continue through the phallic stage. As anyone who has raised children knows, in the oral stage nearly everything seems to enter the mouth. The child ostensibly is trying to "swallow the world." Karl Abraham (Rezmierski & Kotre, 1972) has divided this stage into two substages: the oral dependent, which extends over the first few months of a child's life, and the oral aggressive, which develops at the time that teeth become an effective tool. During the oral dependent stage, the child is seemingly much like a bird, swallowing whatever is presented. If the child becomes fixated at (attached to) this substage, he will likely be overdependent on the world or too optimistic. This child feels the world will take care of him and is therefore easily disappointed. When the teeth erupt, the child has the tools to become much more aggressive; therefore, the child who fixates at this substage may be orally aggressive, verbally attacking, and sarcastic. The child might also use oral means to get the love and attention necessary to function. Whether such a clear division between oral substages is evident in the classroom is debatable, although fixation at the oral stage is often evident with children who are in conflict. The exact substage is relatively unimportant in treatment, at least in an educational setting.

During the second year of life, the anal area of the body becomes the principal region for gratification. Two substages are again delineated: the *anal-expulsive substage*, when the child derives much gratification from expelling of feces, and the *anal-retentive substage*, when gratification is obtained by holding in and controlling the feces. The anal stage of development is usually consummated by the fourth year of life. Problems during the anal stage of development can lead to one of several conflicts. Children may become too orderly, with every pencil and every book in their desks having an exact spot, or the opposite behavior might develop. Children whose behavior is defiant, obstinate, cruel, and destructive have been associated with inappropriate progression through the anal stage of development.

Beginning at about 4 years of age and continuing until approximately 6 years of age, the *phallic stage* becomes dominant. During this stage, children are preoccupied with the genital area of the body. Masturbation, looking at the genitals (the child's own and others), and sex play with other children are common. At this stage children are extremely interested in knowing all about sex, where babies come from, the difference between boys and girls, and the sexual activities of parents. Children are trying to work out their sexual identity, a task beset with difficulty.

The Oedipus complex (attachment of the child to the parent of the opposite sex) was originally used to describe behaviors of both boys and girls. This rather complicated stage begins with the boy feeling very close to the mother. This closeness finally develops into a desire for more intimate contact with the mother, a thought that produces much fear and anxiety for the child. His father, whose role he would like to have, is seen as much more powerful and therefore a real threat to the boy. In fact, the child feels his father may harm him severely for harboring such desires. The ultimate harm a boy could experience would likely be castration; this fear is called *castration anxiety*. This anxiety causes the boy to repress both his sexual impulses for his mother and his anger and hostility toward his father. To cope with feelings toward his father, the son identifies with him (identification with the aggressor). Through the process of identification the boy incorporates much of the father's personality by a process called introjection. As the son incorporates the values of his father, he develops a superego in both its positive (ego-ideal) and negative (conscience) connotations.

It is less easy to explain the Oedipus complex as it relates to girls (Electra complex). Although it develops as a parallel to the Oedipus complex in boys, it has some notable differences. As the girl recognizes that she does not have a penis, she feels cheated and angry, with her feelings being directed toward her mother. This leads to a "cooling off" of her relationship with her mother. To achieve what she does not possess, she turns to her father. From this point the Electra complex develops in a manner similar to that of the Oedipus complex for boys, with guilt and fear of the mother becoming evident. This leads the girl to identify with the mother and to replace the desire of the father with the desire for a baby. Most theorists believe that describing the Electra complex is extremely difficult. Apparently this resolution is more difficult for girls and less clearly made, suggesting that the superego of girls is not as strong as that developed by boys (Hall, 1954; Rezmierski & Kotre, 1972).

By the time the child successfully completes the phallic stage, the id, ego, and superego should be intact and the basic components of personality established.

Problems that occur during the phallic stage of development are apparent with children in conflict. Attitudes concerning the opposite sex that are not resolved at this stage will continue to cause problems in later life. Exaggerated masculinity, including boastfulness, extreme aggressiveness, and other behaviors that bring the child into conflict with peers and authority, may be the result of inappropriate resolution of the phallic stage.

The latency stage comes between the phallic and genital stages. It is really not a stage of development but a rest period between the tumultuous phallic and genital stages. During this period, sex interest is dormant, the conflicts of the phallic stage are resolved, and identification with the parent of the same sex has been accomplished. These are relatively calm years. Boys belong to boys' groups and play boys' games, whereas girls pursue activities of a feminine nature and establish relationships with girls. Learning seems to come quickly at this stage, since other conflicts are now put aside.

The genital stage begins with puberty and leads to the mature adult. During this stage the earlier conflicts of the phallic stage emerge once again. Partial solutions to the oedipal complex now become unacceptable during the more advanced genital stage. It should be pointed out that three basic differences exist between the phallic and genital stages. Although both are concerned with the genital areas as the center of gratification, the focus of this gratification is significantly different. During the phallic stage the child's focus of sexual interest is incestuous or within the family, wheras sexual interest during the genital stage is external to the family. In addition, during the phallic stage the child was seeking satisfaction only for himself, whereas during the genital stage the child seeks to bring satisfaction not only to himself but to the object of his love. Finally, the child now has the physiological capability to act out feelings toward the opposite sex.

In the Freudian view there is little in the way of pathology that cannot be traced to one of the prelatency stages. If the resolution of problems has been successfully completed in the first three psychosexual stages, there appear to be few later concerns.

There are several reasons for problem behaviors developing during the psychosexual stages of development. First, too much psychic energy might have been invested at any one of the various stages. With too much psychic energy expended, there might be too little remaining to negotiate successive stages of development. Second, there is a problem of regression to an earlier stage. For example, a child who encounters problems adjusting to puberty might regress to the oral stage and fixate his behavior at that level. When the prospect of moving from one stage to the next is too threatening, the child might choose to remain at a more comfortable stage, thus creating further conflict as immature behavior is exhibited.

Freudian theory is not the end-all in psychological thought. Although it has opened many avenues of thought for theorists and clinicians, it is admittedly sexist, with women being valued less than men; it is pessimistic in its attitude toward the goodness of man (Horney, 1951), and it looks for causation, which is often seen as a waste of time (Mosak & Dreikurs, 1973). Despite all of these problem areas, it still is the foundation on which other theories were built (Fine, 1973).

Rather than review neo-Freudian theorists, this section will move on to the humanistic psychologists. Although the neo-Freudians depart from the strict Freudian interpretation of personality development, they are still very analytical in their approach to child study. For the teacher interested in the neo-Freudian viewpoint, the works of Anna Freud (1937, 1947, 1949, 1952, 1965) and Otto Rank (1929) of the more socially oriented analytical theorists Harry Sullivan (1953), Karen Horney (1945), and Erich Fromm (1947) are suggested.

Humanistic Psychology. Adler is considered by many theorists to be among the first of the humanistic psychologists (Ellis, 1970; Mosak and Dreikurs, 1973), a group of psychologists who search for truth without using mechanistic and dehumanizing methods (Maslow, 1965). Adler (1870-1937) was born in Vienna, where he was awarded his M.D. degree in 1893. After working as a general practitioner for several years, he turned his attention to psychiatry. At Freud's invitation in 1902, Adler joined Freud's circle of close associates to study the human personality from a Freudian perspective (Mosak & Dreikurs, 1973). In 1911 he separated from Freud's group to start his own school. Adler accepted a professorship at Columbia University in 1926, and from that point in his life he spent most of his time in the United States (Adler, 1970). The influence of the people and culture of this country undoubtedly influenced his theoretical approach, particularly his latest writings.

Adler followed the lead of Freud in his insistence on the importance of childhood as the foundation of a healthy personality. His attitude was not as extreme as Freud's, however, and he leaned toward a social explanation of acceptable and unacceptable behavior. Adler departed from Freud on many issues, including the importance of sexual energy. Adler (1964) believed that all questions of life could be related to three major

problems: that of communal life (community life), of work (occupation), and of love (Adler, 1963, 1970). He repeatedly stressed the problems of the spoiled child and the difficulty of using any system to overcome this basic undermining of the child's ability to function. Adler had an extreme dislike for oversimplification and easy answers, and he recommended leaving no stone unturned in an effort to secure understanding.

Several basic theoretical assumptions separate Adlerian theory from Freudian theory. These are outlined by Mosak and Dreikurs (1973) as follows: Adler, in relation to Freud, is (1) more subjective, (2) more socially oriented, (3) more holistic in his approach, (4) less fatalistic regarding the "goodness of man," and (5) less sexist.

In his review of humanistic psychology, Bugental (1963) outlines eight major parameters of psychology undergoing change in a humanistic approach:

1. A person is a composite of part functions rather than a catalog of individual parts.
2. The original model of science that was borrowed from physics is changing.
3. The medical model that has guided psychological thought is changing toward client involvement in the change process.
4. Changes are occurring in the role of graduate schools as training agencies, isolated theory is giving way to practical application.
5. There is a moving away from statistical analysis as the way to find the truth.
6. A change is occurring in the belief that research must precede practice.
7. The clinical team is being exposed as having often been a myth and in many cases a smoke screen for domination by a single professional.
8. The belief that diagnosis (a medical term) is necessary for treatment to proceed or be effective is being called a fallacy.

The extent to which these changes have taken place varies; however, movement away from clinical observation and dissection is apparent if we read the works of Maslow, Allport, Combs, Rogers, and other humanist psychologists. Only one of these theorists, Rogers, will be reviewed. Although Rogers cannot be considered the torchbearer for humanistic psychology, his theoretical approach supports the general direction of humanism as outlined by Bugental (1963). In his early writing on clinical treatment of the problem child, Rogers (1959) stated his position in regard to behavior change: "In this book we shall deal with the child, not with behavior symptoms" (p. 3). Rogers goes on to describe symptoms of behavior such as stealing, truancy, and thumbsucking, which are not problems and therefore cannot be treated. He concludes:

There are children—boys and girls—with very different backgrounds and personalities, and some of these children steal, and some of them run away from school, and others find satisfaction in sucking their thumbs, or in saying obscene words, or in defying their parents; but in each instance it is the child with whom we must deal, not the generalization we make about his behavior (1959, pp. 3–4).

Rogers's theory is phenomenological (the way in which a child perceives reality at any given moment; the incongruence that develops between the child's self and his experiences). More precisely, psychological conflict, according to Rogers, "exists when the organism denies to awareness, significant experiences, which consequently are not accurately symbolized and organized into the gestalt of the self-structure, thus creating an incongruence between self and experience" (1959, p. 204). Rogers prefers the term *defensive behaviors* for symptoms commonly called neuroses and the term *disorganized behavior* for what has generally been called psychosis.

For the classroom teacher, Rogers (1969) offers a conceptualization of relationships, a modern approach to the value system held in education, and a plan for self-directed change. For many practitioners in the classroom who must deal with behaviors as the behaviors occur, the impact of the phenomenological approach as espoused by Rogers has not been fully realized. Many teachers believe the approach to be more applicable to clinically oriented situations of one-to-one encounters rather than to classrooms. Others believe the theory to be more attuned to adults than to children, a belief supported by Rogers (1959). Rogers has much to offer teachers who are able to use the mirroring techniques of counseling, adapt teaching to include "facilitation of change," develop an attitude of acceptance and trust, and cultivate empathetic understanding.

SCREENING AND EVALUATION PROCEDURES

Psychodynamic screening will probably occur at a later date in the child's life than biophysical screening, since medical screening can begin at birth. Bower (1978) suggests that screening is most effective if it takes place at a time when the child is at a transition point, for example, the child's first year in preschool, first grade, middle school, or junior high school—all points that have been found to be emotionally hazardous for children and parents.

Bower (1978) points out several additional important facts about the screening process: First, screening is not a one-shot affair. It must be an ongoing process that offers continued opportunities for observation. Second, it must produce reliable data gathered in a precise manner. It must not be sloppily done simply because it is a screening process. Finally, the screening process requires sanction and support by those testing and the consumers of the evaluation.

During the past ten years, screening has had a major boost because of congressional action. In 1967 the U.S. Congress added a provision to the Medicaid Act that offered children of eligible familes the right to early and periodic screening, diagnosis, and treatment (EPSDT) for physical and mental defects. Under this Title XIX provision, children from birth to 21 years of age from poor and minority families could receive services that might otherwise be unavailable.

Several attempts have been made to develop a national guide to assessment of children with mental defects. These efforts have generally met with failure. The reasons for this are varied but often include problems of predictability, particularly as predictability relates to reliability and applicability of test instruments; confidentiality; labeling; adequacy of treatment facilities; and need for integration of treatment services (American Orthopsychiatric Association, 1978).

In the absence of a national screening procedure, it is necessary for communities to develop screening routines that fit local needs.

Role of the Teacher

The classroom teacher is the primary person in the screening process using a psychodynamic approach. A teacher's role is also critical, although not primary, during the evaluation, placement, and programming phases.

Although earlier researchers have questioned the teacher's role and effectiveness in the screening process (Goldfarb, 1963; Wickman, 1928), there is a wealth of data that supports teachers as being effective observers of childhood deviance if certain specific procedures are followed (Cartwright & Cartwright, 1974, 1984). Generally, the contributions of the teacher are enhanced by the discreet use of additional tools, but the teacher's involvement in the process is very im-

portant (Bower, 1960; Nelson, 1971; Swanson & Watson, 1982).

Several important factors support teachers as the most logical persons to participate in the identification process.*

1. Teachers are trained in personality development of children.
2. The classroom teaching role provides a variety of normal behaviors on which teachers can base their professional judgment.
3. Teachers interact with children each day for extended periods of time.
4. Both individual and group activities are monitored by teachers, a fact that enhances teacher judgments when compared with clinical interpretation. An interesting and important consideration of the teacher's role in screening was raised by Woody (1969, p. 44) when he asked, "Is it really necessary for teachers to view behaviors in the same manner as clinicians?" From the evidence of research findings and the role assumed by classroom teachers, it would appear that both teacher judgment and clinical assessment are effective in the assessment process; however, for screening purposes teacher judgment appears to be most acceptable.

Bower and Lambert (1971, p. 144) list seven broad criteria for selection of a screening instrument for school use.

1. It should be possible to complete the screening procedure with only such information as the teacher could obtain without outside technical or professional assistance.
2. The procedure should be sufficiently simple and straightforward to undertake without long training or daily supervision.

---

*Persons interested in a summary of teacher growth in attitudes toward behavior problems of children should consult Hunter (1957).

3. The results of the procedure should be *tentative identification* of children with emotional problems—leading the teacher to *refer* to competent specialists those children who could benefit most from thorough diagnosis.

4. As a corollary to 3 above, the procedure should *not* encourage the teacher to diagnose emotional problems, nor to draw conclusions about their causes, nor to label or categorize children; in fact, the procedure should actively discourage the teacher from undertaking any of these highly technical interpretations.

5. The procedure should be one which neither invades the privacy of individuals nor violates good taste.

6. The procedure should be one that does not offer a threat to any child.

7. The procedure should be inexpensive to use.

Selected Screening Instruments

Bower-Lambert Scales. Bower and Lambert have developed a screening instrument that is comprehensive for both the individual child and the range of children served by schools. This scale is designed for both boys and girls from kindergarten through grade 12. It represents a comprehensive model for screening that offers promise for use in the school setting. The procedure covers three domains: the teacher's perception of each child, the child's self-perception, and the perception of each child by his or her peers. Bower and Lambert's screening device could be labeled a semiprojective technique and might be further classified as embodying a psychodynamic orientation to screening. Following is a narrative description by Bower and Lambert (1971, p. 142–148) of their pupil behavior rating scales.

Behavior Rating of Pupils (All Grades)

One of the most important and useful kinds of information obtained by the school is the teacher's professional judgment of children's behavior. Teachers see children over a period of time in a variety of circumstances: in stress situations, at

work and at play. Their judgment and observation have been sharpened by professional training and by day-to-day experience with the normal behavior of children. Often the teacher's rating can be the single most effective index of a pupil's growth and development.

Few professional persons, no matter how well-trained, can make ratings of others with absolute certainty and complete comfort. Don't spend too much time worrying about whether your rating for a particular child is "right" or "wrong." Make your best judgment of each student, then go on to the next. Remember that it is not your judgment alone that will be used to determine whether or not a pupil is developing emotional difficulties. Your perception of a child's behavior will be combined with the perceptions of the child himself and those of his peers—to make the final judgment about screening a child.

The Class Pictures (Peer Rating—Kindergarten to Grade 3)

After you have completed the *Behavior Rating of Pupils*, your next step in screening is to plan for administration of the peer ratings. The peer rating instrument for kindergarten and primary grades, *The Class Pictures*, must be given to each child in your class individually. This may take fifteen to twenty minutes of time for each child. Administration of *The Class Pictures* to the entire class, however, may be spread over a period of time—up to, but not exceeding, one month.

Administer the instrument to children one at a time when the rest of the class is engaged in seat work of some kind or occupied in other activities which do not require constant supervision. Such a schedule will require a minimum of interruption in your regular teaching program.

The Class Pictures are composed of twelve picture cards with a total of twenty scoring items (one or two items on a card). Five of the items are pictures of boys in situations related to emotionally maladjusted behavior; five are pictures of girls in situations related to emotionally maladjusted behavior; five are pictures of boys in situations related to positive or neutral types of behavior; and five are pictures of girls in situations related to positive or neutral types of behavior.

The Class Pictures have been developed as a means of analyzing, in a systematic and measurable way, how children are perceived or "seen" by their peers. The responses of most pupils to the pictures will not surprise you. Some responses, however, may seem unrealistic and inappropriate. *Accept each child's responses without comment unless the child obviously misunderstands directions.* Your role during the administration of *The Class Pictures* is one of test proctor and recorder of responses.

The Class Pictures are used with children who have not yet learned to read or write well. Therefore, the responses of each child will need to be recorded individually by you. You will, of course, have to make special provision for the rest of the class while you are administering *Class Pictures* to individual children. If an additional school person is available, he may work with the class while you administer *Class Pictures*. The actual administration should always be done by you. If you are able to organize the class into working groups, *Class Pictures* may be administered daily to a few individuals during such work periods—but you will decide for yourself how best to accomplish this task.

On the test each child is asked to consider which of his classmates is most like the child in every one of the twenty situations. Some children will pick twenty different names. Others may name one or two peers for several or many different items. Still others may make no response for one or more items. *Do not expect any fixed pattern of responses.*

When the responses for each child in the class are collected, the teacher can tally the number of times a particular child is chosen for each of the twenty pictures. The total number of times a child is chosen for *all* of the pictures indicates how clearly or how vividly he is "seen," or perceived by his peers.

The number of times a pupil is picked for the *negative* pictures indicates the degree to which he or she is *negatively* perceived by his peers. By dividing the number of times a child is picked for the ten negative pictures by the total number of times he is picked for all twenty of the pictures, a percent, indicating the ratio of negative perception by peers, is obtained and used in screening.

The mean or average number of negative selections of emotionally handicapped boys and girls has been found to be significantly different from the mean number of negative selections in the general school population of that grade and sex. Consequently, the percent of negative perception has been found to be a reliable indicator of those children whose behavior, as observed by peers, indicates some degree of emotional difficulty. The higher the percent, the greater the possibility that the child has emotional problems. The percent of negative selections on *The Class Pictures*, when combined with teacher ratings and self-ratings, has been found effective in primary grades for screening children with emotional handicaps.

A Class Play (Peer Rating—Grades 3-7)

A Class Play is a peer rating instrument with greatest applicability in grades, 4, 5, and 6, though it has been used with success in grades 3 and 7. It should be administered reasonably soon after you have completed the *Behavior Rating of Pupils*. It should take no more than 35 to 40 minutes.

Section I of the instrument contains descriptions of twenty hypothetical roles in a play, with instructions directing each pupil to choose a classmate who would be most suitable and natural in each of the roles. Section II of the *Play* elicits from each pupil an indication of the roles he would prefer, or which he thinks other people would prefer, or which he thinks other people would select for him. This section has thirty different quartets of the twenty roles, with a question aimed at finding out how the child sees himself in relation to each role.

The scoring of *A Class Play* is very much like the scoring of *The Class Pictures*. Each pupil names a classmate for each of the roles in the play. By counting the number of times a pupil is picked for each of the roles in the play, and then counting the number of times each pupil is picked for the *even numbered* (negative) roles, a percentage is obtained indicative of the positive or negative perception of each pupil by his classmates. This score is used in the screening.

Student Survey (Peer Rating—Grades 7-12)

The *Student Survey* is the peer rating instrument for use in the junior and senior high schools. In order for this test to have validity, it is necessary to administer it to a class in which the students have had an opportunity for some social and intellectual interaction, as well as for observation of one another in a variety of classroom situations. Previous work with this test has shown that social studies or English classes are usually best for this purpose.

Some students in the junior and senior high school may be sensitive to the kinds of questions on the *Student Survey*. It is important, therefore, that you anticipate the possibility of such sensitivity and take steps to allay any suspicion or resentment. For example, some teachers have found it helpful to have ready an envelope into which all the tests can be placed when the students are finished. This helps to reassure the class that the test results are confidential and reinforces statements made in the instructions that the results will not be discussed with others.

Section I of the *Student Survey* consists of twenty items. Ten are illustrative of maladjusted or emotionally disturbed behavior and ten are illustrative of neutral or positive behavior. For each statement of behavior, the students are asked to list the name of a classmate who is most like the student described in the item.

Section II of the *Student Survey* contains the same twenty behavior statements randomly arranged in thirty groups of four statements each. The student is asked to select one of the four statements in each group as the one which he thinks others in the class might apply to himself. The responses to Section II can be used to compare the peer ratings of a student with his self rating. The value of providing two sections in the *Student Survey*, a peer rating and a self-rating on the same items, is, that after scoring both sections, the teacher is able to measure and analyze how a student sees himself in relation to how he is seen by others.

A Picture Game (Self Rating—Kindergarten to Grade 3)

A Picture Game is designed to give a measure of young children's perception of *self*. It is used along with the *Behavior Rating of Pupils* (teacher rating) and *The Class Pictures* (peer rating) to identify pupils who are vulnerable to, or handicapped by, emotional problems.

A Picture Game consists of 66 pictures, including two sample pictures. Each picture is illustrative of normal home and school relationships and events. With the exception of the two sample cards and the first ten pictures, each picture is emotionally neutral in the portrayal of the relationship or event. The child is asked to sort each picture into one of two categories: "This is a happy picture" or "This is a sad picture." The sorting is done by placing each picture in the "happy" or "sad" side of a two-compartment box, which has a happy face shown on one compartment and a sad face shown on the other. The child categorizes each picture in accordance with his perception of it.

The first ten pictures the child sorts are stereotypes: obviously happy or obviously sad situations. The purpose of including them in the test items is to check on each pupil's understanding of the task. If a child sorts the first ten pictures correctly, you can be fairly sure that he has understood the process well enough for you to use his score in screening. If, on the other hand, he does not sort the first ten pictures correctly, you will need to meet with him individually and ask him to sort the pictures again for you, making certain that he understands the process. Some children *choose* to place pictures differently from others. If you find that such children understand the process but continue, on readministration, to sort the pictures in an independent fashion, make a note of it on the "Class Record Sheet," and use the child's score in screening.

Thinking about Yourself (Self Rating—Grades 3-7)

The purpose of *Thinking about Yourself* is to elicit from the pupil himself an *intra-self* measure of the relationship between a pupil's perception of his environment and his conception of what it ought to be. What is looked for is the degree of discrepancy between a pupil's self perception of himself as he *is* and as he would like to be.

Many pupils with serious emotional problems cannot bring themselves to disclose their difficulties in writing, or are uncomfortable about disclosing them. Their responses will therefore very much resemble those of other children in the class. These youngsters are most likely to be screened by teachers and peers.

There are other pupils, however, who do not manifest their difficulties to teachers or peers, but who rise to the opportunity to express inner discomfort and *can* communicate their disturbance on a self rating instrument. Since the average discrepancy between self and *ideal* self has been found to discriminate between pupils with emotional problems and those with normal behavior adjustment, *Thinking about Yourself* provides a meaningful and useful screening dimension not available from teacher or peer ratings.

A Self Test (Self Rating—Grades 7-12)

Like *Thinking about Yourself*, *Self Test* measures the difference between self and ideal self. To the extent that a student is able to disclose the differences or similarities between these two aspects of self, the instrument is useful in screening. Thus like the previous test, some troubled children are more likely to be identified by teachers and peers in the screening process. For those who *can* communicate their disturbance on a self rating, the *Self Test* provides the opportunity and can be a meaningful screening dimension not available from teacher or peer ratings.

A *Self Test* contains forty statements describing people behaving in a number of different ways. In Section I, the student is asked to indicate how strongly he *would like to* be or *would not like* to be the person described. In Section II, the items are repeated and the student is asked to indicate how strongly he feels he *is* like or *is not* like the person described. The two responses by the student (i.e., whether or not he *wants* to be like and whether or not he *is* like) are then compared in the scoring process, after which the amount of discrepancy between the two "selves" is compared . . . .

The Bower-Lambert scales are an example of a comprehensive screening instrument. Although this system may appear somewhat cumbersome to teachers, it actually includes instruments rather simple to administer and

score. The data from tests are collated and weighted through specific procedures that finally result in a total evaluation for each child.

Observational Screening

One of the most often used and productive screening techniques is professional observation. The teacher has unique opportunities to gain insight into student conflicts. The teacher, along with the social worker, school nurse, school aides, and psychologists, can offer a perspective that contains useful screening information.

Evaluation

Evaluation is the process of studying the youngster to determine specific areas of need and potential intervention. The most common evaluation tools include intelligence tests, personality tests, and interviews (Swanson & Watson, 1982).

Examples of two commonly used individual intelligence scales are the Wechsler Intelligence Scale for Children (WISC) (1974) and the Stanford-Binet test (1973). These tests have received sharp criticism in recent years but still remain the major tools for determining the potential intellectual capacity of a given child (Anastasi, 1968). Before any psychological tests are administered, the psychologist should spend time in the classroom observing the child. Tests that are given by a person not familiar to the child, in strange surroundings, and without prior observation are highly suspect as valid measurement tools (Anastasi, 1968; Ebel, 1972). Although some states still require individual tests of intelligence before special class placement can be made, there appears to be a healthy skepticism developing that will probably diminish "testing for testing's sake."

Although both the WISC and Stanford-Binet test were intended to be used only as intelligence tests, much research has been done to determine their usefulness in assessing other areas, such as personality makeup and learning style (Buros, 1965). Various testing professionals have even proposed that brain damage and mental illness can be determined by using individual intelligence tests (Coleman, 1964). Placing much confidence in the ability of intelligence tests to evaluate areas like emotional stability is highly questionable; in fact, Anastasi (1968) suggests that emotional variables are important factors in the adequate measure of intellectual ability.

Once the test administration is completed, the information should be shared with those who are directly responsible for the correct educational placement of each child. This information should include more than test scores, since the testing situation generally yields extremely important data. Proficient test administrators report that the final IQ score is among the least important data gathered during test administration with children in conflict.

Although teachers sometimes believe that the information gained from the intelligence testing is useless, since it represents something they already knew, they should be aware that the psychologist or psychiatrist is really not gathering new information. The alert teacher will soon develop a sense of knowing the approximate intellectual level at which a child is functioning from various school-related tasks. Common findings should lend support to both the teacher and psychologist. The role of the psychologist in testing helps to verify the teacher's suspicions, but, more important, the psychologist looks at the learning style of the child from another perspective, which can contribute valuable insight for educational programing (Anastasi, 1968). When the psychologist is an active participant with teachers and other staff in a helping team, the interaction adds to

the overall usefulness of the intelligence testing.

In addition to intelligence testing the psychologist will probably want to do other psychological testing as part of routine evaluation. Personality tests of either the projective or nonprojective type might be used. There are a variety of these tests available from which the most appropriate can be selected. Generally, the age of the child and the expertise of the diagnostician are major factors in personality test selection.

Some school districts have negotiated special contractual agreements with mental health centers or professional persons in private practice to evaluate children in conflict. The success of these agreements seems to depend, to a considerable degree, on the process established for assessing behavior of children. Assessment that is done in the isolation of a clinical setting, away from the child's natural world of interaction with other children and adults, is proving to be of limited value for teachers (Ebel, 1972). Under these conditions there tends to be a disruption of interaction and communication between the teacher and clinician. Reports written by clinicians have often been couched in professional jargon; these are of limited value to the teacher in the ongoing educational process. In addition, much of the reporting to teachers concerns static data (the way the child is) rather than process data (the way the child developed). This information is often of limited value, since the teacher generally has good insight concerning the child's present behavior as a result of ongoing classroom interaction. Processing the events that have contributed to the static test information into programing for behavior improvement appears to be the major necessary component of psychological evaluation.

The total evaluation process can be viewed as beginning with the child and gradually including additional people who, hopefully, possess more encompassing skills. The total evaluation process can be conceptualized as concentric circles, with each additional ring showing movement toward a more encompassing evaluation.

Selected Evaluation Tools

Of all the evaluation tools available, astute observation by teachers, parents, and mental health professionals appears to be most crucial for accurate diagnosis (Akhurst, 1970; Sattler, 1974). Skill in observation does not come easily or naturally; it is generally built on an adequate background in and understanding of human growth and development and a basic knowledge of school expectation and the role, effectiveness, and range of formal and informal tests. The teacher who possesses good observational skills can help to avoid unnecessary testing of children. The problems of obtaining accurate assessment with emotional, behavioral, and/or social problems are well documented (Anastasi, 1965, 1968; Davids, 1958; Kleinmuntz, 1967; Lyman, 1971). However, when inappropriate behaviors persist in spite of the best efforts of teachers, additional measures are often indicated. Formalized tests represent one method to verify teacher observations and provide the teacher with a relatively factual method for gathering new information (Anastasi, 1968; Sattler, 1974).

The formal tests reviewed here are not typically used by teachers of children in conflict. They represent professional measures of emotional stability generally employed by psychologists or others appropriately trained to administer them to children. Their usefulness is determined by the ability of the evaluator to make relevant judgments of educational needs and by teachers' ability to implement educationally sound programs to meet these needs.

Intelligence Testing. The study of intelligence testing as it is known today was started with the work of Alfred Binet and Theodore Simon. Binet and his co-workers had been interested in the development of tests to measure intelligence for many years before being commissioned in 1904 by the Minister of Public Instruction to study alternatives to the education of subnormal children who attended schools in Paris. It was to meet this practical demand that Binet, in collaboration with Simon, prepared the first draft of the Binet-Simon scale (Anastasi, 1968). The 1905 scale consisted of 30 items arranged in order of difficulty. A variety of functions were measured, with emphasis on judgment, comprehension, and reasoning.

A major revision of the 1905 test was made in 1908. The number of items was increased, unsatisfactory items were eliminated, and all test items were grouped into age levels. A 1911 revision set the stage for intelligence testing as it is known today. Several revisions of Binet's test were developed in the United States, but the most famous was developed at Stanford University in 1916 under the direction of Terman and called the Stanford-Binet test (Anastasi, 1968).

The most recent major change in either the Stanford-Binet test or WISC came in 1974 with a revision designed to minimize the cultural bias of the WISC.

Personality Tests

Rorschach test. Perhaps the best known of the projective techniques is the Rorschach, developed by the Swiss psychiatrist Hermann Rorschach (Anastasi, 1968). This test, first described in 1921, attempts to predict from the subject's associations to inkblots how he will react to others in his environment. The Rorschach consists of ten cards, each printed with a bilaterally symmetrical inkblot. Five of the cards are done in shades of grey and black, two have additional touches of bright red, and three combine several pastel shades. As the individual is shown each inkblot, he is asked what he sees.

Administering and scoring the Rorschach test is demanding, generally subjective, and the results are often of questionable value for educational purposes. Not only are the responses considered in scoring but other factors, such as popularity of various responses, position in which cards are held, remarks of the examinee, and emotional expressions, are also considered. Scoring is not only difficult and time-consuming, but the final results with children are suspect for many professionals (Kleinmuntz, 1967; Ullmann & Krasner, 1965), since some of the normative data were derived from adult groups. Clinical experience with the instrument also lacks an accumulation of information in the qualitative interpretation of protocols for children (Anastasi, 1968). Presently, it appears that few children who are placed in classes for the emotionally disturbed or behaviorally disordered are being given Rorschach tests. The reason for this is somewhat unclear but probably is related to the behavior bent presently held by many mental health professionals, the difficulty of scoring and interpretation, and the apparent lack of usefulness for educational programing.

Holtzman Inkblot Technique. An alternative inkblot test that is receiving some attention is the Holtzman Inkblot Technique. This test represents a genuine attempt to meet the technical standards of psychometric instruments. The Holtzman test is patterned after the Rorschach test but is sufficiently different to be called a new test, with little data to suggest any true superiority over the Rorschach test. Age range for the Holtzman test is from 5 years to adult, as compared with preschool to adult age range for the Rorschach test (Anastasi, 1968).

Thematic Apperception Test. Another projective instrument that has been developed is the Thematic Apperception Test (TAT). In contrast to the vague inkblots used in the Rorschach test, the TAT uses more highly structured stimuli and requires more complete and better organized responses. To utilize the advantages of the TAT with children, a special Children's Apperception Test (CAT) has been developed. The CAT cards substitute animals for people as stimuli for children; the test is designed for ages 3 to 10 years. The various animals are shown in typically human situations. The pictures are designed to evoke fantasies that children may hold regarding various problems, such as oral problems of feeding, sibling rivalry, parent relationships, aggression, toilet training, and other experiences of childhood (Anastasi, 1968; Kleinmuntz, 1967).

The Blacky pictures. The Blacky pictures, a series of cartoon drawings, are designed to study psychoanalytical concepts of child development (Blum, 1950-1962). Reliability, validity, and normative data for the Blacky pictures have been challenged as being inadequate (Blum, 1950; Zubin, Eron, & Schumer, 1965); however, numerous refinements of the original test have been made (Kleinmuntz, 1967). The test consists of 12 cards depicting a family of dogs in cartoon form. The major character of the test is Blacky, a dog that takes on the role of male or female depending on the sex of the individual being tested.

Word, sentence, and story completion tests. Various projective techniques have evolved from the more formalized projective tests. These include word association tests, such as Jung's list of 100 words, which are presented orally, and the list developed by Kent and Rosanoff. Response to words has been analyzed according to the reaction time of the child, content of responses, nonverbal responses, and frequency of responses (Forer, 1971).

Sentence completion tests, such as the Forer Structured Sentence Completion Test, are used to gain a general diagnostic overview of the child's personality (Forer, 1971). From the individual responses many clinical inferences and behavioral predictions are drawn. Interpretations of fear, hostility, and aggression can be made from sentence completion tests. The Rotter Incomplete Sentence Blank is another example of a sentence completion test (Rotter & Rafferty, 1950). Sentence completion tests are designed for a specific population or situation. Typical examples of individual items might include the following:

My dad always . . .
At night I often . . .
On school days I . . .
My sister . . .
School work is . . .

In the story completion test, the examiner begins a story and the child finishes it. The Madeleine Thomas Stories (MTS) are an example of this projective technique (Wursten, 1960). Story completion tests are really not tests but contain stimuli that encourage children to talk about their inner world freely and with little or no discomfort.

Classroom use of projectives. Educators should avoid the use of projective techniques in the classroom for other than cathartic purposes for children. The teacher can use the techniques as a way of encouraging freer expression in children who would otherwise withhold and repress feelings. The perceptive teacher is usually aware of problem behaviors without having the child do a story completion or word association test. As exercises of creativity, the techniques described can encourage children to express themselves freely. This expression can often "cleanse" the child of various irrational fears, guilt feelings, and internal conflicts. Being able to express these feelings around a picture or story often precedes confronting the problem on a more realistic level, such as in an open discussion of inappropriate feelings with the teacher or parent.

The use of formal diagnostic tests with children to ascertain personality development has generally centered around psychodynamically oriented projectives. Educational evaluation often includes observation and recording of behaviors observable to the teacher. Whereas formalized diagnostic tests serve a useful purpose for clinicians, observation remains the teacher's most often used tool in behavioral assessment and subsequent educational programing for children in conflict.

CLASSROOM APPLICATION OF PSYCHODYNAMIC THEORY

Since children generally have a more limited ability to verbalize than adults, alternate forms of therapy are often necessary to help them assert their feelings in ways that are helpful to the intervention process. Several alternative therapies will be presented for consideration.

Milieu Therapy

Milieu therapy is a French term that means treatment by environment, usually treatment in an institutional or hospital setting. The concept, as described by Redl (1959b) and Lewin (1935), has much to offer school programs that are designed to help children in conflict. Milieu therapy goes hand-in-hand with crisis intervention and life space interviewing. Although most school programs have made concerted efforts to develop a healthy environment for children, these efforts have generally centered around the needs of normal children rather than around children who exhibit deviant behaviors.

Milieu therapy has most often been used in total care programs, for example, institutions for emotionally disturbed children. It cannot be transplanted to public schools without modification, but it includes useful concepts that show promise for those who teach children in conflict.

An example of milieu therapy in schools is difficult to outline in a brief description, but it might include the following characteristics: manipulation of schedules (bus, restroom, classroom, lunchroom, and so forth) for the benefit of a child; organization of staff (teachers, bus drivers, aides, school nurse, and so on) to recognize or avoid reinforcement of certain behaviors; and involvement of significant persons in the child's life (for example, parents, teachers, relatives, and peers) to support positive feelings that the child emits. Milieu therapy is similar to behavioral manipulation of the environment but without specific behavioral activities such as counting and recording of behaviors.

Selecting an appropriate setting for each component of a total program is the first step toward developing an appropriate milieu. Special programs should generally be located in schools whose staffs choose to help children in conflict, where the welfare of all children is important, and where administrative support for the concept is evident.

A second consideration concerns the nature of the therapeutic milieu. No milieu that is established is good or bad in itself (Redl, 1959b); it all depends on the outcome that it helps to promote. The milieu that is established needs careful and continual attention by the total staff so that components of the milieu are not promoted or deleted indiscriminately. Many of the decisions concerning children tend to be made with the group in mind rather than individual children. This practice is defensible to a point; however, the concern for the group can immobilize individualization for children who cannot function in the same manner as normal children are expected to function.

A final consideration involves the degree of deviance that can be tolerated in a school setting. If children are unable to cope with their problems at a very basic level, they may need total environmental support while in school. However, most children will need less than total support. The support level needed and the manner in which it can be effected are concerns for the *total school staff*. Many of the conflicts of children arise in situations and places where the teachers and principal are simply not involved. Parents, aides, custodians, cooks, bus drivers, and other children are often painfully aware of the problems created by and for children in conflict but have little input into the situation. To establish a therapeutic milieu within schools for these children, educators must solicit support from all staff who come into contact with these children, as well as parents.

Crisis Intervention

Crisis intervention is essentially just what the words say: intervention during crises. The crisis teacher is, ideally, an "extra" staff member who is trained to interact with a child during a crisis situation; however, the crisis teacher may be a regular classroom teacher or resource teacher who is freed to work with one child during a crisis. An aide or even a child can monitor classroom activities for a short period of time while the teacher attends to an immediate crisis situation.

The crisis teacher concept as described by Morse (1971) offers the flexibility to serve a broad spectrum of problem behaviors in the school setting. Although a wide variety of crisis approaches have been used, they seem to have several common characteristics.

1. An "extra" staff member is employed to act as a crisis teacher." This person is trained not only in education but in the dynamics of various psychological inter-

ventions, such as life space interviewing, individual counseling, and group interaction.

2. The school provides a small classroom in which the crisis teacher works with one or more children for brief periods of time.

3. A communication system is developed so that the crisis teacher can be made aware of the impending problems.

4. The most important common component of crisis intervention is capitalization on the crisis situation itself. When a child is embroiled in conflict, some of his or her defenses are down, and in many cases the child is open to change. Therefore, emphasis is placed on intervention at the time of crisis, not after a cooling-off period.

The crisis teacher concept lends itself to varying degrees of crisis situations and can be used in a variety of educational settings. It has been used in special schools for disturbed children, in special classes for disturbed children, and in regular school programs with behavior problem children. The expertise of the crisis teacher and the availability of supportive personnel are important factors in determining the kinds of children served. Since no one person is capable of solving all problems that are brought to the attention of the crisis teacher, other professionals must support the crisis teacher if correct solutions are to evolve.

The role of the teacher in crisis intervention is total involvement. The child might be seen at a mental health center or in private therapy in addition to crisis intervention, but this is not mandatory. The crisis teacher not only is available to children but is available to other teachers on the staff. This consultation is vital; the crisis teacher can receive tremendous help from regular classroom teachers and, in turn, can be supportive in problem situations that arise in the classroom.

Pitfalls that have developed from abuses of the crisis teacher concept include (1) using the crisis teacher to complete mundane tasks between crisis situations, such as grading papers, filling out reports, and so forth; (2) having poorly qualified persons fill the role of the crisis teacher, which leads to poor results; and (3) scheduling children into the crisis room, which often diminishes flexibility to the extent that crisis situations cannot be handled effectively when they arise.

Life Space Interview

Life space interview, an approach generally credited to Redl (1959a), is essentially a cathartic technique that lends itself to use during a crisis or potential crisis situation. Redl lists two major components of life space interviewing: (1) emotional first aid and (2) clinical exploitation of life events. An example of these two interventions is described by the following brief encounter.

Your class is ready for lunch. As the children reach the lunchroom, it is discovered that another class has "slipped" in front of your class. A brief period of delay follows at which time pushing and verbal attacks ensue. One of the cooks finally challenges Dennis, one of the instigators of the conflict. At this point Dennis comes "unglued" and runs for the classroom with occasional pauses to deliver very specific verbal barrages.

According to the goals established for life space interviewing, either one of two behaviors would be appropriate: You could return to the classroom with Dennis to reconstruct the events of the crisis in such a way as to get Dennis back to lunch as quickly and painlessly as possible. This would be called "emotional first aid on the spot." Or, you could spend your lunch hour with Dennis to begin piecing together the events that precipitated the problem and to relate these to other similar events in which Dennis typically becomes involved. The goal here is not to "dig up old bones" but to help Dennis gain some insight into how problems begin, develop, and finally end in conflict. Redl calls this technique "clinical exploitation of life events."

Emotional First Aid

Redl (1971) lists five subcategories of emotional first aid that offer specific alternatives for the classroom teacher.

1. *Drain-off of frustration acidity.* Frustration often arises when children must discontinue something they like to move on to another less pleasing activity. Disappointment leads to an explosive situation for the child who has experienced so much defeat and who often has a low threshold for frustration. The life space interviewer might be able to take some of the "sting" out of this frustration by explaining why a change in schedule is necessary or warning of possible changes in time to prevent a crisis from developing.

2. *Support for the management of panic, fury, and guilt.* Children who have too much hate, guilt, anxiety, or anger are particularly vulnerable to their feelings. Often the child not only has these feelings but, in addition, is unable to cope effectively with them, even when these feelings occur at times they should. An adult who is available during times of stress to be supportive, particularly after the episode is completed, seems extremely important for helping the child to sort through the events and to put problems in their proper perspective.

3. *Communication maintenance in moments of relationship decay.* Positive relationships are difficult to maintain when the teacher is forced to intervene in a problem behavior. In the process of stopping inappropriate behavior, the communication link between the child and teacher is easily broken. The teacher must therefore hang on to any thread of communication so that the child does not slip into a totally autistic state of daydreams or self-pity. The child must be free to choose alternative behaviors and still be able to "save face."

4. *Regulation of behavioral and social traffic.* Rules help to establish guidelines for behavior that offer much-needed support for children in conflict. Whereas rules are not a goal in themselves, their consistent application by patient and benign adults will help these children through critical situations where their behavior must come under better "ego control." The adult must not moralize or be dictatorial in the process of pointing out the rules or in helping children live within their intent. Some children need an authority figure in sight to support appropriate rule-following behavior, at least until better inner controls can be developed.

5. *Umpire services.* The role of an adult who can be fair with all sides is vital to children in conflict. Many situations are too dangerous to be left to chance alone. When children begin to develop and, more important, to rely on a sense of fairness with other children, it is vital that an adult sometimes act as umpire. This umpire role is important in both intrachild and interchild conflicts. Interchild services might include acting as an impartial referee during a wrestling match. Helping a child to tell the truth rather than lie is one example of solving an intrachild conflict.

Clinical Exploitation of Life Events. Emotional first aid is a first line of defense against runaway emotions and deviant behaviors. No specific guidelines are suggested for the use of either emotional first aid or clinical exploitation of life events. Redl (1971) suggests that a correct approach cannot be predicted in advance; it can only be arrived at through involvement with the child. Two factors are critical in determining whether to go deeply into clinical exploitation of life events: (1) the time available at the moment of need and (2) the receptivity of the situation to therapy. When time is available and the situation correct, Redl offers five techniques to exploit the crisis.

1. *Reality rub-in* (make the child aware of what really happened). Many children appear to be "perceptually impaired" in their ability to see problems that they have caused. Redl calls this "socially nearsighted" behavior. Other children get caught in a "system of near to delusional misinterpretation of life" (Redl, 1971). Unlike socially nearsighted behavior in which children fail to read the social meaning of their behavior, these children tend to overlook obvious situations that should be interpreted correctly. In both cases reality rub-in is an effective tool to point out inappropriate behavior. Doing so immediately is vital, since any period of delay will only allow the child to rationalize and further overlook the real problem.

2. *Symptom estrangement* (help the child "let go" of inappropriate behaviors). In symptom estrangement, the task of the person doing the life space interviewing is to help children in conflict let go of the symptoms that are ruling their behavior. It is important that other staff who interact with the children also support this letting go of pathological behavior. Children have learned that this kind of behavior does get results even if the behavior is seen as deviant. Educators must tell and show children how they can let go of their symptoms and still reach the goals that pathological behavior has helped them achieve.

3. *Massaging numb value areas* (awaken appropriate values that are dormant). Redl suggests that many children simply have had sensitive areas of their personality numbed by the pathology and resulting conflicts, both internal and external. The life space inter-

viewer can slowly chip away at this numbed area and reawaken the potential for acceptable behavior that exists in most children. This process does not generally produce a dramatic change, rather, it is a painfully slow process both for the child and for teachers.

4. *New-tool salesmanship* (promoting new behaviors as alternatives). A major difficulty of children in conflict is their inability to approach problems with any flexibility (Bower & Lambert, 1971). When faced with a crisis, the child reverts to a common behavior pattern that appears not to vary with experience. Redl suggests that the life space interviewer can offer new alternatives for children in conflict. Giving a child a new, socially acceptable behavior to replace an old unacceptable behavior seems to be necessary to avoid trading one inappropriate behavior for another.

5. *Manipulation of the boundaries of the self* (desensitize the child to deviant behavior). The manipulation that Redl is speaking of concerns the child who is always getting "sucked in" by peers who enjoy seeing the child do the wrong thing and get into trouble. By increasing the number of interviews with the child and providing needed support, he can often be desensitized to the contagion around him and be able to redirect his behavior.

The following example describes how this contagion develops. A group of boys screw out a light bulb until it is about to fall. Then one of the "deviant" kids is told to jump up and touch the light bulb. When the bulb falls to the floor, everyone points the finger at the "culprit," who is subsequently punished for breaking the bulb. This type of setting up a deviant child is common in schools. Punishing those who prey on children in conflict will only make the problem worse; deviant children must be desensitized so as not to be "sucked in" by those around them.

Practical Problems. The teacher who is doing life space interviewing will spend a major portion of time and energy on emotional first aid rather than clinical exploitation of life events. In fact, teachers who are effective in administering emotional first aid will decrease the time spent solving more serious problems.

Teachers who have worked in a life space interviewing role have been quick to point out some of the problem areas. First, a competent person must be selected to do the major share of life space interviewing, particularly if it is used as a supportive technique in a specialized administrative structure, as in crisis intervention. Although many teachers in a typical school probably can and should develop competence as life space interviewers, this is not an easy or quick task for already overburdened teachers. Selecting a resource teacher trained in life space interviewing techniques seems to be a likely alternative. In this way other teachers can share in the expertise exhibited by the trained person while their own personal skills are being developed. Since correct application of life space interviewing skills is relative to the problems presented, it is important that good judgment be used in determining when and at what levels to become involved. The interviewer must also be aware that children may learn to manipulate the teacher so as to receive individual attention through life space interviewing.

A second problem area is communication. How does the classroom teacher communicate in an effective manner with those doing life space interviewing? Those who have worked in clinically oriented systems are aware of the vast amounts of time spent in communication with other staff. Teachers have generally operated in an autonomous environment that easily leads to noninvolvement and isolation. Team teaching situations offer hope that this isolation may be transformed into a cooperative effort with effective communication.

A third problem for the teacher using life space interviewing is timing. What does the teacher do with thirty other children while spending time with one child? If a teacher is not convinced that life space interviewing can work effectively, that teacher will not have the "administrative courage" to give time to one child that needs it—not after school or tomorrow at 10:30 A.M. This problem can be solved by commitment to the concept and a resulting determination to solve the administrative problems. Some teachers have supervised other teachers' classes by combining classes on a temporary basis to free one staff member to help one child. Other programs have used aides, parents, the principal, and more mature children in a temporary role so that life space interviewing could be implemented by the teacher. Using a staff member who is trained to interview children (a crisis teacher) and who is free of other school duties is an ideal solution, but by no means the only solution to the time problem.

A fourth problem centers around the role of teachers who function as life space interviewers. Although the teacher's role cannot be one of junior psychiatrist, psychologist, or social worker, some allied skills are necessary. The teacher using this technique must have an understanding of individual and group personality dynamics, be able to work effectively on a one-to-one basis, and be able to initiate productive educational tasks in short periods of time.

Therapies with Supportive Media

Several supportive therapies have been developed that offer assistance to classroom teachers who must deal with serious behavioral problems. These techniques have developed largely in clinical practice where they continue to be used; however, their strengths are not limited to that setting. Teachers have discovered that many are usable in the classroom. These include play therapy, which is the most sophisticated of the supportive therapies, art therapy, music therapy, occupational therapy, and therapeutic play.

Play Therapy. Play therapy makes use of the child's natural world of play for therapeutic purposes. As a form of psychotherapy, play therapy seeks to unfold the child's inner world and to help the child gain insight into his or her own behavior, to be able to live within limits, and to grow in ability to solve problems (Axline, 1947). Psychotherapists have suggested that the basic principles of play therapy are applicable to the classroom, especially classrooms that are serving children in various stages of conflict (Nelson, 1966). There are definite limits placed on using play therapy in an educational setting; however, the teacher can utilize some of the therapeutic principles that have shown promise in more structured play therapy sessions. The intent of this discussion is to explain how the classroom teacher can use the *philosophy* of play therapy. There is no intent to suggest the establishment of a clinical play therapy situation within a school classroom; however, a therapeutic attitude is a possibility. The principles of play therapy, as outlined by Axline (1947), are summarized here:

1. Permissiveness is allowing the child to be free to express feelings completely. In an educational setting, the expression of feelings necessarily must have some limits; however, allowing the child the freedom to create his or her own painting, to write ideas, and to develop creative talents in music, drama, and free play are all important. Self-expression, though important for the child, does not solve problems the child may have. It only allows the behav-

iors to come to the surface where the teacher can deal with them in a productive manner.

2. Establishing a warm, friendly relationship is generally accepted by teachers in theory but difficult to implement (Fig. 3–1). Children in conflict have often lost their trust in adults, which makes teaching even more difficult. It is a more arduous task to build a warm, friendly relationship in a classroom than in a one-to-one therapy situation, but it can be done if the children are viewed and treated as individuals rather than as an amorphous group. Individual children must be encouraged to interact with the teacher and other children if security and trust are to be developed.

3. Limits are established only as needed to anchor the therapy to the world of reality. In the classroom these limitations must be more numerous and stringent than in individual therapy, but limits are never established just for the sake of having limits. The child should only have enough structure so that he does not injure himself or others and so that property is protected from willful destruction. Limitations are not set out as a list of rules to be followed but are introduced as needed to maintain a productive environment for learning while still maintaining respect for every individual in the classroom. Limitations do not place demands on the child but allow growth within some reasonable structure. Reasonable limits allow the timid child a "safe place" in which to explore and grow and provide needed bounds for the more volatile child.

4. The therapist should be aware of expressed feelings and reflect these feelings back to the child. This guideline has been misinterpreted more often than any of the guidelines of play therapy. Reflecting the child's feelings does not make a mockery

FIGURE 3–1. The teacher can develop a warm, friendly relationship in several ways. Sitting on the floor with a child for a brief period of time is one technique.

of the child nor is it "selling out" to the whims of the child. It is not easy to recognize feelings and to reflect them back to the child. For most teachers it is easier to tell, to explain, and to solve the problem for the child rather than to allow the child the time and freedom to solve his or her own problems. Although some have suggested that teaching and therapy are antithetical, this principle shows that this should not be the case; good teaching and good therapy are parallel, rather than contradictory, activities.

5. Complete acceptance of the child seems to be the most difficult to operationalize of all the guidelines presented. Accepting children completely does not imply that teachers also must accept their behavior. It is relatively easy to accept a child who has limitations that are visibly apparent, such as a broken leg or a severe vision problem. If the handicap is not readily visible, however, teachers may view the child as lazy, uninterested, and rebel-

lious. A teacher's persistence in comparing one child with another in school activities demonstrates an unwillingness to treat each child as an individual. In a clinical setting complete acceptance is more easily effected, since there is no other child readily available for comparison and no implied criticism that can be transmitted to the child as a result of this comparison.

6. A respect for the child's ability to solve his or her own problems must be maintained. This principle is indirectly related to all of the other principles and the structure that regulates behavior during therapy sessions. If the teacher can have respect for the child's ability to make decisions, even though the decisions will probably be different from those the teacher would make, the child will be helped to gain insight into decision-making processes. The teacher must make some logical determination of the level of decision making at which the child is presently functioning. For example, a first-grade child should not be expected to make decisions that will have serious implications for his future existence unless the child is certain to make correct decisions. Whether the child practices words for reading now or two hours later is not too big a decision for a first-grader to make. However, whether the child practices reading words or not is too big a decision to make, since the punishment that might conceivably result from failure in learning to read would be too big a price for the child to pay. If the teacher will allow the child to make small decisions, where the price of failure is equal to the child's ability to handle failure, growth in problem solving should result.

7. The teacher should allow the child to lead the way in both conversation and action. This principle has been successfully dem-

onstrated by the discovery method often used in teaching mathematical concepts, reading skills, and spelling rules. However, when inappropriate behavior is the issue, it is tempting for the teacher to tell, to direct, and to manipulate—temptations that must be avoided if this principle is to be implemented.

8. Therapists tend to think in terms of time, but therapy often does not follow a time schedule. Behaviors that have taken years in formation generally respond slowly to significant change. Teachers understand the process of change in cognitive skills extremely well but often are unrealistic when affective behaviors are under consideration. This principle of play therapy emphasizes the importance of time in changing affective behaviors.

When teachers are able to incorporate the therapeutic principles of play therapy into their teaching style, the atmosphere for learning often is improved for all children.

Art Therapy. Art therapy, as the term is used in this text, is a therapeutic process that provides children with the opportunity to interact with the various visual arts as the vehicle of therapeutic intervention (Fig. 3–2). Finger painting, working with clay, and free-hand drawing would be examples applicable to children in conflict.

The various art media can provide additional channels of communication. Just as play therapy encourages children to express themselves through play activities, art therapy encourages communication through the various art forms. Children can show when they are sad, happy, and afraid; they can share their dreams, ambitions, and innermost thoughts. Art can also show deep psychological conflicts such as aggression, compulsive behaviors, sublimation, substitution, and various unconscious feelings

(Kramer, 1971, Naumburg, 1958). This communication does not preempt the need for other forms of information—it only supports and enhances these forms in most cases. In a situation where a child is not speaking, as might be the case in autism, art therapy can become even more critical as a communication link.

Although children's artwork may hint at inner conflict, this realization only supports the teacher's original concern, since the troubled child will generally give many such indications. The classroom teacher generally should not use art as a diagnostic tool; rather art can be a way for the child to try to express and to identify feelings. For the teacher who is aware of the students' emotional needs and problems, art therapy adds one more dimension of understanding.

Art therapy should be seen as supplementary to other therapeutic interventions, not as an isolated panacea. Art should help children share their inner feelings with the teacher in an acceptable and nonthreatening manner. It also gives children an outlet for the release of inner tensions; this release ultimately can have beneficial effects on future learning experiences that will demand a child's complete attention.

The art therapist should become an ally of the child's creativity. Kramer (1971) says that the therapist should lend both technical assistance and emotional support. By requiring that materials be used to produce works of art, the therapist counteracts any tendencies toward "dissipation into fantasy or play." Kramer suggests that the end product is not the major goal of art therapy. The emphasis is on therapy through the art media. Whereas art therapy is strongly allied to psychotherapy, it does not follow that its use cannot serve other therapeutic models—a behavioral approach, for example—as long as the basic premise of freedom to create is not endangered.

FIGURE 3–2. A, This child's picture takes on a new meaning if you look at **B**. The child views his teacher as an extremely important person in his life and is concerned with how his teacher feels about him. Through art media he expresses these feelings.

Music Therapy. Music therapy is in many ways a parallel to play therapy and can be used to bring out feelings that would otherwise fail to surface. Music has become a way of life in the United States. Everywhere people go they hear music—in church, in bars, at football games, and in the supermarket. Music has various effects on people: it can relax them and put them in a mood for sleep or it can stir them to action. Football marches played on a crisp autumn afternoon have one effect on an individual's feelings, whereas soft dinner music puts the individual in quite a different mood. Music can promote many similar reactions from children.

Soft background music in the classroom will often have a quieting effect on active children and aid in the concentration of children, since it helps to shut out noise that might otherwise be distracting. Teachers have, at times, used music in the classroom only as a reward for appropriate behavior. Since many schools are equipped with classroom speaker systems, there seems to be the possibility of background music for those who would care to implement its use in the classroom. Since there has been little research on the effect of background music on children in conflict in regular classroom settings, teachers will need to develop much of their understanding and techniques through trial and error.

Music can have a therapeutic value in addition to its use as a background stimulus. Singing or playing songs on a piano or other instrument can give the child a feeling of success. Playing certain instruments (drums, piano, clappers) allows the child an acceptable outlet for physical aggression. Music can be a healthy reward activity for less desired tasks, and it provides a medium of self-expression, for example, dancing to the music or acting out the beat.

Music therapy places emphasis on encouraging appropriate behaviors rather than perpetuating existing problems. For example, the overly active child may become even more out of control with certain stimulating music, or the withdrawn child may become more isolated with music that is fear producing. Careful monitoring of the therapeutic situation is needed to ensure productive outcomes.

Occupational Therapy. Occupational therapy is the use of manual activities such as carpentry or building, leather work, and plastic work to treat emotional problems. Occupational therapy has long been accepted as a productive method of treating disturbed children and adults. However, it has been abused in schools that have relied too heavily on it as a tool of pacification. Keeping a child busy and "out of the teacher's hair" has its merits, but it cannot be the goal for any child who is to grow emotionally. Although occupational therapy has typically been a part of institutional therapy, it is often a part of school programs under the guise of arts or crafts. The use of activities that allow children to express themselves, to create, and to be productive with their hands can have many beneficial outcomes for both children and teachers. Many of the same benefits outlined for art and music therapy are also applicable here.

Occupational therapy, as a part of total intervention procedures, seems appropriate for schools. Concentration on an activity that is enjoyable is therapeutic for everyone. In the elementary school these activities generally should be limited to no more than five hours a week with most children. Young adults might reasonably spend more time in occupational therapy.

Therapeutic Play. One of the most promising interventions that can be implemented in the school is therapeutic play—the structuring of play activities so that maximum therapeutic benefits can be achieved. Although most teachers try to individualize educational activities, they often encourage play for individual children that is unsuited to their developmental level; for example, teachers want all children to participate in games during recess. The problem is that all children are not ready for this rather sophisticated level of interaction. With children in conflict it is not unusual to have individuals who cannot yet play effectively alone. They may need to develop satisfactory skills of individual play and parallel play with one other child before proceeding to play with other children. The necessary growth may take weeks or months in some cases, but the time for growth must be taken. The troubled child may initiate interaction with another child by attacking his sand castle or kicking the child's football into the street—both encounters that appear to be of negative value. This stage of relationship development should be tolerated by the teacher only until it can be guided into more cooperative activities.

When a child is able to play alone, it is time to encourage individual skill development. Activities that encourage running, jumping, and climbing are generally appropriate. As muscle coordination develops, the child can be taught individual skill activities such as swimming, table or lawn tennis, bowling, fly casting, wrestling, handball, gymnastics, and camping. These individual skills, along with many others appropriate to various age groups and geographical location, seem to help prepare the child for interpersonal interactions that will follow.

Group activities that require sharing, cooperation, and rule following generally should be delayed until some individual skills have been mastered. If this is not done, group activities are likely to deteriorate into chaotic disputes over rules, who pushed whom first, and eventual refusals to participate.

Other therapeutic interventions include puppetry, Big Brother and Big Sister pro-grams, community recreational programs, scouting, dance therapy, and drama therapy. Many of these activities are supplementary to or could become a part of therapies already mentioned, with the teacher providing the imagination necessary for implementation.

The Mental Health Center Approach. During the late 1950s and early 1960s when schools formally initiated educational programs for the emotionally disturbed, the typical emphasis was the mental health center approach, or "pull-out" program. In this strategy schools handled the academics and the mental health personnel handled the therapy. Often these two areas carried out their roles in isolation.

The mental health center approach, provided cooperative programming takes place, has several advantages:

1. Professionals are available for support and consultation to the teacher.
2. The child and/or parents and other family members might be seen at the local mental health center. Communication of this fact to the school is more likely when a close working relationship exists.
3. Services need not be duplicated; that is, schools do not need mental health services, and mental health programs generally do not need educational programs.

Some weaknesses of the mental health approach have included the following:

1. The child is often out of the mainstream of life for treatment; this approach represents the ultimate in "pull-out" programs.
2. The system is wasteful of human resources, both children and professionals. This intervention simply cannot accommodate the number of children who need help in the public schools.
3. Individual therapy only helps the child. No one else, such as the teacher, has the

possibility of growth. The therapist is the expert, and little communication is possible with any other helping professional.

4. The process often has led to a defensiveness rather than a team effort.

5. Little in the way of verification of success has been demonstrated. Research data are painfully scarce, and when they are available, the interpretation is risky since the school and therapy settings are often physically separate.

6. Too much emphasis is placed on the past status of the child at the expense of programming for the present and future.

In reviewing the strengths and weaknesses of the mental health approach, there appear to be few problems that could not be overcome, at least to some degree, through a commitment to cooperative programing. A major concern of cooperative mental health efforts must include the pull-out nature of such programs—a weakness that pervades all of the areas of concern.

CURRENT STATUS

The psychodynamic approach has achieved much acceptance during this century. It was one of the major therapies during the 1940s and 1950s only to have its theory questioned and challenged by the behaviorism of the 1960s. It appears that with the maturity of psychodynamic theory and its movement away from analysis has come a rebirth of interest.

The psychodynamic consulting model, which emphasizes the importance of input from all those interested in and knowledgeable about a given child, offers a useful tool for practitioners. The teacher's role in psychodynamic theory has changed from that of interested spectator to one of valuable input and leadership in psychoeducational programing.

Teachers interested in psychodynamic

theory have a wide variety of journals from which to choose. Some of these are listed at the end of this chapter. Among the publications available are *The Journal of the American Psychoanalytic Association, The International Journal of Psychoanalysis, The Psychoanalytic Review, Psychoanalytic Quarterly, Journal of Child Psychology and Psychiatry, Psychiatry,* and *The American Journal of Psychoanalysis.* All of the journals mentioned are quite technical and generally appropriate only for the serious student of analytical theory.

With the growth of humanistic psychology have come journals that espouse its values. The major journals dedicated to Adlerian psychology are the *Journal of Individual Psychology* and the *Individual Psychologist.* In addition to these the teacher of disturbed children may find one or more of the titles listed below helpful in keeping abreast of current developments in the field.

The *American Journal of Orthopsychiatry* is one of the best for the professional teacher of children in conflict. Articles of interest appear consistently throughout the year. These articles are of high quality and are readable: characteristics appreciated by busy professionals. Each journal includes sections on research, delivery of services, and clinical practice, as well as literature reviews.

The *Humanist Educator* is the official publication of the Association for Humanistic Education and Development, a division of the American Personnel and Guidance Association. It is directed toward professional educators interested in humanistic education. Although its primary focus is not disturbed children, it provides good insights for teachers who espouse a humanistic attitude toward education.

VIGNETTES

To demonstrate the effectiveness of the various psychodynamic tools with children in conflict, a series of vignettes are presented. These brief case outlines and research studies were selected to (1) show specific psychodynamic techniques and (2) evaluate their use. Most techniques are a combination of two or more psychodynamic constructs, although one may appear to be the dominant tool.

Vignette 1: Music Therapy

REPORTED BY Nordoff and Robbins (1971)

The child in this case was a 9-year-old girl, Y, who was diagnosed as a schizoid personality. Her behavior before labeling has been described as bizarre and hallucinatory. She would attack both physically and verbally when she became angry. The occurrence of this behavior was limited to her neighborhood. In school she was described as withdrawn, preferring to be alone both in the classroom and on the playground. She had no friends among her peers and felt that adults, including her parents and her teacher, were mean and hated her. Y was referred to the music therapist because of her apparent music aptitude. The goals of music therapy were to develop an adequate relationship with an adult, change her attitude toward adults, provide an intellectual challenge, afford group recognition, and provide an acceptable emotional outlet.

Y took piano lessons twice a week for 5 years with the exception of two weeks' vacation each summer. During the first few months, lessons were devoted to learning fundamentals of piano and developing an acceptable relationship with her therapist. During this time she consistently tried to manipulate the therapist into rejecting her. The therapist resisted the temptations successfully by describing the behavior without condemnation. Gradually a warm and friendly relationship developed with the therapist. Y became less shy in school, and she began to play with other children. During her second year this progress continued, as did growth in muscal ability. In her third year outbursts of anger began to develop, which were caused, according to her physician, by her mother's illness, irritability and lack of consistent discipline. A rebellious teenage sister also contributed to the unsettled

nature of the home. This situation continued into the fourth year. At one point Y told her therapist she had picked up a butcher knife and was going to kill her mean old mother but she did not. The therapist said: "No, and you never will. If you start to do anything like that, you will always stop yourself." She then resumed the music lesson. Y played wildly, inaccurately, and loudly for a time after the incident. When she finished her lesson, she left without saying a word, only to return and say to her therapist, "I love you— you are good to me." The therapist reported the incident to Y's psychiatrist so that these feelings could be dealt with in psychotherapy sessions.

Y developed good musical skills, played in school recitals, and, according to her parents, often played the piano for relaxation.

Vignette 2: Life Space Interview

REPORTED BY Newman (1963)

Six severely disturbed preadolescent boys who had spent the previous fives years at the Child Research Branch of the National Institute of Health were integrated into an educational program away from the institute. Newman discusses the role of the life space interviewer, or crisis interviewer, in these cases. The problems that these boys exhibited centered around their poor self-image: that is, uncontrolled behavior, withdrawal, violence, grandiose delusions, and acting-out behaviors. Crisis situations often grew out of otherwise bland situations: a nail that bent in woodworking, a potter's wheel that failed to turn at the right speed, an arithmetic problem that failed to come out right, reading *was* for *saw*, or the cancellation of a promised trip all brought down the wrath of the boys on the teacher.

Over a period of time the life space interviewer was able to deal with these on-the-spot crises effectively. In addition, the life space interviewer was able to disarm potential crisis situations by the following interventions.

1. Warn the boys of changes in routine in advance, for example, "You will have your tutoring session after science today."

2. Help prepare the child for the grade he is going to receive, for example, "What grade do you think you will receive?"
3. Help the child organize himself to do his homework assignment, for example, "What part of your homework do you need for tomorrow?"
4. Practice test taking with the boys to help them master the technique of test taking.

In brief, this report suggested that life space interviewers can work effectively in helping troubled youngsters over the "rough spots" in their everyday life, to avoid problems when possible, and to overcome them when avoidance fails.

Vignette 3: Play Therapy with Puppets

REPORTED BY Kessler (1966)

Ralph was in therapy from the age of 5 years, suffering from several chronic problems including enuresis, phobias, destructive and aggressive behavior, and separation anxiety. After three years of therapy he became interested in puppets, and for the following ten months he was engrossed in making and playing with puppets during therapy sessions. Through the puppets he was able to show the conflict between his wishes and his conscience. Two characters dominated therapy situations: Good Bob (Ralph) and Bad Bill (the therapist). Good Bob had everything going for him; he was a model child, bright and wealthy. Bad Bill, on the other hand, was in constant need of money, brains, friends, and advice. Bill was unhappy and always getting into fights.

Bob was able to reform Bill by showing him how he had trained a room full of wild animals. He said he had trained them through patience, love, and rewards. As therapy continued, Bob began to indulge himself by eating sweets all the time, going to bed when he wished, and spending money at will. The therapist began questioning his position of Good Bob, since he was not living by the rules, and so forth. Bob's behavioral deterioration stopped; however, he continued to be very successful in everything he did.

Bob preferred to relate only to boys, whereas the therapist related to girls, such as Bob's sister

and mother. The therapist could not get Bob to relate to girls or to discuss topics of sex. He would always pretend to know everything there was to know about babies, pregnancy, and so on, but when pressed by the therapist, he would forget the details of information he claimed to have. As the puppets (Bob and Bill) grew older, they went through the stages of being interested in girls, of conflicts with big brothers, and of induction into the armed services. When the therapist suggested they were leaving the world of girls for a world of men, Ralph suggested they return to the age of 10 years. The therapist interpreted this as a desire to regress to a more comfortable state and avoid marrying and making babies.

In this vignette the therapist used puppetry at the child's request to ease the way to change. After Ralph was able to solve his problems through play, he was ready to relate these solutions to real life.

Vignette 4: Art Therapy, Milieu Therapy, and Psychotherapy

REPORTED BY Kramer (1971)

Martin was admitted to Wiltwyck School at the age of 10½ years. He was an only child and was admitted at the request of his mother. Wiltwyck School is a residential school for emotionally disturbed boys from the slums of New York City. The home can serve 100 boys aged 8 to 12 years who have normal intelligence with emotional disturbance that does not require the safety of a hospital setting.

Martin's behavior before coming to Wiltwyck was highly erratic. He was often truant from school, and he had been involved in a number of minor delinquent acts and conflicts with his mother. Martin's father was a seemingly dependent man who was unable to control the family situation effectively. His mother was the major breadwinner and also responsible for monitoring Martin's behavior, which she did by beating him severely after his provocations. Martin's first encounter in art therapy was extremely revealing of his internal thought processes. He came to the art room and drew an island scene surrounded by a dark green sea. When he finished, he picked up several aprons and put them around his neck, ran into the yard, and twirled around in a whirling dance. Then he threw the aprons aside and ran from the area. Later he came back and apologized for his behavior.

The therapists interpreted this behavior in the following way: (1) the painting represented isolation and a preoccupation with faraway places (2) his dance indicated an exhibitionism, and (3) his return and apology represented a desire to maintain a relationship. Martin became one of the most intolerable boys at the school. He was unable to get along at all with men and only occasionally with women. He showed his only real interest in art, and it was in art therapy that the staff was able to tolerate him part of the time.

Martin's art had a distinctly angry tone in its message. He also produced works that showed his intense emotion and strong sexual stimulation. After six months in school Martin was placed in psychotherapy as a supplement to art therapy and milieu therapy. With this team effort he gradually began to grow in his ability to let go of his pathological behaviors.

His therapist reported a major breakthrough that occurred in an art session with prior stimulation during psychotherapy. Martin had been walking in the woods with his therapist when he spoke of one of the many bird's nests in the trees. This led to a discussion about the feelings of a bird that would be robbed of its freedom. Martin said he would give the bird partial freedom by tying a kite string to the bird's leg. Slowly he came to verbalize that the kite string idea was similar to his mother's relationship with him. The following day he came to the art room and painted an intricate picture of an apple with an apple tree inside and branches, leaves, and smaller apples. In the center of the tree was a bird's nest with a mother bird feeding her baby. He had worked for seven hours one day and finished it the following day. When it was completed, he presented it to his counselor, Mr. Frank. This was the first gesture of friendship he had made to any male since he came to the school.

Kramer believed that Martin survived because of art and eventually used art as a form of recognition.

Vignette 5: Crisis Intervention

Behavior. Tom, 9 years of age, is a very angry boy. It has been common for him to hurt other children by pushing, hitting, kicking, and biting them. He also has a history of cutting up baby kittens, killing birds, and even killing trees by stabbing them to death with a sharp object.

Family background. Tom is from an above average income family. The family has been intact, although the mother has some emotional problems. Tom was adopted through a private agency. He has two brothers and one sister, all adopted, also through a private agency. Tom's mother appears to be uncertain in her acceptance of the children. She loves and wants the children badly; however, at times she locks them out of the house until dinner in the evening. Tom has had more than his share of toys, clothes, and other material goods; however, he lacks appropriate adult attention.

Psychological information. Tom's early records show no psychological problems that can be identified. On entering school his behavior problems prompted the parents, on recommendation from the teacher, to seek psychiatric help for Tom. As a result of the psychiatric interview, it is reported that Tom had weak ego strengths and an underdeveloped superego. His intellectual functioning was considered to be above average according to the score achieved on the individual test of intelligence. The parents report psychological problems with Tom in the home but nothing they cannot manage.

Medical information. Physical evaluation shows no abnormalities that would interfere with educational or social functioning.

Educational information. Tom is academically retarded in all skill areas. He is extremely capable in verbal skills but is unable to transform these verbal ideas into written communication. He is an extremely nervous child in school, often biting his fingernails until his fingers bleed. He appears to be seeking constant attention from others.

Placement recommendations. Tom was placed in a regular classroom with support from a crisis intervention teacher. On signal (a buzzer) the crisis teacher would come to the classroom and take Tom for brief periods of time. Tom was to be taken from the classroom only in situations where his behavior was so inappropriate that it could not be tolerated in the regular classroom situation. The classroom teacher was to be the judge of this behavior. The crisis teacher tried various approaches with Tom when he was taken from the classroom. These included (1) ignoring Tom and allowing him to complete whatever work he was supposed to be doing at the time of the crisis, (2) helping Tom with assignments that were being completed at the time the crisis arose, (3) visiting with Tom about his problem and encouraging him to get back to the task that he was working on when the crisis arose, and (4) using life space interview techniques.

Evaluation. Much success was gained through crisis intervention with Tom. Initial problems included Tom's trying to manipulate the classroom teacher so that he could be with the crisis teacher whenever he chose. When it was thought that Tom was manipulating his way out of the classroom and into the crisis situation, he was not allowed to leave the classroom. Developing a more structured crisis intervention system in which Tom could carry on with the same work he had left in the regular classroom also helped solve this problem. As soon as Tom discovered that he could not escape the reality of the classroom by creating a crisis, he began to grow emotionally. Tom's need for support during crisis situations was intense for about six months, followed by a period of approximately one year when occasional support during crisis was needed. After one and one-half years Tom was able to function within the regular classroom situation without intervention other than that normally provided by the classroom teacher.

SUMMARY

The psychodynamic viewpoint postulates that psychological problems or conflicts can cause children to act in deviant ways and that finding these causal factors is important in treatment of these conflicts. Psychodynamic intervention can range from an in-depth analysis of the problems facing the individual to the more commonly used approach of treating symptoms. Regardless of the specific approach used in treatment, the inner self is important to the psychodynamic theorist.

The major psychodynamic approaches have been reviewed in this chapter, including the analytical theory of Sigmund Freud and the more recent humanistic approaches to intervention. Screening, evaluation, and placement procedures have been discussed and specific instruments outlined.

Various educational applications of psychodynamic theory have been proposed, including milieu therapy, crisis intervention, life space interviewing, play therapy, art therapy, music therapy, occupational therapy, and therapeutic play. The chapter concludes with a review of the current status of psychodynamic theory, a listing of journals that feature psychodynamic techniques, and vignettes that describe its use in practical situations.

JOURNALS OF INTEREST

The Journal of American Psychoanalytic Association
International Universities Press, Inc.
Journal Department
315 Fifth Avenue
New York, NY 10016

The International Journal of Psychoanalysis
Bailliere Tindall, 1 Vincent Square
London SWIP2PN
England

The Psychoanalytic Review
Guilford Publication, Inc.
200 Park Ave. 5, Room 1603
New York, NY 10003

Psychoanalytic Quarterly
Psychoanalytic Quarterly, Inc.
175 Fifth Ave., Room 210
New York, NY 10010

Journal of Child Psychology and Psychiatry
Pergamon Press, Inc.
Journal Division
Maxwell House, Fairview Park
Elmsford, NY 10523

Psychiatry
Washington School of Psychiatry
1610 New Hampshire Ave., N.W.
Washington, DC 20009

American Journal of Psychoanalysis
Agathon Press, Inc.
111 8th Ave.
New York, NY 10011

Individual Psychology
University of Texas Press
Box 7819
Austin, TX 78712

American Journal of Orthopsychiatry
American Orthopsychiatric Association
19 W. 44 St.
New York, NY 10036

The Humanist Education
American Association for Counseling and Development
5999 Stevenson Ave.
Alexandria, VA 22304

BIBLIOGRAPHY

Adler, A. (1963). *The problem child*. New York: Capricorn Books.

Adler, A. (1964). *Social interest: A challenge to mankind.* New York: Capricorn Books.

Adler, A. (1970). Depression in light of individual psychology. In H. Werner (Ed.), *New understandings of human behavior*. New York: Associated Press.

Akhurst, B. (1970). *Assessing intellectual ability*. New York: Barnes and Noble.

American Orthopsychiatric Association. (1978). Developmental assessment in EPSDT. *American Journal of Orthopsychiatry, 48*, 7–31.

Anastasi, A. (1965). *Psychological testing*. New York: John Wiley.

Anastasi, A. (1968). *Psychological testing*. New York: Macmillan.

Ansbacher, H., & Ansbacher, R. (Eds.). (1956). *The individual psychology of Alfred Adler*. New York: Basic Books.

Apolito, A. (1978). Primary prevention: A breakthrough in sight. *American Journal of Psychoanalysis, 38*, 121–127.

Axline, V. (1947). *Play therapy*. Boston: Houghton Mifflin.

Baumgartner, B., & Shultz, J. (1969). *Reaching children through art*. Johnstown, PA: Mafex Associates.

Beilin, H. (1959). Teachers and clinicians' attitudes toward the behavior problems of children—A reappraisal. *Child Development, 30*, 9–25.

Blum, G. (1959). Reliability of the Blacky Test: A reply to Charen. *Journal of Consulting Psychology, 20*, 406.

Blum, G. S. (1950). *The Blacky picture: A technique for exploration of personality dynamics*. San Antonio: Psychological Corp.

Bower, E. (1960). *Early identification of emotionally handicapped children in school*. Springfield, IL: Charles C Thomas.

Bower, E. (1978). Pathways upstream: Risks of early screening efforts. *American Journal of Orthopsychiatry, 38*, 131–139.

Bower, E., & Lambert, N. (1971). In-school screening of children with emotional handicaps. In N. Long, W. Morse, & R. Newman (Eds.), *Conflict in the classroom* (2nd ed.). Belmont, CA: Wadsworth.

Bugental, J. (1963). Humanistic psychology: A new breakthrough. *American Psychologist, 18*, 563–567.

Buros, O. (1965). *The Sixth Mental Measurements Yearbook*. Highland Park, NJ: Gryphon Press.

Burton, A. (Ed.). (1969). *Encounter*. San Francisco: Jossey-Bass.

Cameron, J. (1978). Parental treatment, children's treatment, and the risk of childhood behavior problems. *American Journal of Orthopsychiatry, 48*, 140–147.

Cartwright, C. A. & Cartwright, G. P. (1974). *Developing observation skills*. New York: McGraw-Hill.

Cartwright, C. A. & Cartwright, G. P. (1984). *Developing observation skills* (2nd ed.). New York: McGraw-Hill.

Coleman, J. (1964). *Abnormal psychology and modern life*. Glenview, IL: Scott Foresman.

Combs, A. W. (1959). *Individual behavior: A perceptual approach to behavior*. New York: Harper.

Davids, A. (1958). Intelligence in childhood schizophrenics, other emotionally disturbed children, and their mothers. *Journal of Consulting Psychology, 22*, 159–163.

Dmitriev, V., & Hawkins, J. (1973). Susie never used to say a word. *Teaching Exceptional Children, 6*, 68–76.

Ebel, R. (1972). The social consequences of educational testing. In G. Bracht, et al. (Eds.), *Perspectives in educational and psychological measurement*. Englewood Cliffs, NJ: Prentice-Hall.

Ellis, A. (1970). *Reason and emotion in psychotherapy*. New York: Lyle Stuart.

Ellis D., & Miller, L. (1936). Teachers' attitudes and child behavior problems. *Journal of Educational Psychology, 27*, 501–511.

Erikson, E. (1968). *Identity, youth and crisis*. New York: W. W. Norton.

Erikson, K. (1964). Notes on the sociology of deviance. *Social Problems, 1*, 307–314.

Facts on File. (1968). *Weekly World News Digest*. New York: Author.

Felix, R. (1967). *Mental illness: Progress and prospects*. New York: Columbia University Press.

Fine, R. (1973). Psychoanalysis. In R. Corsini (Ed.), *Current psychotherapies*. Itasca, IL: F. E. Peacock Publishers.

Fiske, D., & Cox, J. (1960). The consistency of ratings by peers. *Journal of Applied Psychology, 44*, 11–17.

Forer, B. (1971). Word association and sentence completion methods. In A. Rabin & M. Haworth (Eds.), *Projective techniques with children*. New York: .

Freud, A. (1937). *The ego and the mechanisms of defense*. London: Hogarth Press.

Freud, A. (1965). *Normality and pathology in childhood: Assessment of development*. New York: International University Press.

Freud, A. (1947). *Psychoanalysis for teachers and parents*. New York: Emerson Books.

Freud, A. (1952). Mutual influences in the development of ego and id. *Psychoanalytic Study of the Child, 7,* 42–50.

Freud, A. (1949). Aggression in relation to emotional development: Normal and pathological. *Psychoanalytic Study of the Child, 3–4,* 37–42.

Freud, S. (1949). *An outline of psychoanalysis*. New York: Norton. (First German edition, 1940).

Freud, S. (1953). *The standard edition of the complete psychological works of Sigmund Freud*. London: Hogarth.

Freud, S. (1935). *A general introduction to psychoanalysis*. New York: Liveright. (First German edition, 1917).

Fromm, E. (1947). *Man for himself*. New York: Holt, Rinehart, & Winston.

Gaston, E. (1968). *Music in therapy*. New York: Macmillan.

Glasser, W. (1965). *Reality therapy*. New York: Harper & Row.

Glasser, W. (1969). *Schools without failure*. New York: Harper & Row.

Goldfarb, A. (1963). Teachers' rating in psychiatric case finding. *American Journal of Public Health, 53,* 1919–1927.

Grump, P., & Sutton-Smith, B. (1971). Therapeutic play techniques. In N. Long, W. Morse, & R. Newman (Eds.), *Conflict in the classroom*. Belmont, CA: Wadsworth.

Hall, C. (1954). *A primer of Freudian psychology*. New York: The New American Library.

Hollander, E. (1965). Validity of peer nominations in predicting a distant performance criterion. *Journal of Applied Psychology, 49,* 434–438.

Holmen, M., & Doctor, R. (1972). *Educational and psychological testing*. New York: Russell Sage Foundation.

Holtzman, W. H. (1958). *The Holtzman inkblot test*. Austin: University of Texas.

Horney, K. (1945). *Our inner conflicts*. New York: Norton.

Horney, K. (1951). *Neurosis and human growth*. London: Routledge and Kegan Paul.

Jacobs, J., & DeGraaf, C. (1973). Expectancy and race: Their influences on intelligence test scores. *Exceptional Children, 40,* 108–109.

Jung, C. (1959). *Basic writings*. New York: Modern Library, Inc.

Kessler, J. (1966). *Psychopathology of childhood*. Englewood Cliffs, NJ: Prentice-Hall.

Kleinmuntz, B. (1967). *Personality measurement*. Homewood, IL: Dorsey Press.

Kramer, E. (1971). *Art as therapy with children*. New York: Schocken Books.

Lewin, K. (1935). *A dynamic theory of personality*. New York: McGraw-Hill.

Lyman, H. (1971). *Test scores and what they mean*. Englewood Cliffs, NJ: Prentice-Hall.

Maes, W. (1966). The identification of emotionally disturbed children. *Exceptional Children, 32,* 607–613.

Maslow, A. (1962). *Toward a psychology of being*. Princeton, NJ: D. Van Nostrand.

Maslow, A. (1965). *Eupsychian management: A journal*. Homewood, IL: Richard D. Irwin.

Mitchell, J. (1942). A study of teachers' and mental hygienists' ratings of certain behavior problems of children. *Journal of Educational Research, 36,* 292–307.

Morse, W. (1971). The crisis or helping teacher. In N. Long, W. Morse, & R. Newman (Eds.), *Conflict in the classroom*. Belmont, CA: Wadsworth.

Mosak, H., and Dreikurs, R. (1973). Adlerian psychotherapy. In R. Corsini, (Ed.), *Current psychotherapies*. Itasca, IL: F. E. Peacock Publishers.

Murray, H. A. (1943). *Thematic Apperception Test*. Cambridge, MA: Harvard University Press.

Naumburg, M. (1958). Art therapy, its scope and function. In E. Hammer et al. (Eds.), *The clinical application of projective drawings*. Springfield, IL: Charles C Thomas.

Naumburg, M. (1958). *Psychoneurotic art: Its function in psychotherapy*. New York: Grune and Stratton.

Nelson, C. M. (1971). Techniques for screening conduct disturbed children. *Exceptional Children, 37,* 501–507.

Nelson, R. (1966). Elementary school counseling with unstructured play media. *Personnel and Guidance Journal, 45,* 24–27.

Newman, K. (1963). The school centered life-space interview as illustrated by extreme threat of school issues. *American Journal of Orthopsychiatry, 33,* 730–733.

Nordoff, P., & Robbins, C. (1971). *Therapy in music for handicapped children*. New York: St. Martin's Press.

Perls, F., Hefferline, R., & Goodman, P. (1951). *Gestalt therapy*. New York: Julian Press.

Rank, O. (1929). *The trauma of birth*. New York: Harcourt, Brace & World.

Redl, F. (1959a). The concept of a therapeutic milieu. *American Journal of Orthopsychiatry, 29,* 721–734.

Redl, F. (1959b). The concept of the life space interview. *American Journal of Orthopsychiatry, 29,* 1–18.

Redl, F. (1971). The concept of the life space interview. In N. Long, W. Morse, & R. Newman (Eds.), *Conflict in the classroom*. Belmont, CA: Wadsworth.

Rezmierski, V., & Kotre, J. (1972). A limited literature review of theory of the psychodynamic model. In W. C. Rhodes, *A study of child variance*. Ann Arbor: University of Michigan Press.

Robbins, C., & Nordoff, P. (1968). Clinical experiences with autistic children. In E. Gaston (Ed.), *Music in therapy*. New York: Macmillan.

Rogers, C. (1951). *Client-centered therapy*. Boston: Houghton Mifflin.

Rogers, C. (1959). A theory of therapy, personality, and interpersonal relationships, as developed in the client-centered framework. In S. Kock (Ed.), *Psychology: A study of a science* (Vol. 3). New York: Holt, Rinehart & Winston.

Rorschach, H. (1942). (Transl. by P. Lemkau and B. Kronenburg.) *Psychodiagnostics: A diagnostic test based on perception*. Berne, Switzerland: Hans Huber. (First German edition, 1921; U.S. distributor, Grune & Stratton).

Rosenthal, R., & Jacobson, L. (1968). Self-fulfilling prophecies in the classroom: Teachers expectations as unintended determinants of pupils' intellectual competence. In M. Deutsch et al. (Eds.), *Social class, race and psychological development*. New York: Holt, Rinehart & Winston.

Rotter, J., & Rafferty, J. (1950). *Manual for the Rotter Incomplete Sentence Blank: College form*. San Antonio: The Psychological Corp.

Salvia, J., Schultz, E., & Chapin, N. (1974). Reliability of Bower scale for screening of children with emotional handicaps. *Exceptional Children, 41*, 117–118.

Sattler, J. (1974). *Assessment of children's intelligence*. Philadelphia: W. B. Saunders.

Schultz, W. (1967). *Joy*. New York: Grove Press.

Sharp, E. (1972). *The IQ cult*. New York: Coward, McCann & Georghegan.

Skinner, B. (1953). *Science and human behavior*. New York: Macmillan.

Skinner, B. (1953). *Beyond freedom and dignity*. New York: Bantam Books.

Skinner, B. F. (1972). *Beyond freedom and dignity*. New York: Bantam-Vintage Books.

Stainback, S., Stainback, W., & Hallahan, D. (1973). Effect of background music on learning. *Exceptional Children, 40*, 109–110.

Sullivan, H. (1953). *The interpersonal theory*. New York: Norton.

Swanson, H. L., & Watson, B. L. (1982). *Educational and psychological assessment of exceptional children*. St. Louis, MO: C. V. Mosby.

Terman, L. M., & Merrill, M. A. (1973). *The Stanford-Binet Intelligence Scale* (3rd rev.). Boston: Houghton-Mifflin.

Thorne, F. (1967). *Integrative psychology*. Brandon, VT: Clinical Psychology Publishing Co.

Thorne, F. (1973). Eclectic psychotherapy. In R. Corsini (Ed.), *Current psychotherapies*. Itasca, IL: F. E. Peacock Publishers.

Ullmann, L. & Krasner, L. (Eds.), (1965). *Case studies in behavior modification*. New York: Holt, Rinehart & Winston.

Walker, H. (1970). *Walker problem behavior checklist manual*. Los Angeles: Western Psychological Services.

Waterland, L. (1970). Actions instead of words: Play therapy for the young child. *Elementary School Guidance and Counseling, 4*, 180–187.

Wechsler, D. (1949, revised, 1974). *Wechsler Intelligence scale for children*: Manual. New York: Psychological Corporation.

Wickman, E. (1928). *Children's behavior and teachers' attitudes*. New York: The Commonwealth Fund.

Wolpe, J. (1958). *Psychotherapy by reciprocal inhibition*. Stanford, CA: Stanford University Press.

Woody, R. (1969). *Behavioral problem children in the school*. New York: Appleton-Century Crofts.

Wursten, H. (1960). Story completions: Madeleine Thomas stories and similar methods. In A. Rabin & M. Haworth (Eds.), *Projective techniques with children*. New York: Grune & Stratton.

Zubin, J., Eron L., & Schumer, F. (1965). *An experimental approach to projective techniques*. New York: John Wiley.

4

The Behavioral Approach

INTRODUCTION AND OBJECTIVES

This chapter is divided into six major sections: (1) defining emotional disturbance, (2) basic theory, (3) screening and evaluation procedures, (4) classroom application of behavioral theory, (5) current status, and (6) vignettes.

Objectives of this chapter are to (1) familiarize you with behavioral theory as it relates to children in conflict, (2) identify behavioral causes of deviance, (3) familiarize the reader with screening and evaluation procedures, and (4) explain techniques for treating behavioral problems and developing classroom approaches for intervention.

DEFINING EMOTIONAL DISTURBANCE

A significant contrast to psychodynamic theory is presented by those who espouse the behavioral model. It is unlikely that one definition of emotional disturbance will be acceptable to all behaviorists, however, most will accept something like the following: Behavioral deviance is essentially maladaptive behavior that has been learned. This maladaptive behavior has developed and is maintained just like other behaviors— through positive and negative reinforcement and punishment (Buckley & Walker, 1970). If patterns of behavior deviate sufficiently from accepted behavioral norms, the child might be recommended for special intervention techniques or even excluded from regular classroom activities. Behaviorists generally avoid labeling children "emotionally disturbed," preferring instead to describe the behavior.

BASIC THEORY

Behavioral theory promotes the idea that deviance is a very practical problem with very logical solutions. The theory of treatment for emotional disturbance is essentially the same as that for changing normal behaviors. The critical issues of this theory will be discussed here. Several theoretical constructs of behavioral theory have been operationalized (MacMillan, 1973). From these models, eight common assumptions can be drawn:

1. Most inappropriate behavior is learned as is appropriate behavior (Ullmann & Krasner, 1965).
2. A relationship exists between the behavior a child exhibits and his environment. This relationship can be described as well as predicted if various components of the environment are known (Hill, 1963; Krasner & Ullmann, 1965).
3. Deviant behavior can be changed through the use of appropriate reinforcement techniques (Gagne, 1965; Haring & Phillips, 1962; Ullmann & Krasner, 1965).
4. Looking for causes of deviant behavior is counterproductive, since the original cause of a given behavior is unlikely to be what is maintaining the behavior at the present time (Ullmann & Krasner, 1965).
5. Behavioral theory is a "black box" theory with both environmental inputs (stimuli) to the black box (individual) and outputs (responses) from the black box observed (Rhodes & Sagor, 1974).
6. The relative goodness of any theory rests on its demonstrability and predictability (Rhodes & Sagor, 1974).
7. Behaviorists are reductionists, imposing severe limitations on observation techniques, intervention specifications, and interpretation of data.
8. The goals of behavioral theory are specific (Morris, 1985).

It is important to note that behaviorists generally acknowledge that some deviant behaviors are biologically motivated; however, their concerns are directed toward the response that society makes to the deviant behavior. For example, most behaviorists acknowledge that a child may exhibit deviant behaviors after an accident in which severe brain damage was incurred. The simple fact that brain damage occurred is not the central issue, however. The teacher, parents, peers, and others in the child's environment are also important to the behaviorist, since their reactions to the child will probably shape many behaviors of the injured child. It is not that the behaviorist is uninterested in what caused the deviant behavior. The important thing is what is *maintaining* the behavior at the present time (MacMillan, 1973).

Since behavior modification techniques have generally taken their strength from what behaviorists call "the failure of the medical model," it is well to cite some of the common weaknesses attributed to the medical model (Ullmann & Krasner, 1965).

1. The original cause of a behavior is not what is maintaining behavior later in a child's life. A good example of this might be smoking. A child might begin smoking at 10 years of age because of peer pressure. At 17 years of age the young person is still smoking but for a variety of different reasons. Peer pressure may or may not be a factor. The reinforcers *maintaining* the smoking behavior may center around the taste acquired for tobacco during seven or eight years of smoking. Taking away or changing the peer pressure for smoking would likely have little or no effect on the smoking behavior once other reinforcers are acquired.

2. Finding the original cause of behavior is improbable. In trying to identify good reasons or causes of a child's reading failure, the teacher might identify the following factors: First, reading is not all that important in this particular home. The parents seldom read, and little stimulation for the child to read is apparent. Second, two languages are spoken in the home, with English being used only sparingly. Third, the child has not developed an attention span that will allow any in-depth focus on the reading task. The child is in and out of his seat on the average of ten times every five minutes. Fourth, the child's peer relationships are significant. The child is in constant conflict with other boys and girls, both during and outside of school. The teacher reports that he gets into fights on the average of three times each school day. Fifth, the child has a vision problem; his eyes do not track properly. Given the proposition that all five factors are *probable causes* of the reading failure, what are the odds of finding the one cause or the correct combination of causes? By a simple mathematical process one can determine that given five variables that might *cause* a given behavior to occur, there are 120 possible combinations of these variables. The point is that the odds of finding the cause of any one behavior are relatively slight. Most behaviorists believe that looking for causes is a guessing game that takes a great deal of time and produces few results.

3. Suppose for a minute that a teacher is fortunate enough to find *the* cause of the specific problem just outlined. The teacher determines that two languages spoken in the home is very confusing to the child, and this can be identified as *the* problem that causes the child's reading failure. What can the teacher do to alter this real problem? Can the language structure of the home be manipulated? Should the child be removed from the home? Both of these solutions would probably be a waste of effort on the teacher's part. Therefore behaviorists believe that finding *the* cause is no assurance that the teacher, or anyone else, can change the behavior.

4. Finally, what indications are there that

gaining insight will help change behaviors? Consider again the example given earlier—the child who has been smoking from 10 years until 17 years of age. Will the young person want to quit smoking after he or she gains insight into the smoking behavior? Many behaviorists believe that insight alone will not change the behavior but, in fact, may contribute to the continuance of inappropriate behavior by giving the person a reason, or an excuse, for continuing.

In general, behaviorists tend to believe that it is a waste of time to search for causation of inappropriate behaviors. It is difficult for teachers who have observed the process of referral, testing, conferencing, and placement for several years to remain completely objective in the matter. Even when causes for deviant behaviors are found, teachers are generally unable to change the behavior pattern effectively by other than behavioral manipulation of the symptoms. Many children have been victimized by referral, testing, conferencing, and placement with little or no effective teaching taking place. By the time the child is evaluated and placed, the school year is over, and the process begins again the following year. Most behaviorists believe a more efficient system is available, a behavioral system that tries to determine what is supporting or maintaining behaviors rather than finding the original cause.

Reinforcement

Positive Reinforcement, Negative Reinforcement, and Punishment. Three ideas common to the various behavior modification systems and critical to the modification process are positive reinforcement, negative reinforcement, and punishment.

Reinforcement is an event that immediately follows a target behavior and results in an increase in the frequency of occurrence of that behavior (Skinner, 1938, 1953). For example, ice cream can be positive or negative as a reinforcer; it all depends on whether the person being reinforced likes ice cream enough to change because of it. Whether ice cream is good or not is irrelevant. A reinforcer is positive if the behavior it follows— and this is the key—is maintained at a *high level* or *strengthened*. If a child gets a perfect paper and the teacher says, "That's great!" will the child get more perfect papers, or fewer? If the child thus aspires to achieve more perfect work, the teacher's words are said to be positive.

A reinforcer is negative if its *removal* increases the strength of a behavior. Negative reinforcement appears to have a more limited applicability to the teaching process than positive reinforcement; however, its effective use is often critical in the solution of specific problems. Suppose a child is taken to a time-out room (a room away from the classroom where no positive reinforcement is likely) during a temper tantrum. As soon as the tantrum subsides, the child is allowed to return to the classroom, where reinforcement can again be earned. The child is relieved of the sterile atmosphere of the time-out room by exhibiting the desired behavior. Being permitted to leave the time-out room is therefore the negative reinforcement. Its removal increases the probability that appropriate behaviors will be repeated in the future. Examples of negative reinforcers in the everyday world include buzzers on seat belts and warning lights in automobiles. Although more severe negative reinforcers like bright lights and shock are generally not employed, their use has been demonstrated with severely disturbed children (Lovaas, Schaeffer, & Simmons, 1965).

Punishment contrasts sharply with positive and negative reinforcement. Whereas reinforcement aims at *increasing* behavior, the goal of punishment is to *decrease* specific behaviors. Punishment, as used in this text, means the removal of positive reinforcement or the presentation of a negative reinforcer. As with positive reinforcers, the determination of punishment can only be made by the results. If the behavior decreases, the stimulus is said to be punishment.

Schedules of Reinforcement. The rate at which positive reinforcers are delivered may follow a variety of patterns, called schedules of reinforcement. Reinforcement is generally scheduled according to time intervals (one reinforcer for every 10 seconds, one for every 15 minutes) or according to a ratio of acts to reinforcers (one reinforcer every three acts, one every ten acts). Both interval and ratio reinforcement may be fixed (one reinforcer given after each three acts or one reinforcer given every 15 minutes) or variable (random reinforcement after a varying number of acts or after a varying number of minutes). Although fixed ratio and fixed interval reinforcement are generally considered to be best for learning new behaviors, variable and/or intermittent reinforcement is generally considered to be best for maintaining behaviors at a high rate and is more resistant to extinction over time (Skinner, 1971).

Types of Reinforcers. The continuum of reinforcements used is often a concern of teachers who must work with a number of children at one time. Behaviorists generally believe that whatever works should be used as a reinforcer. It seems, however, that caution should be employed within a school setting to avoid intrastaff and intrastudent conflicts, which are debilitating to student growth. The determination of types of reinforcer employed should be considered a staff responsibility in the same way as establishment of other teaching procedures that concern children. Honest disagreements concerning the kinds of reinforcements that should be made

available to children must be debated openly, and acceptable agreements should be reached if a harmonious and efficient school operation is to be maintained. The comments that teachers and aides frequently make concerning the use of reinforcers indicate that basic disagreements plague the efforts of energetic and capable teachers and cut the learning efficiency of children. Giving dollar bills in school as reinforcers is one example of a reinforcement practice that is likely to create many staff problems.

There are two general guidelines for selection of reinforcers: First, the reinforcer used should not be stronger than is needed to effect changes in behavior. Everyone has heard the saying, "Let the punishment fit the crime." In terms of reinforcement one could say, "Let the reinforcer fit the behavior." The right kind of reinforcement is needed to ensure progress toward goal achievement. Second, the right kind of reinforcer can be determined by assessing the age of the child, the problem involved, and the relative strength of competing reinforcers. Two common errors of reinforcement are (not giving a reinforcement that is sufficiently strong) and (giving reinforcement that is more potent than necessary.) The concern often raised in reinforcement is the assumption that tangible reinforcers are better than social reinforcers. Children are given tokens, candy, and trinkets,—often in lieu of more acceptable social reinforcers (at least to teachers) such as praise and attention. Research in this sensitive area appears to be inconclusive. Although educators have a well-known aversion to extrinsic motivators (Hewett, 1968), there appears to be significant research that supports the use of primary rewards (food and water), toys, and tokens with a small percentage of deviant children (Birnbrauer & Lawler, 1964; Ferster & DeMyer, 1962; Levin & Simmons, 1962).

In deciding which reinforcers to use, the

teacher should consider both long- and short-term goals. For example, candy might serve the immediate needs of the child effectively but pose a real problem for the future. Candy will need to be phased out and replaced with a social reinforcer that is more acceptable in the school situation. If the child will perform efficiently without candy, one step in the modification sequence is avoided by the teacher. In addition, a host of paltry problems that drive teachers to early retirement are subsequently eluded. Complaints of staff members who do not approve of primary reinforcers, parents who believe the reinforcer to be a bribe, and other children who feel they are "left out" by the teacher's actions are only a few of the possible pitfalls that must concern teachers.

Behaviorism—A Critical Review

Any system that grows in popularity quickly is likely to be subjected to severe scrutiny at a later time. Such is the case with behavior modification. Even though behavior modification techniques were used as early as Roman times, their use in education did not have significant impact until the 1960s (Forness & MacMillan, 1970). During the 1960s, behavior modification techniques emerged from the laboratory into the classroom, with an impact unparalleled in education (Goldstein, 1973). Colleges and universities that had never accepted principles of behavior modification hired "behavior mod men" to bolster their staffs. Federal grants written with a behavioral bent suddenly became "the way to get money." In-service education for teachers, stressing the importance of behavior modification, proliferated. The day of accountability was just around the corner.

Many charges and countercharges have been made by the proponents and opponents of behavior modification techniques (Mac-Millan, 1973). Raising theoretical issues

serves a worthwhile purpose in bringing legitimate concerns to the attention of all professionals. It would appear profitable to consider some of the questions being raised by those who are skeptical about the modification process to establish a middle ground for using a technique that has demonstrated promise for boys and girls in conflict.

Behavior modification has given a tremendous lift to teachers who needed a technique that could restore confidence in their own ability to solve problems. After a period in which teachers were often considered second-class citizens as contributing members to various team efforts, behavior modification offers new hope for meaningful involvement with children. Teachers have attributed the rapid growth of behavior modification to the positive attitude of those who used modification techniques and to the antilabeling position taken by behaviorists.

PROCEDURES FOR BEHAVIOR ASSESSMENT

The purpose of assessment is to identify problems and devise intervention strategies. The screening procedures include rating scales, observation, interviews, and self-report.

BEHAVIOR RATING SCALE OR CHECKLIST

Behavior rating scales or check lists offer the teacher an efficient method of determining which children could benefit from further evaluation and intervention. The following are sample tools that emphasize a behavioral approach.

Teacher-made Checklist. School staffs often develop screening instruments that contain behavioral checklists. The behaviors listed are usually like those on the informal screening instrument shown on p. 81. The advan-

Child's name _____ Date _____

Birthdate _____ Evaluator _____

DIRECTIONS: Place a check mark in the column that best describes the child's behavior.

	Usually	Occasionally	Never
1. Misses school	☐	☐	☐
2. Short attention span	☐	☐	☐
3. Aggressive	☐	☐	☐
4. Withdrawing	☐	☐	☐
5. Appears confused	☐	☐	☐
6. Hyperactive	☐	☐	☐
7. Disorganized	☐	☐	☐
8. Displays inappropriate emotional reactions	☐	☐	☐
9. Talks too much	☐	☐	☐
10. Distractible	☐	☐	☐
11. Fearful	☐	☐	☐
12. Lacks consistency of behavior	☐	☐	☐
13. Fights with peers	☐	☐	☐
14. Relates well with adults	☐	☐	☐
15. Is a leader	☐	☐	☐
16. Is a follower	☐	☐	☐
17. Makes new friends	☐	☐	☐
18. Keeps friends	☐	☐	☐
19. Has nervous tics	☐	☐	☐
20. Daydreams	☐	☐	☐

tage of the informal teacher scale is that it includes items important to the teacher.

Walker Problem Behavior Identification Checklist (WPBIC). The Walker behavior checklist consists of 50 items in five behavior areas. These include

1. Acting-out behaviors, such as disruptive, aggressive, or defiant behavior
2. Withdrawal, for example, avoidance and restricted functioning
3. Distractibility, for example, short attention span and inadequate social skills
4. Disturbed peer relations, for example, inadequate social skills and negative self-image
5. Immature or otherwise dependent behavior

Area 1 has 14 items, each with a weighting from one to four. The evaluator simply checks the item if that behavior has been observed. For example, if the child displays physical aggression toward persons or objects, item 30 would be circled.

Area 2 contains five items with weightings from one to four. If the child does not initiate relationships with other children, the appropriate item in this area would be circled.

Area 3 contains 11 items with weightings of one to two. Does the child disturb other children? If he or she does, item 14 is checked.

Area 4 contains ten items with a weighted value of one to four. The child who utters nonsense syllables would be identified by an item from this area.

Area 5 contains ten items with a weighted value of one to four. The child who is seen as tainted or untouchable is a child who would be identified by this area. The test includes a profile sheet for each child so that the teacher can identffy individual strengths and weaknesses at a glance. Any child who has a T score of 60 or higher is identified as needing further evaluation (the cutoff level for boys is a score of 22 or above—for girls it is 12 or above). The WPBIC has been used extensively in both screening and evaluation processes, although it appears to be most suited to screening. The test manual says the instrument should "function as a tool for the elementary teacher in identifying children with behavior problems who should be referred for further psychological evaluation, referral, and treatment" (Walker, 1976, p. 1).

Behavior Problem Checklist (Quay & Peterson, 1967, 1975). The Behavior Problem Checklist consists of 55 items in four behavior clusters: (1) conduct problems, such as acting out; (2) personality problems such as lack of self-confidence; (3) inadequacy-immaturity problems, for example, inattentive-withdrawn and hyperactive; and (4) socialized delinquency.

Although the Behavior Problem Checklist is the most frequently used and widely researched in the field, it is focused on assessment of deviancy. No items assessing positive behaviors are included in the checklist and, therefore, no factors emerge reflecting appropriate social behavior or adjustment (Wells, 1981; Ollendick & Meador, 1984).

Behavior Rating Scale by Walker (1969)—Grades 4-6. The Behavior Rating Scale developed by Walker is designed to follow the **WPBIC,** discussed earlier. The scale requires evaluation of specific behaviors by teachers. A six-point scale is used to indicate the degree to which the behavior is descriptive to the teacher. This in turn will predict the likelihood of referral for more specialized psychological help. Data supporting the instrument are limited at this time; however, the instrument is still in the development stage.

Child Scale B by Rutter (1967)—Elementary Grades. Rutter developed the Child Scale B to aid in psychiatric diagnosis of elementary age children through ratings of classroom behavior. The scale is designed to discriminate between different types of behavioral and emotional disorders, as well as between emotionally disordered and normal children (Rutter, 1967).

This tool does not appear to be more than a preliminary psychiatric assessment tool and should be used in conjunction with other behavioral and professional evaluations.

Devereux Elementary School Behavior Rating Scale (DESB). Spivack and Swift (1967) developed a behavior rating scale for kindergarten through grade 6. This scale was not designed to rate only clinical cases of deviance, as were the Walker and Peterson-Quay scales. Instead, it was designed to rate a child's overall adaption to the demands of the classroom setting and subsequent academic achievement in that classroom (Spivack & Swift, 1973).

The strengths of the DESB include its ease of administration and scoring. The results are reliable, and validating data are strong. The tool is designed for screening rather than clinical evaluation and labeling.

Other screening instruments that feature behavior rating scales have been developed.

The following list includes a few that have shown promise for use in the school.

1. Behavior Checklist by Rulein, Simpson, and Betwee (1966)—elementary grades
2. Child Behavior Rating Scale by Cassell (1962)—kindergarten through grade 3
3. School Behavior Rating Scale by Pimm and McClure (1966)—grade 1
4. School Behavior Rating Scale by Davidson and Greenberg (1967)—grade 5
5. Teacher's Behavior Rating Scale by Cowen and coworkers (1963)—grade 3
6. Child Behavior Checklist by Achenbach (1979)—age 4 through 16.

Behavior rating scales or checklists can be easily used as screening devices to identify potential target behaviors and narrow the range of treatment strategies in the school settings. However, behavior rating scales or checklists should not be used as the only method of assessment since they are subject to interpretive and contextual biases of the informants who filled them out (Wells, 1981).

BEHAVIORAL OBSERVATION

Direct observation of the child's behavior in the natural environment is the hallmark of child behavioral assessment (Ollendick & Meador, 1984). With specific guidelines and practice, teachers may find that behavioral observation can be a very useful approach to behavior intervention in the classroom. According to Swanson and Watson (1982), steps for teachers to follow in observing and recording behaviors include

1. Determine the setting in which the behavior will be observed. Maladaptive behavior is observed in the situation in which the behavior is to be modified.
2. Decide on a method to code target behavior. Observational data are usually coded in a manner efficient to record and use.

3. Determine the interval of time the behavior is observed each day and the number of days observation will take place. A 5-day baseline observation period with approximately a 45-minute observation period is recommended by O'Leary and O'Leary (1977).
4. Become involved in observing and recording a baseline level. The baseline phase is the performance of an individual during the period before any special teaching procedures are implemented.
5. Chart the behavior data on graph and interpret the data collected (p. 288).

INTERVIEW

Behavioral interviews are structured to obtain detailed information about the target behaviors and their controlling variables (Ollendick & Cerny, 1981). The interview is widely used (Swan & MacDonald, 1978) and is generally considered an indispensable part of behavior assessment (Gross, 1984). In the interview, the child is administered a set of structured questions regarding current behavioral and emotional status and school and social adjustment. The child's responses are recorded as the interview proceeds (Wells, 1981). The same procedures can be applied to parents or other family members who know the child well enough to respond to the questions. Remember that this information is tentative, used to formulate or validate the hypotheses about the target behaviors and educational strategies.

SELF-REPORT

Self-report is an indirect approach to evaluate and understand a child's behaviors and the controlling variables. This method involves the child's retrospective rating of attitudes, feelings, and behaviors. A variety of self-report instruments have been recently developed for school-aged populations. The following list includes a few that seem to be appropriate for use with children in conflict:

1. State-Trait Anxiety Inventory for Children (Speilberger, 1973)—age 9 through 12
2. The Fear Survey Schedule for Children (Scherer & Nakamura, 1968)—younger and middle-age children
3. Children's Depression Inventory (Kovacs, 1978)—age 8 through 12

Although these instruments do provide valuable information regarding the child's own perception of his or her behavior, as with other questionnaire surveys, they should be used with caution due to their limitations (Cone, 1978; Ollendick & Meador, 1984).

CLASSROOM APPLICATION OF BEHAVIORAL THEORY

Behavioral theory offers the classroom teacher a practical alternative to psychodynamic theory, which was presented in Chapter 3. There are several distinct theoretical constructs that offer the practitioner a variety of methodological approaches. Three of these systems will be discussed: operant conditioning, contingency management, and behavior modeling.

Operant Conditioning

Behaviorists delineate two basic systems of conditioning: one is classical (Pavlovian), or respondent, conditioning; the other is operant conditioning (Ullmann & Krasner, 1965). In general, respondent conditioning is associated with the involuntary muscular movements, as in the response to touching a hot stove or to a mild shock. Respondent behavior is not used in typical learning situations, although its use has been demonstrated with severely disturbed children (Lovaas, Schaeffer, & Simmons, 1965).

From the time children are born they make an enormous number of random responses to their environment. Children literally "operate" on their environment through motor and verbal responses. Operant behaviors are conscious responses to the child's environment, which are maintained through reinforcement. As such, operant behaviors are clearly a major concern of teachers who attempt to modify children's behaviors. Whether operant behaviors are modified depends on what happens immediately after each operant behavior. If a child completes a good piece of work and is complimented by the teacher, this is likely to affect that child's work in the future. Whether the teacher's compliment will increase the strength of the operant (good work) or not depends on whether the teacher's praise is a positive reinforcer or punishment to the child.

Operant conditioning, in simplest terms, means reinforcing desired behaviors in ways that will cause the child to repeat the desired behavior. Operant conditioning can be used in a simple setting with no formal counting or reinforcement schemes, or it can be part of an extremely sophisticated system in which each behavior is counted, charted, and reinforced appropriately. Whether a teacher uses a simple or a highly sophisticated system often depends on the nature of the behavior being modified. The child who exhibits an occasional moodiness on Monday mornings probably needs no formal intervention, whereas another child who has a major temper tantrum each Monday is an entirely different problem.

Children in conflict who are identified as needing special intervention should be among those whose behavior should be monitored closely to effect desired behavior changes. Operant conditioning should begin as soon as a determination is made that serious problems exist. Hopefully, the child will be observed and inappropriate behaviors counted while he or she is still in the mainstream or as close to the mainstream as possible.

Data Collection. Three steps can be delineated in implementing operant conditioning systems. The first is data collection. Data collected before intervention begins are called *baseline data*. They help the teacher in several ways. First, baseline data help the teacher to determine if a problem actually exists. On one occasion a child in conflict was observed exhibiting "nervous habits" including nose-picking behavior. Over a period of two weeks in which the teacher observed and counted the behavior, it was found that nose picking occurred an average of once every 10 hours, and then for an average duration of 10 seconds. After counting and charting this behavior, the teacher decided that it was not the frequency of the deviant behavior but her dislike for the behavior that caused serious concern. The decision was made not to intervene formally to change the child's behavior, since it was occurring at such a low level of frequency and duration.

On another occasion it was discovered, through counting talk-out behaviors (talking without permission in the classroom), that the rate of inappropriate talk-outs for one classroom was over 70 an hour, with one child contributing over 40 of the total number. The boy who was dominating the classroom was a favorite of the teacher and was never suspected as being a behavior problem, only an outgoing child.

These two examples emphasize the importance of gathering baseline data to determine the exact nature of the behavior being considered for modification. To obtain accurate information, behaviors should ordinarily be counted and charted for a period of one or two weeks. During this time nothing new in the way of intervention should occur. The goal is to establish which behaviors are being exhibited and how often they occur. The teacher can gain information concerning the specifics of behavior counting by reading one of the many fine texts on the subject. Buckley and Walker (1970), MacMillan (1973), and Morris (1985) are examples of easily read texts on the process involved in behavior modification whereas the work of Ullmann and Krasner (1965) represents a more detailed and in-depth study of the process.

Second, baseline information can also help the teacher identify environmental stimuli that are supporting or maintaining the inappropriate behavior and that environmental stimuli would likely produce the desired behavioral change. This step is rather involved and takes considerable thought and skill on the part of the teacher. To determine the reinforcing stimulus (stimulus that follows behavior) or eliciting stimulus (stimulus that precedes behavior), the teacher must observe deviant behavior and also recall what environmental stimuli preceded it. A simple chart can be used to collect data on both reinforcing and eliciting stimuli.

Table 4–1 outlines a series of behavioral events that were either preceded or followed by stimuli. Deviant behaviors often occur in rapid succession, although the events could occur as separate behavioral entities. If a chart similar to this is kept, the problem areas soon become apparent. Table 4–1 shows that the teacher was involved twice in eliciting inappropriate behavior and four times in reinforcing deviance. At other times peers provided eliciting and/or reinforcing stimuli.

Third, baseline data provide teachers with a standard against which future progress can be measured. Without this standard it becomes increasingly difficult to measure success or failure. Teacher's memories tend to

TABLE 4–1. Acting-out behaviors (David, age 12 years)

Eliciting stimuli	Behavior	Reinforcing stimuli
Teacher asks question	David shouts out	Teacher says "Be quiet"
	David mumbles under his breath	Peers laugh
Tim walks past	David hits Tim on the arm	Tim cries
Teacher scolds David	David talks back	Peers all watch David
Tim snickers at David	David swears	Teacher sends David to the principal
	David refuses to leave	Teacher starts toward David
	David runs from classroom	Teacher follows

be inadequate when specific behaviors are compared, especially when several weeks or months have elapsed.

Arranging Consequences. Once the baseline data have been gathered, the teacher must decide whether or not to proceed with an intervention process. If a decision is made to modify specific behaviors, the teacher then determines which of the stimuli are maintaining the deviant behaviors. If either the reinforcing stimuli or eliciting stimuli can be removed, behavior will often change. In Table 4–1, if the teacher could avoid reinforcing David's inappropriate behavior, a noticeable change in the behavior should become evident. However, some cases will require additional intervention for change to occur. The teacher may need to reinforce appropriate alternative behaviors, for example. The successful arrangement of consequences requires specific attention to behaviors and how they are affected by reinforcement—a requirement that makes this a difficult stage of operant conditioning. Arranging consequences requires the teacher to decide (1) which reinforcers to use (types), (2) how much reinforcement is necessary

(rate), and (3) the schedule of reinforcement to employ. Any or all of these variables can contribute to the failure of intervention approaches.

Phasing Out Reinforcers. The third step in operant conditioning is the phasing out of reinforcers so that the child continues to exhibit appropriate behaviors with a "normal" level of social reinforcement. The phasing-out process has not been given as much attention in behavior modification texts as other issues, but it appears to be an important teacher concern. Reinforcers should gradually be reduced in both type and rate to a level acceptable to those with whom the child interacts. The goal is to have the individual feel good about his or her behavior and achieve internal satisfaction. Children vary in their individual need for reinforcement; however, this range has limits beyond which most teachers and parents will not continue (at least for long periods of time) to reinforce behaviors.

Reinforcement Tips for Teachers. Several reinforcement ideas have survived the trial and error of classrooms and have proved useful for teachers (Fig. 4–1). These include the following:

1. The most potentially powerful consequence in the classroom is the teacher (Anderson, Hodson, Jones, Todd, & Walters, 1972). Teacher attention can be in the form of verbal praise, physical contact, attention, allowing special privileges, and so forth. Whether teachers are the most powerful reinforcer in children's lives depends on the age and sex of children and teachers, environmental relationships, and a host of other variables. At any rate the teacher is potentially a high-level reinforcer for children.

2. Behavior modification can be used in a variety of educational settings, but it has no educational content of its own (Gearheart, 1973). Although behavior modification has only been a "technique" for teaching, its use has become so widespread that persons outside education have sometimes misinterpreted the technique as having educational content.

3. Operant conditioning is just as applicable to "normal behaviors" and "regular class" as to "deviant behaviors" and "special class" (MacMillan, 1973). Children can be helped to change deviant behaviors through the use of operant techniques, but appropriate behaviors can also be increased through this technique.

4. Whereas do-it-yourself methods, which are readily available to teachers, can help to foster professional knowledge, they cannot ensure adequate training (Woody, 1969).

5. Behavior modification techniques are actually a refinement of traditional teaching techniques that have been practiced by effective classroom teachers. Many of the common sense ideas teachers have been using are theoretically sound when they

FIGURE 4–1. The faces of the child and teacher both suggest that the reinforcement is having a positive effect.

are compared with "proved" behavior modification techniques.

6. The process of extinction will generally bring an increase in deviant behavior (Ullmann & Krasner, 1965). Teachers have noticed the occurrence of this phenomenon in the case of positive and negative reinforcement as well as during extinction processes. It almost seems that some children are afraid to grow in educational and social skills for fear that it will not last or that the expectation for growth will continue.

7. Three crucial elements of classroom behavioral control include (a) sensible rules, (b) appropriate praise, and (c) planned ignoring of deviant behavior (Madsen, Becker, & Thomas, 1968).

Operant conditioning provides teachers with the theoretical construct to change behaviors. Two systems will be discussed that add form to this theory: one is called contingency management, or contracting, and the other is behavior modeling.

Contingency Management

Contingency management is a close ally of operant conditioning that relies on basically the same concepts as other forms of behavior modification, that is, reinforcing appropriate behaviors by using positive reinforcement, with punishment used sparingly, if at all. The basic difference between contingency management and other behavior modification systems is the degree of structure. Contingency management is essentially a contractual agreement between the teacher and the child. The contract can vary, depending on the needs of the child and the school setting. Generally, more severe conflicts require more structure, whereas less severe problems require fewer external controls.

In contingency management, LPBs (low probability behaviors) are rewarded with HPBs (high probability behaviors). LPBs generally include such things as grading papers, doing homework, and studying for tests; HPBs generally include such things as eating, free time, coffee, and watching television.

An excellent outline of contingency management is available to teachers through the Instructional Materials Center, Special Education, University of Southern California, Los Angeles. This package presents the basics of contingency management by means of cassette tapes, filmstrips, and a written manual. In their contingency management package, Langstaff and Volkmor (1974) outline the basis of contingency management: (1) Of any two alternative behaviors, one is preferable to the other. (2) If the preferred behavior is given only after the less preferred behavior has been performed, the less preferred behavior will occur more frequently in the future. Thus the preferred behavior becomes

"contingent" on the performance of the less preferred behavior.

Contingency management has four basic components: (1) identifying a target task, (2) signing a fair agreement with the student, (3) rewarding behaviors that approximate desired goals, and (4) rewarding performance only after the behavior occurs. A contingent environment encourages a trusting relationship between teacher and student.

1. Contracting must be for a specific amount of work. The child must know what is expected, even if this means that each contract is put in writing and signed by all parties concerned. If a child has lost faith in adults, it may take more than words to assure the child of good intentions. A contract can often be the means to reassure the child.
2. The contract must be fair to both sides involved, not just to the teacher or just to the child. This implies that both sides have agreed to its content.
3. Behaviors that approximate the desired outcome should be rewarded. This is the principle of shaping that allows the child (and the teacher) to have partial successes on the way to goal attainment.
4. Behaviors are rewarded after they occur, rather than in advance. It is necessary to state this principle because teachers often are tempted to reward before the fact or before the contract is completed.

Homme (1970) has written a helpful outline to contingency contracting in the classroom in which he presents ideas useful to the teacher. This easily read and applied text has a self-instructional format, with pretests, intermediate tests, and posttests to guide each step of the instruction.

Contingency management is becoming a popular system of behavior management for use with children in conflict. It is simple, straightforward, and includes input from the child at every step, from deciding on a contract to reinforcement for work completed. The basic assumptions that underlie operant conditioning also apply to contingency management, making it supportive to this powerful modification tool.

Behavior Modeling

Bandura (1965, 1969, 1971) outlines a social learning theory that he calls behavior modeling, which is based on the concept that many behaviors are learned most effectively through modeling, or imitation. Although trial-and-error learning is an effective learning tool, it is extremely time-consuming and, in many cases, may be dangerous to the learner. No thinking parents would allow their children to learn to cross a busy street through trial-and-error learning for fear the punishment would be too great if they were to make an error. Parents take children by the hand and show them how to cross the street. Parents try to present a good model by their own behavior and also through verbalizing their knowledge and concerns.

Batting a baseball, swimming, and driving a car are other examples of behaviors that are best learned through the modeling process, rather than by breaking these complex behaviors into individual components to be reinforced independently. Bandura (1965) delineates what he considers to be the difference in teaching procedure between operant methods and modeling methods. He sees modeling techniques as most viable for learning a new language. The teacher says a word in the foreign language, and the students in the class attempt to imitate the teacher's pronunciation. Once the individual words or language is mastered, operant techniques would be used to increase and improve on the already learned behavior.

It should be pointed out that operant conditioning and behavior modeling are extremely supportive of one another. When a child swings a baseball bat correctly or develops a swimming skill, the coach or parent might reinforce this behavior with appropriate words of encouragement or a pat on the back. In this way reinforcement, as used in operant conditioning, is much in evidence in encouraging the modeled behavior. Bandura found that there are several variables that either enhance or detract from the effectiveness of the model the child is observing. Some of these variables include the sex of the model, the age of the model, and whether the model is live or on film. In short, the prestige of the model as perceived by the student will either encourage or discourage new learning. An example of this might be a high school football star who is demonstrating passing and catching techniques to a group of third-grade boys. In this case the learned behavior would probably be much more effective than if the same demonstration were conducted by one of the local high-school cheerleaders for a group of third-grade boys, even though the techniques might be similarly demonstrated. The high school football player model would probably be accorded a higher prestige value, and therefore modeling would be more easily effected.

Some children model behavior more readily than others. Although some children learn much deviant behavior as a result of modeling, or seeing deviant behavior performed, other children seem to avoid learning of this type. Withdrawn children often regress into a self-stimulating world and do not appear to be affected by those around them who are very active. Other, more outgoing children appear to model much of their behavior from others in the environment. The teacher can determine which children will learn through modeling by observing and determining which children respond to the contagion of behaviors around them.

Children in conflict who react readily to

the behaviors of those around them should be placed in a location in the classroom or in a special classroom where they might imitate appropriate behavior rather than inappropriate behavior. Educators do not have the same concern for children who do not model their behavior after others, since they are less vulnerable to either appropriate or inappropriate behavior.

In a study of the decision-making patterns of normal and educationally handicapped (emotionally disturbed and perceptually impaired) children, I found that many children capitulate to the value judgments of their peers (Reinert, 1968). Whereas it was found that normal children and educationally handicapped children tend to conform to judgments to a similar degree, their conformity took an interesting form. The educationally handicapped children, as individuals, tended to conform either to a small degree or to a great extent. This study seems to indicate that some disturbed children tend to conform a great deal (are followers who might benefit from appropriate models), whereas others conform little (are themselves leaders who are unlikely to follow).

The practice of putting children with certain behaviors into isolated classes with others who have similar behaviors would seem to be highly questionable if one subscribes to the concept that many behaviors are learned through modeling of peer behaviors.

The role of the teacher in modeling needs careful attention, since adults also serve as models. Teachers who are hyperactive themselves, who scurry around the classroom, yell at children, and otherwise present a frantic, disorganized, and uncoordinated model to children, can hardly expect children to be calm, soft-spoken, and quiet in their classroom. The modification of the teacher's own behavior is likely to have a dramatic effect in calming the classroom if the children can

observe this type of model. Many young male teachers have observed that the young boys in their classroom often model their behaviors: copying the belts that they wear, imitating their walk, combing their hair in similar fashion, and trying to imitate speech patterns. Little girls often model their teachers, particularly if they are women, in similar ways.

Bandura (1965) has done many studies to demonstrate the social implications and value of the modeling process. He suggests that no trial learning occurs once a child is under the control of discriminative stimuli. That is, a child can learn from others once he has learned to view others as sources of information.

Behavior modeling is more effective in learning new behaviors when no reliable eliciting stimuli are available to the teacher (Bandura, 1965). For example, how would you teach a child to say "I'm sorry" without using a behavioral model? Would a child ever say "I'm sorry" without ever having heard someone say the words before? Bandura doubts this would happen and therefore believes in the modeling process, a process that avoids the painful slowness of the operant conditioning model.

Although the concept of behavior modeling has been researched extremely well (Bandura, 1969), its use with children in conflict must be considered a part of other modification systems. Modeling becomes a component of change, rather than an isolated change in its own right.

Educational Concerns of Using Behavior Modification

Many claims and counterclaims have been made regarding the use of behavior modification in the classroom. The following guidelines should help the classroom teacher bring some of these concerns into perspective.

1. Behavior modification is not a panacea for all children. It is one technique that offers promise if used with discretion.

2. Behavior modification will not overcome poor teaching. Although reinforcement will never replace a well-planned lesson, it can certainly enhance the lesson if used appropriately.

3. It is unreasonable to believe that a teacher could function without using some behavior modification techniques. Social reinforcement is as real as life.

4. Behavior modification was not invented yesterday. Teachers have used behavior modification techniques for many years, even though the labels of behavior modification were not applied. Many behavioral techniques were not scientifically grounded by research, but they were still being used. For example, the Romans are said to have put an eel into wine glasses as an aversive stimulus for those who had a drinking problem. Teachers have successfully used negative reinforcement, positive reinforcement, and counterconditioning long before theorists developed the supportive research for these techniques.

5. Society is based to a great extent on principles of behavior modification. Individuals receive pay for working, supposedly in some relationship to their contribution to society. If individuals drive too fast, they are punished, if they have an accident-free year, they are sometimes rewarded with a deduction on their automobile insurance premium—a form of negative reinforcement.

6. Proper use of behavior management techniques will help to avoid the conflict between those who support the use of token reinforcers and those who favor only internal controls (an individual's feeling good as a result of his behavior). Children who can function without token reinforcers should be encouraged to do so. (Teachers would never think of putting all the children back into reading readiness material simply because one child in the classroom needed to be at that level.) Neither should teachers use token reinforcers, like candy, for all children when only one child needs this type of reinforcement to function. The goal should always be to achieve as much inner control and motivation as possible for each child.

7. Reinforcement cannot overcome a lack of structure and common sense in teaching children. At times teachers must learn to close doors, to vary schedules, and to separate personalities, rather than use behavioral manipulation to solve problems.

8. Behavior management is not a subversive activity. Teachers have always been interested in changing the behaviors of children they are paid to teach. Whether behavior is changed through the discovery method or through conscious manipulation on the part of the teacher does not really matter; to be effective the one who teaches must have a plan for change. As a change agent, the teacher has certain rights and obligations to students that remain intact regardless of the system advocated in helping to bring about desirable behavior changes. Behaviorists believe that their system is more open and honest than systems that encourage change through discovery or through gaining insight.

9. An often-heard complaint regarding behavior management is that it is unfair to reinforce one child while ignoring another. If that happens, it certainly is unfair, since all children need some reinforcement. Even university students on occasion will let it slip out that they have achieved all A's during a given

quarter. Parents often remind their children of the high marks they received in school. It seems that everyone needs reinforcement, although they generally want this reinforcment to be appropriate to their level of maturity and to the situation.

10. One principle of behavior management appears to be beyond reproach—making systematic observations of what is going on. This is what the push for accountability is all about. No matter what system is used to teach children, teachers need to be accountable to students, to parents, and to whomever else they serve.

Most teachers indicate that behavior management is a powerful tool for behavior change. Still, they are often reluctant to implement it in their classrooms. Teachers apparently view behavior modification techniques with some fear because of this tremendous potential for changing behavior. Most teachers feel a deep obligation to children and are fearful of the ethical implications that manipulation raises. As long as teachers are aware of this powerful tool and desire to help rather than hurt children, there appears to be no real danger of misusing it in the classroom.

CURRENT STATUS

The use of behavior modification techniques for the treatment of emotional deviance continues to be very common. In the mid-1960s teachers were interested in behavior modification but often reluctant or forbidden to use the technique in the classroom. By mid-1970 the use of the technique was not only common but encouraged in the schools. This rapid rise in interest in behavior modification is noted by Benassi and Lansen (1972), who surveyed the teaching of behavior modification in colleges. Hoon and Lindsey (1974) reported that the number of behavioral papers published in 1972 was higher than the number of psychoanalytic and client-centered papers combined. There is little debate that behavior modification has become a popular tool for use with children in conflict. There is considerable concern, however, as to its value. There are three major problems associated with its use. First, there are those who do not believe the technique works. Grunes (1970) and Thorne (1972) have been highly critical of the system. They suggest that if behaviorism works at all, it probably is limited to those of lowered intellectual functioning and the very young. A second group of critics believes that behavioral technology can modify behavior but question the morality of using such a powerful tool to modify behavior—often against the client's wishes. This attitude has prevailed in a case in which the American Civil Liberties Union brought suit against a behavior modification project underway in a Federal prison. As a partial result of this suit, the Law Enforcement Assistance Adminstration decided to curtail funding of behavior modification projects in prisons (Trotter & Warren, 1974). A third major problem is aptly pointed out by Willis and Giles (1978), who suggest that behaviorism has been far too narrow in its approach to learning. It has concentrated on consequent causes and has emphasized the elimination of behaviors rather than developing new ways of reacting to life's problems.

While the debate goes on, it remains obvious that behaviorism is a very popular technique today.

The student of behavior modification currently has an almost endless supply of journals that publish articles associated with behavioral theory. These include *Behavior Therapy, Behaviorism, Behavior Research and Therapy, Behavior Modification, the Journal of Applied Behavior Analysis, the Journal of Behavior Therapy and Experimental Psychiatry,* and the *Journal of Abnor-*

mal Child Psychology. Articles range from highly technical and statistical to ones of general lay interest.

VIGNETTES

Vignette 1: Behavioral Theory

REPORTED BY Patterson (1965)

Karl, a 7-year-old boy exhibited an unusual fear of school (anxiety at separation from his parents), a condition often called school phobia. Karl began to exhibit a fear of leaving home in nursery school. He often needed to go into his house to check on his mother. If she planned to go to the store, he would demand that he also go along. All attempts to keep Karl in school or to avoid his fears of separation were fruitless.

Karl was tested and found to have normal intellectual functioning but was low in reading readiness and rather immature in social interaction skill. Treatment was undertaken in a clinical setting, with reinforcement (candy) given for time spent in the playroom without looking at his mother. During discussion sessions (held after treatment), the mother was encouraged to praise Karl for remaining in the playroom without her. The mother was also instructed to praise Karl for not "checking" on her at home for periods of more than 30 minutes.

Through the continued process of reinforcement of mother separation, Karl gradually allowed his parents to stay in the reception area rather than sit outside the playroom door. Gradually, in sessions 11 through 23, he attended school, accompanied by the special teacher Three months after the individual sessions were terminated, Karl remained in school. Teachers reported a general improvement in school adjustment with no evidence of the return of fearfulness. The process consumed approximately 20 bags of M & M's and ten hours of staff time.

Vignette 2: Contingency Management

REPORTED BY Dee (1972)

Dee reports the uses of contingency management with a crisis class of children experiencing emotional problems. The children involved in the study were placed in the special class as a result of fighting behaviors, hostility to authority, school truancy, and disruptive behavior. Special class goals included modification of existing behaviors so as to allow each child to return to regular class.

The day was divided into work periods and play periods to provide the disturbed children with consistent boundaries. During work periods each child worked from an assignment book individualized to meet his needs. When the work was completed, the child brought the work to the teacher for any help and correcting. The work had to be within the contractual limits established before completion of the task (for example, three mistakes or less). If the contract was completed, check marks were awarded, as agreed on in the original contract. When the specific number of check marks was reached, each child could take his free time, which he monitored with a timing clock.

Free time was spent in a variety of activities, including games, eating, art activities, or any other high probability activities available at the time. The success of individual contracts was based, to a large extent, on the ability of the staff to identify reinforcers of positive value. If a child did not play well, he had to return to academic activities or go to quiet area for a specified period of time, for example, a five minute period, in which no reinforcement was received or work completed (Fig. 4–2).

Classroom example. Fred was in the special class for eight weeks working under a contractual program with the special teacher before he was ready to return to his regular class. He was a belligerent child with average or better intelligence who was considered a potential dropout. His functional academic level in the classroom was extremely low. When Fred entered the special class, he was offered several alternative contracts through which he could earn free time, candy, and teacher attention. He worked well initially but eventually tested the situation to see if there were "holes" in the system. After the honeymoon period he became belligerent and was placed in the quiet area, where he became

FIGURE 4–2. A quiet time-out area where a child cannot receive reinforcement is often helpful for children whose emotions are out of control for brief periods of time.

even more obnoxious. Some of his hard-earned points were then taken away. This case is extremely believable for classroom teachers who must adjust programs for individual children in ways that do not disrupt the good things that are happening in the classroom.

Vignette 3: Behavior Modeling

REPORTED BY Bandura, Ross, and Ross (1963)

This vignette describes a classical study in modeling theory. The study was designed to research the modeling effects of aggressive behavior presented on film. Subjects for the study included 92 children (46 boys and 46 girls) enrolled in the Stanford University Nursery School. They ranged in age from 35 to 69 months, with a mean age of 52 months.

One group of children observed real-life aggressive models, a second group observed the same two real-life models performing their aggressive acts by way of a motion picture, and the third group viewed a film of a cartoon character exhibiting aggressive behavior. After exposure to these aggressive models, each group was subjected to mild frustration (not allowing them to play with some special toys).

The results of the study indicated that children exposed to filmed aggression (both human

and cartoon) exhibited nearly twice as much aggression as did children in a control group who were not exposed to aggressive films. Children who viewed aggression of real-life models showed less tendency toward aggression than either of the groups that viewed filmed aggression and more than children in the control group.

This study is open to many interpretations, but two findings seem important for teachers and parents: (1) both normal and deviant children model aggressive behavior when frustrated, and (2) both boys and girls model aggressive behavior when frustrated.

Vignette 4: Behavior Modification of Selectively Mute Child

REPORTED BY Dmitriev and Hawkins (1973)

Before coming to the Olympic Center, Susie, age 9 years 4 months, had been in a regular kindergarten for two years. She was referred to the center because of a muscular twitching and refusal to talk to anyone outside her immediate family (she talked primarily to her 10-year-old sister).

During her first two years at the center, Susie showed periodic gains but always regressed into periods of twitching and digging at her arms, causing considerable bleeding. Speech was absent in school during this period. Susie was placed full-time in the center for a while, but still speech was absent, although other social gains were reported.

Through the consultation of Valentine Dmitriev, it was determined that the various behavior modification plans that were tried and discarded had failed because the staff was actually reinforcing Susie for *not speaking*.

Treatment centered around giving cues for speaking, that is, "say *chair*," "say *work*," or "say *lunch*." After two years of silence Susie began speaking. The breakthrough came on the fifth day of intervention, when seven of ten cues met with verbal response. This number increased rapidly, until verbal responses reached 421 words on the twenty-second day. Susie returned to public school six months after the procedures for implementing speech were undertaken. The authors report that Susie entered junior high school in 1973 and was doing well in school and community activities.

It should be emphasized that Susie was different from other mute children in that she was selectively mute. Her rapid progress under treatment obviously was a result of this fact. A totally mute child undoubtedly would react differently to treatment.

Vignette 5 describes the basic program used at the University of Northern Colorado Laboratory School. It could be described as a contingency management program with support services from a psychiatrist from the local mental health clinic, the school psychologist, the director of special education, a visiting teacher, and graduate students attending the university.

Vignette 5: Contingency Management in a Special Class

REPORTED BY University of Northern Colorado Laboratory School

John came to the classroom reluctantly one early spring morning (being carried by two husky males). John was 9 years old at the time and had been in school for an average of about 30 days a year through his first four years of school. He was a member of a large migrant family who spent part of their winter in Texas and part of it in Colorado, depending on the work that the father could do.

From John's cumulative folder it was learned that John disliked authority, was hyperactive, and was unable to keep at a task for any appreciable length of time. Our first contingency with John was to have him remain in the vicinity of his desk for five minutes and thereby earn a five-minute break to do as he chose. We were sure that John did not know what *vicinity* meant, and that was all well and good. We could interpret the word *vicinity* as we saw fit and thereby allowed John the freedom to cope with the situation without imposing rigid standards that he perhaps could not meet. For the first five minutes John laid on his chair, sat under his desk, sprawled over the top of his desk, and

looked out the window. He was told that he had done a good job of staying in the vicinity of his desk and had earned five minutes of free time to play outside or in the classroom as he chose. John immediately went out to the playground and found a multihandicapped youngster playing in a wagon. He quickly separated the wagon from the handicapped child and began riding around the school yard. This activity pointed out that the red wagon had a high reinforcing value for John. We made appropriate arrangements with the classroom teacher whose wagon John had commandeered so that John could use the wagon for his reinforcement whenever he was on the playground. John must get permission to use the wagon from the teacher, which she would readily give on his asking, but he must not dump a child from the wagon. In addition, no other children in our classroom were to use the wagon. This was to be solely John's possession when he had earned his reinforcement. The wagon proved to be a highly reinforcing agent for John, since he continued to stay in the vicinity of his chair for five minutes and thus earned five minutes of free time. We allowed this to continue for two days, until John began to show signs of tiring of this activity. During this first two days, which we call the honeymoon period, John tried to manipulate the reinforcement process by overstaying his five minutes with the wagon, even though he had a kitchen timer that warned him when his time was up. When he returned to the classroom, we said nothing but had him continue earning more reinforcement. When he got ready to return to the playground for another five-minute break, we told him that he had overstayed his break time on the previous period and therefore must lose the amount of time he overstayed plus an additional one minute from his next five minutes. This left him only one minute on the playground. We specifically waited until John had earned more free time before breaking the news that he had overstayed his last free time break so that he would not become discouraged. Please note that we did not ask John if he had reset the timer or why he was late returning but simply stated the fact that he had overstayed his time. In this way we tried to avoid the conflict that might arise if we asked questions as to why he did not return.

After the two days of earning reinforcement by staying in the vicinity of his chair, we indicated to John that he would need to sit in his chair to earn his free time. John seemed to be pleased to make this advancement toward the behavior that he was seeing modeled by other children in the classroom. The second phase of modeling John's behavior lasted only one and a half days; then John gave signals that indicated he was ready to do more than sit in his chair. These signals included taking a pencil and paper from his desk and doing some scribbling on the paper, forming a few crude letter symbols, and drawing some pictures. At this point we introduced John to the letters of the alphabet using the Sullivan reading program. John continued to earn five minutes of free time for every five pages of the reading material that he was able to complete correctly. John learned quickly, since he did have good ability and was older. We had few conflicts with John, and he liked school. He even rode his bicycle four miles from his home to school when he missed the bus.

A contingency management program helped John to become responsible for his behavior. The reinforcements that were earned were the type that are acceptable to most teachers in the public school so that John was able to make the transition to regular class without a difficult phasing out of reinforcers. In our program we avoided such reinforcers as candy, gum, and toys, which would not be readily accepted by teachers in future placements. We also found that the social reinforcers that we were using were much more easily phased into a reinforcement system that could be carried out in the regular classroom. Since several graduate students interacted with the children, we were forced to have specific guidelines for interaction so that consistency would be maintained.

The following guidelines were established for all staff:

1. Try to be positive at all times—even when correcting a child's behavior.

2. Prepare all work for the day before school begins. Prepare more work than generally needed so as not to be caught short.
3. Keep lessons short and to the point. Cut through the red tape of learning.
4. Individualize work so that each child can work on his own as much as possible. Each child should have an individual "in" and "out" folder so that he can pick up his work without interrupting others.
5. Check work as soon as possible. Generally, work should be checked immediately so that children receive immediate reinforcement.
6. Children should come to the teacher to have work corrected. The teacher is seated at a table near the entrance to the classroom.
7. Verbalize as little as possible. Show by actions rather than words. Do not argue with children.
8. Be alert to everything positive a child does. Ignore inappropriate behaviors as much as possible.
9. Try to give each child something positive to look forward to the next day.
10. Maintain positive relationships with parents.
11. Always pair reinforcement with a smile or verbal praise.

Reinforcement for the children was not expensive, since we relied mostly on social reinforcers. When token reinforcers were used, they were generally supplied by the children. We allowed children to bring their bicycles to ride during free time, models to build, and games to play. The children played chess, checkers, cards, and dominoes. One of the most novel reinforcers we observed was an old cowboy hat that one boy brought from home. His mother did not allow him to wear it around the house, so he took special delight in having it in school. During his reinforcement period, he would sit in the reinforcement area of the classroom with his cowboy hat on his head and a big grin on his face.

SUMMARY

A critical review of behaviorism and schedules of reinforcement were discussed in this chapter. Procedures for behavioral assessment, including rating scale or checklist, observation, behavioral interview, and self-report were also fully discussed.

Three systems of behavior modification, operant conditioning, contingency management, and behavior modeling, represent efforts to explain and formalize the learning process in schools. Although all are related, each has unique components characteristic of its individual process. Operant conditioning relates closely to the other systems. Contingency management varies from operant conditioning in that it is a contractual arrangement rather than just a process of reinforcement. In the contingency management process, the child is totally involved. The child, hopefully, recognizes the deviant behavior and knows exactly what is being done to help him or her change the behavior. Behavior modeling is also a process of behavior change but is slightly different from contingency management. In the modeling process, the child behaves because of an exemplary model that he or she chooses to follow. Sophisticated behaviors are believed to be more easily taught by use of the modeling concept.

The advantages and disadvantages of behavior modification are also discussed. The use of behavior modification has increased rapidly in the public schools during the past decade. It is proposed that professionals should make a healthy reassessment of its use, so that needed changes can be made. The major concerns delineated include the use of hard-sell approaches to behavior modification in the classroom, the feeling that behavior modification will overcome poor teaching, the ethical implications of behavior modification, and the need for behavior modification techniques to be included in the repertoire of all teachers.

The current status of behavior modification is reviewed. Teachers continue to use the technique in efforts to teach children in conflict. There is still a question of the degree to which the technique should be used. There appears to be a movement toward the use of behavior modification techniques in conjunction with more humanistic approaches.

Chapter 4 concludes with a series of behavioral vignettes that give examples of the practical application of behavioral modification.

BIBLIOGRAPHY

Achenbach, T. M. (1978). The child behavior profile–I: Boys aged 6–11. *Journal of Consulting and Clinical Psychology, 46,* 478–488.

Achenbach, T. M., & Edelbrock, C. S. (1979). The child behavior profile–II: Boys ages 12–16 and girls aged 6–11 and 12–16. *Journal of Consulting and Clinical Psychology, 47,* 223–233.

Altman, R., & Meyer, E. (1974). Some observations on competency based instruction. *Exceptional Children, 40,* 267–271.

Anderson, D., Hodson, G., Jones, W., Todd, F., & Walters, B. (1972). *Behavior modification techniques for teachers of the developmentally young.* Greeley, CO: Rocky Mountain Special Education Instructional Materials Center.

Bandura, A. (1965). Behavioral modification through modeling procedures. In L. Krasner & Ullmann, L. (Eds.), *Research in behavior modification.* New York: Holt, Rinehart & Winston.

Bandura, A. (1969). *Principles of behavior modification.* New York: Holt, Rinehart & Winston.

Bandura, A. (1971). *Social learning theory.* Morristown, NJ: General Learning.

Bandura, A., Ross, D., & Ross, S. (1963). *Imitation of film-mediated aggressive models. Journal of Abnormal Social Psychology, 66,* 3–11.

Benassi, V., & Lansen, R. (1972). A survey of the teaching of behavior modification in colleges and universities. *American Psychologist, 27,* 1063–1069.

Birnbrauer, J., & Lawler, J. (1964). Token reinforcement for learning. *Mental Retardation, 2,* 274–279.

Buckley, N., & Walker, H. (1970). *Modifying classroom behavior.* Champaign, IL: Research Press Co.

Cassell, R.(1962). *The child behavior rating scale.* Beverly Hills, CA: Western Psychological Services.

Cone, J. D. (1978). The behavioral assessment grid (BAG): A conceptual framework and taxonomy. *Behavior Therapy, 9,* 882–888.

Cowen, E., et al. (1963). A preventive mental health program in the school setting: Description and evaluation. *Journal of Psychology, 56,* 307–356.

Davidson, H., & Greenberg, J. (1967) *School achievers from a deprived background* (Project Report No. 2805). Washington, DC: Department of Health, Education and Welfare.

Dee, V. (1972). Contingency management in a crisis classroom. *Exceptional Children, 38,* 631–634.

Dmitriev, V., & Hawkins, J. (1973). Susie never used to say a word. *Teaching Exceptional Children, 6,* 68–76.

Fargo, G., Behrns, C., & Nolen, R. (1970). *Behavior modification in the classroom.* Belmont, CA: Wadsworth Publishing.

Ferster, C., & DeMyer, M. (1962). A method for the experimental analysis of the behavior of autistic children. *American Journal of Orthopsychiatry, 32,* 89–98.

Forness, S., & MacMillan, D. (1970). Origins of behavior modification with exceptional children. *Exceptional Children, 37,* 93–100.

Gagne, R. M. (1965). *The conditions of learning.* New York: Holt, Rinehart & Winston.

Gearheart, B. (1973). *Learning disabilities: Educational strategies.* St. Louis: Mosby.

Goldstein, A. (1973). Behavior therapy. In R. Corsini (Ed.), *Current pyschotherapies.* Itasca, IL: F. E. Peacock Publishers.

Graubard, P. S. (1973). Children with behavioral disabilities. In L. Dunn (Ed.), *Exceptional children in schools.* New York: Holt, Rinehart & Winston.

Gross, A. M. (1984). Behavior interviewing. In T. H. Ollendick & M. Hersen (Eds.), *Child behavior assessment: Principles and procedures.* New York: Pergamon Press.

Grunes, M. (1970). The coming of the westland in contemporary psychology. *Psychiatry and Social Science Review, 4,* 10.

Hall, C. S. (1954). *A primer of Freudian psychology.* New York: The New American Library.

Hall, R., Lund, D., & Jackson, D. (1968). Effects of teacher attention on study behavior. *Journal of Applied Behavioral Analysis, 1,* 1–12.

Haring, N. (1963). The emotionally disturbed. In S. Kirk, & B. Wiener (Ed.), *Behavioral research on exceptional children.* Washington, DC: The Council for Exceptional Children.

Haring, N., & Phillips, E. (1962). *Educating emotionally disturbed children.* New York: McGraw-Hill.

Hewett, F. (1968). *The emotionally disturbed child in the classroom.* Boston: Allyn & Bacon.

Hill, W. (1963). *Learning: A survey of psychological interpretation.* San Francisco: Chandler Publishing Co.

Homme, L. (1970). *How to use contingency contracting in the classroom.* Champaign, IL: Research Press.

Hoon, P., & Lindsey, O. (1974). A comparison of behavior and traditional therapy publication activity. *American Psychologist, 29,* 694–697.

Kovacs, M. (1978). *Children depression inventory (CDI).* Unpublished manuscript, University of Pittsburgh.

Krasner, L., & Ullmann, L. (1965). *Research in behavior modification: New developments and implications.* New York: Holt, Rinehart & Winston.

Langstaff, A., & Volkmor, C. (1974). *Structuring the classroom for success.* Columbus, OH: Merrill.

Levin, G., & Simmons, J. (1962). Response to praise by emotionally disturbed boys. *Psychological Reports, 11,* 10.

Lovaas, O., Schaeffer, B., & Simmons, J. (1965). Building social behavior in autistic children by use of electric shock. *Journal of Experimental Research in Personality, 1,* 99–109.

Lovitt, T. (1970). Behavior modification: The current scene. *Exceptional Children, 37,* 85–91.

MacMillan, D. (1973). *Behavior modification in education.* New York: Macmillan.

Madsen, C., Becker, W., & Thomas, D. (1968). Rules, praise, and ignoring: elements of elementary school control. *Journal of Applied Behavior Analysis, 1,* 139–150.

Morris, R. J. (1985). *Behavior modification with exceptional children.* Glenview, IL: Scott, Foresman.

O'Leary, K., & O'Leary, S. (1977). *Classroom management: The successful use of behavior modification* (2nd ed.). New York: Pergamon Press.

Ollendick, T. H. & Cerney, J. A. (1981). *Clinical behavior therapy with children.* New York: Plenum.

Ollendick, T. H., & Meador, A. E. (1984). Behavioral assessment of children. In G. Goldstein & M. Hersen (Eds.), *Handbook of psychological assessment.* New York: Pergamon Press.

Patterson, G. (1965). A learning theory approach to the treatment of the school phobic child. In L. Ullmann & L. Krasner, (Eds.), *Case studies in behavior modification.* New York: Holt, Rinehart & Winston.

Peterson, D. (1961). Behavior problems of middle childhood. *Journal of Consulting Psychology, 23,* 205–209.

Pimm, J., & McClure, G. (1966). Behavior observations of grade one pupils. In *NEA* (p. 152) Washington, DC: The Council for Exceptional Children, 44th Annual CEC Convention.

Quay, H. C., & Peterson, D. R. (1967). *Manual for the Behavior Problem Checklist.* Champaign, IL: University of Illinois.

Quay, H. C. & Peterson, D. R. (1975). *Manual for the Behavior Problem Checklist.* Unpublished manuscript.

Reinert, H. (1968). *Decision making in the educationally handicapped and normal child: A comparative study.* Doctoral dissertation, Colorado State University, Greeley.

Rhodes, W. C., & Sagor, M. (1974). *A study of child variance: The future.* Ann Arbor, MI: The University of Michigan Press.

Rulein, E., et al. (1966). *Emotionally handicapped chil-*

dren and the elementary school. Detroit: Wayne University Press.

Rutter, M. (1967). A children's behavior questionnaire for completion by teachers: Preliminary findings. *Journal of Child Psychology, 8,* 1–11.

Scherer, M. W., & Nakamura, C. Y. (1968). A fear survey schedule for children (FSS-FC): A factor analytic comparison with manifest anxiety (CMAS). *Behavior Research and Therapy, 6,* 173–182.

Skinner, B. F. (1938). *The behavior of organisms.* New York: Appleton-Century-Crofts.

Skinner, B. F. (1953). *Science and human behavior.* New York: Macmillan.

Skinner, B. F. (1971). *Beyond freedom and dignity.* New York: Alfred A. Knopf.

Speilberger, C. D. (1973). *Preliminary manual for the State-Trait Anxiety Inventory for Children ("How I feel questionnaire").* Palo Alto, CA: Consulting Psychology Press.

Spivack, G., & Swift, M. (1967). *Devereux elementary school behavior rating scale manual.* Devon, PA: The Devereux Foundation.

Spivack, G., & Swift, M. (1973). The classroom behavior of children: A critical review of teacher-administered rating scales. *Journal of Special Education, 7,* 55–89.

Swan, G. E., & MacDonald, M. L. (1978). Behavior therapy in practice: A rational survey of behavior therapists. *Behavior Therapy, 9,* 799–807.

Swanson, H. L. & Watson, B. L. (1982). *Educational and psychological assessment of exceptional children.* St. Louis: The C. V. Mosby Co.

Thorne, F. (1972). Skinnerian psychology, authoritarianism, and tunnel vision. *Journal of Clinical Psychology, 28,* 123–124.

Trotter, S., & Warren, J. (1974). Behavior modification under fire. *APA Monitor, 5,* 1–4.

Ullmann, L., and Krasner, L. (Eds.). (1965). *Case studies in behavior modifications.* New York: Holt, Rinehart & Winston.

Walker, H. (1969). Empirical assessment of deviant behavior in children. *Psychology in the Schools, 6,* 93–97.

Walker, H. (1976). *Walker problem behavior identification checklist manual.* Los Angeles: Western Psychological Services.

Wells, K. C. (1981). Assessment of children in outpatient setting. In M. Hersen & A. S. Bellack (Eds.), *Behavioral assessment—A practical handbook* (2nd ed.). New York: Pergamon Press.

Willis, J., & Giles, D. (1978). Behaviorism in the twentieth century: What we have here is a failure to communicate. *Behavior Therapy, 9,* 15–27.

Woody, R. (1969). *Behavioral problem children in the schools.* New York: Appleton-Century-Crofts.

5

The Sociological and Ecological Approaches

Section One:
The Sociological Approach

INTRODUCTION AND OBJECTIVES

To those who teach emotionally disturbed children the sociological approach offers a rich tradition. Although much of the work has been in institutional and private settings, the impact on schools has been significant. For the past two decades the field of social work, the heart of social theory, has been questioned severely suggesting that social services are of questionable value (Reid & Hanrahan, 1982). Even though the discipline of sociological theory is currently under scrutiny, there is considerable reason for optimism. This hope is due largely to new forms of practice and experimental designs that offer new insights to the effectiveness of social work (Reid & Hanrahan, 1982).

Objectives of this section are to (a) make you familiar with sociological theory as it relates to children in conflict, (b) identify sociological causes of deviance, and (c) outline intervention strategies and potential application of sociological theory.

DEFINING EMOTIONAL DISTURBANCE

During the 1960s a sociological theory of deviance emerged that was called *social-role approach* (Townsend, 1978), *symbolic interactionist, social reaction,* or *labeling theory* (Des Jarlais, 1978). The term *labeling theory* will be used in this chapter since it more clearly describes the process that occurs within the school environment. Labeling theory is relatively new to sociologists who formerly used terms like *social disorganization, delinquency, crime,* and *social problems.*

Labeling theory suggests that the labels we give to people contribute to the behaviors that will be exhibited. Of course, this contribution can be either a positive or negative experience. If we label a child *cooperative* or *good student,* the child will try to fulfill this expectation. If we label a child *poor student* or *behavior problem,* we also contribute to the child's self-perception and behavior.

BASIC THEORY

In his preface to the book of proceedings of the third Vanderbilt Sociology Conference, Grove (1975, p. 1) says, ". . . the labeling perspective has provided the most popular way of explaining stabilized deviant behavior." Labeling occurs when "agents of social control" such as teachers, parents, or psychologists publicly identify a youngster as deviant; an activity that sets powerful social processes into motion (Des Jarlais, 1978). When the public begins to focus on specific behaviors the child exhibits rather than on the child as a person, there is trouble ahead for the child.

The child who establishes an indentity of deviance does so in the same manner as the child who forms a nondeviant identity (Des Jarlais, 1972). In both cases the child conforms to the expectations of others. Usually the deviant child is given a specific label, such as *emotionally disturbed, behavior problem, spoiled, socially maladjusted, retarded.* At times the child is even rewarded for playing out the deviant role in an acceptable manner.

If a society labels children as part of the evaluation and placement process, there is a likelihood that the lives of youngsters will be adversely affected by this procedure. While labeling occurs for a variety of reasons, there is a strong relationship between the needs and values of society and the labeling that occurs in that society.

Even though there has been much written regarding the negative effects of labeling, there is some significant research that questions this widely accepted belief. Morash (1982) studied juvenile offenders and concludes that the importance of a negative label depends on how much the child values the person who uses the label. Since friends are most often seen as valuable, they are the most likely to have an impact on the youngster. Those who are most likely to place a label on a youngster are generally not valued by the juvenile. Of course, the relationship that a teacher has with a child is central to growth, so labeling becomes a critical issue for teachers and other school personnel.

Much criticism has been leveled against special education programs for their labeling aspects. Charges have been made that special programs actually create problems for handicapped children by setting them apart and pointing out their differences (Sye, 1971). Present efforts toward mainstreaming exceptional children are partially a result of efforts to avoid labeling children who have been previously classified deviant. Others contend that deviant children label themselves without any effort from society. When a child violates the rules of society, he or she in effect sets himself or herself apart. A number of theorists believe that the individual is responsible for most of his or her behaviors and that blaming an individual's inappropriate behavior on an anonymous society will do little to solve the problem (Matza, 1969).

Special educators do not have a monopoly on the labeling of children. Ability grouping, a common practice in schools, contributes to lowered self-concepts for the person who is identified as being in a lower group. A study by Elder and co-workers (1981) suggests that ability grouping can lead to teacher-student interaction that becomes self-fulfilling for the student. This finding presents a difficult dilemma for school personnel. In order to meet the needs of children academically, we place them in environments that are designed to meet their academic needs, but in the process we can cause a lowering of self-esteem and teacher expectations—ultimately damaging to the child.

Significant changes have occurred in 20th century society that have had an equally significant impact on children and youth in our schools. A few of these changes are outlines by Odhnoff (1975) in her presentation "Social Planning in a Changing Society." Speaking to a professional group in Stockholm, she suggested that social change in the Western World would have several outcomes:

1. Family Structure. Both the size and structure of the family have undergone dramatic changes. The number of children per household is down dramatically and the number of families with children, parents, and grandparents within close proximity has also dimished rapidly.

2. Family Function. During the early part of the 20th century nearly half of the people of Sweden made their livelihood through their own enterprise (e.g., family businesses, trade, agriculture). Due to changes in industry, urbanization, and agriculture, there is no longer the demand for small family organizations but for a more mobile work force. Therefore, families deteriorate as a necessary economic unit.

3. Standard of Living. As economic structure has changes, so has the standard of living. For the past several decades most people have experienced an increased standard of living. This fact has resulted in more free time for lesiure. In addition, we have more social and job security, better food, easier travel, and improved working conditions. Increased standard of living has also brought more demands by family members, which in turn increased the

pressure for more of these material advantages.

4. **Family Environmental Relations.** As families have extended their relationships outside the family unit, there has been a greater potential for deterioration of intra-family relationships. This extension of relationships has the potential of creating communication problems within the family as well as isolation of individuals in the family unit.

5. **Relationships between Generations.** Nowhere in our social relations has change been so dramatic and far reaching as in relations between generations. Industrial society has destroyed the relationships between families that once existed. Except in limited agrarian situations, parents work away from the home and children. Supervision of the children, which was once a shared parental activity, has become a responsibility of the mother or babysitter (or, more recently, a day care center or school). Margaret Mead (1970) has suggested that parents have seen their role as models, and their authority as parents, diminished by television, pop idols, and other distractors of the times. The strength of the family has also been changed by "shared governance" within the family. Children generally have a greater say in their lives than children of a generation or two ago. In brief, the authority of parents has changed, which has modified the relationships between generations.

6. **Relationship between Sexes.** Our most recent upheaval in Western Culture has been sex-role changes. Our traditionally conditioned behavior has been shaken to its foundation. Debates occur daily in the media regarding the roles of men and women. The role of boys and girls is also being studied and debated. Generally, we are approaching equality in education and the labor market for men and women, at least this appears to be a goal of Western society. All of this change is not without pain and conflict for adults and children.

In addition to the changes pointed out by Odhnoff, there are critical changes occuring in areas of religion, morality, family planning, and international relations that affect children through their interaction with adults. These areas of change are a part of sociological theory, affecting the youngsters we teach in school. As children react to this social environment, the adults who relate to them make judgments about the children's behavior and emotional status.

When one studies the concept of labeling, it quickly becomes obvious that labeling occurs for a variety of reasons, with none seeming to dominate all others. Sometimes youngsters are labeled *deviant* because they break the rules of the school (fighting and out-of-seat behavior). At other times youngsters are labeled without having broken any school rules (e.g., withdrawal and failure to respond to affection). Even though we label children *conformists* or *nonconformists*, the process really is not that simple; nonconformists generally *follow* the rules of society. They usually dress according to school rules, have friends and are able to live in some harmony within their neighborhood. Most conformists, on the other hand, have broken many rules. They occasionally are late to school, fail to pay attention at all times, are not always honest and may even run in the halls or chew gum! It all depends on which rules are broken, how often, and the conditions under which the rules are broken.

There appear to be two practical reasons people label children in conflict. The first is to capitalize on resources available for program funding. Funds are frequently not available unless labels are attached that target specific monies to a specific need.

A second reason for labeling, which has much practical merit, is to facilitate programming for children. A label often acts as a signal for special techniques such as play therapy or reality therapy to be initiated. It provides the encouragement for specially trained professionals to become involved with the child and encourages the use of specialized materials. When children are labeled, these three ingredients (specialized techniques, special teachers, and special materials) often become available to the children. If applying labels helps to facilitate evaluation and placement into viable programs that secure help for children, labeling will not have been in vain. If, however, labeling only allows expedient disregard for the needs of children, it cannot be tolerated.

Rule Breaking and Rule Following

Rule breaking and rule following are often suggested as major ways in which the deviance or normalcy of an individual is established. From a sociological viewpoint, deviance includes breaking the rules that society has set. The child is labeled according to the types of rules broken and the conditions under which rules are broken. If a child breaks more clearly defined rules, for example, takes things that belong to others or tells lies, he or she might be labeled as a thief or a dishonest child. However, if the child violates rules that are less obvious, for example, does not make eye contact during conversation or does not use appropriate facial expression or proper voice inflection, the child might be given a less specific label, for example, *withdrawn* or *emotionally disturbed*.

Social agents that enforce rules and label rule breakers may include parents, police, courts, and teachers. From the vast number in society who break the rules, only a few are chosen to be labeled deviant. The agents mentioned often play an initial and continuing role in this process. It is important to note that social rules are broken by most individuals, even though they are labeled conformists. And most of those who are labeled deviant follow the rules much of the time. The child who is labeled deviant might, in fact, follow the rules set down by the school in all areas except one in which his or her behavior is so nonconforming that a deviant label is attached. An otherwise normal child who exhibits himself or masturbates in the classroom would be one example.

Erikson (1957) suggests that the uncertainty of mental illness often leads individuals who are ill to exaggerate their symptoms so as to erase any doubt concerning their condition. In that way individuals can be legitimate in their claims of illness.

In general, children who are in conflict with their environment are treated differently from children who have physical illnesses. Children in conflict are expected to attend school and are generally given some responsibilities to perform. Except for extremely serious emotional disturbances, children are held responsible for the problems they present to society. This is probably true because there are no good or reliable indicators of the disturbance. If a child has a broken arm, there is a cast for all to see. In the case of emotional problems or other conflicts, there are only the external components of the conflict to observe. Since the cause of the problem cannot be seen, people tend not to believe that a cause exists and therefore blame the child for the deviant behavior.

In comparing the role of the child who is physically ill with that of the child who breaks the rules society has established, one realizes that physical illness is a different role. The child who is physically ill is generally compliant, whereas the child in conflict is usually not attentive to socially acceptable standards of behavior. The physically ill child is treated with compassion, whereas the child in conflict may get no attention until he comes into serious conflict with the law. Finally, there is a definite stigma attached to emotional and social conflict that generally is not attached to physical illness. It would seem that physical illness and social and emotional disturbance are not comparable ideas when one considers their effect on children (Des Jarlais, 1972).

Social Forces

Other theorists (Durkheim, 1951; Merton, Reader, & Kendall, 1957) propose that mental illness results from social forces that exert themselves on the individual. *Anomie* is the predictable result of social change that occurs at a rate faster than society can establish appropriate group norms (Des Jarlais, 1972).

Durkheim's theory of anomie is similar to Freud's theory. Both describe the human being as having potential needs that are inexhaustible (Des Jarlais, 1972). Whereas Freud used the id to describe the needs of an individual, Durkheim used the individual as a total entity. Both theories emphasize the controls that are placed on the individual. Freud used the concept of the ego, whereas Durkheim describes society as the controlling agent.

An example of anomie would be found in the Industrial Revolution. The rapid social changes brought about by industrialization encouraged disruptive human relations and anomie. Society placed a high value on wealth and then limited the individual's ability to achieve this end. The resultant conflict is called anomie. Wealth was desired, but limitations were placed on its achievement.

Although Durkheim's theory was developed with adult society in mind, its principles seem to have specific relevance to children, who are products of that same society. When rapid change occurs within a child's life without the attending social structure to guide his or her needs, frustration results. The child's needs are infinitely expandable and require external points of reference the same as those required by adults. As the needs of the child expand beyond any reasonable level of fulfillment, conflicts are inevitable.

Anomie also appears to be a plausible way of looking at children in conflict. In a society where rapid change is occurring, the role and function of children are often unclear. Changes that occur in the home, school, and community all contribute to this lack of clarity and resulting frustration for the child. As the child's needs expand and find a mixed structure of guidance for growth, this frustration may change to hate, distrust, withdrawal, or other forms of coping that may lead to deviance.

The theory of anomie was designed to explain a social pathology rather than an individual pathology. If many people in a society suffer from severe emotional disintegration, one can utilize the theory of anomie to understand possible causation. Although anomie generally is less helpful in describing the behavior of one individual, this construct will be explored.

Durkheim's theory, although logical, suffers from the same problem as Freud's theory. It is difficult, if not impossible, to test operationally (Des Jarlais, 1972). Table 5–1 compares the basic components of anomie with Freud's theory of personality organization.

Both anomie and personality organization are control theories, the id being controlled by the ego and the individual being controlled by society. If society fails to exercise its role of setting limits on the individual, deviance results. This theoretical approach was a product of Durkheim's theory of suicide, the ultimate in escape and personal pathology.

Merton (1949) set forth his concept of anomie as an example of social interaction produced by conflict between culturally approved goals and institutionally provided means to achieve these goals Merton's formulation was made with adults in mind,

TABLE 5–1. Comparison of personality development and anomie

Personality organization (Freud)	Anomie (Durkheim)
Needs of id (unlimited)	Needs of individual (unlimited)
Restrictions of ego	Restrictions of society
Intrapersonality conflicts (id-ego)	Intrasociety conflicts (individual-society)

TABLE 5–2. Modes of individual adaptation*

Modes of adaptation	Culture goals	Institutionalized means
I. Conformity	+	+
II. Innovation	+	−
III. Ritualism	−	+
IV. Retreatism	−	−
V. Rebellion	±	±

* Adapted from Merton, 1949.

however, there seems to be real application to children as well. An effort is made to make generalizations from adults to children and still keep Merton's basic theory intact. Table 5–2 outlines the various interactions envisioned by Merton. Five types of adaptation are shown schematically. The + signifies "acceptance," the − signifies "rejection," and ± signifies "rejection of values as they now stand and the desire to substitute new values."

Merton's conceptualization refers to role behavior of society in specific situations, not to the personality of one individual. A person does and probably should take different roles in different situations. A child may reject specific goals without any warning of a change in attitude. Merton was considering the economic structure when he formulated his theory and therefore considered wealth as a worthwhile goal. In making a generalization to children, other goals must replace the overall economic goal considered by Merton. Doing well in school or school achievement might be considered as an acceptable goal for children. Each of the five modes of adaptation will be considered using this goal as an example.

1. Conformity (acceptance of cultural goals and institutional means) is the basis of the goals of school achievement. If school achievement were not generally accepted as a logical goal and its institutional means, "study," were not an accepted route to achievement, schools would be considerably different in their structure. Conformity to this goal and to the institutional means of achieving this goal exists in most schools. This is considered normal behavior for boys and girls of school age.

2. Innovation (acceptance of cultural goals but not the institutional means) is a source of many problems for teachers at all levels of education. School achievement is an acceptable goal, but study is not the only route to achievement. Cheating on examinations, copying school work, or other unacceptable behaviors may be a few of the innovative efforts of children whose behavior falls into this second mode.

3. Ritualism (the rejection of cultural goals but the acceptance of institutional means) appears to be a problem for children who see no way to succeed in the system of education but who do not have the security to break completely with the system. Children who are of low ability or whose background has not prepared them for the rigorous competition they face in school are examples. These children may reject the possibility that the goals established by society might be achieved. School achievement is therefore rejected as a personal goal; however, they might con-

tinue to go through the ritual of study without any hope of achievement.

Schools that put a great deal of emphasis on achievement or, more specifically, signs of success such as grades, run a risk of ritualism developing among students. The competitive struggle for grades is exhilarating for those who are able to achieve, but it is extremely debilitating to those who fail to achieve. There is still hope for ritualistic children if they do not break ties with the school, but ritualism is risky because it is difficult to determine what the problem really is. Does the child suffer from a learning disability, a physical problem, or low ability? It is a difficult task to identify the child who is going through the motions in ritualistic fashion and even more difficult to remedy this behavior.

4. Retreatism (the rejection of both cultural goals and institutional means) is probably the least common of all the modes of adaptation discussed. When retreatism does occur, the child is extremely difficult to reach. The child may withdraw into a shell or may drop out of school if old enough to do so legally.

   Severe forms of retreatism could include autistic behaviors, psychotic tendencies, and addiction to drugs (Des Jarlais, 1972) These children have retreated from the real world to one more acceptable to them.

   Children who retreat from the world of school are often ignored by the school, get few if any of the rewards of school, but also have few of the problems of school. In their world of retreat they may find a solitude stimulating to themselves, without regard for others and the strife that others impose.

5. Rebellion (rejection of both cultural goals and institutional means and the substitution of new goals and means) is a severe

departure from other modes of adjustment that have been discussed. Children who rebel are not only rejecting that which is generally accepted—achievement and study—but replace this goal and means to the goal with their own goals. This presents the teacher with a most serious challenge, since the behavior is now tainted with distrust, rebellion, and often hate. Children in rebellion have been classified variously as socially maladjusted, personality disordered, and delinquent.

Anomie occurs as the child becomes alienated from society and develops a feeling of not belonging. Retreatism can be the ultimate result of not establishing meaningful connections between the goals of society and acceptable means of reaching those goals. Merton's theory of anomie has not been highly successful in describing the causes of mental illness from a scientific base, since establishing proof of a system that depends on a complex social interaction is difficult. For the teacher who is more interested in everyday interaction with children than scientific proofs, this theory offers a way of looking at children in conflict that may provide direction for intervention not offered by other systems.

SCREENING AND EVALUATION

The screening procedures used by social theorists are very similar to those described in Chapter 3. The emphasis is on gathering social information. Data gathered from these screening and evaluation instruments would be "laundered" to extract the sociological components. Behavior checklists such as the Walker checklist can be completed by parents or "significant others" in the child's social environment.

Sociometrics

Various forms of sociometrics have been used by teachers for a number of years. For classroom teachers, sociometric tests are a simple measure of the attractions and repulsions within a given group of children. Fig. 5–1 shows the results of social questions within a small class of boys.

Several important concerns regarding sociometric tests should be considered before this measure is used for classroom screening (Moreno, 1943).

1. Questions used to stimulate pupil selection should be simple enough to be understood by everyone in the group.
2. Children should be allowed to make choices in private.
3. The limits of choices should be clearly indicated to all children.
4. Children should be permitted an unlimited number of choices or rejections.
5. Each choice should be made with a particular activity in mind.
6. Children should be reacting (as much as possible) to a real situation that will be affected by their decisions.

Sociometric data provide additional information for the classroom teacher. A sociometric test is generally not intended to be used as an isolated screening instrument but to obtain supportive information.

In an effort to determine several criteria for identification, Kessler (1966) outlined several variables that are important in identification of children for referral. These include (1) the discrepancy between chronological age and behavior, (2) the frequency of symptom occurrence, (3) the number of separate symptoms that alienate the child from those around him, (4) the view that the child holds toward himself, and (5) the resistance of behaviors to change.

Evaluation

Once screening has been completed and children in need of further evaluation identified, the first stage of the total evaluation process is completed. Next the educator is ready to evaluate each identified child to determine, as far as possible, specific reasons for deviance to be exhibited. Only those children who are screened out as high-risk cases are usually provided with a more complete evaluation. States that have established special funding for emotionally disturbed or behaviorally disordered children generally require specific information before special placement is made. Required information may include observation, psychological or psychiatric interview, individual intelligence tests, achievement tests, medical examination, personality testing, and professional judgment. These evaluations are required to avoid duplication of services and to ensure proper placement for each child. Through the use of evaluative instruments and professional observation, the determination of major problem areas is made. When the decision is made to evaluate an individual child, the parents should become involved. This is necessary from ethical, practical, and legal points of view.

Children in conflict can be affected by a variety of other problems. They may be visually impaired, hearing-impaired, or physically handicapped; they might also be mentally retarded or suffering from organic problems that might necessitate special placement. The process of sifting through the various physical, mental, perceptual, and emotional processes to determine the major cause of disability is being seriously questioned by teachers, parents, and others interested in the welfare of children. Understandably, educators do not want children whose only problem is a physical handicap, for example, to be placed in a special program

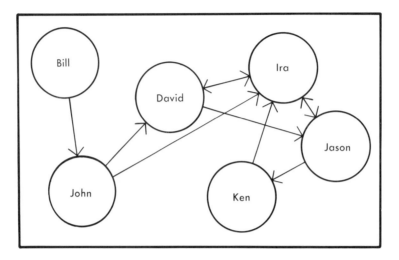

FIGURE 5–1. Sociogram of special class of boys.

designed to serve emotionally disturbed children. In many cases, however, it is extremely difficult to determine which handicap is presenting the major problem for the child. Mental health and adequate interpersonal relationships are not achieved in isolation, nor are they limited to those who do not have other problems. With the growing shift in emphasis on schools toward the resource room and away from the special class model, many of the categorical breakdowns of the past are being minimized. Resource teachers are trying to help the child without determining the specific weighting that should be applied to each problem area. Granted, the child who has a visual limitation, hearing impairment, or other physical limitation is generally more vulnerable to intrapersonal and interpersonal conflicts. The degree of conflict a child experiences can be viewed as the result of two factors: the child's adjustive resources and the degree of stress under which each child lives. Fig. 5–2 shows this conceptualization graphically.

Fig. 5–2 outlines the relative interaction of four children with two factors: adjustive resources and degree of stress. Mary has a high level of coping skills and a low level of problems in her life. She is able to get along well in school. John has a high number of problems and low ability to cope. He presents serious problems in school. John may have physical, social, hearing, and visual problems in addition to emotional problems. He needs help to strengthen his ability to cope, and at the same time the number of problems that he must face needs to be reduced if possible. Susan has a low number of problems and has few resources for coping. Her functional level is adequate as long as she continues to be free of stress. Her adjustive resources must be strengthened, since her life will include problems with which she must cope effectively. Bill has a great number of problems but also copes well, which allows him to get along adequately in school. Whereas educators might work with all of these hypothetical cases at some time in school, they generaly are most concerned with Susan and John, who have poor adjustive abilities. Secondary handicaps such as vision or hearing problems must be considered in the degree of stress under which a child must function. Although vision and

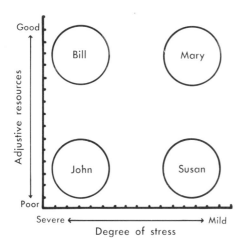

FIGURE 5–2. A comparison of adjustive resources and degree of stress with four chlidren.

hearing problems should be corrected as much as possible and accommodation of the disability emphasized, the emotional impact often remains. In brief, it is important that emotional problems be dealt with, even if other handicapping conditions are present within the child's behavioral pattern.

Children who are suffering from various physical or mental handicaps may have developed adequate emotional relationships with those around them and achieved an internal self-acceptance. If this is the situation, there is no more need to establish special services for these children than for normal children.

One instrument that is getting attention in the sociological area is the Piers-Harris Children's Self Concept Scale (*The Way I Feel about Myself*) (CSCS) (1969).

The CSCS consists of 80 first-person questions to which the child responds "yes" or "no." Approximately half of the questions are worded to indicate a positive self-concept and about half are worded to indicate a negative self-concept.

The scale is designed to be used in grades 3 through 12. It takes very little teacher time to administer, although younger children would need to have questions read to them.

Although research on the instrument with disturbed populations is limited, this scale offers professionals a standardized instrument that can provide insight into personal feelings of children in conflict.

Personal interviews that emphasize the social nature of the child continue to be the most commonly used evaluation tool. Generally, these evaluations are conducted by the social worker, psychologist, or school nurse, although the teacher may contribute information if other professionals are not available.

Individual evaluation is often done for a variety of reasons, including classification or labeling, educational placement, funding, establishing the number of handicapped children to be served, and development of an educational blueprint. Of these and other reasons for evaluation, there appears to be only one that is educationally valid and defensible—to establish an educational blueprint for action. Screening and evaluation are reasonably easy operations that can be effectively performed by trained professionals, but what happens after evaluation is closely related to the quality of the diagnostic process and will ultimately determine the success of the program. Professionals seem to have become so enamored of the process of diagnostic evaluation, they have lost sight of the most important factor in their original plan.

CLASSROOM APPLICATION OF SOCIOLOGICAL THEORY

Of all the interventions for children in conflict, the sociological approach is probably the most difficult to implement. Critics question whether sociologists have any practical input into social problems facing our nation (Whyte, 1982). When we apply practical intervention to this theory, we need to re-

member that sociological theory includes belief systems imposed on individuals, such as
labeling, and the effects of social forces on
individuals.

Social theorists have made us aware of the
impact our actions have had on children in
conflict. Two areas of current concern for
social theorists are labeling and mainstreaming. With the advent of Public Law 94–142,
we began "mainstreaming" children in conflict whenever possible, to minimize the
effect of labeling and the isolation that resulted in placement of youngsters in special
classes. Gresham (1982) suggests that
mainstreaming has not provided the answers
we thought it would, for three reasons. First,
mainstreaming has not resulted in increased
social interaction. Second, the quality of social interaction has deteriorated. Third, behavior modeling has not materialized.

Overcoming societal problems for the
child in conflict is a very difficult problem,
for some of these obvious reasons:

1. The child's home and community, which
   contribute to deviant behavior, are often
   ignored in favor of more expedient areas
   of intervention that essentially avoid attacking the causes of the problem.
2. Many problems in the classroom are related to the "assembly line" aspects of
   education. Impersonal tactics in the classroom are very difficult to change significantly because of cost, efficiency, and
   tradition.
3. Children who are pushed into the deviance role through the labeling process are
   often treated, when it is society that needs
   to be changed. Labeling occurs in an
   effort to create a feeling of control or
   progress. The labeling process is apparently an easier problem to deal with than
   a change of societal behavior.
4. School personnel generally have minimal
   training in sociological aspects of change.

5. Programs designed to help those who are
   different are often funded on the basis of
   labeling, and certification for teachers is
   generally categorically based.

Sociological intervention is difficult. However, interventions can be made. Des Jarlais
(1978) suggests that sociological intervention
would modify social situations so that deviants would adjust to the social order and the
nondeviants would adjust to the deviants.
This concept is very close to the ecological
construct that will be discussed in Section
Two of this chapter.

While some argue that mainstreaming has
failed to solve education and social problems
of the child in conflict, it is obvious that
removing the concept of mainstreaming
would be unacceptable. An alternative would
be to modify the components of integration
that have not worked. Gresham (1982) suggests that we need to undertake social skills
training with handicapped youngsters in order to prepare them to interact more effectively with their nonhandicapped peers.

In the 1960s, teachers of the emotionally
disturbed paid considerable attention to social interaction skills of the youngsters who
were to be integrated into the regular classroom. With the advent of PL 94–142, teachers came to believe that mainstreaming was a
necessary reality for handicapped no matter
what the consequences. Perhaps teachers
have not been as diligent in the social preparation of children in conflict as they should
have been. Perhaps it is necessary to prepare
handicapped and nonhandicapped to relate
more effectively before mainstreaming.
There is also the need to pay more attention
to mainstreaming as a necessary follow-up
activity. If we do not attend to these socialization issues, the least restrictive concept for
which we have strived will not be reached
(Gresham, 1982).

It is refreshing to read articles written

especially for teachers that speak specifically to the concern of social intervention techniques as a need of professionals. Hardin (1982) speaks to this issue in her recent article, "Designing Continuing Education Programs for Special Educators." She says that the field of education will always be confronted with the need to add to its professional culture and improve competence among its professionals.

We are coming to grips with cultural issues. As a result of court cases, school personnel are being sensitized to the disproportionate numbers of youngsters being served in special education. However, there are still many concerns that need attention.

Mental health centers, which began in the 1950s and received legislative support in 1963, have had a tremendous impact on the sociological nature of mental illness. Public school programs, developed "in concert" with mental health centers, have benefited directly from this sociological impact. These centers initiated attempts for prevention of mental illness, organizing community services, and educating the public about the nature of mental illness. Mental health center staffs have provided professional counseling and therapy to parents and others in the child's environment. Mental health workers have had to provide services to a wide variety of community members rather than to just the mentally ill (Des Jarlais, 1978).

Bloom (1971) identified several strategies that were developed by social reformers, including crisis intervention in suicide prevention, crisis centers, and identification of persons suffering from extremely high levels of stress.

A broader-based outcome of social change in relation to deviance is evident from the acceptance level of school personnel and boards of education. One realizes the dramatic changes that have occurred when one recalls the practices of the 1950s and compares them with those of 1982. In the 1950s it was common practice to expel students who were pregnant. In the 1950s a student might be expelled from school for smoking or drinking on school property. Students who experienced severe emotional disorders were generally not in school in the 1950s. (Recently, I was delighted and amazed to see a pregnant woman in a maternity referee smock officiating at a high school volleyball game. Guidelines of acceptability have changed!)

Other changes that have been made in schools include an extension of the open classroom to include specialist personnel, such as teachers of emotionally disturbed, social workers, and psychologists, who work in the regular class rather than in isolation. Changes that have results from a sociological emphasis also include the implementation of humanistic curriculum experiences, mainstreaming with handicapped populations, and family therapy as an extension of the school.

CURRENT STATUS

The sociological approach has become one of the more utilitarian approaches for those working with children in conflict. As program leaders have recognized the importance of productive interchange with parents and others in the child's environment, the need for enlightened professionals and sociological techniques has grown. Program leaders of the 1980s have come to understand the importance of this interaction and have been providing social work services.

Professional social workers can provide leadership in areas where teachers need assistance, working with children in therapy and interfacing with parents and others as a liaison from the school.

Journals that emphasize the sociological approach include the following:

American Sociological Review, a bi-monthly journal, is published by the American Sociological Association.

Social Casework, is a monthly journal dedicated to issues important to social work practitioners and educators interested in social issues. Emphasis is on professional research that relates to social problems.

Social Psychology publishes articles concerning products and processes of social interaction. Professionals interested in research and practice in social science will find this quarterly useful.

Sociological Inquiry is a quarterly publication of the National Sociology Honor Society, Alpha Kappa Delta (AKD). The journal is dedicated to the scientific aims of AKD. In general, the journal has a research orientation that emphasizes the adult functioning levels of society.

Social Psychiatry is a quarterly dedicated to the scientific contributions of social conditions to behavior and social environment and psychiatric disorders. This journal has an international flavor, with contributions from scientists around the world. Each issue features a theme, for example, "Attitudes Toward Mental Illness."

Section Two:
The Ecological Approach

INTRODUCTION AND OBJECTIVES

A theoretical construct that comes closest to an integration of techniques is offered by the ecological approach. It not only borrows heavily from various other theoretical positions but also encourages other approaches to use the techniques from ecological theory. Its strength comes from a dedication to observation, thinking through problems, and evaluation of all aspects of an issue before making judgments of success.

Objectives of this section are to (a) make you familiar with ecological theory, (b) identify ecological causes of deviance, and (c) explain intervention procedures and classroom application of ecological theory.

DEFINING EMOTIONAL DISTURBANCE

The origin of the word *ecology* is unknown; however, its use is attributed to the German naturalist, Heinrich Haeckel (1834–1919) (Sears, 1950). The dictionary defines *ecology*

as (a) "the science of the relationships between organisms and their environments, also called *bionics*" and (b) "the relationship of organisms and their environment" (The American Heritage Dictionary of the English Language, 1976).

The use of ecology in education emphasizes the interaction between the child and the environment. Disturbed behavior resides in the system of which the child is an integral part (Hobbs, 1982).

BASIC THEORY

William Rhodes is perhaps the most eloquent spokesman for ecological intervention with children in conflict. The term *ecological* perhaps conjures up a variety of interpretations, but to Rhodes (1970, p.310) a specific meaning is attached. Ecological intervention

. . . attempts to shift the locus of the disturbance from the child to an encounter point between the child and the micro-community or communities which surround him. It addresses itself to the ecological exchange nature of the disturbance. It searches for an intervention which will address itself to the shared process which is occurring between the child and the micro-communities he is encountering.

Rhodes does not advocate doing away with other modes of intervention, such as psychotherapy or behavioral intervention; however, he suggests simultaneous intervention directed toward the conditions of the child and the surroundings of the child. Intervention in the behavior of the child is not enough, since the child's behavior is only one part of the problem. As the child acts on and reacts to his or her surroundings, a relationship is established that contributes to the child's emotional stability. If this interaction is detrimental to the child's development, the entire constellation must become a part of the intervention process. When a satisfactory relationship is not established, the child must continually return to an environment that is hostile to continued emotional stability, and any growth is probably lost. Rhodes (1970) discusses several basic tenets of ecological theory:

1. Ecological theory sees the conflict as one that encompasses both the child and his or her community rather than only as a pathological condition of the child or of the community.
2. It is generally easier to intervene only with the child or with the community.
3. The ideal intervention would trace problems to their cultural source during treatment.
4. Intervention of an ecological type recognizes the totality of the problem.

The basic premise of ecological systems just described has implications for intervention that, in the view of the proponents of this theory, must be considered in planned change. This theoretical approach would frown on any system that attempts to modify behavior of the child or change his or her environment without attending to the quality and nature of the interactive process between child and environment.

Ecological theory has not developed a coherent framework for understanding emotional problems in children. Swap (1978) proposes a "nested" system of three levels: the behavior setting such as the classroom, patterns of behaviors, and the community and culture. This conceptualization allows us to view various levels and components of ecological theory without debating issues of narrow or broad interpretation.

Ecology is a new concept to educators and does not yet have a strong following in the school, even though it has had an impact in legislation and mainstreaming. At the school level, ecology has had effects on curriculum, and it has changed the concept of the classroom unit and school design. The net outcome of ecology and the school is one of adaptation, with the child living in harmony with the environment. We have become aware of the impact of a child's deviance on the classroom unit. At the same time, we have become concerned about what placement elsewhere can do to the child and those around the child. We can no longer look only at the needs of the child or at the needs of the groups with whom the child interacts. The placement of individual children has new significance for those who adopt an ecological perspective.

Rhodes and Paul (1978) speak of emotional disturbance as alien niches. The deviant individual is shunted into or finds her way into these niches. Deviant categories, such as *emotional disturbance, mental illness,* and *children in conflict,* provide society with ecological niches in which individuals can function without disturbing the mainstream of society.

The school system has a major impact on defining the niche for each child. Mercer (1973) believes that if the school assigns a label of deviance it is adopted by other agencies, for example, corrections. If Mercer is correct, and the evidence suggests she is, then we need to examine closely our evaluation, labeling, and placement of youngsters.

Ecological theory is essentially a holistic approach to children in conflict. Holistic theory by definition emphasizes the importance of the whole and the interdependence of its individual parts.

CLASSROOM APPLICATION OF ECOLOGICAL THEORY

Project Re-Ed

One of the most widely publicized and duplicated sociological/ecological systems is Project Re-Ed, which stands for "a project for the re-education of emotionally disturbed children" (Hobbs, 1966). The program described here represents a compilation of interpretations (Hobbs, 1966; Lee, 1971; Lewis, 1967; Weinstein, 1969). Although no major variance of description occurs with the writers who describe the Re-Ed process, there appears to be a healthy variance in program implementation. The intention here is to discuss briefly the Re-Ed process from a theoretical viewpoint and then to describe its implementation in one school setting.

The Re-Ed approach holds to the principle that the conflict is within the child but maintained through inappropriate interface (interaction) with the environment. Lewis describes this conflict as a discordance between the role prescriptions of the primary socializing systems with which the child interacts and the child's role performance. This discordance may develop for one of three reasons: (1) the child may not have the ability to perform the role prescription, (2) the child may not be aware of this role prescription; or (3) the child may find the consequences of competing role prescriptions more attractive than those of expected roles. Fig. 5–3 de-

picts the ecological system as interpreted by the Re-Ed approach.

As indicated by Fig. 5–3, there is a close relationship among various components of the child's primary socializing systems. Traditional psychotherapy, including the exploration of inner personal dynamics, transference, and intrapersonal conflicts, is avoided in the Re-Ed process. Since inappropriate behaviors are seen as bad habits that have been learned by the child in conflict, major emphasis is placed on establishing improved relationships between the child, family, and home community (Hobbs, 1966).

The Re-Ed approach is generally labeled a pull-out program by those who favor keeping children in the mainstream of education. Those who espouse the Re-Ed approach believe that a temporary pulling out from the regular school situation, which is contributing to the disturbance, is a positive factor. The environmental setting established by the Re-Ed process is a residential, 24 hour care unit that focuses its attention on the educative process. To maintain some orientation to reality the children return home each weekend to be with their families.

The center of the intervention system is the teacher counselor. Teachers selected for this role are generally those with teaching experience and a year of special training for emotionally disturbed children. The teacher counselor is assisted in program development by consultants from social work and mental health and by a liaison teacher. These consultants do not interact directly with the child but consult with the teacher counselor concerning the child's specific needs.

The philosophy of the Re-Ed approach is well stated by 13 processes of reeducation, as described by Hobbs (1966).

1. Life is to be lived now. This process points out a basic difference between Re-Ed and traditional approaches, which

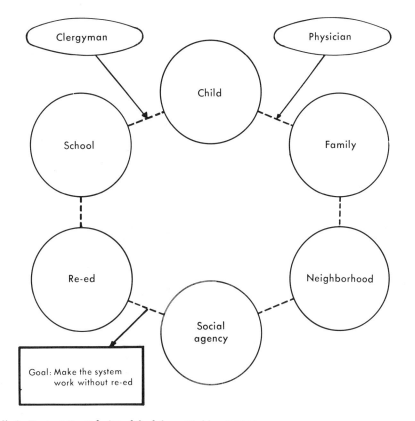

FIGURE 5–3. Project Re-Ed. (Modified from Hobbs, 1966.)

often look to solutions to problems in terms of a therapy hour. The Re-Ed approach does not put the child in a "holding pattern" for another intervention to effect change. Re-Ed is the change agent; each hour is important to the child and the reeducation process.

2. Time is an ally. This process supports the concept that time heals. When a child is taken from her home, the family is often at a low point in its ability to cope with the child. Things must get better. Re-Ed tries to capitalize on this belief without sentencing the child to a two-year stay before she can "get well." The goal is to use time for the advantage of the child, with six months considered a justifiable period of stay.

3. Trust is essential. Children in conflict have often lost all trust in adults. They have been let down too often, they have been coerced in various ways by adults and often resent the intrusion into their lives. To teach, to change, and to reeducate the child, first reestablish trust. Hobbs suggests that teaching this skill to adults is impossible; this would underscore the importance of the selection of teacher counselors rather than training.

Hobbs (1979) believes that we fail most often with children whose experiences have taught them to distrust adults. Children in conflict have generally learned that adults cannot be trusted or can be trusted only within limited settings. In order to overcome or minimize this problem, teachers must recognize that a problem exists and that building a trusting relationship will have direct value in educational growth for the child.

4. Competence makes the difference; we perceive others based on what they do. In teaching it is necessary to begin with the acceptance of some children's limitations and lack of competence; however, we must show them that they are *good* at some things! Disturbed children often lack school achievement; therefore, in the Re-Ed approach, school is important. It is part of the change process, not to be put off. In addition to gaining competence in school subjects, individual skills are stressed.

Opportunities for growth in academic skills often come from building on previous learning. This fact presents a problem for the school in working with disturbed children, for whom school has meant failure. In order to overcome this problem with trust, look outside the school for growth opportunities (Hobbs et al., 1979). Success and growth may come from volunteering or learning to swim, dive, skate, paddle a canoe, shoot baskets, or dribble a basketball. The building of competence comes from within the child with each new skill balanced delicately on previous experience.

5. Symptoms can and should be controlled. This process points out a specific difference of the Re-Ed process from traditional interventions. In psychotherapy, for example, symptoms often go untreated, with emphasis being placed on the underlying conflict. Re-Ed theory encourages the study and control of symptoms whenever possible. Symptoms are behaviors that can endear children to those around them, or symptoms can alienate children. It is important that symptoms that alienate children be changed or replaced by more acceptable ones.

Re-Ed uses explanations of inappropriate behavior that assume minimum pathology (a behavioral belief), rather than explanations that assume underlying psychological causation.

In addition to the psychological relationships associated with physical well being, we are becoming increasingly aware of our diet's effect on our mental health and learning. Although conclusive evidence is not available at this point, there appears to be good reason for teachers to become concerned with the effects of poor diet on the behavior of children.

6. Cognitive control can be taught. Emotionally disturbed children can learn to monitor their own behavior if taught to do so. Emphasis is on today and tomorrow, on immediate and short-term goals. Such teaching can be done by teacher counselors interacting with the child around life events that are underway. Much talking is done to develop personal insights into social occurrences. Each night a group session or council ring is held to talk over what went right and what went wrong during the day and to encourage appropriate changes for the following day. The youngsters are encouraged to verbalize their problems so that eventually self-control might be brought under the child's own verbal control. It is hoped that verbal interaction will carry over into the home, with a strengthening effect for that relationship.

7. Feelings should be nurtured. In contrast to those who would turn feelings off, the Re-Ed approach encourages the healthy expression of feelings. Feelings that have been blunted by experiences with adults

or other children are not easily restored to their full resiliency. The child might first wish to establish a relationship with an animal before entering into a more complex human relationship. This approach also emphasizes the release of feelings in productive ways, such as throwing clay on a potter's wheel, drawing, painting, or writing the script for a puppet show.

8. The group is important to children. A sense of belonging, of comradeship, and of responsibility can all be encouraged through group processes. Groups are kept small, usually around eight persons. Various sharing activities, including the council ring or pow-wow, are made possible through the group interaction.

9. Ceremony and ritual give order, stability, and confidence. In an effort to bring order to otherwise chaotic lives, the Re-Ed philosophy encourages rituals, such as regular meetings, a nightly back rub, or other small but important occurrences. The healthy family traditionally has developed rituals that are important to and held sacred by family members. Celebrations around family successes, parties, and family outings can never be replaced by rituals developed in a residential setting, but a certain closeness can be developed.

10. The body is the armature of the self. A wholesome physical self-image seems to be associated with a wholesome psychological self-image. To enhance the psychological self, the Re-Ed approach encourages physical activities such as swimming, canoeing, climbing, tumbling, and walking a monkey bridge.

11. Communities are important. Families of disturbed children often have failed to develop adequate community ties. The child can be encouraged to be aware of community activities and to participate in them. Field trips to the police and fire stations, health department, and community recreation facility might be helpful in pointing out useful community relationships. A boy might be encouraged to become actively involved in Boys' Club or Young America Football to help develop a positive association with community agencies.

12. A child should know joy. Joy is promoted by the teacher counselor who knows each child and what he or she enjoys. Re-Ed schools believe that joy is more than reinforcement given for some minute behavior. The child should have something to look forward to each day that will promote joy and a desire to anticipate coming events.

13. Middle-class values should be taught. Children who are considered "normal" by their peers can deviate considerably in their relationships with others and still be seen as normal. Children whose behavior has been inappropriate are often labeled as *deviant* and have a more difficult time expressing themselves in acceptable ways. Children in conflict must learn good manners, cleanliness, and acceptable language to be accepted by middle-class teachers. Often their behavior must be superior to that of "normal" peers.

The Re-Ed process offers one way to deal with the child in conflict as an indivisible unit, that is, child, school, home, and neighborhood. Its goals are concerned with reality and self-fulfillment rather than illness. Teacher counselors are employed as change agents, and specialists are used only in a consultant role. In addition, the Re-Ed process capitalizes on the abundant energy of young teachers, thus allowing professional expertise, which is in short supply, to be spread to the population of children in need.

CURRENT STATUS

The ecological approach to education is an emerging theory that offers professionals an opportunity for integration of all theoretical approaches. Its strength lies in the integration of the components needed for a holistic educational program. Its unique approach to deviance requires professionals to study the child, the environment, and the interaction between them in order to formulate a therapeutic intervention. The technique is receptive to all theoretical approaches that offer insight and/or solutions to maladaptive behavior. Ecological theory offers unique insights to those who believe that emotional problems are complex problems likely to require complex solutions.

Journals that emphasize the ecological approach for disturbed populations are not as well focused as journals in other theoretical areas. Journals featuring ecological perspectives include the *American Journal of Sociology*, *Social Psychology*, and *Social Psychiatry*.

In addition, the *American Journal of Orthopsychiatry*, the *American Journal of Psychiatry*, and the *New England Journal of Medicine* offer readers occasional information regarding this area.

Three journals dedicated to special education all have featured articles that relate to ecological management of disturbed children. These are the *Exceptional Child*, *Exceptional Children*, and the *Exceptional Parent*.

VIGNETTE

Sociological/Ecological Theory

REPORTED BY Project Re-Ed, State of Tennessee

Jimmy, age 6 years 3 months, was enrolled in the first grade of an elementary school in Tennessee. Jimmy was originally recognized as a serious behavior problem. He had been seen at a mental health services clinic earlier because his mother thought he was mentally retarded or organically damaged. His behavior included a preoccupation with knives and hatchets, a serious lag in educational achievement, and inability to control his anger. According to a problem behavior checklist, the teacher indicated 24 separate behaviors that were severe problems in the classroom.

Jimmy was evaluated for the Re-Ed school at the age of 7 years. On the Stanford-Binet test he was found to have normal intellectual ability but was thought to have perceptual and emotional problems. On the WISC Jimmy's scores were: verbal scale, IQ 89; performance scale, IQ 89; and full scale, IQ 88. Subtest scores were as follows:

	SCALED SCORE
Verbal	
Information	7
Comprehension	11
Arithmetic	8
Similarities	8
Vocabulary	7
Performance	
Picture completion	11
Picture arrangement	12
Block design	10
Object assembly	6
Coding	3

The scatter noted on the subtest scores indicated the possibility of learning disabilities, whereas the mannerisms and explosive reactions to the testing situation prompted the examiner to believe that Jimmy was experiencing emotional difficulties.

Other tests were administered after intake. These included the Metropolitan test, in which he scored at the 67th percentile; the Illinois Test of Psycholinguistic Abilities and Frostig test, which indicated acceptable functioning, although some scatter; the Wepman Auditory Discrimination Test, which was normal; the Beltone Audiometric Analysis, which was normal; and the Keystone Visual Survey Test, which placed him in the unsatisfactory range, with correction possible.

In all academic areas Jimmy was considered to be functioning below normal, although some scatter was noted. A comprehensive educational program was developed to remedy areas of educational concern.

Jimmy's early childhood was a stormy one. His mother and father experienced continual marital problems, which ended when his father was killed in an automobile accident. Jimmy was the oldest of three children; the youngest child his half-brother and the second child his sister. The mother generally believed that Jimmy was having some difficulties but less than others believed he was having.

In Project Re-Ed a behavior modification program was used with Jimmy, including positive social reinforcement, a token economy, and point systems. He became a member of the Tomahawks, a group of 12 younger boys from 6 to 8 years of age. Camping experience, a structured environment, and group rituals were among the many activities in which Jimmy was involved.

A Family Service Agency caseworker was assigned to the family to help improve any home situations needing attention. Communication with the home indicated steady and continual growth.

Jimmy was 7 years 2 months old when he entered the Re-Ed program. He was terminated at 7 years 9 months. At termination his academic achievement was average and his social relationships were adequate. The growth demonstrated during his brief stay can best be indicated by a statement in the case report: "Jimmy was a little bitty baby when he came to Re-Ed. He was a second grade boy when he left" (State of Tennessee, p. 77).

SUMMARY

Sociologists have studied deviance from both medical and deviance perspectives. From a medical viewpoint, the illness can be studied much as one would study physical illnesses. Emphasis is placed on finding medical causes of the disease, who has it, and under what condition the illness appears. From a deviance perspective, emotional problems center around the concepts of rule breaking and rule following. Through the process of rule setting by society and rule breaking by the child, the label *deviant* may be used. From a sociological viewpoint, the child is considered deviant because of inappropriate societal influence on the child.

Ecology as applied to children in conflict is a study of the dynamic interaction between the child and the environment. A child's emotional well-being is established on the basis of this interaction. This theory has significance for teachers who believe in treating the whole child.

This chapter includes both sociological and ecological theory because they are so closely related in their view of deviance. By placing the two theories side by side, one can readily see how their definitions of deviance, their screening and evaluation techniques, and their approaches to intervention are related. The vignette reported by Project Re-Ed shows this relationship very nicely.

BIBLIOGRAPHY

American Heritage Dictionary of the English Language. (1976). Boston: Houghton Mifflin.

Bloom, B. (1971). Strategies for the prevention of mental disorders. In G. Rosenblum (Ed.), *Issues in community psychology and preventative mental health.* New York, 1971, Behavioral Publications.

Des Jarlais, D. (1972). Mental illness as social deviance. In W. C. Rhodes, *A study of child variance.* Ann Arbor, MI: The University of Michigan Press.

Des Jarlais, D. (1978). Labeling theory: sociological views and M approaches. In W. Rhodes & L. Paul (Eds.), *Emotionally disturbed and deviant children.* Englewood Cliffs, NJ: Prentice-Hall.

Durkheim, E. (1951). *Suicide: A study in sociology.* Translated by John Spaulding and George Simpson. Glencoe, IL: The Free Press.

Eder, A., Grumiller, I., Jandler-Jager, E., & Springer-Kremser, M. (1981). The psychological background of mental illness: An empirical study of the frequency and economical aspects of impairments of health, partly psychological in origin, in nonpsychiatric medical practices and hospital departments. *Social Psychiatry, 16*(3), 151–161.

Erikson, D. (1957). Patient role and social uncertainty. *Psychiatry, 20,* 263–268.

Gresham, F.M. (1982). Misguided mainstreaming: The case for social skills training with handicapped children. *Exceptional Children, 48*(5), 422–433.

Grove, W., (1975). *The labeling process.* New York: Sage Publication.

Hardin, V.B. (1982). Designing continuing education programs for special educators. *Exceptional Children Quarterly, 2*(4), 69–76.

Hobbs, N. (1966). Helping disturbed children: Psychological and ecological strategies. *American Psychologists, 21,* 1105–1115.

Hobbs, N. (Ed.). (1979). *Exceptional teaching for exceptional learning: A report to the Ford Foundation.* New York: The Foundation.

Hobbs, N. (1982). *The troubled and troubling child.* San Francisco: Jossey-Bass.

Kessler, J. (1966). *Psychopathology of childhood.* Englewood Cliffs, NJ: Prentice-Hall.

Krasner, L., & Ullmann, L. (1965). *Research in behavior modification; New developments and implications.* New York: Holt, Rinehart & Winston.

Lee, B. (1971). Curriculum design: The re-education approach. In N. Long, W. Morse, & R. Newman (Eds.), *Conflict in the classroom.* Belmont, CA: Wadsworth.

Lemert, E. (1962). Paranoia and the dynamics of exclusion. *Sociometry, 25,* 1–20.

Lewis, W. (1967). Project Re-Ed: Educational intervention in discordant child rearing systems. In E. Cowen, E. Gardner, & M. Zax (Eds.), *Emergent approaches to mental health problems.* New York: Appleton-Century-Crofts.

Lindzey, G., & Borgatta, E. (1954). Sociometric measurement. In G. Lindzey (Ed.), *Handbook of social psychology.* Cambridge, MA: Addison-Wesley.

Matza, D. (1969). *Becoming deviant.* Englewood Cliffs, NJ: Prentice-Hall.

Mead, M. (1970). Pastoral psychology: The next 20 years as seen by a social scientist. *Pastoral Psychology, 21*(201), 8–15.

Mercer, J. (1973). *Labeling the mentally retarded: Clinical and social system perspectives on mental retardation.* Berkeley, CA: University of California Press.

Merton, R. (1949). *Social theory and social structure: Toward a codification of theory and research.* Glencoe, IL: The Free Press.

Merton, R., Reader, G., & Kendall, P. (Eds.). *The student physician: Introductory studies in the sociology of medical education.* Cambridge, MA: Harvard University Press.

Morash, M. (1982). Juvenile reaction to labels: An experiment and an explanatory study. *Sociology and Social Research, 6*(1), 76–88.

Moreno, J.(1943). Sociometry in the classroom. *Sociometry, 6,* 425–428.

Odhnoff, C. (1975). Social planning in a changing society. In L. Levi, M.D. (Ed.), *Childhood and adolescent.* New York: Oxford University Press.

Piers, E.V., & Harris, D.B. (1969). *The Piers-Harris Children's Self-Concept Scale.* Nashville, TN: Counselor Readings and Tests.

Reid, W., & Hanrahan, P. (1982). Recent evaluations of social work. *Social Work, 27*(4), 328–340.

Rhodes, W. (1967). The disturbing child: A problem in ecological management. *Exceptional Children, 33,* 449–455.

Rhodes, W. (1970). A community participation analysis of emotional disturbance. *Exceptional Children, 36,* 309–314.

Rhodes W., and Paul, L. (1978). *Emotionally disturbed and deviant children: New views and approaches.* Englewood Cliffs, NJ: Prentice-Hall.

Rhodes, W., and Sagor, M. (1974). *A study of child variance: The future.* Ann Arbor, MI: The University of Michigan Press.

Rhodes, W., and Tracy, M. (1972). *A study of child variance.* Ann Arbor, MI: The University of Michigan Press.

Sears, P. (1950). *Charles Darwin: The naturalist as a cultural force.* New York: Scribner's.

State of Tennessee (1974). *One child: A case study.* Department of Mental Health grant from National Institute of Mental Health.

Swap, W. C. (1978). Interpersonal attraction and repeated exposure to rewarders and punishers. *Personality and Social Psychology Bulletin, 3*(2), 248–251.

Sye, W. (1971). Social variables and their effect on psychiatric emergency situations among children, *Mental Hygiene, 55,* 437–443.

Szurek, S. (1956). Psychotic episodes and psychic maldevelopment. *American Journal of Orthopsychiatry, 26,* 519–543.

Tannenbaum, F. (1938). *Crime and the community.* Boston: Ginn Company.

Townsend, J. (1978). *Cultural conceptions and mental illness.* Chicago, The University of Chicago Press.

Tracy, M. (1972). Conceptual models of emotional disturbance: Some other thoughts. In W. Rhodes (Ed.), *A study of child variance.* Ann Arbor, MI: The University of Michigan Press.

Weinstein, L. (1969). Project Re-Ed: Schools for emotionally disturbed children—Effectiveness as viewed by referring agencies, parents and teachers. *Exceptional Children, 35,* 703–711.

Whyte, W. (1982). Social invention for solving human problems. *American Sociological Review, 47,* 1–13.

6

The Counter Theory
Approach

INTRODUCTION AND OBJECTIVES

The counter theoretical view of children is one of the most diverse and controversial of all classroom interventions. Gibbons and Tracy (1978, p. 288) say, "Behavior, in counter theoretical terms, is studied, not to devise remediation or therapy but rather for the purpose of promoting diversity, for . . . celebrating deviance . . . and for facilitation . . . [of] choice by each individual." This approach not only reflects divergent views concerning classroom practices, but also incorporates such general concerns as normalcy, socialization patterns, and institutional reform.

Diversity is the unique contribution that this theory offers. While most writers of counter theory agree that variety in behavior is a desirable goal in the classroom (Gibbons & Tracy, 1978; Tracy, 1974), counter theorists can also be identified by their own theoretical divergence on how this is accomplished. If they have a common bond, it probably is their distaste for schools as they now exist (e.g., Melton, 1975; Kozol, 1967).

DEFINING EMOTIONAL DISTURBANCE

Counter theory is not a single philosophical or theoretical approach, but represents a number of individual approaches that have one common thread—they all are in opposition to the established theoretical approaches described in Chapters 2 through 5.

Chapter objectives are to (a) make you familiar with the basic concepts of counter theory, (b) identify causes of deviance from a counter theory approach, (c) identify screening and evaluation procedures, and (d) evaluate classroom application of counter theory.

BASIC THEORY

Anyone who spends any time browsing in a bookstore will be impressed with the number of books that are critical of the practices within public schools and education in general. Some of these books are by counter theorists. The targets of these attacks are wide-ranging. Teachers are often identified as the culprits in the "conspiracy" of the schools; but others, including psychologists, social workers, and administrators are also vulnerable. Parents and various childrearing practices are favorite targets of those who espouse the counter theoretical approach. Titles such as *The Myth of Mental Illness* (Szasz, 1961, 1974), *Death at an Early Age* (Kozol, 1967), *The Student as Nigger* (Farber, 1970), *Our Children Are Dying* (Hentoff, 1966), *The Way It Spozed to Be* (Herndon, 1968), *Growing Up Absurd*, and *Stranger in a Strange Land* (Heinlein, 1961) are a few examples that will catch your eye.

Some counter theorists abhor the status quo of traditional theory. They refuse to be put into a theoretical straightjacket in which the way it has been is the way it should be.

Counter theorists have several things in common. First is their "hard sell" approach, which proposes a new panacea for all children. Those parents and professionals frustrated by an apparent lack of progress with children often are ready consumers of counter theory because it is so critical. For example Melton in *Burn the Schools and Save the Children* (1975), states, "If you are convinced that your children are getting the best education possible, then there is no reason for you to read this book." Unfortunately many counter theory approaches are prescriptions for practical application without rationale.

Second, since counter theory springs from discontent with more traditional approaches, from a sense of frustration, or from a desire to solve problems in ways never before attempted, counter theorists generally have in common their support of a freer concept of education (Goodman, 1964; Gross & Gross,

1969; Kohl, 1969; Neill, 1960). This "freer concept" means that most counter theorists relate in a humanistic way toward children and education, reject the extreme views of Freudian theory and do not believe in behavior manipulation (Tracy, 1974). Counter theorists think the school curriculum is irrelevant to life, that labeling is a poor practice, and that children should have more say in their educational destiny (Glasser, 1969; Goodman, 1964; Hentoff, 1966; Holt, 1972; Reimer, 1972).

Third, counter theorists have in common a view of schools as the major institutional structure for dehumanization in our culture. They see today's system of education as an arena for mass production, analogous to the automobile industry or modern farm production, in which the goal is production of the most, with the fewest resources, in the shortest period of time (see Melton, 1975; Reimer, 1967). According to writers such as Melton (1975) and Reimer (1967), many children fall off the assembly line and need to be put back on. Along the line children are sorted on the basis of physical characteristics, intelligence, and behavior; thus the growth of the field of special education. Other children continue in the regular system but do not have the "quality" expected and are gradually taken off the line. Still others become disillusioned with the process and take themselves off the line. The normal continue toward their goals. Several theorists such as Goodman (1964), Kozol (1967), and Hentoff (1977) believe that much of what teachers do in school (rather than helping children) is to preserve the assembly line system.

Obviously there are many questions in education that have no definite answers. For example, there is the question of philosophical directions. Should we (or can we) make education humanistic? Counter theorist Neill (1960) suggests that we should modify schools to allow for student freedom. Children

should have an equal voice on school policy, with few demands placed on them. Several others (Goodman, 1964; Hentoff, 1966; Kozol, 1967) would like modification in the goals of curriculum, such as the inclusion of materials and methods concerning affect or emotion, interpersonal relationships, and concepts of interdependence. Others have more radical suggestions; Melton (1975) suggests "Some [school] buildings will be constructed. . . . Some [schools should] be burned" (p. 260).

One concern of counter theorists is how to bring about educational change. Most of them (Gibbons & Tracy, 1978), feel that this change can take place in a "community" in which there is integrity, interdependence, and respect, in which there is emphasis on the development of interpersonal relationships. As relationships between the teachers and children develop, no single approach to a child's education becomes dominant. Therefore, children and teachers confront one another, each confident that they have a say in the educational process, neither feeling like an outsider. Children and teachers would determine their goals together, in an atmosphere of positive interaction (Allen & Hecht, 1974; Friedenberg, 1959; Rogers, 1969; Schutz, 1974).

What, then, are the problems that the counter theorists wish to fix? And how, specifically, will it work? Their issues seem large, sometimes vague without clear methods for change. For example, Reimer (1967) is against school-propogated "social domination." Reimer says that schools teach children to follow only the rules that can be enforced, and to break those that cannot. Those who flagrantly break the enforced rules either drop out or are pushed out; the rest become good producers and consumers of the technological society for which we all work. Though to society this progression may be seen as efficient and useful, the counter theorists argue it is not the best way life can work. But practically, how do teachers change this problem? Teachers who try to implement the concerns of the counter theorists into classroom practice may create chaos unless they choose with extreme care and fit each idea into a sound theoretical framework (Glasser, 1965).

Some counter theorists disagree with commonly held societal values. Since one of the goals of education is to carry on the values of society, there is immediate confrontation. Counter theorists would argue that education should not foster the absurdities of society's goals and means (Goodman, 1960). They feel that they will have changed the world for the better if they can accomplish their goals by constantly challenging education.

DE-EMPHASIZING LABELS

Counter theory rejects the tendency of analytical theorists to label deviance (e.g., Glasser, 1965; Neill, 1960). Counter theory calls for a freer concept of education—one with a humanistic style, which looks first to the needs of children as described by counter theorists.

Counter theorists object specifically to the concept of normalcy. They argue that deviance may be created or expunged by changes in the world's notion of normalcy. For example, the categorization system of grades, competencies, and behaviors is viewed as arbitrary (Kohl, 1967; Kozol, 1967; Melton, 1975; Neill, 1960).

The study of how labels are applied and removed in the social context is an intrinsic part of counter theory. Emotional disturbance, as discussed in Chapter 5, may be explained in counter theory as an adaptive process to an unhealthy school environment. Counter theorists, operating under a value system that espouses child diversity, are critical of rules that define "deviant" acts and those that define "deviant" role characters. Counter theory also distinguishes between children's value systems and institutional goals. According to counter theorists, how a child is labeled depends arbitrarily upon who is affected by the action, the witnesses, and the personal perspective of the person doing the labeling. This subjective process applies to most social and cultural forms. Counter theorists criticize the development, transformation, and analysis of specifically labeled acts, whether they be individual or group enterprises; the ongoing labeling activity of educational systems, and children labeling themselves; the establishment of networks of moral, emotional, and material dependence to foster labeling; and the creation of comparative classification systems for children such as diagnostic evaluations (Schutz, 1974; Reimer, 1967; Szasz, 1970).

DIVERSITY OF CHILDREN

Counter theorists have stated that the study of emotional disturbance should no longer be limited to the framework of scientific logic for predictive purposes but should also include the unique experiences that each child brings to the classroom (Gibbons & Tracy, 1978; Fromm, 1960).

This view of the child in conflict differs in several interesting ways from those discussed in earlier chapters. First, counter theorists advocate diversity. There is greater emphasis on philosophy than is true of most other intervention approaches. Second, there is less concern with actual intervention techniques in the classroom than is characteristic of most emotional disturbance models. Not only do adherents of this view write very little about actual techniques, but they sometimes criticize any concern with them (Melton, 1975; Rogers, 1969), noting that intervention is likely to interfere with the essence of the child's uniqueness.

While the differences just mentioned are not representative of all counter theorists (e.g., Glasser, 1965), they are true of most counter theoretical approaches. Basically, in this approach the teacher attempts to understand the "being" of the child as a unique person. A classroom goal is to increase the child's awareness of her own experiences and values, rather than making the child feel like an object.

SCREENING AND EVALUATION PROCEDURES

More radical counter theorists generally do not support the concept of screening and evaluation processes either since these lead to labeling and placement in special programs. Counter theorists believe in the modification of educational programs to allow for deviance rather than in the development of niches for the control of deviance. Generally, counter theorists support holistic views of the child rather than the fragmented views so often used in screening and evaluation.

More moderate counter theorists would support educational evaluations that have been developed for specific cultures or socio-economic groups. An example of this is the System of Multicultural Pluralistic Assessment (SOMPA) developed by Mercer (1977).

Counter theorists are concerned with administering tests in the dominant language, in a familiar setting, and by someone who can relate effectively to the child. Generally, more moderate counter theorists would support the use of a wide range of formal and informal measures, interviews, and observations rather than one standardized evaluation.

CLASSROOM APPLICATION OF COUNTER THEORY

Counter theory has adherents among those who teach children in conflict. As previously mentioned, although counter theorists vary in their ideas, they do agree on many points about what is wrong with education. Tracy (1974) lists several assumptions made by traditional educational institutions that are opposed by counter theorists. To summarize:

1. Counter theorists oppose the idea that education consists of a quantifiable set of knowledge that should be passed on to generations of children.
2. They reject the idea that the role of the teacher is a reservoir of knowledge that is to be siphoned to each student.
3. Literacy, part of a value system generally accepted in American society, is seen as a political tool for spreading political information to the populace.
4. The institutional character of schools and the destruction of individual personality that results from schools are further concerns.

Some writers would abolish the formal educational system as we know it, whereas others would only seek to modify its structure severely (Reimer, 1972; Tracy, 1974).

Counter theorists have been proposing changes in the educational system for years. In general, they are dissatisfied with the "system" of education that has evolved (Cleaver, 1968; Farber, 1970; Glasser, 1969; Goodman, 1964). They are also generally dissatisfied with the medical model of deviance (Szasz, 1961, 1970). Bron aptly stated the position of counter theorists (1972, p. 464):

There are no organizations, schools, publications, or authors which can lay exclusive claim to the title and thereby define the parameters to be explored. Each person is left to apply the label to whatever overlapping and divergent views strike some chord of recognition, some feeling of "ah, here seems a thread of counter psychology."

Counter theory is needed. It adds a new dimension to educational thought. Although controversy often accompanies a new theoretical approach, there seems to be new growth by all professionals as a result of the theory.

The most immediate outcome of the efforts of those who advocate counter theory is the lessening of emphasis on special programs and labeling. Even Public Law 94–142 is under attack by those who advocate the complete normalization of handicapped youngsters.

In this section the contributions of four counter theorists, T. Szasz, A. S. Neill, William Glasser, and James Dobson, will be discussed. Szasz's work demonstrates the degree to which some theorists believe that mental illness is actually a part of our folklore, a figment of our imagination. Neill promotes a freedom-oriented, residential approach. In contrast to Neill, Glasser encourages mainstreaming (without labeling). Glasser represents a humanistic-behavioral approach that emphasizes an individual's own responsibility towards mental health. Dobson's book, *Dare to Discipline* (1970), is a message against permissiveness, coupled with a basic belief in God.

Szasz: The Myth of Mental Illness

Thomas Szasz shocked the psychiatric establishment with his thesis that mental illness is not a disease (Szasz, 1960). He suggests (1960, 1970, 1974) that the medical model is of historical value, but of little or no scientific value. He argues further that the major goal of the medical model is to label the patient and serves no greater utility than attributing deviance to the gods or the deity (Szasz, 1974).

Szasz offers several ideas for teachers. First, teachers should avoid labeling since this is the root of the child's problem. Second, the child herself should be taught to become a person who can control her own

behavior (rather than giving control to someone else).

Thus teachers should help the child become independent, rather than dependent. In addition, teachers should guard against road blocks surrounding personal development in order to enable the child who is experiencing problems to be free to grow. Finally, teachers should establish a school environment that is free of "growth retardants" such as arbitrary rules and capricious judgments that are designed more for adults than for children.

Summerhill School: A. S. Neill

The basic thesis of *Summerhill* (1960) is teaching without the use of force by developing the child's self-motivation. Teachers must not only avoid overt force ("You must do this or else") but also avoid covert force (a hidden power system that manipulates anonymously). As Fromm (1960) puts it, parents and teachers have confused non-authoritarian education with "education by means of persuasion and hidden coercion."

Summerhill's principles are embodied in these 10 philosophical statements:

1. Children are, by nature, good.
2. The aim of education and of life is to find happiness.
3. Education must embody both intellectual and emotional development.
4. Education must be at a level needed by and within the capacity of the child.
5. Discipline and punishment create fear; fear begets hostility.
6. Freedom does not imply license to do as one wishes.
7. The teacher must be honest and sincere with children.
8. Children must, sooner or later, cut their primary ties to parents.
9. Guilt binds the child to authority.

10. The *Summerhill* School is aimed toward praising God through happiness of man.

Neill criticizes society's absurdities and feels that we now educate children to become unhappy persons. Focus on students should not be to make them successful in worldly terms, but to help them develop their human potentials.

Reality Therapy

One of the most complete and best accepted of all counter theories is reality therapy as developed by William Glasser. Although the theory appears to have a strong humanistic flavor, it does not embrace Freudian psychoanalysis. Instead, it emphasizes three factors: reality, responsibility, and a sense of right and wrong. Glasser suggests that if these become a part of a person's behavior, there will be appropriate mental health. Glasser says that teachers must maintain an acceptable standard of behavior in order for children to feel worthwhile. Morals, standards, values, right and wrong—these are all needs to be fulfilled. People must learn to live within these values—to correct themselves when they are wrong and to credit themselves when they are right. Strong emphasis is placed on increasing accomplishments for children rather than lowering goals. Reality therapy emphasizes fulfilling needs without interfering with the ability of others to meet these needs. It encourages teachers to support and strengthen the functioning of the children's sense of right and wrong. The teacher helps the children reject their irresponsible behavior and offer better ways to behave (Glasser, 1965).

Glasser believes that many children have not experienced warmth for a long time. A close relationship between teacher and child is necessary in order to change behavior. (Glasser does suggest objectivity, however, when the teacher views the irresponsible behavior of a child). Becoming effectively involved is often difficult with children who have rejected adults and school. As Glasser indicates (1965, 1972), teachers naturally begin to feel discouraged when their efforts to relate are ignored or rejected. At these times teachers must try to maintain a constant image of trust and concern. He suggests that at times a nonverbal cue will build bridges, or a friendly word.

Once a level of involvement is reached, the teacher must help the child deal responsibly with problems. Obviously the rejection of irresponsible behavior is a delicate task. The child has developed that way of behaving for "good" reasons. In many cases the child has found it works and is extremely reluctant to try another way to solve difficulties.

The teacher must reject the behavior but not the child. For example, the child may feel a strong need to be liked by other students and to do well in school. To accomplish this, the child may cheat on tests. While the behavior is irresponsible, the needs and feelings surrounding the behavior are understandable. The child needs to be helped to accept new patterns of coping with feelings. The need to be liked should not be diminished, but more responsible ways to reach the goal need to be developed.

Reality therapy can be done in groups because (Glasser, 1965) members help to move individuals toward reality. The therapist guides the group toward increasing involvement and makes suggestions for members on how to cope with reality better. A classroom teacher deals with much less severe behavior than a counselor, but the same procedure may work: Establish group and/or individual interaction, guide individuals and groups toward increased involvement, and make suggestions for coping with reality in a better way.

William Glasser was trained as a dynamically oriented psychiatrist. During his training he became convinced that traditional therapy, which stressed transference, exploration of the past, the unconscious, and interpretation of behavior, was not meeting the needs of those under treatment. In his book *Reality Therapy*, Glasser did not attempt to soften the Freudian concept but adopted a theoretical position that in many ways is in opposition to Freudian theory.

Glasser (1965) is opposed to labeling, and the system he proposes is geared to the mainstream of education. His opposition to labeling is based on the premise that deviance is an indication that the person is not meeting her essential needs. The degree of deviance is determined by the extent to which needs are not being met. Glasser is unable to explain why patients exhibit such a wide variety of inappropriate behaviors. In an effort to fulfill their needs, these patients deny the reality of the world they live in. Glasser puts it this way:

In their unsuccessful efforts to fulfill their needs, no matter what behavior they choose, all patients have a common characteristic: they all deny the reality of the world around them. Some break the law, denying the rules of society; some claim their neighbors are plotting against them, denying the improbability of such behavior. Some are afraid of crowded places, close quarters, airplanes, or elevators, yet they freely admit the irrationality of their fears. Millions drink to blot out the inadequacy they feel but that need not exist if they could learn to be different; and far too many people choose suicide rather than face the reality that they could solve their problems by more responsible behavior. Whether it is a partial denial or the total blotting out of all reality of the chronic backward patient in a state hospital, the denial of some or all of reality is common to all who exhibit deviant behavior. Therapy will be successful when they are able to give up denying the world and recognize that reality not only exists but that they must fulfill their needs within its framework (1965, p. 6)

Glasser defines reality therapy as "a therapy that leads all patients toward reality, toward grappling successfully with the tangible and intangible aspects of the real world" (1965, p. 6).

The basic needs that are mentioned so often in reality therapy include the need to love and be loved and the need to feel worthwhile to ourselves and to others. These two basic needs are closely related, but they can and do stand alone. Human beings must not only love but be loved. Children must not only achieve for the satisfaction of those who care for them but must feel worthwhile themselves. Glasser says that, to be worthwhile, human beings must maintain a satisfactory standard of behavior by learning to correct themselves when they are wrong and to approve or reward themselves when they exhibit correct behavior.

The ability of individuals to fulfill their needs in a way that will not deprive others of the ability to fulfill their needs is called responsibility or acting responsibly. The responsible child then is the healthy child, whereas the irresponsible child is emotionally disabled (Glasser, 1965).

The task for teachers is to teach children to become more responsible. This is not an easy task; it takes extreme courage and unheralded dedication to stand firm in the process of teaching children in conflict. Holding firm in the face of a child's anger has given many teachers sore shins and broken noses to others. Giving in to irresponsible behavior has caused much more serious and lasting damage for the child, even though the teacher might escape personal attack.

Glasser does not propose that teachers should become psychiatrists or usurp the professional relationship of the psychiatrist with the child. He suggest that teachers work more in a role of preventive therapy in the classroom. The difference is one of intensity; the psychiatrist works on a more intense level with children who are acting out their irresponsibility in ways totally unacceptable in the school situation.

Whether the therapeutic intervention is attempted by the psychiatrist, the teacher, or the parent, there are three basic steps to intervention: (1) the therapist must achieve some level of involvement with the child; (2) the therapist must reject the inappropriate behavior; and (3) the therapist must teach the child more appropriate ways to fulfill her needs. The teacher has a real advantage in this scheme of intervention since involvement is not only the cornerstone of therapeutic intervention but of good teaching as well.

Reality therapy is concerned with behavior as well as with attitudes. It aligns itself with the behavioral approaches and with psychodynamic theory. However, reality therapy does not rely on exacting behavioral techniques such as counting, charting, and direct reinforcement of appropriate behaviors, nor does it utilize strict psychological interpretation of life events and labeling as in a dynamic orientation. It is concerned with psychic surface, with behavior that occurs now, and with the reality of these current behaviors. Although Glasser carefully avoids labeling himself, his behaviors seem to categorize him as a counter theorist.

James Dobson

James Dobson believes that permissiveness does not work. He believes that love is not enough. It must be supplemented with structure and, at times, punishment in order to provide the guidance needed for some children to become mature adults.

Dobson lists five key elements needed in teaching children:

1. Instill respect for the parents
2. Communicate after punishment
3. Control without nagging
4. No excessive materialism
5. Avoid extremes in control and love

Dobson follows the principles of modern behavior modification, including techniques of Thorndike and Skinner. He interweaves Christian principles as valuable. His system is the direct opposite of A.S. Neill's.

Dobson suggests that most (not all) deviance is a failure of parents and teachers to mold the child properly. Dobson's approach to education and discipline (more moderate than other fundamentalist writers) is a useful one to consider as a possible compromise with parents who are supportive of more conservative techniques.

CURRENT STATUS

There are many reasons for closely examining counter theories. Counter theories do not support the typical ways of doing therapy, they ignore vigorous research questions, and they challenge the assumptions of literacy that educators hold dear. Despite all these negatives, counter theories offer promise for the more traditional educator. They make a strong case for humanizing education; they reject helper-recipient contracts as being heavily in favor of helpers; they object to the self-serving, self-sustaining nature of service agencies; and they reject the concept of labeling and categorization.

Whether counter theorists have solutions to these rather complex problems remains to be seen. Certainly they are proposing answers, which is a beginning. A few of the many solutions offered for modifying schools are included in the writings of Dennison (1969), who describes the first street school, and O'Gorman (1970), who outlines the concept of freedom schools (storefront schools) in urban areas. Kozol (1967), Goodman (1964), and Hentoff (1966) have outlined modifications for curriculum, and Melton (1975) has described ways to destroy the school.

Affective development is emphasized in the writing of Glasser (1969), Neill (1960), and Grossman (1972). More radical theorists suggest that advocates of deviance are needed. Marcuse (1964) advocates the recognition and acceptance of deviance. He suggests that tolerance implies that deviance is undesirable. Marcuse believes that deviance should be as acceptable as normalcy.

Whereas much of current counter theory writing about schools is in book form, there is also an emerging press that features articles and news releases. *This Magazine: Education, Culture, Politics* offers articles of a radical nature for those interested in writers who challenge the status quo of education. This journal was formerly called *This Magazine is About Schools.*

One of the newer and more controversial approaches reviewed is Robert Zaslow's Z Therapy (1973). In its modified form, this approach offers the teacher a technique with possible application for troubled children.

Three vignettes are presented that illustrate the practical application of counter theories.

VIGNETTES

Vignette 1: Dare to Discipline: Developing a Respect for Parents

Dobson believes it is critical for children to develop a respect for their parents since their attitude toward parents provides the basis for interactions with other people.

One afternoon a client came to Dr. Dobson to discuss Becky, his teenaged daughter. Becky's father related the following story to Dobson: Becky had gone through her 15 years never having had to respect her parents. As a result, their lives were in severe conflict. Mrs. Holloway was sure that Becky would become more manageable as she grew older and matured. The expected improvement never came. She held her parents in utter contempt from early childhood. She was sullen, selfish, disrespectful, and

uncooperative. The parents did not feel they had the right to make demands on Becky so they tried to make the best of the bad situation by smiling and ignoring the problems presented. As Becky approached adolescence she became even more unmanageable, and her parents tried even harder to meet her demands. They were afraid to antagonize her because she would throw violent temper tantrums. At this point Dobson believed they were under emotional blackmail and were powerless to cope with the situation. In an effort to pacify her, they attempted to buy her cooperation by installing a private phone in her bedroom. She generated a gigantic phone bill the first month. Their final act was to have a party for her. She invited a group of dirty, rowdy, and profane youngsters who proceeded to destroy personal belongings in the home.

During the evening Mrs. Holloway said something to Becky that angered her. When Mr. Holloway returned he found his wife, injured by Becky, in a pool of blood on the bathroom floor, while Becky was in the yard with her friends.

Dr. Dobson discusses the tragedy that will follow the three family members the rest of their lives if they do not change. He suggests that the problem is like terminal cancer with little hope that a "cure" can be found. The problem is deep and has been going on for too long. Where did the family go wrong?

Dr. Dobson suggests that the parents were at fault for not instilling respect in Becky as a youngster. They did not set rules. They did not deal with bad behavior swiftly and decisively. Dobson believes that punishment can be given and still demonstrate love and affection, when coupled with kindness and understanding. The tone of the punishment is to help the child mature, not to get even.

Respect is something that the parents may have to teach. Firmness with caring is the key to developing a relationship that can endure the stormy years of adolescence.

Vignette 2: Project R-5

Project R-5 is an alternative school for teenagers in Mesa County, Colorado. R-5 stands for readiness to learn and work, relevancy of that to be learned, reinforcement of desired behavior, responsibility to oneself and others, and respect for law, order, and authority. The program serves approximately 120 potential or actual dropouts of high school age. Students placed in the program are not labeled in any manner; however, many students were in conflict with the educational program from which they came.

The program represents a blending of several unique activities as well as a unique staffing pattern. Students who attend R–5 do not return to their regular high schools but remain in the special school until they complete requirements for graduation. The program's success is partially because of the student-staff ratio: 120 students to 6 teachers, 7 teacher aids, and 1 counselor, 1 reading specialist, 1 secretary, and the principal.

Students must apply to the school and are generally placed on a waiting list. During this time students take a battery of tests and spend several days visiting the school. Courses are divided into very small units. For example, a student can take a course for 1/8 credit, which can be completed in as little as two weeks. Longer courses are available for those who can cope with the additional length and intensity.

Regular coursework includes emphasis on occupations as well as English and math.

The program combines a behavioral approach with a strong humanistic attitude among the staff. Three R–5 programs have applied theories that differ from traditional practice into a successful program format.

Vignette 3: Reality Therapy with an Entire Sixth-Grade Class

Description of class. Children from this sixth-grade class included 29 boys and 6 girls. They are from the lowest section academically of all the sixth-grade students, numbering approximately 120. They live in a middle to lower middle class environment, and their parents have occupations including skilled labor, blue collar work, unskilled labor, and some unemployed. The boys were generally showing acting-out, aggressive behavior, whereas the girls tended to be very withdrawn.

Educational information. The grade point average for this class was about 2 years below expected grade achievement. The parents were generally supportive of school activities but tended toward punishment as a way of solving educational problems that their children encountered. There was a noticeable lack of interest in educational activities by the students. Homework was seldom if ever completed, and classroom assignments generally were ignored.

Psychological information. Group intelligence testing indicated that the class was in the normal range of intelligence. A few of the children had been identified as having emotional problems, and some borderline retarded children were included in the class. In addition, two mildly crippled children and one visually impaired child were members of the class. There were extensive psychological work-ups available to the classroom teacher for the exceptional children.

Implementation of reality therapy. It was decided to implement reality therapy techniques for two basic purposes: (1) to hold students in the classroom responsible for their own behavior and (2) to establish group meetings each day to get individual children's feelings out into the open where they could be dealt with.

Evaluation of reality therapy. Through continued efforts of the classroom teacher to hold each pupil responsible for his or her own behavior, students gradually developed more self-responsibility. The aggressiveness, fighting behavior, and tattling behavior decreased remarkably. This was a slow process with many regressions. The group meetings generally deteriorated into gripe sessions about other teachers and about other kids on the playground. After the first three weeks it was decided to suspend the group meetings of a therapeutic type, except when classroom situations indicated a need. Other class meetings were held around academic areas, with discussion topics announced previously and each child doing a small amount of research to prepare for the discussion. With this method, the class meetings improved significantly. Problems around behavior, social interaction, and feelings were handled in class meetings, but these occurred only sporadically throughout the school year. The students learned many discussion skills and were able to give and take, to take turns, to listen, and to evaluate ideas through the process of group meetings. In addition, class meetings proved to be highly supportive for those who needed to let their feelings out in a group situation. Some of the children never felt comfortable in the class meetings and continued to withdraw from interaction with more than one person. As a result of this experience, the classroom teacher believed that class meetings, designed for therapeutic value, were unnecessary on a daily basis and should be used only as needed to support individuals within the class. Other days could better be utilized in educational types of meetings as described by Glasser (1969).

Vignette 4: Veronica

REPORTED BY Forest Heights Lodge and the International Society for the Advancement of Z Therapy (1973)

Veronica was a 7-year-old who was pretty, uncooperative, nasty to her younger brother, very disobedient, and petulant. She exasperated her parents. Veronica was brought to the therapist's office amid whines, wails, and pleading, and the door was closed. During the first therapy session, Veronica controlled the total situation. She played when and with what she wished. She talked when she wanted to, and she avoided contact when she chose. Before the following therapy session, the therapist decided to use a different approach, modified Z therapy.

On the next visit Veronica stood in the center of the floor twisting her dolly's hair, just as she had done previously. This time the therapist put her on his lap with her legs straddling his knees. He held her chin in his right hand and put his left hand behind her back. In this position he could look directly into her eyes.

He opened the session by saying, "When I'm in this office and you are in this office, who is the boss?" She answered with astonishment, "You are." He continued with rapid-fire statements and questions: "When you come in here and refuse to talk, looking at the floor and not looking at me, who's trying to be boss?"

VERONICA: "I am."

THERAPIST: "That's right, you are trying, but are you the boss?"

V: "No."

T: "You bet, so what are you going to do right now?"

V: "Take off my coat."

T: "Right on, and where are you going to look at me when you talk?"

V: "In your eyes."

T: "Right." The therapist hugged Veronica and put her off his lap. She slipped off her coat and walked over to the toy shelf.

T: "What do you want to play with?"

V: "I don't know."

T: The therapist whipped her back onto his lap. "Who's boss?"

V: "You are."

T: "Who's trying to be boss?"

V: "I am."

T: "How?"

V: "By saying I don't know what I want to play with."

T: "Okay. Do it right. What do you want to play with?"

V: "Crayons and paper."

T: The therapist gave her a hug and said, "Great, let's go." Veronica went to the toy shelf and selected yellow paper and a yellow crayon. The therapist put her back on his lap and said.

T: "What did you do wrong?"

V: "Picked a color so you couldn't see what I draw."

T: "Who's trying to be boss?"

V: "I am."

T: "Who's boss at your house?"

V: "I am."

The therapy session continued, with the therapist continuing to demand attention and identification as the boss. During the latter part of the session, Veronica drew a picture of her family and talked to the therapist about her brother Mark, who she felt was her mother's favorite.

When Veronica's father came she said: "That's my dad. You'll tell me when I'm done? You're the boss in here. I want to show my dad how fast I can read—can I do that, boss?"

Veronica opened the door and let her dad in. She snuggled up to the therapist and read to her father. He was stunned. He shook his head as he left and said, "Far out!"

The therapist points out several things that occurred during therapy.

1. The therapist was in control.
2. The therapist made requests.
3. Requests were reasonable.
4. The child responded to the requests.
5. Both the child and therapist felt good—both were winners.

SUMMARY

The popularity of counter theorists in the mid-20th century has caused many educators to reconsider their former positions on teaching children in conflict. Counter theorists have divergent points of view, but most have several common beliefs. They generally agree that the following are inappropriate for education:

1. The idea that education possesses a quantifiable set of knowledge that should be passed on to generations of children.
2. The role of the teacher as a reservoir of knowledge to be siphoned to each student.
3. The question of literacy as a value system that is used as a political tool.
4. The destruction of individual personality that often results from schools.

Counter theorists have contributed educational strategies that have dared to be different. Although counter theorists have generally established approaches from a basis of more traditionally oriented theories, such as psychoanalytical or behavioral thought, they have added some of their own originality to develop a significant direction in working with children. Four counter theorists, Szasz,

Neill, Glasser, and Dobson, are given as examples.

First the theories of T. Szasz were profiled; his thesis is that mental illness is not a disease and that the role of teachers is to help children become independent.

The Summerhill residential school concept of A. S. Neill is then presented. Ten principles are outlined that guide the work carried on in Summerhill: (1) A firm faith in the goodness of the child is maintained. (2) The aim of education is to find happiness. (3) Education is both intellectual and emotional. (4) Education must be geared to the capacities of the individual child. (5) Extensive disciplining of the child should be avoided. (6) Freedom is important, but it is a mutual arrangement. (7) The child must be told the truth by teachers. (8) Primary ties with parents must eventually be severed. (9) Guilt feelings impede growth toward independence. (10) No specific religious training is fostered. The Summerhill concept represents one of the most controversial of educational programs. It has been called a fraud, a myth, and a contradiction of reality.

The third counter theorist is William Glasser, who defines his practice as therapy that "leads all patients toward reality, toward grappling successfully with the tangible and intangible aspects of the real world." Much of Glasser's theory also encompasses a humanistic bent that relates more closely to psychodynamic theory.

James Dobson was the last counter theorist presented in this chapter. He is representative of the fundamentalist group of Christian theorist who believe that school personnel and parents have become too permissive in their approach to child rearing and teaching. Dobson challenges those who teach to discipline children, even though it is difficult to do. He encourages parents and teachers to use corporal punishment when necessary to impress upon the children that they cannot openly defy rightful adult authority without paying the price of confrontation. Dobson represents a growing number of theorists who are critical of the public schools, but is moderate in his solutions to the perceived problems. His suggestions seem to be very useful to teachers working with children in conflict.

BIBLIOGRAPHY

Allen, D., & Hecht, J. (1974). Structure and function in the classroom. In J. Cooper, *Controversies in education*. Philadelphia: W. B. Saunders.

Bron, A. (1972). Some strands within counter psychology, In W. C. Rhodes, *A study of child variance*. Ann Arbor, MI: The University of Michigan Press.

Cleaver, E. (1968). *Soul on ice*. New York: McGraw-Hill.

Dennison, G. (1969). *The lives of children: The story of the first street school*. New York: Random House.

Dobson, J. (1970). *Dare to discipline*. Wheaton, IL: Tyndale House.

Farber, J. (1970). *The student as nigger* (2nd ed.). New York: Pocket Books.

Faris, R. E. L., & Dunham, H. W. (1939). *Mental disorders in urban areas*. Chicago: University of Chicago Press.

Feagans, L. (1972). Ecological theory as a model for constructing a theory of emotional disturbance. In W. C. Rhodes, *A study of child variance*. Ann Arbor, MI: The University of Michigan Press.

Felix, R. (1967). *Mental illness: Progress and prospects*. New York: Columbia University Press.

Friedenberg, E. (1959). *The vanishing adolescent*. Boston: Beacon.

Fromm, E. (1960). Forward. In A. S. Neill (1960). *Summerhill: A radical approach to child rearing*. New York: Hart.

Gibbons, S., & Tracy, M. (1978). Counter theoretical views and approaches. In W. C. Rhodes, and L. Paul, *Emotionally disturbed and deviant children*. Englewood Cliffs, NJ: Prentice-Hall.

Glasser, W. (1965). *Reality therapy*. New York: Harper & Row.

Glasser, W. (1969). *Schools without failure*. New York: Harper & Row.

Glasser, W. (1972). *The identity society*. New York: Harper & Row.

Goffman, E. (1963). *Stigma: Notes on the management of spoiled identity*. Englewood Cliffs, NJ: Prentice-Hall.

Goodman, P. (1960). *Growing up absurd*. New York: Random House.

Goodman, P. (1964). *Compulsory miseducation: Community of scholars*. New York: Vintage Books, Inc.

Goodman, P. (1970, October). High school is too much. *Psychology Today*, p. 25.

Gross, B., & Gross, R. (1969). *Radical school reform*. New York: Simon & Schuster.

Grossman, H. (1972). *Nine rotten, lousy kids*. New York: Holt, Rinehart & Winston.

Haring, N., & Phillips, E. (1962). *Educating emotionally disturbed children*. New York: McGraw-Hill.

Hart, H. (Ed.). (1970). *Summerhill: For and against*. New York: Hart.

Heinlein, R. A. (1961). *Stranger in a strange land*. San Bernardino, CA: Borgo Press.

Hentoff, N. (1966). *Our children are dying*. New York: The Viking Press.

Hentoff, N. (1977). *Does anyone give a damn?* Westminster, MC: Namar Productions, Ltd.

Herndon, J. (1968). *The way it spozed to be*. New York: Simon & Schuster.

Hewett, F. (1968). *The emotionally disturbed child in the classroom*. Boston: Allyn & Bacon.

Holt, J. (1972). *Freedom and beyond*. New York: E. P. Dutton & Co.

Kohl, H. (1967). *36 children*. New York: New American Library.

Kohl, H. (1969). *The open classroom: A practical guide to a new way of teaching*. New York: Vintage Books, Inc.

Kozol, H. (1967). *Death at an early age: The destruction of the hearts and minds of Negro children in the Boston public schools*. New York: Houghton Mifflin.

Marcuse, H. (1964). *One dimensional man*. Boston: Beacon.

Melton, D. (1975). *Burn the schools—Save the children*. New York: Thomas Crowell Co.

Mercer, J., & Lewis, J. (1977). *System of multicultural pluralistic assessment: Adaptive behavior inventory for children*. New York: The Psychological Corp.

Neill, A. S. (1960). *Summerhill: A radical approach to child rearing*. New York: Hart.

O'Gorman, N. (1970). *The storefront*. New York: Harper & Row.

Reimer, E. (1967). *Unusual ideas in education*. Garden City, NY: Doubleday.

Reimer, E. (1972). Unusual ideas in education. In W. C. Rhodes, *A study of child variance*. Ann Arbor, MI: The University of Michigan Press.

Rogers, C. (1969). *Freedom to learn*. Columbus, OH: Merrill.

Schutz, R. (1974, March). The bad-mouthing syndrome in education R & D. *Educational Researcher*, 5.

Szasz, T. (1960). The myth of mental illness. *American Psychologist*, 15, 113.

Szasz, T. (1961). *The myth of mental illness*. New York: Dell.

Szasz, T. (1970). *Ideology and insanity*. Garden City, NY: Doubleday.

Szasz, T. (1974). *The myth of mental illness*. New York: Harper & Row.

Szurek, S. (1956). Psychotic episodes and psychic maldevelopment. *American Journal of Orthopsychiatry, 26*, 519–543.

Tracy, M. (1974). Conceptual models of emotional disturbance, some other thoughts. In W. C. Rhodes, *A study of child variance*. Ann Arbor, MI: The University of Michigan Press.

Zaslow, R. (1973). *Forest Height Lodge and the International Society for Advancement of Z Therapy*. Evergreen, CO: Forest Height Lodge.

7

A Synthesis of Theoretical Approaches and Classroom Application

INTRODUCTION AND OBJECTIVES

The most difficult part of the educational process is programming because it must blend individual needs with available intervention methods. This chapter emphasizes putting the various theoretical approaches together into an effective program.

Chapter objectives are to (a) develop a basic approach that accommodates the concerns of each theory in a workable technique; (b) identify methods usable for specific behavior problems; and (c) formulate a technique for mainstreaming and gaining support of the regular school staff.

BASIC THEORY

So far we have reviewed several theoretical approaches to understanding and teaching children in conflict. This chapter targets the merging of these theories into a workable plan for youngsters who have more than one need. Children typically have multiple problems that must be addressed if growth is to take place. To cope with the numerous problems presented by children in conflict and to prepare to interact with a variety of professionals and staff, the teacher must be able to orchestrate many points of view, to select the deeper problems from the superficial, to choose the appropriate technique for each problem, and to have the patience and determination to follow through when frustration and perhaps rejection of the child are natural reactions.

The differences between theoretical approaches generally become less pronounced in practice. Figure 7–1 illustrates how this reconciliation can be made. How approaches relate are shown:

1. The child is the center of the theoretical construct, not only being acted on by those around him/her, but also, in turn, interacting with the environment.

2. Biophysical factors form the base on which the child develops. When biophysical factors are intact, the child has a solid foundation on which to develop. Conversely, if the child is impaired through prenatal or postnatal injury, genetic accident, or a chemical imbalance, she will grow unsteadily.

3. The sides of the triangle include the behavioral and psychodynamic factors that help shape the child into a wholesome individual. Behavioral factors include learned behaviors, both appropriate and inappropriate, that shape a child's future. As the child grows, her psychological development effects her personality. The resolution of childhood conflicts and child-rearing practices help to determine the child's eventual mental health.

4. The two concentric circles totally surround the child and all other theoretical constructs. Sociological and ecological theory bring a wholeness to the otherwise fractured interpretation of personality.

5. Counter theory is then seen as a constant re-examination of what the whole schema means.

Looking at only one theoretical approach, ignoring the others, is similar to looking at only one portion of this diagram. Just as one portion of the diagram represents only a small segment of the total figure, one approach represents only a small segment of the total personality and educational needs of a child.

If the teacher decides to use a holistic approach, a number of problems arise. Of course no one person will have expertise in all theoretical areas, so the teacher needs to rely partially on ancillary personnel to offer the child a good program. Timing is also a problem. After an initial emphasis on the biophysical factors, placement can be made. This strategy assures that all medical con-

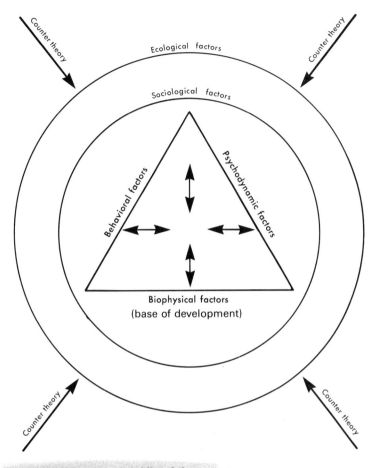

FIGURE 7–1. Theoretical diagram of childhood deviance.

cerns that might affect educational development are addressed.

A team approach is usually the best for planning and intervention with the handicapped (Pfeiffer, 1982). The team should be comprehensive without being too large to be efficient. Probable members include the teacher, a psychologist, social worker, school nurse, and the administrator or program coordinator. In some situations the counselor and school physician would also take part. Team members need to have an active and continuing interest in the children and not serve merely as consultants. It is hoped that such expertise can be found within the school so that the need for outside assistance is limited. During the evaluation process *each person* gathers information, independent of other viewpoints, so that no one opinion is predominant. Thus no one person makes all the decisions while other group members remain just support staff.

Throughout, a caring approach to the classroom process is maintained, with the inclusion of various focused techniques such as behavior modification, social interaction, parent involvement, and community concerns. In the next section several techniques are identified for each of several behavior types.

Section One: Specific Methods for Behavior Change and Classroom Placement

This section emphasizes techniques for those on the firing line. The first part will focus on the regular classroom situation; in particular, how to identify which children need help and how to remedy their problems. These will be "first-aid" type techniques. This list is not meant to be exhaustive. The ideas presented are intended to stimulate professional staff in the development of their own techniques for coping with similar problems.

Areas of deviance will be divided into four basic behavioral problem areas with a variety of techniques for behavior change presented so that a selection process is feasible. The four basic behavioral types that will be discussed include acting-out, withdrawing, defensiveness, and disorganization; these behaviors were discussed in Chapter 1. Each of these four behavioral types will be identified, alternative solutions will be proposed, and finally, methods that have generally *failed* to produce desired change will be discussed.

ACTING-OUT BEHAVIORS

The statements that follow are representative of teacher descriptions of acting-out behaviors. Most of these are observable and occur in groups rather than in isolation.

1. Talks out in class without regard for others
2. Does not attend to classroom directions
3. Often does not listen
4. Cannot stay at own desk
5. Touches or pushes others to irritate
6. Is easily distracted
7. Both physically and verbally aggressive in behavior toward others
8. Slams doors
9. Talks back to the teacher and other authority figures
10. Abuses other children
11. Is disruptive in the classroom
12. Is out of control
13. Often has temper tantrums
14. Makes loud clicking noises; yells in the classroom or in the hallway
15. Swears
16. Runs around the room, talks, does not work
17. Argues
18. Hurts other children
19. Refuses to cooperate
20. Is stubborn and disrespectful
21. Is always goofing around
22. Interrupts others
23. Harasses other children
24. Becomes rowdy
25. Cannot control anger
26. Must always be first in line
27. Fights
28. Refuses to work

Children in conflict put teachers under a great deal of stress. If the teacher is unprepared to cope, the stress can become critical. Of all the behaviors that children in conflict demonstrate, the most wearing on the teacher are these acting-out behaviors. When the conflicts in the classroom become too overwhelming, the teacher, naturally enough, may withdraw and give in! A comment often heard by those who interact with teachers is "I have tried everything, and nothing works with John." But what, actually, has the teacher tried? Perhaps the teacher moved the child to the front of the classroom or to the back of the classroom. Moving the child around cannot represent the complete repertoire for dealing with acting-out children. Here are some suggestions.

First show the child what her behavior is like and that it is inappropriate:

1. Have the child view herself on video. Seeing one's behavior is often self-revealing.
2. Have her count her own behavior and chart it.
3. Teach another child, who is under control, to count her inappropriate behaviors.
4. Count her acting-out behavior and later review the findings with her.

Once behavior is counted or otherwise observed, the teacher and child should review the findings very carefully. The teacher should relate to the child how he feels about the behavior and, in turn, listen to what the child has to say about it. At times this strategy will be sufficient to encourage change.

Another suggestion for change is behavior modification. It is a powerful technique but has limitations, particularly with older children, because of the range of reinforcers useful with adolescents. We would hope that most young adults would have their acting-out behaviors under personal control. For those who do not, suggested reinforcements include free activity time, earning academic credit, and time to work on paying jobs (Ullmann & Krasner, 1965; Woody, 1969).

For reinforcement programs to be effective with young adults, there generally needs to have been some prior pattern of appropriate behavior. If not, the staff will need to provide many success experiences for the youngster before change can be expected. If a child has been able to manipulate the environment to meet personal needs over a period of several years, change is very painful and difficult to manage (MacMillan, 1973).

Before beginning a system of behavior change in the classroom, teachers need to consider their approach to teaching:

1. Is the classroom atmosphere conducive to learning?
2. Is the material relevant and interesting to those using it?
3. Is each child working at a success level?

Alternative Solutions

Planned Ignoring. Ignoring is one of the most often used methods of modifying inappropriate behaviors. This technique has been used with mild talk-out behaviors, with attention-getting behaviors such as hand waving, and sometimes with out-of-seat behavior. The older child who attempts to manipulate or alienate teachers through behaviors that are in conflict with the value system of adults can often be changed through ignoring. Teachers have found that ignoring some behaviors will do more to change the behavior than attending to it with verbal reprimands or other forms of punishment.

Some acting-out behaviors that are potentially dangerous to the child cannot be ignored. For example, the young child who runs from the playground into the street must be attended to, since ignoring might cause serious harm to the child. The same is true for an older student who is behaving inappropriately in his automobile around the school grounds. Ignoring the potentially dangerous behavior may prove to be harmful to both the student and other children in the vicinity of the school.

Behaviors that provide their own reinforcement value often do not respond to planned ignoring. For example, hitting behaviors, slamming doors, fighting, harassing others, hurting behaviors, stealing, and swearing all seem to have reinforcing properties of their own. The teacher will have to decide which behaviors can and cannot be ignored and which will probably respond to planned ignoring.

Reinforcement. A second approach in changing acting-out behavior is to capitalize on the need of the student to play a leadership role. This can often be done by assigning the student extra duties such as coming in before and after school to perform tasks for the teacher. This seems to work with both young children and older students. However, an appropriate level of reinforcement activity needs to be established for different age levels. The younger child might clean off the chalkboards before school or help the teacher take down decorations from the bulletin board after school. Older students, however, may wish to help the coach clean out the locker room, prepare materials in the office, put chalk lines on the athletic fields, or help in the nurse's office.

Counterconditioning. A third technique for changing acting-out behavior is to encourage a behavior in the classroom that is incompatible with the acting-out behavior. For the younger child this might be as simple as reinforcing behaviors that require the child to be actively engaged in a behavior that cannot be done at the same time as acting-out behaviors. (The child who is busy working at arithmetic cannot fight with the child across the aisle.) This method is effective with older children, who can be productively involved in athletic teams and musical groups. These groups give the student appropriate attention so that the youngster's need for inappropriate attention is often decreased.

An Office. Setting up an office or study carrel for children who cannot otherwise keep their behavior under control can be helpful. This is not a place where students are sent as punishment but a place that allows them freedom from distracting stimuli present in the classroom. In extreme cases, a child may desire to remain in the isolated setting for an entire period; however, a few minutes is generally sufficient.

Counseling. The techniques that have been discussed in Chapter 3 should be considered viable alternatives for intervention in acting-out behaviors. Life space interviewing, mirroring feelings, listening, and accepting the child while rejecting behaviors all represent usable examples.

Contingency Management. Contracting, or contingency management, is an excellent technique for use with acting-out children. With this technique the child and teacher contract for an amount of work that must be completed before the student can earn free time to do what he or she wants or have special privileges in the classroom. This technique seems to work with both younger and older children, provided the reinforcer established is appropriate to the age level. Contingency management can be used with an individual, with a small group, or with an entire class.

Satiation. Satiation means allowing inappropriate behavior to continue or insisting that it continue until the inappropriate behavior is satiated or unlikely to return. Many teachers have used satiation as a way of stopping inappropriate behavior with younger children. This might include saying or writing inappropriate words over and over, or filling a wastebasket full of spitballs. With older children this technique has been used in similar ways. One example was a teacher who "allowed" a group of boys to continue chewing tobacco when they wanted to leave the room to spit it out. This resulted in mild nausea and at least temporary satiation for tobacco.

Teaching Technique. The classroom teacher should strive to establish a classroom structure that is unambiguous, simple, and to the point. Often, unclear directions lead students to a frustration level that promotes acting-out behavior.

1. *Giving clear, concise directions.* Directions that are straightforward, simple, and given one at a time in a clear, understandable fashion are better than directions that are unclear, ambiguous, and given over and over for clarification. Repeating directions for clarity also leads to inattentiveness, since listening is of little value if directions are going to be repeated several times.

2. *Limiting assignments.* Many children are overwhelmed by the amount of work that teachers give to them at one time. Work should be presented in assignment formats that the child can tolerate. One apparent way to cut down on the amount of an assignment is to divide the paper in thirds with a colored pencil. The child is asked to work down to the red line before having it checked, then work to the blue line, and finally work to the end. Cutting the paper in half with scissors and allowing the child to do the first half and, on completion, do the second half is another way to accomplish this same goal. Children in conflict often have a tendency to give up too easily when assignments appear so overwhelming that failure is certain.

3. *Providing for physical movement.* Children can be given appropriate reasons to leave their seats to work off some excess energy. No adult would be able to tolerate sitting in seats for as long as some students are expected to sit. The child should be given the opportunity to move about the classroom for meaningful purposes. If the teacher does not do this, the acting-out child will find excuses to move around the classroom. Allowing the child to come to the teacher's desk when the assignment is completed, having centers or work areas to which the child can move as needed, and establishing learning activities that require physical involvement

or movement can all promote an atmosphere in which the child does not feel tied to his desk.

Seating Variables. Often the acting-out child can be seated near the teacher, where touch control and visual contact can be maintained. In this way the teacher can physically touch the child on occasion to reinforce appropriate work and to give the child the necessary assurance to be able to maintain appropriate behaviors. Children who are acting out often get attention by being told to sit down, to be still, and to leave someone alone. The teacher should use nonverbal cues as much as possible to modify the child's behavior. Taking the child back to his seat without saying anything can often be effective. The teacher should try to avoid verbal cues, which are often highly reinforcing to the child.

Running from the classroom is a behavior often attributed to impulsive, acting-out children. To avoid the inevitable problems that develop from running behavior, the teacher should arrange the classroom to minimize this possibility. Establishing a work station near the door will allow the teacher to be near the door much of the time. Once the child has turned his or her back on the teacher and has left the room, it is extremely difficult, if not impossible, to get the child back to the classroom without a confrontation. Putting a child in an embarrassing position in front of several students will undoubtedly force the child to save face by running away from the situation.

Presenting a Low Profile. The ability to teach acting-out children successfully depends, to a great extent, on the teacher's attitudes toward teaching and children. The teacher's ability to relate to children in a low-key but resolute manner will do much to quiet an acting-out child and will help to maintain tranquillity within the classroom.

Encouraging Children to Monitor Themselves. If acting-out children are somewhat cooperative during better moments, the teacher can work out a way for them to keep a record of their own behavior progress. The teacher should have the child try to increase the amount of time spent on appropriate behavior by a system of record keeping. The child should monitor only one behavior at a time, since a behavior change will probably have a positive effect on other inappropriate behaviors. The child does not have to change all the behaviors at one time.

Relaxation Exercises. For the younger child relaxation exercises are often helpful. For an older child, activities that can use up some excess energies, such as athletic activities, can be helpful. A punching bag, a blocking dummy that can be hit and kicked, or a dart board can all be helpful in alleviating hostility and pent-up anxiety in the student.

Minimizing Rules. The acting-out child often tries to manipulate the rules that are set. Rules that are necessary should be few in number, simple, and consistently administered. Consequences to rule breaking should be clearly set so that ambiguity of interpretation is minimal. The acting-out child should not be threatened. If the teacher intends to punish the child, the child should be punished. If the teacher intends not to allow the child to do something, he or she should not be allowed to do it. But the teacher should not harass, threaten, or accuse the child of inappropriate behavior.

Reinforcing Appropriate Behaviors. When the student is acting appropriately, the teacher should be attentive to this good behavior. It should not be ignored. Sometimes teachers believe that a student who is acting appropriately should not have his "chain pulled," so they ignore appropriate behavior when it does occur. If teachers are going to ignore appropriate behavior, there is no reason for the child to exhibit this behavior.

Students who are in conflict with the system often dislike being reinforced in public. A quiet word away from the other students, a smile, or a nod can often be very appropriate for an older student, whereas a verbal reinforcer could be extremely punishing if overheard by other students. The teacher should discuss the acting-out child's problems in private, either at the child's desk, in a quiet area of the classroom, or away from other students. Students should not be given the reinforcement of discussion or arguing a point in front of all the other students. Communication that is nonverbal in nature can be understood by the student so that the teacher does not have to verbalize all feelings.

Encouraging Peer Reinforcement and Ignoring. Students are excellent modifiers of behavior. At certain age levels peers are the best reinforcers for both appropriate and inappropriate behaviors. Getting other students to reward appropriate behavior and to ignore inappropriate behavior will go a long way in changing an acting-out child's behavior.

Assignment to a Buddy. The buddy system is particularly effective for new children in class (Fig. 7–2). The buddy system can give a new child a feeling of being welcome and can also give needed responsibility to a child who is playing the helping role.

Providing Success. Success brings success, especially with children who have failed so often. This means success in school as well as success in behavioral tasks.

Reducing Auditory and Visual Stimulation. Acting-out children often cannot cope with visual and/or auditory stimulation without becoming involved in the action. Using visual and auditory barriers between these

FIGURE 7–2. A buddy system can be an effective tool for controlling behavior and providing a leadership role for another child. This helping relationship can often grow into a friendship.

children and activity areas of the class can be helpful.

Consistency. Acting-out children need to know where the teacher stands on various issues. They need to know that the teacher will behave the same today, tomorrow, and next week.

Methods That Have Generally Failed

Teachers can do well to make a list of teacher behaviors that have failed to change acting-out behaviors, so that they can be avoided. A partial list might include the following:

1. Using force
2. Ridiculing the behavior
3. Taking away privileges
4. Forcing a child to admit lies or errors
5. Punishing the child
6. Demanding a confession of guilt
7. Confrontation over issues
8. Asking the child why he or she acts out
9. Comparing the child's behavior with other children's behavior

WITHDRAWING BEHAVIORS

The withdrawing child is often inconspicuous in the classroom and therefore can be ignored by the teacher. The following are examples of behaviors that might lead the teacher to believe that the child is withdrawing from the reality of the classroom:

1. Not responding when spoken to
2. Thumb-sucking, chewing on pencils, or chewing on clothing
3. Failure to talk even though the skill to talk is properly developed
4. Rocking or other self-stimulating behavior
5. Attending more to animals or toys than to people
6. Sitting and playing alone when other children are nearby

Alternative Solutions

Encouraging Parallel Activities. Withdrawn children should not be forced to interact with other children. Often the best that a teacher can hope for is parallel activity. From parallel play the child can often be involved slowly in a more active role.

Encouraging Activity with the Environment.

1. Art activities—clay, water, fingerpainting, drawing, and manipulation of materials
2. Role playing with puppets
3. Hiking, wading in water, and climbing activities
4. Music therapy—drums, piano, and shakers

Guaranteeing Success. By using short experiences of an appropriate level of difficulty, the teacher can often encourage involvement. A quiet manner, along with understanding and an accepting attitude, will also encourage participation.

Pets in the Classroom. The younger child can often relate to pets in the classroom before relationships with people are possible. Allowing the withdrawn child to care for pets is an excellent technique for involving the child in a meaningful activity.

Group Projects. The older child can often be involved in group projects so that individual abilities are diluted among those of others. The child who would cringe with fear at the thought of singing solo will sometimes feel secure singing in a group.

Establishing Guidelines for Behavior. Establishing some guidelines for behavior will often allow withdrawn children greater freedom in their relationship with that limited environment. Withdrawn children need a time and a place within the school environment to be alone during the day. This gives them an opportunity to withdraw when they really need to withdraw and be alone.

Allowing Physical Involvement to Replace Verbal Involvement. The teacher should not force participation, especially when oral language is involved. Involvement should center around physical involvement rather than verbal involvement, at least in the beginning stages. The child might hold the chart for the group, hand the teacher materials to put on the chart, or point to pictures that others name. In this way the child is involved, if only peripherally.

Empathizing with the Child. When contact can be made, the teacher should empathize with the child. The teacher might explain about his or her own problems in becoming involved with certain school activities. Some of the things the teacher did to overcome this lack of involvement can be offered. Often the child will begin to realize that other people have felt the same way he or she is feeling.

Informal Conversation. Informal conversation groups among children can be encouraged so that the child can become involved in small talk before being encouraged to interact in a more formal atmosphere. Any participation by the child should be encouraged. However, the teacher must not rush children into involvement for which they are unprepared. Withdrawn children are suspicious of being pushed too quickly and thus being embarrassed by a situation in which they cannot succeed.

Methods That Have Generally Failed

Methods that have generally failed when used with withdrawing children include the following:

1. Forcing the child to become involved
2. Embarrassing the child
3. Ignoring the behavior
4. Asking the child why he or she does not want to take part
5. Comparing the child with other children

DEFENSIVENESS

Defensive behaviors are behaviors that allow children to protect themselves from failure, from embarrassment, and from the truth and to take the focus from themselves. Defensive behaviors are necessary and appropriate for children at various times. They are dangerous for children when they become a way of life rather than a way of handling isolated problems. If the children lie when the truth would be easier, their defensiveness is getting in the way.

Following are several rather typical behaviors that indicate a defensive behavior pattern:

1. Unwillingness to accept assignments
2. Forgetting or not doing homework
3. Avoidance behaviors in the classroom
4. Losing things such as papers, homework, and clothes
5. Exhibiting an I-don't-care attitude when faced with failure
6. Crying behavior and frustration
7. Manipulation behavior of the situation
8. Saying the water is too cold in the swimming pool to avoid going into the water
9. Lack of responsibility and not attending to tasks
10. Compulsive eating
11. Tattling behavior
12. Asking questions after being given an assignment
13. Saying, "I'm too tired to work" or "I can't remember"
14. Out-of-seat behavior
15. Wasting time with a pencil or a ruler
16. Playing with objects in school
17. Missing school
18. Becoming ill at specific times during the day
19. Wetting pants to avoid something in the classroom
20. Crying
21. Practical jokes
22. Coming in late for class
23. Running away from school
24. Messy work, particularly in writing
25. Cheating
26. Daydreaming
27. Sleeping during class
28. Giving unreasonable answers
29. Lying

Alternative Solutions

Since defensive behaviors are often an indication that the child is afraid to become involved because of the fear of failure, the fear of not measuring up to himself or others, or a fear of embarrassment, it is important that the teacher involve the child at a success level. A few ideas that have worked with children with defensive behaviors follow.

Being Truthful with Children. Adults often force children to become defensive by their line of questioning and skeptical attitude. If a teacher knows that a child did something wrong, the teacher should not ask the child if he or she did it: for example, if a teacher sees a child take a dollar from another child's desk, the teacher should not ask, "Did you take some money?" Rather, the teacher might say to the child: "I saw you take the dollar. What shall we do about it?"

Planned Ignoring. Defensive behaviors can manifest themselves in a variety of ways. Planned ignoring of defensive behaviors is appropriate when allowing the behavior to continue for a brief period will not cause serious problems.

Reinforcement. When children approach problems with realistic behavior, they should be reinforced appropriately. A teacher must be extremely alert in such cases so that proper reinforcement is given. Children who use a variety of defensive behaviors are often difficult to reinforce because teachers fail to observe appropriate behaviors that are exhibited.

Using Nonverbal Responses. Nonverbal responses often effect greater change than verbal responses. Children become so familiar with verbalization that they often ignore it.

Giving the Child Something to Look Forward To. The child who is continually late or who does not come to school can be helped by anticipated events. All children need something to hope for. Small surprises or something special for tomorrow can often encourage children to be on time or to come to school when they might otherwise be absent.

Giving Choices. Children who fear work are sometimes afraid of the work the teacher gives them. If choices can be made, the fear is often allayed. The teacher can give parallel choices so that similar learning takes place regardless of the choice made.

Assuring Success. The best antidote for defensive behaviors is realistic success. It will take many success experiences to change defensive behaviors. Often success experiences in one area of the child's life will spread to other areas.

Other Alternatives. Teacher alternatives outlined for acting-out and withdrawal behaviors are also useful here. It has been suggested that acting-out and withdrawing behaviors are in fact both defensive behaviors.

Methods That Have Generally Failed

Methods that have generally failed when used with children who behave defensively include the following:

1. Telling the child he or she is trying to avoid work, school, or reality
2. Taking away privileges
3. Comparing behavior with other children's behavior
4. Threatening the child
5. Punishment
6. Telling the child you are aware of his or her gimmicks
7. Suspending a child for a few days if the child skips school
8. Taking the child out of activities he or she likes to do

DISORGANIZATION

Children who exhibit severe disorganization will generally not be placed in a regular classroom. In fact it is questionable whether disorganized children will even be maintained in a special class in the public school except in a one-to-one relationship with the teacher. These children might be confused in terms of time, place, and their education placement. They might not have speech skills and often will not relate to people. Although significant progress has been made with these children on a one-to-one basis, the prognosis for mainstreaming or part-time placement in a regular classroom is problematical at best. Emphasis in a special class will generally be on (1) building interpersonal relationships, (2) communication, (3) developing work habits, and (4) self-care skills.

The teacher who works with disorganized children should certainly be in contact and collaborate with other professionals, such as the school psychologist, psychiatrist, pediatrician, and social worker, who might lend professional support. In addition, the teacher needs ongoing classroom support from the school staff, including enough aide support for one-to-one interaction with these children.

REINFORCEMENT GENERALLY ACCEPTABLE IN SCHOOL

Much can be said for teachers' use of reinforcement in the classroom, regardless of the educational approach being used. Most children are more productive if rewarded appropriately rather than ignored when they exhibit correct behaviors. Teachers generally have a ready supply of highly reinforcing activities at their disposal. The age of the children, their individual needs, and the relationship established between the teacher and students will determine the reinforcement value for each of these activities.

1. Having a good citizen sign on the desk
2. Access to quiet play area
3. Access to art area
4. Helping to clean the teacher's desk
5. Access to science area with slides, fossils, terrarium, aquarium, microscope, and so on
6. Monitoring classroom activities
7. Working on a bulletin board
8. Helping to correct work of others
9. Helping to dispense reinforcers to other children
10. Being in charge of sharing time
11. Erasing the chalkboard
12. Sweeping floors
13. Washing desks
14. Cleaning the aquarium
15. Coming early in the morning to help get the room ready
16. Cutting paper
17. Being errand boy or girl
18. Answering the door
19. Taking messages
20. Answering the telephone
21. Working in the office
22. Cleaning erasers
23. Writing daily lesson plans on the chalkboard
24. Watering plants
25. Tutoring a less able child
26. Collecting papers
27. Getting out gym equipment
28. Passing out books
29. Taking roll
30. Acting as line leader
31. Leading the morning pledge to the flag
32. Leading songs
33. Choosing stories to be read in class
34. Being captain of a team
35. Pronouncing the spelling words
36. Choosing a new seat in the room
37. Helping in the school office
38. Visiting in another classroom
39. Going to lunch at school or going home
40. Being allowed to move to another activity
41. Being allowed to read the directions to other children
42. Helping in the cafeteria
43. Assisting the custodian
44. Using colored chalk
45. Using a typewriter
46. Running the copying machine
47. Stapling papers together
48. Feeding the fish or animals
49. Giving a message over the intercom
50. Writing and directing a play
51. Picking up litter on the school grounds
52. Holding the door during a fire drill
53. Serving as secretary for class meetings
54. Raising or lowering the flag
55. Emptying the wastebasket
56. Carrying the wastebasket while other children clean out their desks
57. Operating a slide, filmstrip, movie projector, and so on
58. Recording own behavior on a graph
59. Correcting papers
60. Teaching another child
61. Playing checkers, chess, cards, or other table games
62. Choosing a game to play
63. Working with clay
64. Doing "special," "the hardest," or "impossible" teacher-made arithmetic problems
65. Reading the newspaper
66. Listening to the radio with an earplug
67. Arm wrestling
68. Learning a magic trick
69. Lighting or blowing out a candle
70. Going to the library
71. Helping the librarian
72. Making or flying a kite
73. Popping corn
74. Making a puppet
75. Carrying the ball or bat to recess
76. Visiting with the principal
77. Doing a science experiment
78. Telling the teacher when it is time to go to lunch
79. Sharpening the teacher's pencils
80. Opening the teacher's mail
81. Sitting next to the teacher at lunch
82. Doing crossword puzzles or mathematics puzzles
83. Weighing or measuring various objects in the classroom
84. Adjusting the window shades

These reinforcers and numerous others are available to most teachers. Reinforcers

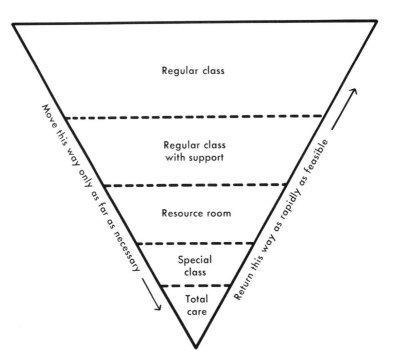

FIGURE 7–3. Cascade of services for children in conflict.

such as candy, money, and trinkets are generally less acceptable to other teachers and parents and probably should be avoided if the child will show adequate growth through the use of more socially acceptable reinforcers.

CLASSROOM PLACEMENT

Cascade of Services

A variety of placement possibilities must be provided to meet the needs of all children in conflict. Deno (1970) proposed what she termed the Cascade System of Special Educational Service. Fig. 7–3 shows how this system would provide service for children with a wide range of educational needs. Four classroom settings by Deno will be discussed: (1) regular class placement with support, (2) the resource room, (3) special class placement, and (4) total care programs. The Cas-

cade System of Special Education Service was part of the policy statement that was approved by the 1973 Council for Exceptional Children (CEC) Delegate Assembly.

Regular Classroom Placement with Support. For children in conflict to be maintained in a regular classroom, educators must provide the teacher with support. This support must be more than verbal and must stop short of removal of the child from the classroom. The specialist assigned to aid the classroom teacher is generally expected to integrate findings from the evaluation and to help the regular classroom teacher develop appropriate educational interventions. The resource teacher can provide this support by working in the classroom whenever possible. The relationship established will often depend on the personalities of the teachers, the needs of the child, and the willingness of each to grow. Often the specialist can best work as an assistant to the teacher. This enables total classroom coordination to remain with the classroom teacher and provides a nonthreatening atmosphere in which cooperation can flourish.

Working in the classroom marks a dramatic departure from traditional approaches, which often encourage pulling children out of the classroom in favor of a more secluded atmosphere. Although it takes a great deal of effort and professional confidence to display one's expertise in full view of one's peers, several advantages of this mode of operation seem appropriate to mention. First, the child remains in the regular classroom, where the necessity for labeling is decreased and where the trauma that often results from pull-out programs is avoided. The child in conflict continues to be part of the class even though there are problems. Second, it discourages the classroom teacher from giving up on the child and turning to the experts for answers. Third, working within the classroom provides the advantage of the sharing of information between the special teacher and classroom teacher. Both have much to offer in the understanding of and programing for a given child that might be lost in a segregated setting. Pull-out programs, by their design, have often encouraged teachers to regress into isolated positions rather than to grow in their understanding and coping ability with children in conflict. Fourth, integrated programing allows children to make use of the modeling process. Children in conflict who are isolated have less appropriate behavior on which they can model their own behavior. This can result in a potentially unhealthy situation developing (Reinert, 1968). Reality demands that normal children interact and relate with those who are different from themselves, since the world is filled with diversity of thought and of action. The normal adult must be able to cope with this divergence. One way to prepare children for

this diversity is to allow them to interact with children who are, in some ways, different. The deleterious effects of homogeneous grouping have been well documented (Coleman, 1966; Dunn, 1968; Meyerowitz, 1967). Part of the teaching process seems to be neglected if educators fail to help every child interact with peers who are different.

Specialists who have capitalized on the opportunity to interact with regular classroom teachers around the needs of children in conflict seldom want to return to the position of isolation that they once knew. But how does the school change direction once a pull-out program has been well established? Obviously, many alternatives exist, ranging from simple reassignment of all pupils to regular classrooms to gradual mainstreaming through the interaction of specialists with regular classroom teachers. Compulsory reassignment seems to be just as inappropriate as the original assignment to special programs. Establishing an organizational structure that supports continual reappraisal of the educational placement of all children seems to be a feasible goal for most schools.

The Resource Room. For some children the regular classroom needs to be supplemented with interaction on a one-to-one basis or with small group activity. One approach to meet this need is the use of a resource room, which is a concept that offers several alternatives to the child in conflict so that a child can receive help in the resource room for varying periods of time throughout the school day. For instance, if a crisis develops in the regular classroom that requires the removal of one or more children, the resource room is available as a temporary intervention site. Theoretically, a child could function in the resource room for as little as a few minutes a week to nearly full time during some difficult periods. This is largely theoretical because the resource room is rarely used in this manner. In a sincere effort to serve more children, teachers often schedule specific times for children to come to the resource room. Some scheduling is necessary, but when this scheduling becomes rigid, children often are unable to receive help when it is needed. With rigid scheduling a child cannot have a crisis at times other than from 2 to 2:40 P.M. on either Tuesday or Thursday, for example. The child is out of luck as far as the resource room is concerned if his or her problems do not occur at appropriate times during the day or week.

A major problem of the resource room concept is the emphasis on expertise and authority of the resource teacher. As long as the resource teacher works in isolation from the regular classroom teacher, there is little opportunity for sharing of ideas. Under isolated conditions, little personal growth occurs, fears grow, and defensive attitudes often develop. To counteract this somewhat natural division of activity, the resource teacher should program as much time as possible in the regular classroom. Time in the regular classroom should be spent in working with children seen in the resource room, in supporting the teacher in curriculum development, in observation, and in working as a co-worker or professional aide to the classroom teacher.

A second problem area of resource rooms is the role of the resource teacher. Many resource rooms have become no more than glorified study halls, with the resource teacher being the study supervisor. The classroom teacher makes assignments that are brought to the resource room for completion. There seems to be little justification for this relationship—not that study periods and teacher assistance are not important or needed, but the employment of a specialist who is trained to treat emotional problems as a daily study hall supervisor does not appear to be an economical or effective use of pro-

fessional personnel. A partial justification for this role might be to develop a relationship with a classroom teacher who is initially reluctant to establish a more meaningful interaction, but this should be only a temporary situation.

There is no one established role for the resource teacher to assume. Some believe a crisis role is the only acceptable alternative, others believe a remedial role is appropriate, whereas others can accept only emphasis on therapeutic intervention. It seems that strict differentiation of roles for the resource teacher and classroom teacher is necessary to avoid costly duplication. An attempt will be made to provide a simple role definition, with the understanding that conflicts in the classroom are never so simple or easily categorized.

Teachers generally establish their roles according to two major factors: what they are hired to do and the strengths they possess. Being relative, the strengths possessed cannot be discussed in any practical way. In general, resource teachers for children in conflict are hired to act as change agents to help children establish more appropriate ways of interacting with those entering their life space, whereas regular teachers are employed to teach basic educational skills in large group situations.

If educators keep these general job expectations in mind, they will be unlikely to experience serious role conflict. The specialist will generally work with the weaknesses of personality or behavior problems exhibited by the child, whereas the regular classroom teacher will accommodate the deviant behavior as much as possible and at the same time capitalize on things the child can do. A child who is unable to attend to classroom activities and therefore is not learning might be an appropriate example. The resource teacher works specifically on attending behavior each day in the resource room or regular class. By

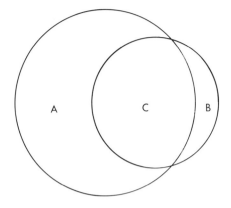

FIGURE 7–4. The role of the regular class teacher as opposed to the role of the resource teacher.

using game activities and positive reinforcement, the specialist might try to increase the attending level until the child is attending to the activity at a desirable level.

The regular classroom teacher would also be interested in the attending behavior but would not work directly on the problem. Instead, highly motivating activities, touch control, and other methods aimed at minimizing the opportunity for inattention are employed. This division of effort will help to assure the child a balanced educational program with emphasis on both education and personality development. Another way of explaining this role separation is that specialists work on the child's weaknesses, whereas the regular teacher capitalizes on the child's strengths. Fig. 7–4 depicts graphically the relative roles of the regular class teacher and resource teacher in relation to the child in conflict.

Three basic interactions are delineated by this diagram. Area *A* represents the efforts put forth by the regular classroom teacher. Using highly motivating activities, touch control, and other methods of minimizing inattention, the regular teacher tries to accommodate the weakness. Area *B* represents the efforts of the special teacher to increase attending behavior by using game activities

along with positive reinforcement. Area *C* represents the interaction between the regular and special teacher. This might include the specialist's working in the regular classroom and consultation. Much of the effort invested by the special teacher is integrated into the regular class structure, with only a small portion available for isolated activities.

The traveling resource teacher or itinerant teacher is an adaptation of the role of the resource room teacher to offer services in schools that could not otherwise be provided with services, often because of small enrollments.

Special Class Placement. During the 1960s special class placement grew rapidly as an alternative for children in conflict. Generally, the relative importance of special classes has diminished in recent years in favor of more integrated approaches; however, there is still a need for special classes for some seriously disturbed children. Children with serious autistic behaviors who have no speech or personal interaction skills represent behavioral types that are difficult to integrate into the most accepting of environments. Integrating these children into routine school activities with normal children seems impossible given the present concept of education. Similarly, severely aggressive children who try to injure themselves or others in a physical way cannot be maintained in less than a special class setting without greatly increased outlays of human resources that are presently not possible for schools.

The educational goals for special class are considerably different from those described for a resource setting. The special class teacher is generally responsible for the total intervention process, with additional help from supportive persons, such as one or more aides assisting in the classroom so that a ratio of one adult to every three or four children is maintained. The goals for each child are often limited almost totally to social interaction, for example, developing talking skills and cooperating with others at a minimal level. Once social interaction is established and some minimal cooperative level achieved, partial placement in a resource room should be considered. For some of these children, integration into a regular classroom will never be a reality. Some will continue to be maintained in a special class for emotionally disturbed children, whereas a few might require placement in a total care facility if they cannot be maintained in the home.

Total Care Programs. Only the most extreme cases of children in conflict should be considered for total care placement, and then only if the child cannot be maintained in the home or in an appropriate home substitute, such as foster care. Children tend to become institutionalized in total care placement, which complicates future placement in more normal education situations. When total care is indicated, it should be considered to be only temporary, generally not to exceed six months in length. During the child's stay in a total care facility, there should be intervention with the home or home substitute to help establish a suitable environment for the child's return. Parents should understand that total care placement is only temporary and that much of the responsibility for eventual reintegration will rest on the home, with staff support from the total care facility.

Program goals for total care are similar to those for special class, with the added dimension of programing for after-school hours. The child's unacceptable behaviors must be modified to an acceptable level during his stay, and academic skills must be maintained at the highest level possible. Total care programs sometimes represent a capitulation or giving up on children with severe problems. Recent litigation in several states is challenging public schools to provide services for all children, regardless of problem severity. The extent to which legal guidelines are followed will undoubtedly depend on several factors: age of the child, the specific type and severity of disability, prognosis for change, relative intactness of the home, and the ability of a given community to respond to individual needs of children (size, location, wealth, and local efforts).

The major goal of placement is one of facilitation—facilitation of the educational process and its attendant intervention techniques.

Guidelines for Program Redevelopment

The following guidelines are offered for those who wish to establish new programs or redevelop those already functioning.

1. Establishing administrative support
   a. Legislative action has put a great deal of weight behind those who wish to provide programs for all handicapped children, including the emotionally disturbed. This legislative posture was adopted during the Eisenhower administration and has continued since that time.
   b. Available financial support should be explored as an incentive to those who begin programs to serve handicapped children.
   c. Administrative routes must be found to gain building level support for children in conflict if programs are to be successful. The principal can often be as effective as the teacher in the outcome of a given program.
2. Priorities
   a. It is necessary to decide on the population to be served (ages, severity, and so on).
   b. A procedure should be developed for referral, screening, evaluation, and so forth.
   c. The location and role of special programs should be determined.
   d. Needed staff and materials that are presently unavailable should be acquired.
   e. The continuum of services to be provided should be outlined.
   f. The budget necessary to fund the needed services must be determined.

3. Developing an educational strategy
    a. Emphasis should be made to keep children as close to the regular classroom as feasible.
    b. Individual programing should be the goal whenever possible.
    c. A team approach should be encouraged in addition to reliance on individual problem solving.
    d. Alternative programs should be provided for those who cannot function in the mainstream.
    e. Contracts should be made with external agencies for ancillary services not available within the schools.
4. Provision of in-service training
    a. Goals of the in-service program should be outlined.
    b. Trainers for the in-service program should be selected.
    c. Delivery alternatives should be negotiated.
    d. The in-service training must be provided.
    e. The results of training should be evaluated.
5. Alternatives to in-service training
    a. Professional leaves for renewal of skills (for example, classroom visitation, sabbatical leaves).
    b. Grade level and school staff meetings.
    c. Extension courses from colleges.
    d. Consultants (for example, textbook and equipment companies, colleges).
    e. Workshops.
    f. Professional conventions.
    g. Professional library.
    h. District, state, and regional newsletters.

Section Two: Mainstreaming and the Educational Team

MAINSTREAMING

The concept of mainstreaming is not a new idea; recently we are rethinking how it can be best used. The concept is not without its critics (Gullotta, 1974; Jordon, 1974; Martin, 1974; Payne & Murray, 1974; Smith & Arkans, 1974). Some specifically are critically examining its process and intent (Gresham, 1982, Reinert, 1968).

Smith and Arkans (1974) have attempted to show that the special class is definitely needed—probably to a greater extent now than ever before. They outline several reasons to support this need:

1. States are mandating education for all of their handicapped children.
2. The number of severely handicapped identified in a given community is increasing as more community-based resources become available.
3. A regular class teacher cannot be expected to meet the needs of 20 to 40 children when several of them have severe handicaps.

Although these conclusions are focused on the severely handicapped, the ideas are essentially the same for the severely emotionally disturbed.

Martin (1974) supports mainstreaming but believes it is not the answer to all educational problems. He raises questions and offers several useful suggestions regarding mainstreaming:

1. What are the attitudes, fears, and anxieties of those who must teach handicapped children and those who will associate closely with them—parents,

teachers, principals, peers, and teacher aides?

2. Training for regular teachers needs to be concerned with attitudes as well as with skills.

3. Logistical problems can upset the school; for example, children coming from and going to classes at unusual times, using different materials, and having separate budgets from which to work.

4. Evaluation, including the effectiveness of mainstreaming on emotional and social characteristics of children, needs to be routinely carried out.

5. Mainstreaming has a mythical quality, a faddish appeal, that must not cause educators to avoid the truth.

As we near the end of period in which mainstreaming has been used as a major concept in the education of handicapped, most professionals seem to favor the concept. A number of recent articles, however, are cautioning practitioners regarding the concept and have raised the concern of parents and professionals. Powers (1982) outlines some useful guidelines for mainstreaming and the inservice education of teachers. These ideas include such things as format, design and methods used, content of the inservice, location and scheduling, evaluation and incentives for participants, as well as selection of training personnel and involvement of school administrators. The success of mainstreaming seems to be equivocal at the present time. At a meeting of the Council for Exceptional Children's Invisible College on mainstreaming, several important concerns were discussed. These concerns are summarized by Jordan (1974, pp. 31–33):

1. First of all, children are children. They have similar needs; they develop similarly. The problems or the handicaps children have must be dealt with on an individual needs basis.

2. Parents of these children also have needs which the public school system has a responsibility to deal with.

3. The public education system has an obligation to all children, which must be fulfilled in a responsible and responsive manner.

4. There are many processes being implemented all over the country dealing with mainstreaming. These approaches seem to have many common facets and these common facets have been dealt with by the faculty.

5. It's clear to everyone that educational change is, for all of us, a way of life. It must be carefully planned in order to be directed so it will lead into constructive service. Yet we know little about the phenomenon called change. It often occurs without our knowing why, without our assistance, and sometimes in spite of us. Most of us know even less about the power which determines, generates, and guides change.

In addition to the five statements regarding the philosophy of mainstreaming, the 12 participants offered many positive guidelines for the mainstreaming process. These include the following:

1. Mainstreaming helps in the more meaningful involvement of large numbers of parents in school activities.

2. A school tends to become a more child-centered community when mainstreaming is implemented.

3. Instruction is individualized for more regular class pupils when mainstreaming occurs.

4. Progressive inclusion is a process which provides a workable approach to the accomplishment of mainstreaming.

5. A team approach to assessment, program planning, and review is superior to anything else we know, especially when that team includes persons with key responsibilities for what is going to happen later—persons such as the parents, the referring teacher, the educational diagnostician, the special education teachers, and the principal. Local school terms also should have substantial responsibility and authority and have ready access to another team of systemwide scope.

6. Trade-off is an established part of the dynamic relationship between regular and special education teachers. It results in help for all children who need some particular kind of attention, whether identified as belonging in special education programs or not.

7. Open spaced school arrangements were felt by some to be conducive to more successful mainstreaming.

8. The board of education and the school system staff must be committed to the adopted policy. They then operate as a power base and as enablers.

9. Program implementation should begin slowly and carefully. Principals and teachers should be patiently moved along each step of the way showing positive results with a few beacon light cases, wherever possible, and providing specific help to teachers on the problems that teachers consider important.

10. Mainstreaming may be difficult but it certainly is possible. More importantly, it's desirable and perhaps imperative for the sake of all of us, not just the children.

11. This group voiced a real concern that the whole story be told. Mainstreaming should not be offered as a panacea. Instead, the dynamics of idea development should be presented.

12. It is important in telling the whole story that mainstreaming be presented as something that is not yet fully proven to be the most appropriate way of organizing for instruction. Of course, in that sense it is not any more fully proven than any other way of supplying special education.

13. Society has a mainstream into which not all are allowed to merge on their own terms. This problem has yet to be resolved. For example, is the special education resource room just an instance of tokenism regarding exceptional children?

Beery (1972) has listed nine questions that he believes schools must answer as they wrestle with the concept of appropriate pupil placement in special education. Appropriate mainstreaming models will have answers that are affirmative on most of his nine questions.

1. Does the model recognize and provide for a *continuum* of programs for children who are experiencing difficulty? Some people are taking what I regard to be an unrealistic view that *no* children should ever be removed from regular classrooms. In my opinion, we will always need a wide variety of educational environments available to children, ranging from all-day, self-contained special education classrooms to individualized regular classrooms in which specialists may come into the classroom but pupils are never pulled out for remedial purposes.

2. Does the model consciously work towards and actually accomplish reduction of pull-out programs? Some profess to, but it doesn't seem to happen.

3. Does the model call for specialists to work in regular classrooms as much as possible?

4. Does the model encourage regular classroom personnel to use special classrooms and equipment?

5. Does the model concentrate on assisting classroom teachers to increase personalization and individualization for *all* children in the classroom?

6. Does the model provide for an *on-going*, meaningful staff-development program which is oriented toward *praticum* and seminar work among staff? Does the staff-development program focus on individualization and have classroom and resource personnel working together?

7. Does the model involve the principal in such a way that he or she is intimately involed as educational leader in the staff-development and special education programs?

8. Is cross-fertilization between schools within and/or across district lines encouraged so that teachers are observing other classrooms—exchanging ideas and moral support?

9. Are interrelationships between the school and local colleges encouraged so that interns and professors are working *in* the school?

Beery's list is not intended to be all inclusive. Additions or deletions may be made as needed to meet individual differences. His view of mainstreaming is more than having normal children sit next to handicapped children: it is a system of human interaction that encourages interrelationships among everyone concerned with the continuous growth of children.

The issues that have been raised regarding mainstreaming for exceptional children must obviously be raised in regard to children in conflict. Although most children in conflict have been and will continue to be educated in regular classes, there are some who will need more intensive psychoeducational intervention. The extent to which this support can be given will undoubtedly underscore successes and failures in the integration process. There are indications that massive efforts must be made if educators are to integrate behaviorally disordered children into regular classes for much of a school day (Martin, 1974).

It is understandable that distrust, disillusionment, and fear continue to be expressed by teachers who are asked to work with children whose behavior is significantly different from what is considered acceptable in the classroom. With adequate support these anxieties often can be allayed. This support must be more than giving the classroom teacher new skills to deal with deviance, more than a new gimmick or shortcut to success. Support means *working together* for the benefit of all children.

Beery (1972) proposed that most school staffs have the capability to meet the needs of exceptional children if they pool their resources effectively. To do this, the teacher must be working in a stimulating, cooperative, and enjoyable environment. Beery calls this a *growth environment.*

Many special education programs were founded on the premise that regular classroom teachers were not doing an adequate job educating all children, that they probably could not do a good job under their present conditions, and that specialists had many of the answers to the problems presented by exceptional children. Training programs also contributed to the problem by training only for regular classroom duties or only for special duties. Over a period of years regular classroom teachers became specialists in teaching normal children, whereas other specialists were prepared to work only with exceptional children. The cleavage in training and expectations was widened by privileges granted to specialists, such as decreased duties and/or an increased stipend for working with special education children. In recent years the frustration has mounted, with increasing funding for special programs while regular classroom funding has been held at a lesser growth rate.

It is indeed unfortunate that such a situation was able to develop among professionals dedicated to the same goal of helping children. The first steps for changing the present situation have begun to be implemented. Common salary schedules are being adopted when educational requirements are similar and when extra time is not required. Whenever possible, children are left in the regular classroom, with the specialists working closely with the classroom teacher. Cooperation is replacing isolation.

Beery (1973) has detailed one method of developing a cooperative effort for teaching exceptional children. The project is called Catalyst and is designed for maximum pupil, teacher, and principal growth. The growth process is based on democratic processes, with all staff sharing in the action. Initial response to this system is extremely encouraging to those who support the concept of integration. The Catalyst method provides the stimulus for each school within a district to develop its own unique formula for mainstreaming exceptional children. The Catalyst concept provides for each attendance unit to differ in its approach, attitude, and implementation of mainstreaming. Consultants are utilized only as stimulators, not as guides. The school staff develops its own potential for expertise in a shared environment, with goals established by the entire staff for their school and their children.

In the early stages of program development, the team concept was one of the more popular ways of handling the problems presented by children in conflict. The proposal that follows is based on the team concept with some notable changes stimulated, to a large degree, by Berry's work in mainstreaming.

THE EDUCATIONAL TEAM

The educational team is suggested as one alternative for providing teachers with the support they need in the development of an educational program for all children in the classroom. The educational team is similar to the diagnostic or staffing team concept in that it represents a group effort in problem solving. At this point, however, much of the similarity ends. Table 7–1 compares the basic conceptualization of the two systems.

Each of these roles will be discussed in more detail to outline the specifics of the educational team concept.

1. *Leadership is determined by role, ability, and interest.* The traditional staffing team is often headed (by state regulation in many states) by the school psychologist, the director of special services, or other professionals because of the position they hold within the school district. Leadership by position often leads to a hierarchy of power so that members do not share on equal terms in discussion and decision making.

2. *Membership is determined by the interest in and working with the child.* A flexible membership that is based on interest in the child and working with the child or family helps to ensure a stronger commitment to the child. Generally, membership will be limited to those who are associated with a single school. Professionals are not excluded from membership. For example, the director of special education might be a team member on all the teams in a district only if he or she is actively involved with all exceptional children. A psychologist would only be a member of teams from the schools he or she serves and then only of those with which he or she interacts. The same would be true for nurses, social workers, and teachers. That is, the team's basic structure would generally come from only one school, with each school having its own educational team or teams as needed. By this method, much flexibility could be achieved. Expertise that is present in every school building would be encouraged to grow rather than be stymied by the traditional concept that expertise comes from outside the school. Under this structure, membership would generally be considerably different from that in the staffing team. Members of the team might include the custodian, bus driver, art teacher, minister, and the child's parent. Teachers who work with the child would be included, as would the principal, psychologist, or psychiatrist who is actively involved with the child. Professionals who are not actively working with the child could contribute their diagnostic findings to the team but would otherwise not be involved in team proceedings.

Many teams have operated under relationships that were antagonistic at best. Team members had no common goals, they shared little of professional importance, and they set the teachers up for failure. It might be like a Republican caucus collaborating to select political candidates for the Democratic primary. Both parties are, hopefully, working for better government. This analogy seems far-fetched but actually represents what has occurred when professionals are assigned to diagnostic teams on the basis of position rather than involvement. An example of the

TABLE 7–1. Comparison of the staffing team and educational team

Traditional staffing team	Educational team
1. Leadership of team by position	1. Leadership determined by role, ability, and interest
2. Membership often determined by professional position	2. Membership determined by interest in and working with the child
3. Membership is static	3. Membership varies with needs
4. Staff all children into and out of special programs	4. Team not responsible for staffing children
5. Team direction often determined by team leader	5. Team direction generally determined by a democratic process
6. Emphasis on evaluation (pre- and post-evaluation)	6. Emphasis on evaluation programing and follow-up

lack of understanding that can occur when a direct relationship is not maintained with the child follows.

At the end of our weekly staff meeting, the psychiatrist (who was also the team leader) made a revealing faux pas. As he gathered his materials he said: "Ah! Now I know who we were talking about today. I have had her mother in therapy." Unfortunately, even after an hour of staffing (the third he had participated in concerning this girl) he did not have the right child in mind.

One thing can be said for this team and for this psychiatrist. Had the psychiatrist been working directly with the child, this lack of communication would not have developed. Whereas his honesty was admirable, the situation raises serious questions as to the value of his contributions to the team. It is generally believed that the quality of decision making will be superior if those involved are both interested in and working with a child.

3. *Membership varies with needs.* This principle helps to ensure that team members will do more than meet and share ignorance. Expertise that is needed could be sought out by the team to help in solving specific prob-

lems. The key factor would be *what is needed for each child.* For example, one child might have a severe vision problem in addition to emotional problems. A person with expertise in helping low vision children, hopefully from within the district, could be consulted and perhaps added to the team. This person would not only participate in discussions concerning the child but would work with the child and/or support the classroom teacher or resource teacher as needed.

Usually, more than one team would be functional within a given school. Table 7–2 shows how this could be arranged.

From these three examples one can see the variety of persons who could become members of a given team. The number of team members should range from three to seven to maintain a workable group size.

4. *Educational team is not responsible for staffing children.* Many states specify the competencies that must be present on a staffing team that makes placement decisions. The educational team would not normally serve in this capacity, although theoretically it could satisfy this function if its membership were appropriate according to state staffing guidelines. Membership on the

TABLE 7–2. Educational team membership

Jon	Sheri	David
Mr. C. (regular teacher)	Mr. W. (homeroom supervisor)	Ms. W. (regular teacher)
Ms. E. (resource teacher)	Mr. J. (bus driver)	Ms. T. (school psychologist)
Mr. L. (parent)	Ms. P. (school clerk)	Tom (peer)
Mr. V. (custodian)	Ms. T. (school psychologist)	
	Sheri (student)	
	Dr. M. (psychiatrist)	

team should generally not be altered just to provide for staffing role, since this could destroy the major reason for the team's existence. The staffing team was often the result of a need to staff children and was never intended to serve as an ongoing support for classroom intervention. The educational team is not designed to replace the staffing team but to complement its function.

5. *Team direction is generally a democratic process.* Leadership of an education team is generally emergent rather than appointed or decided by rank. Some groups have been able to function without a specified leader, however, this is a decision of the group. During the course of helping a child, various team members can take leadership roles depending on the needs of the child, the situation, the relative ability of each member to lead, and willingness to play a leadership role.

6. *There is an emphasis on programming.* The general emphasis of the educational team is on programing for children in conflict rather than evaluation and placement, which are often responsibilities of the staffing team. Whereas some ongoing evaluation and adjustments in placement would be considerations for the educational team, they are not a major function. This is a working team, interested in detail, and supportive of any techniques that will ultimately help the child.

Educational Team Philosophy

The philosophy that sustains the educational team is simple: *Schools have within their walls sufficient expertise to solve most of the educational and behavioral problems that need to be solved.* The process of shared growth will provide staff with the opportunity to grow in their ability to provide for the needs of all children. The practice of providing experts and specialists to solve problems within a school has often undermined the confidence of teachers, staff, and parents in their ability to solve their own problems. This practice has developed, to a large extent, because of a ready supply of professionals (special education teachers, remedial reading specialists, psychologists, speech therapists, and so forth) who were willing and in some cases anxious to tell teachers how to deal with a given child. In many school districts children in conflict were actually removed from the regular classroom so that they could benefit from total immersion in a special class. We can hardly blame teachers if they exhibit a reluctance to become involved in efforts to maintain a child in their classroom when only a year earlier they were asked to refer this child for special class placement.

The educational team should be an informal arrangement that falls somewhere on the continuum between the formal staffing team and informal coffee lounge discussions about children. Guidelines for the team need to be established so that members know their position within the school framework. Team members need to be aware of any constraints on their decision-making power. Whether or not the team can exclude a child from school, reassign the child to another class, call in parents, consult with the school psychologist, or use alternative techniques to effect change; all need to be carefully spelled out in advance or wasted effort will undoubtedly result.

Establishing an Educational Team

The educational team should be established as a result of needs to help children grow. If a school is working effectively with all children, there is no need for this system. However, if use of the educational team could help to solve educational problems, there are several guidelines helpful for implementing the concept.

1. The team should outline the major concerns or problems that they believe need to be modified before a child can grow educationally and socially. This is generally done individually by each team member after observing, counting, and charting deviant behaviors.

2. From the total list of concerns, the team should identify one or two problem areas as starting points. These can be decided on by (a) selecting only a serious problem that concerns all team members, (b) selecting a behavior that is observable, (c) selecting a behavior that will likely respond to change, or (d) selecting a behavior that will probably have a positive spread effect to other behaviors.

3. The team should discuss alternative measures for changing the selected behavior

and decide on the simplest measure that also offers reasonable odds for success.

4. The team should evaluate the success of intervention by comparing baseline data with present functioning level. Team efforts should be redirected as necessary.

The educational team concept represents a renewed faith in the local attendance unit and new hope for meaningful teacher involvement. Although it recognizes the role of mental health professionals, it clearly establishes the teacher's role as a bona fide change agent and a contributor to team efforts to meet the needs of each child in an economical, efficient, and effective manner.

System of Data Collection

As educational teams are formed, they will need to develop a viable system of data collection. Individual child folders often contain excellent data for use by the team, but they generally are not presented in a format that is readily usable. In Figs. 7–5 to 7–7, components of a data collection system that have been found to be functional for classroom use are presented. They are offered as a guide to assist professionals to condense the more comprehensive data generally found in individual folders, as a quick reference, and as a means of keeping up-to-date records with a minimum of time expenditure. They should generally serve only as a guide to the more personalized needs of an individual school or teacher.

Developing a meaningful individual record for each child receiving attention from the educational team can have positive effects on the staff as well as the child.

1. It encourages staff to review the specifics of a case in detail.

2. Sharing information often encourages positive attitudes to develop rather than negative feelings.

EDUCATIONAL TEAM

PERSONAL DATA FORM

Student's Name __Ron B.__   Date __1/5/87__

Date of Birth __11 3 75__   Sex __M__
                Month Day Year

Teacher __Ms. V.__

Name of Parent or Guardian __Mr. B.__

Address __217 Levis Rd.__   Telephone __555 - 1891__

Emergency Contact Person __Mr. W.__   Telephone __555 - 6093__

Medical Doctor __Dr. L.__   Telephone __555 — 7096__

Miscellaneous Information:

Need information from master file for conference —
to be held in 3 wks.

FIGURE 7–5

EDUCATIONAL TEAM GUIDE

Name __Ron B.__   Date __1/23/87__

Team Members   Working Relationship to Student

(1) Ms. V.   Home room teacher

(2) Ms. S.   Reading Specialist

(3) Mr. B.   Ron's father

(4) Ms. S.   Bus Driver

(5) Ms. L.   Music teacher

(6) Mr. J.   School psychologist

(7) Mr. J.   Resource teacher

Major Concerns of Team Members   (In Hierarchy)

(1) Ron's foul mouth

(2) Fighting behavior

(3) Doesn't finish school work

(4) Talks back

(5) Doesn't listen

(6)

FIGURE 7–6

EDUCATIONAL TEAM GUIDE (Con't.)

Intervention Procedure

(1) Teacher & psychologist will visit with Ron re. swearing & fighting
(2) Reward appropriate language — Ignore foul lang.
(3) Set up contract for appropriate lang. — Reinforcement will be free time in gym.
(4) Lay off academic pressures

Responsibilities of Team Members

(1) Mr. J. & Ms. U. outline contingency plan
(2) Ms. S. plan Re. program for bus
(3) Mr. T. outline schedule of Re.
(4) Mr. J. Contact M.D. for info.

Results

Classroom & bus behavior improved — Art a disaster

Recommendations

Take Ron out of art for 2 wks. — Visit with art teacher
Continue all other plans.

FIGURE 7–6 (continued)

EDUCATIONAL TEAM BACKGROUND INFORMATION FORM

Name Ron B.   Age 12-0

	Date	Information	Source
Behavioral	10-86	Fighting daily - Terrible language	ms. F.
	10-86	WRAT: Rdg. 3-8 ; math 5-0	ms. F.
	10-86	Iowa Test: Rdg. 3-9; math 5-1	ms. V.
		Fighting in school & on bus - Swearing - Doing nothing in school	ms. V.
Psychological	1-85	PPVT M.A. 8-5	mr. J.
	1-85	Durrell - Oral 2-5 ; Silent 2-4 ; Listening 3-0	ms. S.
	10-85	WISC Functioning in ave. range	mr. T.
	11-84	Behavior Count (swearing 15 per hr.; fighting 5 per wk.; 1/4 work turned in)	ms. V.
Sociol./Ecological	8-86	3 children (Boy 14; girl 2) Mother abandoned	Father
	9-86	Children placed in foster home	S. W.
	3-86	Father remarried (children returned home) Two step daughters —	Father
	9-85	Father reports need for school support	
Biophysical	10-84	Complete physical (No report)	Sch. Nurse
	11-85	Ron having fainting spells	Father
Needed	11-84	Follow-up report on fainting	Team
	11-85	Observe to see what Ron works for	
	11-86	Evaluation of home situation — Ck. with Doctor to get medical report	

FIGURE 7–7

3. Outlining information from the folder helps to put all of the available information into perspective.

4. Reviewing folders can point out information gaps to the team.

5. Developing individual folders gives the teacher a classroom record to use for ongoing record keeping.

Section Three: Case Studies

The case studies that follow all represent real cases involving children who have been identified as having various behavioral or emotional conflicts. They come from a variety of settings and represent a cross section of problems in school. Specific cases were selected for their interest, genuineness, and usefulness for discussion. Names, places, and any other factors that might lead to specific identification of children have been changed to preserve the anonymity of all concerned.

CASE 1 (TONY P.)

Personal Data

Tony is a 14-year-old boy whose small stature (4 feet 9 inches, 82 pounds) and young features give him the appearance of an 8- or 9-year-old instead of a teenager. He is Chicano and speaks fluent Spanish (mainly in the home), although he has no Spanish accent when speaking English. He is a very attractive boy physically.

Tony has two older brothers, Alberto, 16 years, and Roberto, 15 years, and one younger brother, Richard, 9 years. Tony has two younger sisters, Maria, 6 years, and Belin, 1½ years. All the children except the baby are attending the public school and are doing extremely well. Tony is the middle child and is the only one who did not adjust well to school.

Tony lives with his mother and stepfather (whom she married in 1981) in project housing. His stepfather works at night as an assemblyline man in a mattress factory. He is a rather passive man (34 years old) who speaks little English. Tony's mother is a lively woman (30 years old) who did most of the talking during the interview. One of the first things she said was that Tony had a normal childbirth, although she went into some detail in saying that she was running from Tony's natural father when she was pregnant with Tony and had a terrible fall. She states that Tony slept "day and night" after birth until he was about 1 year old. She stated that when she wanted him awake, she had to keep him awake and even this did not work. Since he seldom cried, she never sought a medical examination or advice concerning his sleeping problem. Mrs. P. stressed that Tony's natural father is an alcoholic. She said that Tony was very close to his natural father and may have been hurt by their divorce in 1980.

There seems to be a symbiotic relationship between Tony and his mother for several reasons. Tony was sick as a child and required much more of his mother's time than did the other children. She was constantly trying to meet his needs, and for unknown reasons she has continued to relate to him as more important than the other children. She seems guilty and defensive about her marriage to her present husband to the extent that she may be feeling that Tony's needs should come before hers. If she projects this feeling to Tony, the relationship of his behavior to the home situation becomes clear. His acting out began at the same time she remarried. He exhibited temper tantrums regularly to assert his need to be of first importance to his mother. This problem is further compounded by the fact that Mrs. P. must spend time away from the home helping to support the family.

Behavior

Tony has had a history of deviant behavior both during and outside school. School problems include erratic school performance, tantrums, and emotional outbursts. Tony's activities outside school were largely responsible for his being labeled as deviant and in need of special help.

Tony was somewhat successful at stealing; however, this activity led to serious problems with police. He was charged with a total of nine burglaries, although the police believe he was involved in approximately 125 such actions. He is presently serving a 2-year probation term.

Psychological Data

Wechsler Intelligence Scale for Children
Full scale   IQ 73
Verbal scale   IQ 74
Performance Scale   IQ 78

On the triad of subtests most specifically related to verbal comprehension, Tony attained a pro-rated IQ of 69. On the triads related to attention-concentration and perceptual-analytical factors, Tony attained prorated scores of 62 and 80, respectively. From this information one could judge Tony's performance to be in the low normal range.

Bender-Gestalt test. There is evidence of perceptual difficulty. Tony exhibited three rotations of 180 degrees as well as some more minor difficulties in angulation and closure of figures. At times during this test, he switched his pencil and seemed confused as to which hand he should write with. There are indications that he may have a generalized difficulty in laterality and problems crossing the midline.

Rorschach test. There is some indication of pathological thinking and also evidence of confused thinking processes. There was, for example, a fusion of responses on two cards so that the same part of the blot was two different

objects at the same time as far as Tony was concerned. It is difficult to tell whether this relates to primarily emotional or primarily perceptual difficulties.

Educational Information

Tony's functional level in school-related tasks was extremely low. He is working at a first-grade level in both reading and arithmetic.

Chronological age 14-0
Peabody Individual Achievement Test

	GRADE EQUIVALENT
Reading recognition	1.4
Reading comprehension	Preschool
Spelling	1.4
General information	4.0
Wide Range Achievement Test	
Mathematics	3.6
No other WRAT scores available	

Teacher evaluation: Functioning much below grade level

Medical Evaluation

All areas of the medical evaluation were within the normal range, including physical examination, visual acuity, and auditory acuity. Tony's electroencephalogram was in the borderline range, although this is not indicative in itself of an organic pathology.

Summary Statement

In summary, Tony can be considered a moderately disturbed youngster who, under conditions of stress, is capable of functioning in a psychotic fashion. It would not seem appropriate to label him a childhood schizophrenic. There is evidence of a moderate perceptual difficulty, and there is some substantiation for organic difficulty in a borderline abnormal electroencephalographic record. It would appear that the emotional difficulties in conjunction with an underlying perceptual deficit can well acount for periods of erratic and sometimes explosive behavior.

Intervention Strategies

From all that can be learned from this case, it is apparent that the school and community made minimal efforts at solving Tony's problems. He received some individual help in school but nothing of great duration or intensity. The lone exception to this was a 6-month placement in a nearby residential treatment center for emotionally disturbed children. He apparently adjusted well to this situation, but little change occurred.

Shortly after Tony's return to the community and school, he was caught burglarizing a home in the neighborhood (fingerprint identification). He went to trial in the fall of 1984 and was found guilty. His probation officer is attempting to have him placed in a closed treatment center for adolescents.

Theoretical Interpretation

In this section we will attempt to raise specific questions and in some cases make recommendations regarding the case under discussion. These recommendations are made after reviewing the data and visiting with concerned persons surrounding the case.

Each case in this chapter will be approached in essentially the same way: (1) by viewing the case from each theoretical position, that is, psychodynamic, behavioral, biophysical, sociological/ecological, and counter theory, and (2) suggesting alternative courses of action if appropriate. We will not attempt to raise *all* of the possible questions that could be considered, but only practical ones that might be realistically pursued.

Psychodynamic position. Several questions regarding Tony's personality development could be explored.

1. Has Tony's only success been in stealing?
2. What is the specific nature of Tony's apparent pathological relationship with his mother?
3. What is the mother's emotional maturity in regard to her family and her husband?
4. What recommendations could the psychologist make to the school regarding Tony's abnormal Rorschach test?
5. What is the family relationship?

Behavioral position

1. What problem behaviors actually exist (baseline information)?

2. What is reinforcing the stealing behavior?
3. What is reinforcing Tony's avoidance of learning tasks?
4. What is reinforcing Tony's tantrum behaviors?

Biophysical position

1. Are there other factors, such as biochemical imbalance or diet, that should be evaluated?
2. Could perceptual problems have significant impact on Tony's performance of educational tasks?
3. Would drug therapy affect his extreme tantrum behaviors?
4. Is Tony receiving adequate rest and a proper diet?

Sociological/ecological position

1. Is Tony's tantrum behavior a legitimate effort on his part to gain his mother's attention?
2. What is the dynamic interaction that exists within the family constellation?
3. What is the present family posture in terms of supervision outside of school?

Counter theory position. It is difficult to consider individual concerns that might be raised in this case, since counter theorists do not follow any predictable pattern (other than divergence).

Questions that could be asked might involve the following considerations:

1. The need for Tony to learn the educational skills required by the school.
2. The relative problems of Tony as opposed to those of a "sick" environment that (a) allows children to go unsupervised, encourages family problems through job scarcity, and forces both parents to work to supply necessary material goods; (b) requires success in superficial and unimportant school activities; and (c) discriminates against minority groups, which often adds to school frustration.

Alternative Courses of Action

When everything is considered, it seems that Tony's case evolves around two important issues: (1) the social and cultural interaction, which is generally inappropriate, and (2) educational programing, which appears to be far less than might be expected. These two problems are mutually supportive in that they often lead to a circular stimulation that grows to encompass more of Tony's life. Although other theoretical concerns should not be ignored, the social/ecological, the behavioral, and to a lesser degree the psychological area should be emphasized. The following procedures would appear to be helpful.

1. A complete family social evaluation should be undertaken to determine the interaction of Tony and his family. This evaluation should lead to a determination of goals and activities within the family that could promote (a) attention and reinforcement for appropriate behaviors, (b) realistic monitoring of after-school activities, and (c) additional activities.
2. If at all possible, Tony should be maintained in his home with support to the family or in a structured group home rather than a state institution.
3. Family support as needed should be made available to ensure Tony's success in the home environment.
4. A structured behavior management program appears to be a viable alternative for Tony during school time. Tony should be allowed to earn free time or tokens that could be turned in for small objects. The ability to earn small items and receive attention for this could have a positive effect on his stealing activities.
5. Educational tasks need to be geared to Tony's chronological age level of interest while remaining concrete enough to allow success. Work-oriented emphasis would seem to be appropriate.
6. Relationships between the home and school need to be nurtured through the efforts of the teacher or a specialist.
7. In addition to the behavior management program developed at school, the parents might be trained to recognize and reinforce appropriate behaviors as they occur within the family.
8. Crisis intervention in the form of life space

interview techniques should supplement the natural consequences of the reinforcement system.
9. Family therapy sessions designed to modify and work through family problems might serve a useful purpose. Much of this effort would depend on the outcome of the family evaluation (item 1).

CASE 2 (KENNY)

Personal Data and Behavior

Kenny is now 12 years old. He is the third child of a family of four children and has two brothers, ages 16 and 18 years, and a sister, age 8. Both parents are well educated. The father, with a Ph.D., works in a specialized scientific field, and the mother, with a master's degree, is a full-time homemaker. Family life appears to be stable although not a typical life-style. Kenny is a handsome child who appears to be loved and well cared for. He can be sweet and loving with an endearing quality that is irresistible. He is aware of his charm and often uses it for his own purposes.

At the age of 4 years Kenny attended a special school where he exhibited hyperkinetic behavior, expressed wishes to burn the school, and verbalized his desire to attack teachers. His psychiatrist recommended patience, firmness, supervised large muscle play, and constant presence of an authority figure to help control his impulses.

Kenny has been a student in an open space concept school for almost six years and has not been labeled as emotionally disturbed but integrated into regular class activities with all modifications of work or therapy done in the class setting. This is not to say that anyone is unaware that he is different. His bizarre behavior is unlikely to go unnoticed by teachers, classmates, neighbors, or even casual visitors to the school.

Kenny has had and continues to have a problem in relationships with his peers. Because of behavior patterns that are rarely acceptable by social standards, many parents do not consider Kenny a good playmate for their children. Those who do accept him as a friend find it difficult to understand his uncontrolled outbursts. Adults often find the outbursts, foul language, inappropriate gestures, refusal to cooperate, and lack of responsible behavior intolerable.

Psychological Data

Extensive testing has been done with Kenny. The following test scores are representative.

Chronological age 6-3
Wechsler Intelligence Scale for Children

Verbal scores	5-5	20%	Slow learner
	(mental age)		
Peabody Picture	5-10	41%	Average
Vocabulary (mental age)			
Test			

Bender-Gestalt Test
    Koppitz scoring: Maturation level is prekindergarten; many psychological indicators of brain dysfunction

Personality Assessment

Children's Apperception Test: Emotionally disturbed
Wechsler Intelligence Scale for Children

Verbal Scale	IQ 87

Educational Information

Chronological age 10-5
Peabody Individual Achievement Test

	RAW SCORE	GRADE EQUIVALENT
Mathematics	15	1.1
Reading recognition	27	2.6
Reading comprehension		No basal
Spelling	27	2.5
General information	23	3.4

Illinois Test of Psycholinguistic Abilities

	RAW SCORE	AGE EQUIVALENT
Auditory reception	38	9-2
Visual reception	27	8-10
Visual memory	8	3-10
Auditory association	35	10-1
Auditory memory	30	8-8
Visual association	24	7-2
Visual closure	25	7-6
Motor expression	32	10-4

Auditory channel appears stronger than visual; visual sequential memory is very impaired and area needing most help

Peabody Picture Vocabulary Test

Chronological age 12	IQ 106
Raw Score 89	
Percentile 73	Mental age 12-9

Detroit Tests of Learning Aptitude
Chronological age 12-5

	RAW SCORE	AGE EQUIVALENT
Verbal absurdities	28	13-0
Verbal opposites	42	10-6

Informal Reading Inventory
    IRI word recognition list—grade equivalent
        Independent level 4-1
        Instructional level 4-5
    Informal reading passages—Betts series based
        Independent level 3-5
        Instructional level 4-1

Kenny has developed good word skills and makes use of them in decoding words in a list. Good comprehension is lacking in silent reading. In directed oral reading, comprehension is adequate at the fourth-grade level. Reading level is subject to variation according to emotional attitude at the time of testing.

Medical Evaluation

Kenny was born after a full-term pregnancy and was of normal weight. His mother reported no medical problems other than some bronchial problems during pregnancy. Kenny did not walk until 2½ or 3 years of age. He did not talk until 3 years of age. At 2 years of age he had surgery for muscle imbalance in his right eye. At 4 years of age he had an operation on his left eye. He began receiving psychotherapy in the city of his former residence at the age of 4 years.

An electroencephalogram done in June 1979 was within normal limits. Hyperactivity and distractibility were not modified by methylphenidate (Ritalin) in 1979. He has not received such medication since.

At the present time (1984) Kenny appears physically healthy and of normal size and strength for his age.

Intervention Strategies

The efforts of the school to keep Kenny in the mainstream of educational reality are commendable. The teacher reports that Kenny has made some academic gains but still lacks friends among children of his own age. His relationships with adults are still erratic, although there is some improvement. A regular classroom placement has been chosen for Kenny because he tends to mirror the behavior of those around him. Providing appropriate behavior models was believed to be helpful for this reason.

Kenny is being seen by a psychiatrist in private practice who has been helpful and supportive to teachers and parents. He has basically been advocating the use of a behavioral approach, although some play therapy, leathercraft, music therapy, and puppetry have been used. With so many different adults interacting with Kenny, it is difficult for everyone to be consistent with their expectations and reward systems. There are some indications that Kenny is capitalizing on this by manipulation of the situation whenever possible.

Theoretical Interpretation

Psychodynamic position. Several questions arise from statements that teachers have made and behaviors Kenny has exhibited:

1. Several recent behaviors, including bringing soiled diapers to school daily for several weeks and "finding" matches in great numbers, could be explored with Kenny.
2. Now that Kenny is 12 years old, could he talk through his problems with the psychiatrist in addition to the behavior modification techniques being applied?

Behavioral Position

1. Kenny's teacher reports that he responds well with consistent treatment. Could a management system be employed that would ensure consistency?
2. Emphasis on punishment should generally be avoided. Kenny apparently allows punishment to take away his guilt for inappropriate behavior: for example, he often washes his mouth out with soap (voluntarily) when he says a nasty word.
3. Behavioral emphasis on building peer relationships could be encouraged more strongly.

4. What is reinforcing Kenny's lack of responsiveness to his peers?

Biophysical position. The electroencephalogram report for Kenny stated that everything measured within the normal range. No physical disabilities were noted, and no medical problems are suspected. Although his behavior sometimes indicates an internal drive that could be biophysically oriented, no objective measures that have been used support this idea.

Sociological/ecological position. The school has apparently done a good job in the social area. Labels have been generally avoided, and intervention efforts have been developed. The teachers and family know Kenny needs help and are getting help for him. Little has been said regarding the relationship of the parents to Kenny, except that the father holds a Ph.D. and the mother a master's degree. It might be helpful to explore the ongoing interaction between Kenny and his parents as well as his brothers and sisters. Having parents who are well educated has certain advantages and certain disadvantages and cannot be judged on external appearances alone.

Counter theory position. A case could be made for allowing Kenny to work more independently within the school as long as he would pay a price for inappropriate behavioral choices. He comes from a well-educated family and has a different life-style from that of most children. A school environment that would allow the freedom to choose, to decide, and to do with only the natural consequences of success and failure might provide Kenny with the treatment he seems to want and perhaps need.

Alternative Courses of Action

The behavioral approach seems to offer the best hope for Kenny at present. When the demands are simple and inappropriate behavior is met with the expected response, Kenny seems to get the security he needs. He likes token rewards but is becoming more able to exhibit appropriate behavior merely for the reward of a pat on the shoulder or a sincere word of praise. He also responds well to the reward of added responsibility that improves his self-concept, for example, being allowed to assist with media equipment for other areas, to help younger children with simple drill work, or to perform on the drums for younger children, although he cannot yet handle this with his own age level. His teacher believes that he would make progress if he had one accepting, primary relationship with someone with whom he could identify. Although several people have partially filled this role, his teacher believes he has not yet developed adequate primary relationships.

It appears that the school and home are providing a good program for Kenny. One notable exception exists. Coordination of effort seems to be a problem that threatens to disrupt progress. This coordination could probably be developed through brief meetings (maybe once a week for a few minutes) of all those interacting with Kenny or through the efforts of one adult, for example, the classroom teacher or resource teacher, coordinating the work with Kenny.

CASE 3 (BOBBY)

Personal Data and Behavior

Bobby is 9 years 4 months of age; he appears well-kept but is slightly heavy for his age and height. He seems to be in constant motion—shifting his feet, cracking his knuckles, and moving his eyes. In times of stress his eyelids drop half-shut, and he seems to peer from under them.

Bobby's mother works to support Bobby and herself. She has been divorced for two years and dates frequently. She is concerned about Bobby but confused about ways to handle him. She is willing to come to conferences and to supply Bobby with the support she can offer.

Bobby is unable to contain his impulses in neighborhood activities. He has no apparent respect for property boundaries or landscaping niceties. He is destructive with his own toys and others' toys. He uses obscene language, and neighborhood parents do not allow him to play with their children or to come into their homes. During leisure time Bobby often loiters in the nearby shopping center or watches television.

Bobby demonstrates aggressive behavior in all school activities. He uses verbal and physical aggression in the classroom—teasing, ridiculing, hitting, and tripping his peers. His acting-out behaviors disrupt playground activities and cause him continually to be involved in fights. He has no close friends but seems to attract others into breaking the rules with him, after which he loudly blames them for his troubles.

Psychological Data

Chronological age 9-4
Wechsler Intelligence Scale for Children

Full scale	IQ 91
Verbal scale	IQ 83
Performance scale	IQ 98

The drawing Bobby made of himself was only 1½ inches high, with no facial features except the ears, only one hand, and no other distinctive body parts included.

Educational Information

Chronological age 9-4
Illinois Test of Psycholinguistic Abilities
    Language age   8-10
Peabody Individual Achievement Test

	GRADE EQUIVALENT
Reading recognition	1.8
Reading comprehension	2.0
Spelling	2.4
Arithmetic	3.1
General information	3.7

Medical Evaluation

Bobby is within the normal range in both auditory and visual acuity. He is physically healthy and normal, as documented by an apparently comprehensive medical examination.

Intervention Strategies

Bobby has been maintained in the regular classroom with the help of professional staff, consisting of a resource room teacher who works with him for 30 minutes, four days a week, and counseling at a local mental health center. He is also being seen in the corrective reading program within the school. In addition, Bobby has been on 10 milligrams Ritalin, morning and noon.

Bobby has made little, if any, progress in developing satisfactory emotional stability; however, a limited gain in academic progress has been noted. His social relationships are bitter and frustrating to him, and his aggressive behavior continues.

Theoretical Interpretation

Psychodynamic position. This case certainly raises some serious questions regarding Bobby's level of personality development and his self-image. Both the drawing of himself and teacher observations support this contention.

Since Bobby has been receiving therapy at the local mental health center without apparent success, it seems that a change in strategy would be indicated. It appears important for the therapist and teacher to decide on future therapy in terms of the following questions.

1. Should therapy continue?
2. Should the therapy become part of daily school activities or be isolated from school?
3. What is the relationship between Bobby and his mother?
4. Could some male adult relationships be developed for Bobby?
5. Would further psychological evaluation be of any benefit?

Behavioral position. The record indicates that the behavior modification techniques employed with Bobby were of little sophistication, since his teacher, in her first year, was at a loss as to the correct teaching procedures. Several questions might help bring out important behavioral concerns.

1. What is maintaining Bobby's aggressive and antisocial acts?
2. What is the exact nature of Bobby's problems (number of times deviant acts are exhibited and so forth)?
3. What contingencies would Bobby work for?
4. Could behavior modification techniques be used to build a better self-image for Bobby?

5. Could behavior counting and charting help to identify areas of success and failure?

Biophysical position. The medical information makes no mention of any medical problems; however, medication is being prescribed with no evidence of success. It seems that this practice should be explored carefully by those competent to evaluate such procedures. Unless some defensible rationale and/or success with medication can be shown, it should be discontinued in favor of other intervention techniques.

Sociological/ecological position. A study should be made to determine Bobby's relationship to his mother, other adults, and children in his school environment. The personal records yield little information regarding social history. Bobby's problems appear to include more than school conflicts. A comprehensive evaluation of these relationships would be helpful in planning a coordinated effort between home and school in helping Bobby to solve his problems. Three comments made in the cumulative record indicate that many of the problems could be related. These are: (1) the child's father has moved out of state and has no contact with Bobby; (2) Bobby's mother dates frequently; and (3) the father does not support the family, so that Bobby's mother must work outside the home. These comments could be useful leads in gaining the information necessary to develop a program for Bobby.

Counter theory position. Several questions might be asked by those who look at this case from nontraditional viewpoints.

1. Is Bobby really the problem or are his reactions correct in view of the situation? Bobby has had little opportunity to develop a male image and has been deserted by his father, and his mother has had a series of male companions. What does this do for his self-image?
2. Is Bobby simply fulfilling the expectations of a system that labels him as deviant both overtly and covertly?
3. What is the probability of success for Bobby as long as he is forced to live in an environ-

ment that is hostile to the goals he is asked to achieve?

Alternative Courses of Action

Since almost every child is adequate in some areas, whether art, music rhythms, identifying dinosaurs, assembling things, telling time, or whatever, this is an area for beginning remediation. Bobby's scores on the Peabody Individual Achievement Test indicate an adequacy in mathematics, in which he performs at grade level. This seems an excellent place to afford him more feelings of success. He could be paired with a child who has great difficulty in mathematics so that he could be helpful and improve his own self-image. Since his visual perceptions are adequate and his general information level is at grade level, he evidently has interests and is absorbing information from his environment. His interests should be discovered, and learning activities with visual emphasis could be launched from these interests. Praise for small successes should be enthusiastic and direct. Approximations of assignments should be accepted and validated in the same way. "Sandwich praise," a kind of praise often used by teachers and parents, which places the compliment between two requirements or criticisms—should be avoided. Details are unimportant in the beginning and should be ignored if the learning activity has been completed and understood.

Since Bobby will make little progress academically until he learns to control his behavior and to attend, both of these areas must be remediated. A behavioral system might be set up to modify his disruptive activities and help him work toward a goal of self-control. He probably would need a token economy initially; hopefully, as his self-image improves, it could change to a social reward system—something that would bolster pride in accomplishment. Any behavior that reflects a change toward better social adjustment must receive immediate and enthusiastic reinforcement.

Academic work that Bobby can handle and that seems pleasant, such as dot-to-dot mathematics and phonic activities, maze puzzles, film loops for viewing and writing about, and pro-

gramed reading materials, might help Bobby to lengthen his attention span. A token economy of behavior modification might be helpful here too.

Although a teacher can use behavior modification, a humanistic approach, and emotional first aid on the spot with each disruptive action that Bobby demonstrates, these will not be adequate interventions to treat his basic problems. He is in need of every supporting service available. If possible, he should be referred for counseling both at school and at a mental health center. A social worker could help in the home, giving Bobby's mother support in mediating the neighborhood situation. Bobby could also receive valuable therapy from a "big brother" program that would fill his need for a male image or model.

Of primary importance for all professionals who are helping Bobby is the establishment of rapport and a relationship of trust with him—becoming real friends. His anger, frustrations, and verbal and physical aggressions must not be accepted; however, he must be recognized as a person while inappropriate behaviors are changed. Acceptable alternative behaviors should be suggested, and, at the same time, impending aggressive behavior should be prevented if possible. Rules should be clearly defined; Bobby should be reminded of the rules occasionally and supported even when he breaks them.

The class as a whole will be well aware of Bobby's problems from his behavior, and they can be a reservoir of support or of frustration for him. Sessions in Magic Circle (a discussion technique) could be helpful in stimulating emotional growth and in understanding feelings surrounding Bobby's situation. The ability of individuals to know and respect their own and others' feelings, the ability to recognize their own and others' energy and how individuals do and do not control this energy, and the consequences of these feelings and energies can all be explored in Magic Circle. Bobby would need to interact with the group in these sessions and, hopefully, would eventually respond to the motivations evident in these activities. The other children will also be made aware of how Bobby manipulates their own feelings and will become less vulnerable to his attempts to lure them into deviant behaviors.

Behavior counting would seem to be mandatory, regardless of the therapeutic approach undertaken, to determine the effects of the intervention. In addition to this monitoring process, close communication must be maintained with the total staff and with the home and community.

At the same time that efforts to alleviate emotional and behavioral disorders are undertaken, Bobby's academic shortcomings must be considered and defined, and specific teaching methods must be prescribed. A unit approach developed around Bobby's interests could be used with a small group and Bobby. Assignments could be based on a contract system, which should have several requirements for success. Completion of approximations of assignments should have immediate rewards, based on accomplishment and not obedience. The terms of the contract should be specific, positive, and fair and should be used systematically for all members of the group. To help Bobby perform well, contract activities should be short and could include puppet plays, listening and viewing activities, and discussion.

A suggestion has been made previously for activities in mathematics—of Bobby being responsible for helping a less able student. If this should prove to be unsuccessful, either in the peer relationship aspect or in the aspect of evident progress, programed materials and behavior modification may have to be used to help Bobby participate in activities that will be worthwhile to him.

Since Bobby's auditory perceptual problem is evident in the Illinois Test of Psycholinguistic Abilities, care would be necessary to ensure that he understands verbal directions, and actions should accompany all instructions. Bobby should be brought to the attention of the specialist in learning disabilities for concentrated remediation or compensation of his apparent learning disability. Classroom procedures might include listening activities, with accompanying visual materials to help him compensate for the disability.

A child generally responds to someone who cares—perhaps not immediately and perhaps never with complete freedom—but enough to begin a relationship that involves understanding, acceptance, and validation. Bobby could surely use a positive relationship with his teacher. Perhaps a male teacher, one who wants to teach Bobby for positive reasons, would be helpful in building understanding, acceptance, and a more healthy self-image.

SUMMARY

This chapter suggests ways in which the staff can synthesize the various approaches presented in Chapters 1–6.

Four behavioral types are presented and reviewed, including acting-out, withdrawing, defensiveness, and disorganization. For each of these behavioral categories, deviant behaviors are outlined, alternative solutions are proposed, and methods that have usually failed to produce desirable outcomes are discussed. The proposals made are for behaviors that generally can be dealt with in the regular classroom. Behaviors that are unlikely to respond to surface treatment are indicated.

Alternative models for the delivery of services are presented and discussed, as is the concept of the educational team. Included are recent discussions of the concept of mainstreaming as well as the discussion of educational priorities after several years of using various mainstreaming concepts.

Three case studies outline the various efforts at synthesizing alternative techniques into a workable educational program for children in conflict.

BIBLIOGRAPHY

Adler, A. (1962). *The neurotic constitution: Outlines of a comparative individualistic psychology and psychotherapy.* New York: Dodd, Mead, & Co.

Beery, K. (1972). *Models for mainstreaming.* San Rafael, CA: Dimensions Publishing Co.

Beery, K. (1973). *Catalyst profiles and faces (experimental edition).* San Rafael, CA: Dimensions Publishing Co.

Birnbrauer, J., & Lawler, J. (1964). Token reinforcement for learning. *Mental Retardation, 2*, 275–279.

Blanco, R. (1972). *Prescriptions for children with learning and adjustive problems.* Springfield, IL: Charles C Thomas.

Christopols, F., & Renz, P. (1969). A critical examination of special education programs. *Journal of Special Education, 3*, 379.

Coleman, J. (1966). *Equality of educational opportunity.* Washington, DC: U.S. Government Printing Office.

Deno, E. (1970). Special education as developmental capital. *Exceptional Children, 37*, 229–237.

Despert, L. (1985). *The emotionally disturbed child: An inquiry into family patterns.* Garden City, NY: Anchor Books.

Dunn, L. (1968). Special education for the mildly retarded—Is much of it justifiable? *Exceptional Children, 35*, 5–22.

Glasser, W. (1965). *Reality therapy.* New York: Harper & Row.

Glavin, J., Quay, H., Annesley, F., & Werry, J. (1971). An experimental resource room for behavior problem children. *Exceptional Children, 38*, 131–137.

Glidewell, J. (1961). *Parental attitudes and child behavior.* Springfield, IL: Charles C Thomas.

Glueck, S., & Glueck, E. (1950). *Unraveling juvenile delinquency.* New York: The Commonwealth Fund.

Gresham, F. (1982). Misguided mainstreaming: The case for social skills training with handicapped children. *Exceptional Children, 48*, 422–433.

Gullotta, T. (1974). Teacher attitudes toward the moderately disturbed child. *Exceptional Children, 41*, 49–50.

Haring, N., & Phillips, E. (1962). *Educating emotionally disturbed children.* New York: McGraw-Hill Book Co.

Hewett, F. (1968). *The emotionally disturbed child in the classroom.* Boston: Allyn & Bacon.

Jones, R. (1972). Labels and stigma in special education. *Exceptional Children, 38*, 553–564.

Jones, R. (1974). Student views of special placement and their own special classes: A clarification. *Exceptional Children, 41*, 31–33.

Jordan, J. B. (1974). Invisible college on mainstreaming addresses critical factors in implementing programs. *Exceptional Children, 41*, 31–34.

Karnes, M., Zehrbach, R., & Teska, J. (1974). Involving families of handicapped children. In T. Kelly, L. Lyndall, and M. Dykes (Eds.), *School and community resources for the behaviorally handicapped.* New York: MSS Information Corp.

Kirk, S., & Weiner, B. (Eds.). (1963). *Behavioral research on exceptional children.* Washington, DC: Council for Exceptional Children.

Levin, G., & Simmons, J. (1962). Response to praise by emotionally disturbed boys. *Psychological Reports, 11*, 10.

Levy, D. (1943). *Maternal overprotection.* New York: Columbia University Press.

Long, N., & Newman, R. (1971). The teacher and his mental health. In N. Long, W. Morse, & R. Newman (Eds.), *Conflict in the classroom.* Belmont, CA: Wadsworth.

Mackie, R., Kvaraceus, W., & Williams, H. (1957). *Teachers of children who are socially and emotionally handicapped.* Washington, DC: U.S. Government Printing Office.

MacMillan, D. (1973). *Behavior modification in education.* New York: Macmillan.

Martin, E. (1972). Individualism and behaviorism as future trends in educating handicapped children. *Exceptional Children, 38*, 514–517.

Martin, E. (1974). Some thoughts on mainstreaming. *Exceptional Children, 41*, 150–153.

Menninger Clinic Children's Division Staff. (1969). *Disturbed children.* San Francisco: Jossey-Bass, Inc.

Meyerowitz, J. (1967). Peer groups and special classes. *Mental Retardation, 5*, 23–26.

Morse, W., Cutter, R., & Fink, A. (1964). *Public school classes for the emotionally handicapped: A research analysis.* Washington, DC: Council for Exceptional Children.

Noshpitz, J. (Ed.). (1973). Report of the Committee on Clinical Issues. In S. Lustman, *The mental health of children: Services, research, and manpower.* New York: Harper & Row.

Payne, R., & Murray, C. (1974). Principals' attitudes toward integration of the handicapped. *Exceptional Children, 41*, 123–125.

Peter, L. (1965). *Prescriptive teaching.* New York: McGraw-Hill.

Pfeiffer, S. (1982). The superiority of team decision making. *Exceptional Children, 49*, 68–69.

Powers, D. A. (1982). Mainstreaming the inservice education of teachers. *Exceptional Children, 49*, 432–439.

Rank, B. (1949). Adaptation of the psychoanalytic technique for the treatment of young children with atypical development. *American Journal of Orthopsychiatry, 19*, 130–139.

Reinert, H. (1968). *Decision making in the educationally handicapped and normal child: A comparative study.* Unpublished doctoral dissertation, Colorado State College, Greeley.

Shotel, J., Iano, R., & McGettigan, J. (1972). Teacher attitudes associated with the integration of handicapped children. *Exceptional Children, 38*, 677–683.

Smith, J., & Arkans, J. (1974). Now more than ever: A case for the special class. *Exceptional Children, 40*, 497–502.

Ullmann, L., & Krasner, L. (1965). *Case studies in behavior modification.* New York: Holt, Rinehart & Winston.

Valletutti, P. (1969). Integration vs. segregation: A useless dialectic. *Journal of Special Education, 3*, 405–408.

Wallace, G., & Kaufman, J. (1973). *Teaching children with learning problems.* Columbus, OH: Merrill.

Whelan, R., & Haring, N. (1966). Modification and maintenance of behavior through systematic application of consequences. *Exceptional Children, 32,* 281–289.

Woody, R. (1969). *Behavioral problem children in the school.* New York: Appleton-Century Crofts.

8

The Adolescent in Conflict

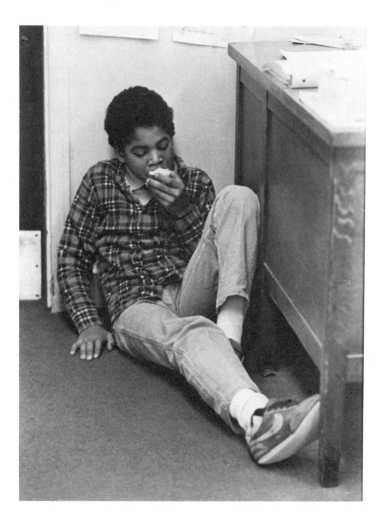

INTRODUCTION

After many years of focusing on children, the field has finally begun turning its attention to the adolescent in conflict. This chapter will discuss youths in grades 7 through 12 and will cover six areas of interest:

1. What are the major behavior disorders of this age group and who is considered to be "in conflict"? Additionally, what is the relationship among such terms as *seriously emotionally disturbed, behaviorally disordered, socially maladjusted,* and *emotionally disturbed*?
2. What are the major problem areas for adolescents in conflict?
3. What are the major treatment techniques used?
4. What are the major delivery styles provided in the public schools?
5. What screening and evaluation techniques are used in secondary schools?
6. What are the training needs for those who teach adolescents in conflict?

The major objectives of this chapter will be to (a) identify the major disorders of those considered to be in conflict and to describe the relationship among those disorders; (b) identify the major problems of adolescents in conflict; (c) describe the major teaching strategies and therapeutic interventions among this group; (d) describe screening and evaluation procedures in secondary schools; (e) describe the major intervention techniques used in educational programs; and (f) identify the training needs of those who work with adolescents in conflict.

MAJOR DISORDERS OF ADOLESCENTS IN CONFLICT

Before launching into a dissertation of the disorders of children in conflict, let us review the terminology. These terms typically in-clude *emotional disturbance, behavior disorders, delinquency,* and *social maladjustment.* For our purposes, we will use the term *behaviorally disordered.* Local school districts serve a variety of behavioral disabilities—the term is very broad. In spite of the limitations placed on districts by P.L. 94–142, they continue to serve a much broader population. The trend is to label all of the disorders mentioned earlier as *seriously emotionally disturbed* (Grosenick & Huntze, 1980). We all realize that at the present time P.L. 94–142 excludes the socially maladjusted unless they meet the requirements for severely emotionally disturbed. However a significant portion of our public schools ignores the ruling and calls the socially maladjusted *seriously emotionally disturbed.* To take the problem of labeling one step further, we must consider the term *severely emotionally disturbed.* As Grosenick and Huntze (1980) suggest, such labeling is doing many emotionally disturbed children a disservice since many are, in fact, not "severely" disturbed. In this chapter we will talk about behavioral disorders as being "severely" disturbed, knowing full well that in this population are the not necessarily "severely" delinquent, emotionally disturbed, socially maladjusted, and behavior disordered.

DISCIPLINE PROBLEMS

Discipline problems in junior and senior high schools have been the subject of extensive study during the past several years. Nicholson, Stephens, Elder, & Leavitt (1985) make numerous suggestions regarding discipline needs in the school. While all of these discipline problems do not relate directly to adolescents in conflict, many do (Grosenick, 1981). Nicholson et al. suggest that literally hundreds of crimes are committed regularly in school, including vandalism.

For 17 consecutive years the attitudes of Americans toward the public schools have been measured and reported by the Gallup polls. Each report shows that the behavior of students is not what the parents and patrons of public education would like it to be.

Sixteen of the 17 Gallup polls have shown people think that discipline is the major problem facing American education. Since discipline is generally seen as a bigger problem at the high school level than at lower levels, one can readily appreciate the tremendous problem being faced by junior and senior high school staffs. Furthermore, several of the top 10 problems mentioned in the survey have a direct relationship to the discipline issue. For the first 10 years respondents listed

1. Lack of discipline
2. Use of drugs
3. Lack of adequate financial support
4. Integration, segregation, and busing
5. Poor curricula and low standards
6. Difficulty of hiring good teachers
7. Large size of classes and schools
8. Lack of interest in school on the part of students
9. Crime and vandalism
10. Lack of interest by parents (Gallup, 1978)

The top problems as perceived by respondents are very similar through the years. The results of the Gallup educational survey (Elam, 1985) reveal that lack of discipline again heads the list, followed by use of drugs, poor curriculum standards, inability to find and hire good teachers, lack of financial support, lack of pupil interest and truancy, and school overcrowding.

Although there is no reliable estimate of the incidence of severe behavior problems among high school youth, estimates range from 1.5% (U.S. Office of Education, 1975) to 30% (Cowen et al., 1966).

Violent Schools, Safe Schools (1978), a report by the National Institute of Educa-tion, confirms that 1 of every 9 high school students have something stolen, 1 of every 200 secondary school teachers are physically assaulted, and 1 of every 80 students are physically attacked during *any one-month time period*! A decade ago violence and vandalism in schools were seen as troublesome, but not as critical problems. In some schools these problems have escalated to a point where learning is no longer possible (NIE, 1978).

In recent years school personnel have tried several methods to get these problems solved; including alternative school programs, vocational programs, counseling services, special education programs, suspension of violators, and various "push out" tactics that allowed the school to be rid of such students.

And what do school administrators think? Duke (1978) indicates that while school administrators do list many problems with skipping class, truancy, tardiness, profanity, fighting, drug use, and disrespect, most of them said that personal attacks, vandalism, and thefts were either no problem or only a moderate problem in their schools (NIE, 1978). Seventeen percent of the principals reported these to be a moderate problem, 6% viewed them as a fairly serious problem, and only 2% reported them to be a very serious problem. Secondary school principals reported higher levels of school crime than did elementary school principals.

What is the relationship between school violence, discipline problems, and emotional disturbance? What is the role of special education? On one hand, there are those who ask: "What difference does it make what the cause of the behavior is, as long as deviance from the norm is severe?" Others believe special education cannot solve all of the problems of the school, no matter how good our intentions or how much money we spend.

Two things seem clear in all the debate regarding the severe behavior crisis facing public education. First, special education has a role. Second, the job of providing educational programs cannot be left solely to special education. Special programs that appear most vulnerable to becoming "dumping grounds" for discipline-problem youth include those for the mentally retarded, learning disabled, and emotionally disturbed. Correct placement is easier if we recognize that (a) discipline is a problem for the entire school and community, and (b) discipline problems are likely to have a positive response to treatment.

Problems of Adolescents in Conflict

In their excellent study of emotionally disturbed adolescents, Grosenick and Huntze (1980) identify five major concerns that state personnel have identified regarding P.L. 94–142.

The first major concern is with the label *seriously emotionally disturbed*, which tends to focus attention on adolescents who have psychiatric disorders. Most troubled youngsters, however, are not defined in this way.

Second, the label *severely emotionally disturbed* is very stigmatizing. The children are done a disservice. Their parents feel victimized because it suggests they are to blame. Sometimes they are; but for the most part, they are not.

Third, by using the term *severe*, we wonder if lawmakers are including the continuum of emotional problems from mild to severe. If they are limiting the definition to only severe populations, they are not consistent in the other exceptionalities that do not use the word *severe* to describe the populations served.

Fourth, there is concern about the definition itself. Many states used Bower and Lambert's definition of *emotional disturbance* for many years prior to its adoption

under P.L. 94–142. During that time school personnel identified a range of emotional problems from mild to severe using the Bower-Lambert definition. Though under P.L. 94–142 the definition remains the same, the label is now one of *severe disorders*. How can the definition mean two different things simply because the federal government says so?

Last, what of those children who are seriously emotionally disturbed but not socially maladjusted?

For states struggling with these problems, there seems to be no clear answer. It appears that some states are interpreting the law to be more in harmony with definitions used in other handicapping conditions. Grosenick and Huntze suggest adding the phrase, "The term includes children who are emotionally disturbed, autistic, and socially maladjusted." They also suggest substituting *behavior disorders* for *severely emotionally disturbed*.

Treatment

Public schools serve approximately 75 to 95% of all handicapped youths labeled *behaviorally disordered* (Grosenick, 1981; Grosenick & Huntze, 1980). Generally, the most popular option is a self-contained classroom, with or without integration for part of the school day. The next most popular option is the resource room, followed by crisis teacher (or teacher consultant, diagnostic teacher) programs. Special schools, out-of-district placement, and homebound services are also used (Grosenick & Huntze, 1980). The number or percentage of students in any one service mode varies markedly from state to state.

One of the most troubling practices of public schools is the use of various forms of expulsion to solve the problems of the emotionally disturbed (Grosenick, 1981). These include

1. In-school suspension, where a youngster is placed (for a few hours, up to several days) in an alternative class or classes. In some cases this indefinite suspension may go on for weeks. Often the student is put in an isolated place with little or no schooling.
2. Repeated suspensions amounting to continuous absence. Most school districts prohibit more than 10 days continuous suspension; however, the district bypasses this rule by using an unlimited number of brief suspensions.
3. Shortened school days lasting from three to four hours.
4. Homebound instruction, which is misused in many instances to effectively bar a student from special programs.
5. Alternative school placement, used with the student who is a borderline case or as a phase-out program for the student who is exiting the special program.
6. Ignored truancy. In some cases it truly is believed that students simply cannot be controlled in an adequate fashion, while in other communities the school simply does not value such follow-up.

Although special programs have been slow in coming for the adolescent in conflict, there are programs being developed that show promise for adolescents (Center, 1986).

Many authorities on education have written books on the importance of producing an effective learning environment in the schools by introducing more effective methods of teaching. None of them, however, seems to understand the shocking fact that the learning environment in thousands upon thousands of schools is filled with violence and danger. Violent crime has entered the school house, and the teachers and students are learning some bitter lessons.

Dr. Owen Kiernan, executive secretary of the National Association of Secondary Principals, told the subcommittee: "Ten years ago, in the secondary schools of this nation, violence and vandalism were remote problems. Occasionally we would have a so called 'blackboard jungle school,' but this was quite unique. This is no longer the case."

The NIE Safe School Study (1978) indicates that violence and vandalism in schools have leveled off from their peak during the early 1970s, there is still considerable cause for alarm. The study indicates, for example, that students are in fact in greater risk in school than elsewhere. Teenagers spend about 25% of their waking hours in school; 40% of the robberies and 36% of assaults on urban teenagers occur in schools. The report indicates that the risks are especially great for youngsters from ages 12 to 15, with 68% of robberies and 50% of assaults on youngsters of this age occurring at school, whereas only 17% to 19% of violent offenses against youth in this age range occur in the streets.

The problems of violence and vandalism are so widespread that 11% of the high school students of our nation have something of value (more than $1) stolen from them in any given month. One-fifth of the thefts involve property worth $10 or more.

There appear to be several factors that are associated with school violence. The age of the child in the secondary school is one factor. Seventh-grade youngsters are most likely to be attacked, whereas twelfth graders are least likely to be the victims of attack. The risks of violence are greater in schools whose student body is less than 40% white. Also, the risks of attack are greater for those students, white or black, who represent the minority in a given school. Another important factor in the crime rate in schools is the neighborhood where the school is located. The higher the crime rate in the neighborhood, the higher the crime and violence in school. Schools with more single-parent families tend to have more property loss due to vandalism. Schools with a higher proportion of male students suffer more violence, since boys tend to exhibit more violent behaviors than do girls.

In addition to the serious immediate implications of violence against teachers and students are the long-range problems for schools. Teachers are increasingly inclined to leave teaching jobs because of fears for their well-being. Promising students are dropping out of school because of fears of crime and violence. Numerous parents are transferring students to private schools to avoid the inevitable discipline problems confronting public schools.

There no longer is a question of whether a problem exists in secondary schools. The question is what to do about the problem.

THE RELATIONSHIP OF DISCIPLINE TO YOUTH IN CONFLICT

The problems of discipline in the American public schools are quite clear. Discipline problems of all types plague our schools— violence and vandalism are being taken for granted. Where do we go from here? Who owns the problem? Is it a problem of the courts, the school, counselors, psychologists, parents, police, or teachers? Obviously, the problem belongs to all society. The school is in a critical position since the school day comprises approximately 25% of a young person's waking hours.

School violence and discipline problems cannot be attributed solely to the school any more than the common cold can be blamed on crowds. However, the school certainly is a factor in deteriorating behavior problems. Neill (1978) evaluated the literature on school violence and vandalism, the testimony at Congressional hearings, and interviews with school officials, police, students, and juvenile workers. She lists several factors commonly blamed for the deteriorating conditions in schools:

1. An upsurge in youth crime.
2. Deteriorating living conditions in large cities and white flight to the suburbs.
3. The ease of availability of guns and drugs.
4. Changes in the attitudes of teachers, parents, and administrators regarding the responsibility for behaviors.
5. A belief by some educators that the involvement of courts in discipline has "tied their hands" in disciplinary matters.
6. Depersonalization in the schools because of large classes, large schools, and excessive use of corporal punishment, suspension, and expulsion.
7. Neglect of "hard core" youth.
8. Violence on television.

In addition, other commonly identified causes include

1. Breakdown of the American family.
2. Number of one-parent families.
3. Increased affluence.

SCREENING AND EVALUATION IN SECONDARY PROGRAMS

Although we generally think of screening as a process of the elementary school and the preschool, there is no more important time for screening than the beginning of junior high. The adolescent in our society is faced with enormous changes: physical, psychological, behavioral, social, and interpersonal. In addition, the adolescent is expected to assume a new role in society—that of a productive member. With all of these changes coming into focus, it is imperative that screening for emotional difficulties be undertaken.

Evans and Evans (1985) have identified several factors to consider in the assessment process when school violence is involved. These include the following:

1. *Home and community factors.* Learned or otherwise sanctioned behaviors, lack of

supervision, family trauma, or violent community influences.

2. *School factors.* Alienation, punitive grading systems, or irrelevant school curriculum. School violence also increases with higher class numbers.

3. *Personal factors.* Psychological or behavioral disorders, and poor impulse control.

The screening process for this age group involves the same steps as earlier screening practices, with the exception of the tests administered. The following instruments are appropriate for this age group.

Bower-Lambert Scales

The Bower-Lambert Scales include sections appropriate for use with high school youth. This instrument has been reviewed extensively in Chapter 3 and therefore will not be discussed further in this chapter.

Quay-Peterson Behavior Problem Checklist

The Quay-Peterson Behavior Problem Checklist, which was reviewed in Chapter 4, is appropriate for use with seventh- and eighth-grade youngsters. This is a behavior checklist that is easy to administer and efficient.

Hahnemann High School Behavior Rating Scale (HHSB)—Grades 7-12, by Swift and Spivack

The HHSB was developed using the same methodology and rationale used in developing the Devereux Elementary School Behavior Rating Scale (DESB), reviewed in Chapter 4. The HHSB was developed to measure the overt classroom behaviors of youngsters in grades 7 through 12. The primary focus of the instrument is to measure behaviors that reflect the child's adjustment to classroom demands (Spivack & Swift, 1973).

The initial pool of items included 102 behaviors that were gathered from weekly small-group discussions with 26 teachers of emotionally disturbed and normal youngsters of secondary school age. Following these ratings, 80 teachers made 882 ratings of "normal" public school children and 672 ratings of "emotionally disturbed" youngsters of the same ages who were placed in a residential treatment school. Both groups were equivalent in intelligence scores.

The HHSB includes 45 items. Areas tested include the following, which are negatively related to academic success:

1. The degree to which children view school work as too much or too hard
2. The level of restlessness, interfering with the work of others, and the degree of teacher intervention necessary
3. The degree to which a child gives up under difficulty
4. The degree of negative and critical verbal behavior in the classroom
5. The extent of forgetting or misplacing materials
6. The degree to which a student is oblivious, uncommunicative, and lacking in social skills
7. The degree to which the child's opinions are closed to interaction
8. The display of outward nervousness

Areas tested that relate positively to academic success include:

1. The student's ability to apply principles, draw inferences, and grasp concepts in the classroom environment
2. The degree to which youngsters suggest unique or original ideas and materials to be explored by the class
3. The extent of positive verbal involvement in class discussions
4. The degree of responsiveness and friendliness in interactions with the teacher
5. The extent to which an individual mas-

ters the work assigned and goes beyond the work assigned

The HHSB has good validity, is practical to use, and provides norms and methods for typing the entire behavior profile. Its goal is to focus attention and reflect the youngster's ability to adapt to the total demands of the classroom. The test is not designed to give a measure of personality type or to provide a formal clinical diagnosis (Spivack & Swift, 1973).

Pupil Behavior Inventory (PBI)—Grades 7-12, by Vinter, Sarri, Vorwaller and Schafer

The PBI is designed to measure the "behavioral and attitudinal factors that affect the degree of success a pupil will have in accomplishing his educational objectives" (Vinter et al., 1966).

This screening instrument is designed to be used to obtain information about junior and senior high school youth before they are referred to agencies for treatment.

The major weakness of the instrument is that its total norming population was male. Test items are divided into four categories. Each of the 30 items are rated to give information on five factors: (a) classroom conduct, (b) academic motivation and performance, (c) social-emotional state, (d) teacher dependence, and (e) personal behavior. Although the instrument appears to be a very usable scale, the reliability and validity data are sparse, with no norms available.

A review of the literature indicates that aggressive, acting-out behaviors are most often tapped by the screening instruments, whereas withdrawing behaviors are least often used. This corresponds to the fact that boys who exhibit acting-out behaviors are most often identified in programs for emotionally disturbed, whereas girls exhibiting

withdrawing behaviors are least often identified.

Spivack and Swift (1973) point out that measurement of overt behaviors in classrooms has been motivated to a large extent by mental health interests rather than by educational interests. With this concern in mind, these scales, checklists, and inventories should be used only after critical review by those who will use them, to determine if they meet the specific needs of the group.

The evaluation of student behaviors at the secondary level presents challenges similar to those at the elementary level. School personnel will need to continue their dependence on interview techniques, observation of behavior, home visits, and formal psychological testing by psychologists and psychiatrists. Generally, the findings of these professionals will be discussed and decisions made through a team approach. The safeguards provided by Public Law 94–142 should enable the difficult decisions to be made with as much accuracy and care as is possible with our limited technical assistance.

Overview of Assessment Devices

As one can readily see, assessment is not an easy or quick solution to problems. Data need to be gathered from a variety of sources, including checklists, observation, interviews, and formal testing. These data, when compiled in a non-judgmental manner, can yield a variety of information about each youngster that can be translated into meaningful programming.

PROGRAM ALTERNATIVES

The provision of services for high school-age youngsters has been severely limited. Morse, Cutler, and Fink, in their classic study (1964), reported that only 32% of school districts that had programs for emotionally handicapped students offered classes at the junior high level and only 11% at the senior high level. Since the original survey indicated that very few high school programs were available, a disproportionate share were included in the review.

Bullock and Brown (1972) studied 126 institutions in 16 Florida counties. Fifteen percent of these were offering programs for adolescents, whereas 69% were serving younger children.

The scarcity of secondary programs has been attributed to several factors. Nelson and Kauffman (1977) suggest that the structure of secondary schools including departmentalized subjects, classroom switching, and an emphasis on academic achievement, may limit program options. In addition, they list a shortage of qualified teachers and of programs to prepare these teachers as reasons for the dearth of educational programs (Berkowitz, 1974). There is also the suspicion that schools have little holding power once students reach 16 years of age and school attendance becomes optional. Approximately 30% of pupils do not finish high school. Of this percentage, approximately half show serious social maladjustment (Ahlstrom & Havighurst, 1971). Morse, Cutler, and Fink summed up the issue on behalf of the disturbed population very succinctly:

By the time disturbed children reach high school age, they are much more difficult to handle, their pathology is likely to be deeply ingrained, and their antisocial behavior as often as not has taken them out of school into the hands of a secondary social agency. Their less bright prognosis, and the limited efficacy of educationally oriented remediation makes the schools less willing to undertake special programs of this sort for them (1964, p. 21).

A number of principles have been identified as useful in establishing a philosophical basis for intervention in secondary programs. Although some school personnel have developed education programs that meet the needs of all youngsters, a majority are struggling with students who are in conflict with the system. The principles listed below will undoubtedly suggest that secondary schools are having problems with some youngsters. This is true; the more quickly we adults can admit this fact, the sooner we can honestly seek solutions.

The following attributes of secondary programs are suggested to improve the educational climate for youngsters in conflict; they were identified in the Preliminary Report of the Subcommittee to Investigate Juvenile Delinquency (1977).

1. Staff members are selected who are dedicated to working with all high-school students. Staff members should be selected not only for their academic skills, but also for their ability to work effectively with those youngsters who are resistive to the system. In brief, staff should be selected who are advocates of students.
2. In schools where the ratio of troubled youngsters is higher, we should consider a lower ratio between students and adults. Successful programs such as Project R-5 in Grand Junction, Colorado have consistently demonstrated the need for the close contact afforded by smaller student numbers.
3. Effective involvement of parents in all aspects of the program is a critical component of change. Professionals who have been successful working with high-school youth with serious behavior problems often report that parent involvement was essential to change.
4. A by-product of small class size is individualized instruction. Individualized programming carried on in small groups or individual work sessions is important to meet the individual needs of students who have failed significantly in school.
5. Programs should emphasize the improvement of the basic academic performance of students. Many secondary programs have "short changed" students by failing to pro-

vide the necessary academic tools for meaningful change to occur over a significant time period. Students are led to believe that, if their behavior is moderated and they stay in school for three to five years, they will automatically and miraculously be transformed into the "educated" persons that industry and business will be needing to fill their ranks. Such is not the case. Students who leave school under a system of social promotion are no better prepared to meet academic needs of a job than if they had left schools before social promotion.

6. A flexibility in curriculum organization, administration, and program development that allows for difference without losing sight of basic goals is needed to be an advocate for change. Flexibility does not mean unthinking behavior without definable goals. It means having several alternatives to reach reasoned goals and the willingness to adjust program activities in order to achieve success.

7. One of our long-range goals for all high-school students should be to return the youngster to the mainstream or most "normal" environment possible. For high school youth, this is extremely difficult if the "normal" placement is a high school program that includes all of the things the special program has tried to avoid—large classes, impersonal relationships, a staff dedicated to the system, isolation of parents, and inflexibility.

8. Coordination with other social agencies is critical if we are to develop a holistic approach to intervention. Many secondary programs are actually counterproductive; activities encourage the development of "splinter skills" rather than useful social techniques. This practice is not only ineffective, but has been costly in both human and monetary resources.

9. Students should share in the definition of personal and program goals. One of the key ingredients of secondary programs is the active and meaningful involvement of the students the program serves. This involvement should be a continuous collaboration in the interest of program improvement rather than the sporadic, "crisis-oriented" involvement so common in public education.

In addition to developing a philosophical basis for education change, it is important for school personnel to identify alternative educational formats for coping with individual needs. This is often necessary because the "system" now in place in the schools was not designed with a philosophical base like the one suggested above. Many schools find it impossible to make the necessary changes within the school structure; therefore, developing a new format is necessary if change is to occur.

The number of alternative school programs for youth in conflict has grown rapidly in recent years, from fewer than 100 in 1968 to more than 5,000 in 1975 (Center for Options in Public Education, 1975). This is not to mention special classes for emotionally disturbed and socially maladjusted students that have been started in recent years.

Several basic models for alternative education programs have developed in recent years. A brief review of these follows:

1. *Schools or classes within schools.* This is one of the more popular modes of coping with special needs of youngsters. In this model the school provides for learning centers or special classes within the larger structure of the school. In this smaller and more intimate environment, the individual needs of students receive special consideration. In some cases the concept can lead to a core of classes that forms a school within a school. Generally, however, the individual student spends only part of the day in the special class or learning center, with the remainder spent in the regular program or work-study area.

2. *Schools without walls.* Programs that emphasize real-life situations are becoming a

more popular means of coping with troubled youth. These programs may include frequent field trips or learning experience in the community rather than studying about the community solely within the classroom. Some variations of this model include outdoor education programs and work apprenticeship programs.

3. *Continuation centers.* A variety of programs have developed that emphasize education away from the school environment. These include street or storefront schools, often housed in vacant stores in core areas of cities or in church basements or other neutral, or nonthreatening, environments. Continuation centers not only include programs that parallel public school programs but also those that emphasize retraining, such as community college and various city activity programs that feature skill development and personal improvement.

4. *Separate schools.* One of the more popular methods of dealing with youth in conflict has been separate schools away from the regular public school site. This form of alternative program is generally the most drastic departure from mainstreaming. Those who work in this setting say that the development of a new ecological environment is necessary in order to change the philosophical structure from one committed to the system to one committed to kids. A brief statement on behalf of these schools from Smith and co-workers (1974) is indicative of the concerns of those who advocate alternative schools.

Whenever we talk with students or teachers, from optional schools, they assure us that their school is more "humane" than the conventional schools they were in previously. At least part of this feeling is a response to the smaller size of the optional school. At the secondary level many of these students and teachers have come from high schools or junior high schools that enrolled over 1,000 students. Inhumaneness may be directly related to size. Certainly a school for 6,000 must

have more rules and bureaucratic constraints than a school for 60. In many optional schools students and teachers know the names of every student and every staff member. Whether it is humaneness or choice, directors of optional alternative schools frequently report less truancy, less vandalism, fewer discipline problems and less absenteeism.

Sinner and Sinner (1978) say that in their Vermont school they use some of the same crude behaviors that other high schools use to combat "intolerable adolescent nonsense." But they indicate they recognize that discipline problems stem directly from the school's inability to meet the human needs of students. "At our school, we feel that in order to attack the fundamental human problems of boredom, frustration, loneliness, anxiety, fears, and powerlessness, we must make our school less a factory and more a family" (Sinner & Sinner, 1978, p. 407).

The Sinners outline seven programs that are available on a voluntary basis at Union High School in Hinesburg, Vermont. A brief review of each follows:

1. *Do Unto Others (DUO).* The DUO program was developed at the suggestion of the Vermont state department of education. It allows high school credit for experiential learning in community services and apprenticeship positions. Students have worked as veterinary assistants, with attorneys, and with medical doctors. From 1974 to 1978 a total of 1,581 students participated in the DUO program. The program has a full-time director, a part-time teacher, a half-time community coordinator, and a full-time secretary. A considerable amount of counseling, evaluation, and follow-up is involved in the program. Although teachers cannot veto a student's participation in the program, they do voice their concerns regarding the student's abilities to participate. Since the program requires a student to miss one day per week, some students might suffer detrimental effects in their classroom studies through participation.

2. *Boys' Life.* This program is a self-contained program apart from the Union High School program. The program can support up to 25 volunteers. Each student in the program contracts weekly to complete academic work, for vocational assignments, to keep a journal of daily activities, for physical fitness activities, and for cleanup duties. The school staff includes a full-time teacher/director, a full-time aide, and part-time consulting teachers from the University of Vermont.

The Boys' Life program emphasizes democratic shared governance. It is incorporated as a profit-making enterprise, and students can earn the equivalent of 18 Carnegie units toward their high-school diploma.

3. *Summer Challenge.* This program is modeled after the Outward Bound programs, which emphasize self-sustaining behaviors. In addition to the rigorous and stressful outdoor training, students experience vocabulary building and writing skills development, all for graduation credit.

The Summer Challenge is a 25-day volunteer experience including backpack construction, hiking, cooking, rock climbing, swimming, team building (for cooperation), competitive sports, and 56-hour solo experience.

The staff includes two teachers and three junior leaders who have successfully completed the project in earlier years.

4. *Summer Site Betterment Project.* This project was a one-summer venture that could become an annual event. It was a combination of several activities, including tree planting, school mural painting, and construction of a green house, that culminated in beneficial community and school improvements. Also, the students kept journals of their activities, which helped to improve writing skills during summer months.

5. *Girls' Life program.* This project was started in the interest of fairness and in response to Title IX regulations. It is a parallel to Boys' Life, which was described earlier in this review of Union High School programs. The Girls' Life project provided services for as many as 25 young women who contract for such skill development areas as child care, nutrition, money management, and legal rights and resources. Academic subjects and a counseling program are also included in the project. Staff members include one full-time teacher and one half-time nurse as well as a consulting teacher aide.

6. *Peer counseling.* This project trained 31 students and two teachers in the skills of peer counseling. Areas of concern for counseling included drugs, sex, and alcohol, as well as teaching students the basic skills of counseling. Counseling was done in a nondirective, nonjudgmental fashion, with good listening skills emphasized. The peer counselors were trained to help others make decisions rather than making decisions for the student.

A peer counseling resource room was a spin-off of the project. This center provided a place for students to come to relax and get support and caring.

7. *The Learning Place.* The newest of the alternative programs for Union High School youngsters, the Learning Place is designed to meet the need of those who act out severely against the institution. It is designed to help youngsters who are more committed to drugs, cutting classes, and dropping out than to academic development. The unique components of this program include democratic shared governance between teachers, students, and administration. The negotiated contracts cover such areas as objectives, evaluation means, governing the program, program design, and staff selection.

The wide range of programs outlined by Sinner and Sinner (1978) represents a laudable attempt to meet the needs of all students in Union High School. Although some of the programs are very new, the data presented indicate that district personnel are trying to evaluate the effectiveness of the programs. The Union programs are highlighted because of their comprehensive nature.

One of the more successful programs for youngsters who are in conflict with the system has been demonstrated in the Grand Junction, Colorado schools. This program, described by Swanson and Reinert (1979), offers students a mature, caring, and realistic atmosphere where production is important.

Long, Morse, and Newman (1977) have suggested that the most effective program for problem youngsters over 16 years of age is exclusion. Although many of these students decide for themselves that they no longer want to continue in the system, others need and receive pressure from the school staff to leave.

Some of the more traditional programs for dealing with behaviorally disordered youth have been outlined by Nelson and Kauffman (1977). The self-contained classroom is the most popular option (Bullock & Brown, 1972; Hirshoren et al., 1970; Morse, Cutler, & Fink, 1964). The special class has become popular ostensibly because integration is very difficult. Morse, Cutler, and Fink (1964) reported only 1% of the schools attending regular classes. A decade's experience in the Grand Junction, Colorado, public schools indicates very little success with integration back into regular high school programs. Program officials now believe that segregated programs are meeting their needs more effectively.

A popular way of dealing with maladjusted and delinquent adolescents has been New York's "600 schools." The program features small classes (12 students per class in schools of about 200) with homeroom teachers responsible for all academic subjects. Students are also provided instruction in remedial reading, shop, physical education, and music. Several support staff are provided, including a full-time guidance counselor, a part-time school psychologist, part-time psychiatrist, and nurse. The curriculum is self-paced, with emphasis on reading. Older students are offered skills in vocational areas as well (Budnick & Andreacchi, 1967).

Hawthorne Cedar Knolls, one of the better-known facilities for severely maladjusted youth, is described by Cohen (1963). The program features a basic academic program complemented by industrial arts shop.

Detention homes are also a popular mode for dealing with problem adolescents. Dorney (1967) has described Youth House in New York City. This rather large program housed over 500 youngsters with a staff of approximately 40 teachers. The curriculum, which was highly flexible, included basic academic subjects and social living skills.

In addition to the more traditional models, Nelson and Kauffman describe several newer derivations being used in emerging secondary programs. These methods include the consultant teacher approaches described by Newman and co-workers (1971), Tharp and Wetzel (1969), and Morse (1971). In these programs, the consultant works with teachers rather than students; although the crisis intervention teacher does interact on a limited basis with youngsters. Other intervention procedures that indicate good promise of success include those outlined by Beck (1985), Ruhl (1985), Hughes (1985), and Bullock, Donahue, Young, and Warner (1985). A sample of quality programs (Smith-Davis, 1985) provides the interested reader a variety of successful programs.

Although the number of high school programs for youth in conflict is growing rapidly, it is obvious that we have only scratched the surface as far as programming is concerned. We do know that whereas program style is an important determinant in the youths' change, the major ingredient is obviously the program staff and the attitudes and methods they use to promote growth.

For current criteria being used by practitioners to identify behavioral disorders and emotional disturbances, refer to Kavale, Forness, and Alper (1986). These researchers say that diversity is the byword in those fields, with little evidence of standardization.

THE TRAINING NEEDS OF THOSE WHO TEACH ADOLESCENTS

Two major categories are identified under training needs: preservice and inservice. Preservice includes college courses taken to gain certification and/or a degree in a specified field of study. Inservice includes courses, workshops, and other activities taken after employment is secured. The inservice may be sponsored and directed by the employing agency, or by an outside agency (as directed by the employment agency).

Preservice

Most programs for training teachers of emotionally disturbed are K–12 programs. Very few are limited to or emphasize secondary-level training. Within the secondary program several components are prominent (Grosenick & Huntze, 1980):

Adolescent psychology
Methods courses such as behavior management, materials, evaluation and curriculum designed specifically for the adolescent
Career or vocational education
Practicum (advanced student teaching)

Other emphasis areas include characteristics of the behaviorally disordered adolescent, drug and alcohol abuse, juvenile delinquency, and abnormal psychology.

Limited enrollment in secondary programs as well as limited faculty skill and experience inhibit the growth and quality of these programs. Teaching in a secondary level program is not, obviously, an easy task. Often, our strongest and best trainees fail to meet the expectations of the secondary school. While part of the problem lies with the training received, much of the blame must be shared by the secondary school. Teachers in secondary programs often do not want emotionally disturbed youngsters in their school or classes. Nevertheless they are seen as a facilitator of those students. Under these conditions cooperation and enthusiasm for change are difficult. The teacher must work with reluctant staff, parents who have often given up, and students who often would prefer being anywhere but school! Teaching becomes a juggling act. The teacher of adolescents must be a very special person.

The inadequate training received by most secondary special teachers, along with the limited number of trained teachers, make secondary programming risky business. It is, however, an area of teaching that can bring rich rewards to those who have the desire to work.

Inservice

There is much inservice training provided public school teachers once they are on the job. Much of it is of the proverbial "dog and pony show" type where someone lectures for a two-hour period. Typically the inservice group has had no preparation, little time for change, and not much follow-up and evaluation. Much of inservice training is of general school interest and but not very specific about the emotionally disturbed.

Personal Qualities of Excellent Teachers. The teacher is one of the most critical components of any successful educational program. Tschudin (1978) has identified 17 items that differ significantly between ordinary teachers and what she terms "A+ teachers." These resulted from the identification of 311 "A+ teachers." Teachers were identified using three criteria: 73% were nominees for or winners of "Teacher of the year" awards, 16% were nominated by other teachers or administrators, and 11% were identified because of media coverage of their teaching activities. This group was compared with a control group of 109 teachers representing entire school faculties.

After an analysis was made of 420 questionnaires from these two teacher groups, some items were identified as significantly different for the two groups. Those excellent teachers offered these behaviors:

1. Established goals that developed student confidence.
2. Gathered ideas for teaching from a wide variety of sources.
3. Developed better plans—and were more willing *to deviate from them*!
4. Designed better classrooms.
5. Used common materials in unusual ways.
6. Disciplined with less punishment.
7. More effectively provided individualized instruction.
8. Used a wider spectrum of techniques.
9. Provided an array of activities that students found attractive.
10. Got their students actively involved.
11. Used effectively the help they did get.
12. Assigned *less* homework.
13. Used teacher-made tests *less* frequently.
14. Used a variety of alternatives to evaluation.
15. Became more involved with students outside the classroom.
16. Offered enthusiasm and humor.
17. Worked hard to succeed.

Although Tschudin's study was done with classroom teachers, a generalization to specialists would be possible. All these factors are certainly motivating when we think of our own personal improvement.

SUMMARY

Adolescents in conflict are being heard by administrators and staff in the public schools. The Gallup polls of the attitudes of Americans toward education have shown consistently that Americans believe behavior and discipline to be our major educational problems. Surveys by the National Institute of Education and hearings conducted by Senator Birch Bayh's congressional subcommittee support these findings.

Special education programs for emotionally disturbed and socially maladjusted children offer help but cannot solve all of the school's problems. Comprehensive school programs, supported by community involvement, show the most promise in meeting the needs of these youngsters.

This chapter identified the major behavior disorders, outlined the major problem areas for adolescents in conflict, suggested major treatment techniques, and suggested alternative delivery styles provided in public schools. Training needs for those who wish to teach adolescents were also identified.

Several screening instruments are now available to aid in the initial identification of potential problem youth. Instruments for evaluation are generally lacking for secondary populations; most teachers and clinicians are relying on various intelligence, personality, and educational measures.

A large number of alternatives in programming are being used by teachers to meet the educational needs of youth. None of these measures has proved to be superior to all others. In fact, efficacy studies are few in number and inconclusive in results.

A need exists for broad-based support of educational programs for high school youth in conflict as well as of the ongoing evaluation of such efforts. In addition, a vehicle is needed for sharing the results of these activities, so that people in the "trenches" benefit from these studies.

BIBLIOGRAPHY

Ahlstrom, W. M., & Havighurst B. J. (1971). *Four hundred losers: Delinquent boys in high school.* San Francisco: Jossey-Bass.

Beck, M. (1985). Understanding and managing the acting-out child. *Pointer, 29*(2), 27–29.

Berkowitz, P. H. (1974). In J. M. Kauffman & C. D. Lewis (Eds.), *Teaching children with behavior disorders: Personal perspectives* (pp. 24–29). Columbus, OH: Merrill.

Bower, E., & Lambert, N. (1978). In-school screening of children with emotional handicaps. In N. Long, W. Morse, & R. Newman (Eds.), *Conflict in the classroom* (3rd ed.). Belmont, CA: Wadsworth.

Budnick, A., & Andreacchi, J. (1967). Day schools for disturbed boys. In P. H. Berkowitz & E. P. Bothman (Eds.), *Public education in disturbed children in New York City* (pp. 57–77). Springfield, IL: Charles C Thomas.

Bullock, L., Donahue, C., Young, J. & Warner, M. (1985). Techniques for managing physical aggression. *Pointer, 29*(2), 34–44.

Bullock, L. J., & Brown, R. K. (1972). Educational provisions for emotionally disturbed children: A status report. *Florida Education Research and Development Council Bulletin, 8,* 1.

Center, D. B. (1986). Educational programming for children and youth with behavioral disorders. *Behavioral Disorders, 11*(3), 208–212.

Center for Options in Public Education. (1975). *Changing our schools* (Issue No. 12). Bloomington, IN: Indiana University.

Cohen, H. (1963). The academic-activity program at Hawthorne: A specially designed educational program for the troubled adolescent. *Exceptional Children, 30,* 74–79.

Cowen, E., Zax, M., Izzo, L., & Trot, M. A. (1966). Prevention of emotional disorders in the school setting: A further investigation. *Journal of Consulting Psychology, 30*(5), 381–387.

Dorney, W. P. (1967). Growth and development of education in a detention setting. In P. H. Berkowitz & E. P. Rothman (Eds.), *Public education for disturbed children in New York City* (pp. 124–142). Springfield, IL: Charles C Thomas.

Duke, D. (1978). How administrators view the crisis in school discipline. *Phi Delta Kappan, 59*(5), 325–330.

Elam, S. M. (1985). The Gallup educational surveys: Impressions of a poll watcher. *PDK, 65*(1), 26–47.

Evans, W. H., & Evans, S. S. (1985). The assessment of school violence. *The Pointer, 29*(2), 18–21.

Gallup, G. N. (1985). The seventeenth annual Gallup Poll of the public's attitudes toward the public schools. *Phi Delta Kappan 67*(1) 35–47.

Grosenick, J. K. (1981). Services for severely disordered youth within public schools and facilities for the neglected or delinquent. *Education Unlimited, 3,* 23–28.

Grosenick, J. K., & Huntze, S. L. (1980). *National needs analysis in behavior disorders: Adolescent behavior disorders.* Columbia, MO: Department of Special Education, University of Missouri.

Hirshoren, A., Schultz, E. W., Manton, A. B., and Henderson, R. A. (1970, December). A survey of public school special education programs for emotionally disturbed children. *Special Education Monograph* (No. 1–70). Urbana-Champaign, IL: Department of Special Education, University of Illinois at Urbana-Champaign.

Hughes, C. (1985). Physical intervention: Planning and control techniques. *Pointer 29*(2), 34–37.

Kavale, K., Forness, S., & Alper, A. (1986). Research in behavioral disorders/Emotional disturbance: A survey of subject identification criteria. *Behavioral Disorders, 11*(3), 159–167.

Long, N., Morse, W., & Newman, R. (1977). *Conflict in the classroom* (3rd ed.). Belmont, CA: Wadsworth.

Morse, W. C. (1971). The crisis or helping teacher. In N. Long, W. Morse & R. Newman (Eds.), *Conflict in the classroom* (2nd ed.) (pp. 294–302). Belmont, CA: Wadsworth.

Morse, W. C., Cutler, R. I., & Fink, A. H. (1964). *Public school classes for the emotionally handicapped: A research analysis.* Washington, DC: Council for Exceptional Children.

National Institute of Education (NIE). (1978). *Violent schools, safe schools: The safe school study report to Congress.* Washington, DC: Department of Health, Education and Welfare.

Neill, S. (1978). Violence and vandalism, dimensions and correctives. *Phi Delta Kappan, 59*(5), 302–307.

Nelson, C., & Kauffman, J. (1977). Educational programming for secondary school age delinquent and maladjusted pupils. *Behavioral Disorders, 2*(2), 102–113.

Newman, R. G., Bloomber, C., Emerson, R., Keith, M., Kitchmer, H., & Redl, F. (1971). Psychoeducational consultation. In N. J. Long, W. C. Morse, & R. G. Newman (Eds.), *Conflict in the classroom* (pp. 275–286). Belmont, CA: Wadsworth.

Nicholson, G., Stephens, R., Elder, R., & Leavitt, V. (1985, March). Safe schools: You can't do it alone. *PDK, 66*(7), 491–496.

Preliminary Report of the Subcommittee to Investigate Juvenile Delinquency. (1975, April). *Our nation's schools—A report card: "A" in school violence and vandalism.* Washington, DC: U.S. Government Printing Office.

Quay, H. C., & Peterson, D. R. (1975). *Manual for the*

behavior problem checklist. Unpublished manuscript.

Ruhl, K. L. (1985). Handling aggression: Fourteen methods teachers use. *Pointer, 29*(2), 47–50.

Sinner, G., & Sinner, J. (1978). Options in high school discipline. *Phi Delta Kappan, 59*(6), 407–409.

Smith-Davis, J. (1985). A sampler of educational programs for adolescents. *Pointer, 29*(2), 47–50.

Smith, V., et al. (1974). Optional alternative public schools, Bloomington, Indiana. *Phi Delta Kappan Educational Foundation*, p. 14.

Spivack, G., & Swift, M. (1973). The classroom behavior of children: A critical review of teacher-administered rating scales. *Journal of Special Education, 7*(1), 55–89.

Swanson, L., & Reinert, H. (1979). *Children in conflict: Methods and materials.* St. Louis: C. V. Mosby.

Tenth Annual Gallup Poll of public attitudes toward the public schools. *Phi Delta Kappan, 60*(1), 33–45.

Tharp, R. C., & Wetzel, R. J. (1969). *Behavior modification in the natural environment.* New York: Academic Press.

Tschudin, R. (1978). What makes an A+ teacher? *Phi Delta Kappan, 60*(1), 267.

U.S. Office of Education. (1975, May). *State education agency estimates unserved by type of handicap.* Washington, DC: Bureau of Education for the Handicapped.

Vinter, R., et al. (1966). *Pupil behavior inventory: A manual for administration and scoring.* Ann Arbor, MI: Campus Publishers.

Williams, J. (1979). Discipline in the public schools: A problem of perception. *Phi Delta Kappan, 60*(5), 385–387.

9

People Who Make the System Work: Parents, Teachers, and Ancillary Personnel

INTRODUCTION AND OBJECTIVES

Those who are actively involved in changing the behavior of children include parents, teachers, and ancillary personnel. These are the people who make the system work, who orchestrate the modification process, and who bring about a lasting change to children in conflict. Without their shared expertise, change is only a hollow ritual—without reason, form, or direction. No single group is more important than the others; each has its own job to do. First we will talk about the parents because of their very committed role to their children in terms of time and caring.

THE FOUNDATION OF CHANGE— THE PARENT

During a child's early years, parents and teachers are the significant figures who, separately and together, provide the opportunities for learning and growth (Kroth, 1975).

How much schools have interacted with parents has ebbed and flowed throughout the history of formal education. As programs have developed for disturbed children, the trend has been the same. As Stendler (1950) so aptly points out, in many cases professional advice to parents has been less than adequate and more confusing than helpful. For example, during the latter part of the 19th century, parents were urged to be sweet and generally permissive. The early part of the 20th century brought rigid habit training. By the middle of the 20th century, this rigidity had given way to demand feeding of babies; more recently nursing, cuddling, and close association with the baby during the early years have been advocated.

Despite the variation in advice to parents, professionals have consistently valued the parent-child and parent-school relationship. Most teachers agree that a positive, supportive relationship is essential for positive emotional development of children labeled *emotionally disturbed*.

Perhaps one of our problem areas with parents has been an emphasis on advice-giving rather than on cooperative problem solving. We must begin to view the parent as more than someone to blame when things go wrong. Parents must be involved if a "ripple effect" to the home and community is to develop.

The importance of parents in the education of their handicapped child is underscored most strongly by the mandate for their involvement by Public Law 94–142. Essentially, this involvement begins with the evaluation process and continues into placement and programing. Although this law is a big step toward assuring the potential involvement of parents in the education of their handicapped child, many questions remain as to their most useful role in the process. Yoshida and co-workers (1978) have studied the areas of potential parental involvement with interesting results. Only two areas of involvement received more than 50% support from planning team members: (1) to present information relevant to the case and (2) to gather information relevant to the case. At the 40% level, only one item was supported: to review the student's educational process. It was rather revealing to find that fewer than 40% of team members responded positively to items like (1) using student needs as guidelines for judging programing alternatives, (2) suggesting student's subject matter needs, (3) reviewing continued appropriateness of student's program, (4) interpreting information relative to the case, and (5) finalizing decisions. From this study one can conclude that parents are not viewed as having a significant role in the educational process, even though their participation is mandated by law.

Although schools generally welcome the involvement of parents in the educational programing of their children, much uncertainty remains regarding how they may best participate. This question must be answered so that parental involvement may become a reality.

The role of parents in program redevelopment is an essential one. Often their presence and support determines district decisions in regard to financing new programs, hiring additional staff, and other important fiscal matters. Hobbs (1978) believes that parents have to be recognized as the primary educators, and professional people, teachers, pediatricians, psychologists, and others, have to learn to be consultants to parents.

Most teachers believe that parents of children in conflict are worthy of much program emphasis; many colleges offer one or more courses that emphasize the counseling aspects of working with parents; and nearly every school system encourages its staff to interact with parents. What is the net result of this emphasis? Special programs for handicapped children have expanded in both number and scope, with many children receiving educational services. This growth cannot be attributed totally to interaction with parents, although this is certainly one positive indicator of parental support. Programs that have capitalized on parental involvement report positive dividends in increased parental support, community acceptance, and successful intervention with children.

Overall, however, it appears that efforts with parents of children in conflict have been inadequate. Teachers still blame parents for inadequacies that appear to have been caused by several factors—teachers and schools included. Teachers generally have had only a one-way relationship with parents, with little sharing of ideas.

The Role of Parents in the Deviance of Their Children

Information about parents of children in conflict is noticeably lacking. There are many how-to books on child rearing but few good research efforts to determine if parents of deviant children are different from parents of normal children. In 1983, Casey reported that only about one-third of behaviorally disordered children live with their mother and father.

Teachers and other professionals can sometimes be heard to say things like: "Jennie's mother is working, and you know what that means," or "Didn't you know Bobby's mom and dad are divorced?" or "David's mother and father were killed in an automobile accident when he was four years old." On one hand these statements suggest that teachers believe good parents and wholesome family life are important to the development of healthy personalities in children. On the other hand these statements imply parents are to blame for their children's troubles.

In her book on emotionally disturbed children, Despert (1965) devoted one section to the families of disturbed children. In a highly emotional narrative, she is critical of parents and society on several issues.

1. Despert claims that although ours is the age of the vitamin pill, scientific formula, and worship of children, that one essential seems to be lacking in our mothers—love. Despert attributes much of the mother's problems to changes in society that have affected her role: smaller families, a mobile society, and a disappearance of the extended family. Despert (1965) puts it: "Instinctive motherliness is being smothered in the material wealth of modern life" (p. 248).

2. One thing that mothers need cannot be taught—feelings that can help to guide her behavior with children. Too much attention has been paid to those who have prepared "cookbooks" for motherhood. The young mother feels trapped by her role. She responds to this frustration by

overindulgence in her children on the one hand and punishment on the other.

3. A mother has little time or energy to adjust to the role of motherhood if she must rush off to a job each day. In addition, the children must often come home to an empty house or a babysitter. At times the mother must leave home before the father is ready to leave. Despert believes the confusion of this arrangement can gradually grow into unsolvable problems within the home.

4. Role confusion has developed because of pressures toward a career and the knowledge that it is difficult to be a mother and career person at the same time. Advertisements portray a modern kitchen as a place that all but prepares dinners and does the dishes. Young girls often come to marriage totally unprepared for the tasks that await them.

5. The care of the baby has been one area where mothers have given up much of their natural feelings for the conveniences of modern life. Breastfeeding is given as a notable example. Despert believes that mothers and babies have suffered because mothers are so concerned over giving the baby what the baby needs that no time is left to pay attention to what the baby wants.

6. Discipline is difficult for the mother because of the guilt of being absent. In addition, she does not get to know her child intimately enough for adequate discipline.

7. Emotional disturbance in the child is often related to inadequate mothers, to those who are alcoholics, psychotics, and drug addicts.

8. Children have not had the opportunity "to be a part of the family" and thereby learn the process of decision making and enjoy the resulting emotional growth. Despert believes that children learn the role of

healthy family relationships from their mothers and fathers, not from books.

Despert takes what many might believe to be a regressive position; however, she represents a professional opinion that should demand the attention of educators. She refuses to be overwhelmed by a modernism that robs parents and children of their humanity.

One of the early attempts to study parent-child relationships was made by Adler (1926), who believed that childhood neurosis resulted from parental overindulgence, pampering, and overprotectiveness. Adler's contention was supported by Levy (1943), who found that many emotional abnormalities were caused by maternal overindulgence. Glidewell (1961) summarized the studies of maternal attitudes as having contributed much important information, including a loss of socialization caused by (1) extremes of control (overcontrol or indulgence) and autonomy (ignoring or overprotecting); (2) extremes of acceptance and rejection; (3) variables of confident spontaneity in the acceptance of the maternal role; (4) the capacity of the mother to find real satisfaction with dependent children; and (5) the lack of consistency in the first four dimensions.

In a report by the Joint Commission on Mental Health, Noshpitz (1973) suggests that much uncertainty surrounds the relationship of parents to the mental illness of their children. Some believe that the cause is parental mishandling, others believe that the causes are unknown, whereas many believe that inborn congenital problems are to blame. Noshpitz believes that many problems are caused by the reluctance of teachers, pediatricians, and friends of the family to recommend therapy for children in need of help. Instead they continue to recommend therapy for parents.

Most of the research on child rearing is centered around the role of the mother. This emphasis appears to overlook several important role factors.

1. The sex role provided by fathers seems to be critical for boys and girls. This is particularly important because women generally dominate the lives of young children.
2. Fathers often play a role of helping children set limits that are realistic. Limit-setting is particularly important early in life until the child can develop internal controls.
3. Fathers equalize the fantasy and wish fulfillment of mothers by their attachment to reality (Noshpitz, 1973).

In an early study of atypical development of children, Rank (1949) found three factors to be important in a child's early life: (1) a serious disturbance in the early relationship between the mother and child, (2) a serious disturbance in the early relationship between the father and child, and (3) traumatic events that affect the child. All of these factors are related to the importance of parent-child relationships in developing emotional health.

Although the research presented indicates that parents play an important role in the formation of emotional health, there is no solid evidence that parents of emotionally disturbed children follow a behavioral pattern from which deviance of their children can be reliably predicted. It appears that when deviance is caused by inappropriate parental behavior, it results from an unhealthy interaction between parents and children rather than from any particular behavioral trait of the parents.

The Family

Karnes, Zehrbach, and Teska (1974) have outlined several assumptions regarding families of handicapped children that appear to have much validity for teachers and parents of children in conflict. A summary of these assumptions follows:

1. Families are interested in their children and would like to improve their interaction with their children.
2. Families can be helped to improve their interactions skills.
3. Parents can work in a classroom setting in which their own child is a member.
4. Families will find time to become involved with children if their involvement is meaningful.
5. Family members will learn to interact appropriately when their training is to the point and when direct application is possible.
6. Families are easiest to involve when there is a close match between their goals and values and those of school personnel.
7. When there is a large discrepancy in the match, a greater flexibility will be required of the program.
8. Families will become involved in direct proportion to their ability to participate in decision making.
9. Families will involve themselves most when they are getting positive feedback.
10. Families will involve themselves more when they receive genuine interest as individuals from professionals.
11. Involvement is greatest when trained personnel are working with the family.
12. Families will involve themselves when their involvement is individualized.
13. Families will become more involved if they can pass their information on to others.
14. More positive attitudes will be developed when involvement is successful.
15. Families will need less staff help as they develop skills.
16. Families may develop the skills necessary to be helpful to other families.

This list outlines many of the activities that school personnel should keep in mind as they involve parents in the educational programs of their children.

Activities with parents can be effective and rewarding for teachers, children, and parents. Teachers who have the skills and interest in parent interaction should use their ability to promote a cooperative relationship between the home and school. Those who do not have the skills should learn the skills or rely on another teacher, a social worker, or a school nurse with this competency.

Teachers generally will not have the answers for parents; however, through a sharing of ideas with other educational team members, acceptable solutions to problems can often be achieved and growth can result.

Kroth and Otteni (1983) define the parameters of a comprehensive parent involvement program in a public school system through their Mirror Model of Parental Involvement. Identified by them as important competencies required of the teacher of exceptional children for successful interaction with the children's parents are understanding parental needs and family dynamics (Kroth, 1975, 1985; Simpson, 1982), good listening skills (Benjamin, 1974; Kroth, 1975, 1985; Simpson, 1982), and trust (Kroth & Simpson, 1977; Rutherford & Edgar, 1979; Simpson, 1982).

THE FOCUS OF CHANGE IN SCHOOL—THE TEACHER

Competent teachers are worthwhile to all children; but for children with emotional problems, the teacher is critical for change to occur. Whereas there are many components to a successful program for children in conflict, none is so critical as the teacher, whether it be the teacher of the regular class or the specialist who assists the regular classroom teacher.

The Regular Classroom Teacher

The classroom teacher is the front line of any educational offensive. Although at times education specialists have claimed that classroom teachers could educate effectively only average children, this is obviously untrue. But the results of these claims were that "special educators" have been created for the average child. And efforts to develop better special education programs, education specialists segregated, separated, and splintered the efforts of regular teachers, to the extent that fragmentation of teaching and learning was inevitable.

As education specialists slowly begin changing their emphasis from isolation to encouraging cooperation between regular and special teachers, defenses against change and fears about maintaining role identity will probably develop. Regular classroom teachers who have been asked to refer children in conflict to specialists are now being asked to maintain these children in regular classrooms. This all-or-nothing attitude held by some special educators is disquieting to teachers, who must wonder what is coming next. Most special educators believe that all children in conflict cannot be maintained in the regular classroom and are seeking for these children a continuum of services that will allow each child to function as closely as possible to their peers.

Teacher Competencies. There is no comprehensive guide available to suggest exactly which traits are best for regular classroom teachers who interact with children in conflict. Several characteristics or teacher behaviors appear to be significant, as determined by a study of classrooms where successful integration is taking place. These include the following behavioral traits:

1. *Group management.* Some of the most important skills of regular classroom teachers include group management techniques. Sev-

eral components of classroom management behaviors have been delineated; however, it is debatable whether these skills can be taught. A variety of management skills are necessary, including both small and large groups and individual interaction. In classrooms in a variety of educational settings, classroom management appears to be one of the more serious weaknesses of classroom teachers. When classroom management techniques of a teacher are weak, the addition of children in conflict to the classroom will often create chaos for the entire class.

It is difficult for training institutions to prepare teachers to manage an entire classroom because preservice stations often do not allow classroom management to be placed totally in the hands of untested teachers. It is important for practicum students to be placed with strong supervising teachers who can allow students some failure and still maintain positive control over classroom activities.

2. *Reluctance to give up.* When classroom teachers are bombarded with new expectations almost daily, it is inviting to give up on problem children. There has been little encouragement to do otherwise. In selecting placement sites for children in conflict, education specialists should consider teachers who are not easily discouraged by lack of observable growth in children.

3. *Security in teaching ability.* The regular classroom teacher must be secure in the ability to teach while working as part of a team. This requires an ability to give and take without feeling threatened by the specialists with whom the teacher interacts or being threatening to other team members.

4. *Willingness to teach through strengths.* The regular classroom teacher will generally try to circumvent problem behaviors whenever possible. This requires the teacher to work through each child's strengths to reach stated goals. Looking for the causes of devi-

ant behavior is often an attractive pastime but is a luxury not afforded the regular classroom teacher.

5. *Ability to motivate students.* Much student activity in the regular classroom is self-directed with routine follow-up by the teacher. The ability to motivate self-direction with many students is essential if any individualization is to occur with other children.

6. *Willingness to give more of self.* The classroom teacher who wants to teach children in conflict must be willing to pay the price required. This price often includes extra time in preparation, meetings with educational teams, conferences with parents, and interactions with the resource specialist. Many of these responsibilities will need to be met after school hours and at night. These children are demanding. Change sometimes occurs between 9:00 A.M. and 3:30 P.M., but it often requires longer hours and some inconvenience to the teacher's normal routine.

The Special Teacher

The skills required of the special teacher are essentially the same as those required of good regular classroom teachers. The implementation of these skills does present some difficult problems, however. Various studies of teacher competencies needed have largely related to teachers who work in isolation from the regular class (Bullock & Whelan, 1971; Mackie, Kvaraceus, & Williams, 1957). In their study on characteristics of teachers of the emotionally disturbed, Algozzine, Schmid, and Wells (1982) reveal that modeling appropriate behavior patterns and showing intact personality structure are the most important roles for the teacher of children in conflict. From initial observations of programs in operation, state certification guidelines, and review of literature, it appears that special skills are necessary for resource specialists who work with children in conflict. These include the following competencies:

1. *Flexibility.* The special resource teacher must interact with several teachers during each school day and communicate with the educational team on a regular basis. This requires flexibility and a willingness to adjust to a variety of teaching styles of regular classroom teachers. The specialist cannot and should not change the regular classroom to fit a prescribed mold, but instead, he must often adapt techniques to fit the needs of each classroom unit.

2. *Ability to share expertise.* Professionals who possess special skills have often protected those skills as though sharing might be dangerous. The resource specialist must break with tradition and share expertise with the regular classroom teacher so that cooperation and growth take place. This sharing of skills will encourage the classroom teacher to communicate more fully with the specialist, which should result in more efficient educational programming for all children.

3. *Understanding of techniques for relieving conflict in the regular classroom.* The resource specialist must provide assistance and innovative leadership in approaching recurrent problems facing classroom teachers. Regular class teachers can get into a rut working with behavior problem children. The specialist must be a catalyst for fresh ideas while sustaining the teacher's confidence in managing the classroom learning situation.

4. *Ability to unify.* The resource specialist must be willing and capable of coordinating information from various members of the educational team into a workable plan or program. This requires a low-key but stable approach that lends support to all members and threatens as few as possible. The child in conflict often exhibits behavior that causes tensions within the classroom and among adults trying to help the child.

5. *Willingness to share the glory of success with others.* Experience indicates that the ability to give credit for success to the classroom teacher and other members of the educational team pays high dividends in future cooperation and success. Conversely, taking much of the glory of pupil growth often assures the specialist poor cooperation and failure. It is not unusual to find teachers with fewer curriculum skills who are able to work more effectively in a cooperative setting than teachers with greater skill development. Situations have been observed in which the teacher seemed to become less effective in human relations as teaching skills were developed. Specialists need to develop the knack of saying: "I don't have the answer. Can you help me?" and "Let's work it out together." Asking for help and giving credit to others may be among the most important skills a specialist can develop.

Aside from the general competencies listed for special teachers, there are many specific skills that are generally taken for granted. These include an understanding of exceptional children, the ability to remedy academic weaknesses, an understanding of curriculum and methods used in the regular class, and a desire to learn from others. Many administrators believe that similar competencies are needed by those who act as resource specialists, itinerant teachers, and special class teachers. Although there are similarities in role expectations, there are basic differences that must be considered. With more integration, the specialist must work more closely with classroom teachers; this requires greater skill in areas of human relations and professional interaction. The teacher who works in the isolated setting of a special class needs to be self-motivating, innovative, and capable of functioning with much less professional support. University training programs have been taking a close look at the product that they prepare, trying to supply public schools with well-trained specialists who have the versatility to fit into the pattern of various school districts. Preservice does have many limitations, one of them being the inability to prepare students who can work successfully in all role expectations.

One of the most difficult tasks for school districts is to define clearly the kind of educational programs they want to implement for children in conflict. An early study that compared various programs for emotionally disturbed individuals supports this claim (Morse, Cutler, and Fink, 1964). The science of changing human behavior is surely an inexact science. To bring some order to this inexact process education specialists must carve out some logical goals to help guide their efforts.

Maintaining the Teacher's Mental Health

Teachers are sometimes placed in situations in which no alternatives to failure exist. Some children are so out of touch with reality during part or all of the school day that an adult needs to be with them almost constantly. In addition, teachers need to have interaction and support from "people who count." In a regular classroom the teacher often receives reinforcement from children, from parents, and from ongoing success in the classroom. These reinforcements are often unavailable to special teachers who are working with children in conflict. Reinforcement is often replaced by punishment, which is adroitly administered by children, parents, and even other teachers. Several ideas for maintaining the mental health of the teacher will be considered.

1. *Adequate preparation.* There seems to be no alternative to adequate preservice for teachers. The turnover or dropout rate of teachers who begin teaching children in conflict before they are fully trained is far too high. Being responsible for the educa-

tional program of seriously troubled children is no way to gain teaching competence any more than jumping into ten feet of water is an appropriate way to learn swimming skills.

2. *Adult support.* Conscientious teachers need the support of significant adults if a high level of teaching efficiency is to be maintained. This support must be based on an understanding of program goals and how these goals are being met. The therapeutic team can lend significant support to the classroom teacher, since their interest is verified by interaction with the child.

3. *Human beings first.* Teachers who work with children in conflict are people first and teachers only as a choice of occupation. As people they should engage in stimulating and rewarding activities outside the classroom. Working with children who take rather than give requires the teacher to be renewed constantly. Hobbies, sports, and free time just to relax are all possible renewal activities. A teacher needs to face each new day fully recovered from the problems that were faced the day before.

4. *Awareness of self.* There is no mold of mental health from which teachers should be cut. The fact that teachers exhibit a variety of feelings is actually a strengthening feature of special programs. Each teacher has special strengths and weaknesses of which he or she should be aware. No teacher will enjoy all pupils equally well or be effective with all personality types. As long as this awareness exists, effective programing can be maintained through proper pupil placement. The teacher must feel comfortable in admitting dislike for particular children if acceptable matching of pupils and teachers is to be assured. It is difficult to describe specific personality patterns that seem to work best with children in conflict. Teachers who appeared to be slightly neurotic and/or compulsive have often been observed to do an outstanding job in the classroom with troubled children.

5. *Patience.* Teachers who have not taught children in conflict have a difficult adjustment to make in terms of the time it takes to change behaviors (Fig. 9–1). When children are first screened for special programs, they are often 9 to 11 years of age. These children did not develop problem behavior overnight. Children often feel comfortable with their deviance and will resist change, even if the change is toward more acceptable behavior. Under the best conditions this takes time; "two steps forward and one step back" is often acceptable progress. The teacher who is unable to notice tiny gains or who must compare growth with what is considered "normal" will often become extremely discouraged.

6. *Therapy for the teacher.* It has been suggested that teachers of disturbed children need to receive some form of therapy (Long and Newman, 1971). Although teachers need therapy at the same rate as all other professionals, those who work with children in conflict often need some additional emotional first aid. It was suggested earlier that this can be gained through interaction with the educational team. Long and Newman suggest that a human wailing wall is often needed to help the special teacher. A sympathetic ear needs to be more than just someone to listen; it must be the ear of an informed person who knows the situation and is able to be supportive to the teachers.

Through the years many young and talented teachers have completed the special education training program at the University of Northern Colorado and left to enter a new teaching career. These have been mostly experienced teachers who have already been successful in the classroom. Although most of them have adjusted to the role and expectations of specialists, there have been some notable exceptions. Following are some complaints that often have led to disenchantment and finally to a change in career teaching goals.

1. Some blame the principal. "Our principal doesn't understand special education and what we are trying to do. He acts as though he is afraid of us, never coming near the classroom. We are treated as outcasts (our classroom is where the storage room once was, next to the furnace). We have invited our principal into the classroom, but he is always too busy to come. I can accept the fact that he is busy, but I get the message that he wants to be left alone."

2. Others blame the staff. "The teachers act as though I caused the kids to act the way they do. It's not "our kids" but "your kids." When I try to integrate a child in one of their classes, they do it as a favor to me, not to help the child. One teacher told me she would help me any way she could, but not to send Greg back to her classroom. I want to be part of the staff, but I am always made to feel different."

3. The "system" is blamed by some. "We have a complete special education program in our school, all in my classroom. I'm supposed to be teaching children who are emotionally disturbed, but I teach every conceivable problem. Some of my kids are retarded, some have serious sensory problems, and last week they brought me a physically handicapped child. My room is the dumping ground for all of the kids no one else wants. I'm supposed to work with children for a part of the day and have part of each day to work with teachers, but I have nearly twice as many kids as state regulations allow. When I do a good job, I get reinforced by getting more kids. Some have not been properly evaluated when I get

FIGURE 9–1. Patience can be exhibited in a variety of ways. This teacher has decided to relax and allow the child to learn in a relaxed atmosphere.

them. I'm supposed to be on the evaluation team, and I haven't been called for a meeting for over a month."

4. Parents are sometimes blamed. "The parents of my kids are completely oblivious as to what I'm trying to accomplish. They won't come to school, they won't answer my notes, and they won't invite me to visit their homes. I don't know what they are interested in, but it certainly isn't their kids."

Other problem situations that are often mentioned by discouraged teachers include too many children, no time allowed for planning, inadequate salaries, extra demands made on teachers such as supervising school activities, and lack of supportive personnel. The problems enumerated by special teachers are common to regular classroom teachers as well.

There is no standardized mental health approach for schools to follow. The educational team, described earlier, offers a positive outlet for teachers who interact with other professionals around the needs of children in their classes. This concept could be enlarged to create a focus of discussion for an entire school. Most schools appear to have the professional competence to promote healthy environments for their members. Often this competence has been allowed to become dormant or has been used ineffectively. Teachers and administrators can take the first step by developing a system that is open to discussion, innovation, and appropriate change. In cases of serious morale problems, professional assistance might be needed to get some positive direction.

Support Staff

Although teachers and parents generally spend a greater number of hours with children in conflict than do ancillary personnel, the involvement of this latter group is critical in a holistic approach: For example, a competent teacher aide has always been recognized as one of the essential variables for a strong program in the field. The role played by each of these personnel will vary according to the approach; for example, the social worker's role will generally be different in a behavioral program than in a psychodynamic program.

As Apter (1977) points out, special programs need a unifying force in the identification of a model to serve handicapped children. A model must be developed that capitalizes on the various personnel available to serve the disturbed child. Currently, there is no unified model that specifies the individual role of each professional. It is unlikely that a model which identifies specific roles that will be accepted and adhered to by school administrators will be forthcoming.

Restricted funds and decreasing student population will, of necessity, force administrators to look for less restrictive roles for staff members rather than more restrictive roles. In future educational planning, individuals are likely to be identified by their skills rather than the degree they hold.

In view of the preceding discussion, I will discuss professional needs of children in conflict first and then identify professional persons who could possibly fill these roles.

Student Evaluation. One of the major support functions needed by teachers of children in conflict is the student evaluation. The person most often charged with this responsibility is the school psychologist. Initial evaluation is done before a student leaves the regular classroom, and an exit evaluation should be done before the child is returned full-time to the regular classroom.

Others who participate in the evaluation process include the medical doctor, the school nurse, and the social worker. In some states a psychometrist is responsible for coordination of screening and testing services. When this practice is followed, the psychologist is freed for more concentrated interaction with teachers and students.

In unusual cases, other clinical consultants may participate in the evaluation of a child. These might include a child psychologist, psychiatrist, and pediatrician. Special vocational evaluation often is done by a vocational rehabilitation counselor. This could include evaluation for work, evaluation for possible training programs, job-related counseling, and job placement. Generally, vocational evaluation services would be available only for older students who are nearing working age.

Program Support. In-house program support is a component frequently missing from school programs. The teacher of disturbed children is often responsible for learning experiences for preschool through upper middle school. To expect the teacher to be proficient in all subject areas across a broad range of abilities is an unrealistic expectation in most cases. Reading and mathematics specialists can be of significant assistance in suggesting methods for individual and group interventions as well as remedial interventions.

Regular class teachers should also be involved with the ongoing program of children in conflict. This involvement should begin with program planning and continue through implementation.

Liaison to the Home and Community. The liaison who works with parents, "significant others" in the community, and mental health agencies is a critical person in any successful program. Several different professionals would be acceptable for this role. The skills needed are knowledge of specific program goals, the ability to relate effectively with a wide variety of professional and lay persons, and the ability to work in a coordinating and unifying role. The school nurse, school psychologist, social worker, and classroom teacher all have demonstrated effectiveness in the liaison role.

Programs that do not have the services of a liaison person often are fragmented and without common goals. The liaison person serves as a contact with local mental health agencies, physicians, and other community and school-based agencies. The skilled liaison can offer much insight into the school operation through collaboration with professionals from legal agencies and detention centers. The liaison person is removed far enough from the classroom to have a healthy perspective but is still close enough to be involved and concerned with the growth of the program.

Crisis Intervention and Therapy. The classroom teacher is usually responsible for crisis intervention; however, some classroom units have used counselors, social workers, and psychologists to fill this need. Although teachers are often the most logical for this role, others, with critical attention to coordination, can fulfill this need.

Educational therapy can take several logical directions. Although all of the therapies are not necessary for every student, a choice should be possible for individual concerns. Art, music, and recreational specialists offer skills in their respective areas that are beneficial to children in conflict. Specialists working in these areas are still, unfortunately, very rare in both public school and clinical situations.

SUMMARY

Several key personnel must be effective agents of change for children in conflict.

The vital role of parents is outlined. As agents of change, parents can be some of the stronger co-workers with teachers if allowed to participate in the change process. A posture of cooperation is all that is needed in many cases to stimulate this change.

Parents of emotionally disturbed children have been the subject of many studies that attempt to discover their unique qualities. Most of these are weakened because they focus only on the mothers of disturbed children. Emotional disturbance in children appears to result from an inappropriate interaction that develops between parents and the child rather than because of any specific behavioral traits of parents.

The special teacher needs to have a certain flexibility and ability to share expertise with other professionals, an understanding of techniques to relieve conflicts in a regular classroom, an ability to unify, and a willingness to share the glory of success with others.

Teachers must not only be psychologically healthy on entry to the classroom but able to maintain their mental health. Adequate preparation, adult support, self-awareness, and patience are a few of the important factors in remaining healthy.

Ancillary personnel are discussed in relation to both the teacher and the child. These include the psychologist, counselor, social worker, art and music therapists, and other specialists who often are supportive to the educational endeavors of teachers.

The various roles of support staff are identified and the value of shared responsibility, planning, and intervention is discussed.

BIBLIOGRAPHY

Adler, A. (1926). *The neurotic constitution: Outlines of a comparative individualistic psychology and psychotherapy.* New York: Dodd, Mead & Co.

Algozzine, B., Schmid, R., & Wells, D. (1982). Characteristics of teachers of emotionally disturbed adolescents. *Adolescence, 17*(65), 167–175.

Apter, S. J. (1977). Applications of ecological therapy: Toward a community special education model. *Exceptional Children, 43,* 366–372.

Benjamin, A. (1974). *The helping interview.* Boston: Houghton Mifflin.

Bullock, L. M., & Whelan, R. J. (1971). Competencies needed by teachers of emotionally disturbed and socially maladjusted: A comparison. *Exceptional Children, 37,* 485–489.

Casey, R. (1983). *The relationship between school performance during residential treatment and post-discharge school adjustment of emotionally disturbed children.* Unpublished doctoral dissertation, University of New Mexico, Albuquerque.

Despert, L. (1965). *The emotionally disturbed child: An inquiry into family patterns.* Garden City, NY: Anchor Books.

Glidewell, J. (1961). *Parental attitudes and child behavior*. Springfield, IL.: Charles C Thomas.

Glueck, S., & Glueck, E. (1950). *Unraveling juvenile delinquency*, New York: The Commonwealth Fund.

Hobbs, N. (1978). Classification options: A conversation with Nicholas Hobbs on exceptional child education. *Exceptional Children, 44*(7), 474–497.

Karnes, M., Zehrbach, R., & Teska, J. (1974). Involving families of handicapped children. In T. Kelly, L. Lyndall, & M. Dykes (Eds.), *School and community resources for the behaviorally handicapped*. New York: MSS Information Corp.

Kroth, R. L. (1985). *Communicating with parents of exceptional children* (2nd ed.). Denver: Love Publishing.

Kroth, R. L. (1980). *Strategies for effective parent-teacher interaction*. Albuquerque, NM: University of New Mexico, Institute for Parent Involvement.

Kroth, R. L. (1975). *Communicating with parents of exceptional children*. Denver, CO.: Love Publishing.

Kroth, R. L., & Otteni, H. (1983). Parent education programs that work: A model. *Focus on Exceptional Children, 15*(8), 1–16.

Kroth, R. L. & Simpson, R. L. (1977). *Parent conference as a teaching strategy*. Denver: Love Publishing.

Levy, D. (1943). *Maternal overprotection*. New York: Columbia University Press.

Long, N., & Newman, R. (1971). The teacher and his mental health. In N. Long, W. Morse, & R. Newman (Eds.), *Conflict in the classroom*. Belmont, CA: Wadsworth.

Mackie, R., Kvaraceus, W., & Williams, H. (1957). *Teachers of children who are socially and emotionally handicapped*. Washington, DC: U.S. Government Printing Office.

Morse, W., Cutter, R., & Fink, A. (1964). *Public school classes for the emotionally handicapped: A research analysis*. Washington, DC: Council for Exceptional Children.

Noshpitz, J. (Ed.). (1973). Report of the Committee on Clinical Issues. In S. Lustman, *The mental health of children: Services, research, and manpower*. New York: Harper and Row.

Peter, L. (1965). *Prescriptive teaching*. New York: McGraw-Hill.

Rank, B. (1949). Adaptation of the psychoanalytic technique for the treatment of young children with atypical development. *American Journal of Orthopsychiatry, 19*, 130–139.

Rutherford, R. G., & Edgar, E. (1979). *Teachers and parents: A guide to interaction and cooperation*. Boston: Allyn & Bacon.

Simpson, R. L. (1982). *Conferencing parents of exceptional children*. Rockville, MD: Aspen Systems Corp.

Stendler, C. (1950). Sixty years of child training practices: Revolution in the nursery. *Journal of Pediatrics, 36*, 122–134.

Yoshida, R. K., et al. (1978). Parental involvement in the special education pupil planning process: The school's perspective. *Exceptional Children, 44*, 531–534.

10

Program Development: Techniques and Materials

INTRODUCTION AND OBJECTIVES

Teaching children in conflict is now an accepted reality in almost every community in the United States. Even though many programs cannot be considered to be mature examples of good programs, there has been remarkable improvement during the past decade.

The objectives of this chapter are to review the present state-of-the-art programming for the emotionally disturbed and to acquaint teachers with a variety of techniques and materials available for their use. In recent years the number and quality of affective materials available to teachers have grown dramatically. Materials are now available for all age levels, from preschool through adulthood. Many of these materials will need to be adapted to the needs of individuals and groups.

There is no systematic model to research the specific instructional requirements of such children (Swanson & Reinert, 1984). Most private and agency-sponsored efforts have been toward the identification, evaluation, and cataloging of the materials available to teachers and clinicians. This approach appears to be working effectively for teachers who build individual programs around their students' needs. Material selections are made according to the goals and objectives for each child and only those materials that show promise of meeting individual objectives are used.

Recently the flexibility and teaching potential of small, personalized computers has offered exciting possibilities for teachers of children in conflict. Their potential will be reviewed in this chapter.

Swanson and Reinert (1984) outlined several important aspects of materials selection; these can be used as a guide in the choice, adaptation, and development of educational materials.

1. Materials should consider affect and behavior problems of the child.
2. Materials should be sequenced.
   a. The beginning of each material should reflect the simplest level necessary for a student's comprehension.
   b. A series of tasks are present, each of which represents a prescribed increment of difficulty over the previous one.
   c. Each task in the series should embody or build upon all the previous ones. The first would present the concept in its simplest form or at the highest level of difficulty with which the child can cope. The second contains the idea of the first task in a slightly more difficult form, and so on through the series of tasks.
   d. The amount of increment in difficulty is, if possible, exactly what the child can negotiate, no more, no less.
3. Materials should be reduced to their major components. The teacher should decide on the major points of the curriculum content and see if they can be presented by being condensed, rewritten, or presented through another sensory modality and programmed to promote retention.
4. Materials should have "success insurance": built-in opportunities for success in an accumulative manner within a firm structure to help the student perform in a productive, consistent manner.
5. Materials should capitalize on the student's interests and/or age level and peer interest.
6. Materials should approximate the content level of that for the student's peers.
7. Materials should be used that are at the leading edge of the student's ability level.
8. Interest should be enticed, created, or magnified by the use of color, game or puzzle contexts, picture completion tasks, or similar techniques that enhance active involvement.
9. Materials should be analyzed through different sequenced approaches to a single goal objective in a horizontal analysis of the subject area.
10. Materials should be selected, adapted, or created to meet predetermined objectives.

11. Materials need to have immediate checks to indicate successful performance.

When deciding whether to use commercially available materials, adapt new materials, or create new ones, teachers should ask themselves the following questions (from Swanson & Reinert, 1984):

1. Do the materials move the student to the selected objective?
2. Have these materials been developed elsewhere? Where can I get them?
3. Can they be adapted for use with another student?
4. What will they cost in both money and teacher time?
5. Are the materials reproducible, or can they be used only once?
6. Will they take time I can best spend on another task? Can I reach the objective in another way?
7. How valuable will they be to this child and others?

Microcomputers

Though we are only in the beginning stages of programming for education through computer technology, the future is bright, with enormous potential. Leneway and Montegomery (1981) state that "the lives of many handicapped persons have been vastly improved by computer technology . . . but millions wait to be served" (p. 49). Computer applications in special education are numerous. For example, classroom management systems enable teachers to tailor curriculum to individualized education plans; a talking wheelchair will assist nonverbal students to communicate with others; a computer language called Logo is giving children with learning dysfunctions the key to unlock their own potential; and Versabraille/Braille Edit, a computer program, immediately translates written materials into braille. In the near future, it will be a required competency for teachers to be able to incorporate this expanding technology into their practice.

Hardware and Software

There is microcomputer hardware available for nearly every budget and need. Hardware consists of the computer, the disc drive, a monitor, and a printer. While all of these components, other than the computer, are not essential, they become so once you begin using the equipment seriously. The cost of this equipment varies widely, but can cost as little as $2,500 or as much as $10,000. For those working in schools, the selection of hardware might be made for you. If you are going to buy equipment for your personal use, you may want to consider how the school's equipment and programs will interface with yours so that you can carry your work home, as many professionals seem to do.

Schools that are considering acquiring hardware should consider a lease arrangement, since hardware is changing so rapidly. When one buys hardware the equipment may need to be kept beyond its most useful time period.

Once the decision to buy or lease is made, the program will need to consider the kind of system needed. Generally, there are several staff members who are interested, knowledgeable, and willing to help select hardware. A small group can be very effective in deciding what the needs of the program are and how they can be met most effectively. Once the needs are established, it makes the elimination and selection of hardware a much easier task.

The selection of software for purchase should be made only after an interested group studies the alternatives and selects software that serves the needs of the program most effectively. A major component of instructional planning is the development and implementation of the Individual Educational Program (IEP). Software is available to make this process more efficient and useful.

The IEP program can store goals and objectives and facilitate the performance of other repetitive tasks. Team members can work together from the monitor to select appropriate goals for the child under study. In addition, lists of teaching strategies (along with appropriate identification of the most useful application of each) can free staff members of both tedious identification and matching of needs and techniques. Some programs permit the entire IEP—from identifying information, anticipated duration of services, goals and objectives, placement, evaluation, materials, and teaching strategies—to be programmed and managed by computer (Bennett, 1982).

Supplementing instruction is useful for some handicapped students, particularly those who find interaction with adults difficult. Individual lessons can be programmed so that children can learn at their own rate. Thus there is no frustration on the part of the instructor and, likely, less frustration on the part of the learner. The Kurzweil Reading Machine (KRM) uses the microprocessor, optical scanner, and voice synthesizer to produce synthetic speech. It can read books, magazines, and other printed material (Weinberg, 1980). Teachers of children in conflict can develop many uses for the microcomputer for individualizing materials in non-threatening formats.

In recent years there has been much concern regarding the amount of actual instruction each youngster receives in the classroom. The microcomputer offers the opportunity for meaningful, individualized computer-assisted instruction and provides time for the teacher to interact personally where needed in the classroom.

Related services such as counseling, various therapies, and communication offer additional avenues for the use of microcomputers. The number of software packages available is increasing dramatically. These materials will be useful for specific types of handicapped children who have unique needs.

In addition to the uses of computers outlined by Bennett, there are other uses being proposed. Hofmeister (1982) suggests staff development through computer-assisted instruction (CAI) as one way to increase the personnel's computer literacy. He also suggests using computers for vocational guidance, and electronic mail for faster and more efficient communication.

With all of the emphasis presently being placed on microcomputers, it is easy to overlook the potential pitfalls. A major concern is poor quality software. As teachers become more literate in computer processes, there will be better interfacing of education and technology.

PUBLISHED MATERIALS

The published materials identified in this section were selected because (a) they are being used successfully (or show promise) with children in conflict; (b) they have affective components; and (c) they are useful for school-age persons.

Computer Hardware

Apple Computer
10260 Bandley Drive
Cupertino, California 95014

Atari, Inc.
1265 Borregas Avenue
Sunnyvale, California 94086

Commodore Computer Systems
681 Moore Road
King of Prussia, Pennsylvania 19406

Epson America, Inc. (dot-matrix printer)
3415 Kashiwa Street
Torrance, California 90505

Heathkit Electronics Corp.
P.O. Box 167
St. Joseph, Michigan 49805

IBM
P.O. Box 1328
Boca Raton, Florida 33432

Non-Linear Systems (Kaycomp II)
533 Stevens Avenue
Solana Beach, California 91202

North Star Computers, Inc.
14440 Catalina Street
San Leandro, California 94577

Osborne Computer Corporation
26500 Corporate Avenue
Hayward, California 94545

Otrona Corporation (Attache Computer)
4755 Walnut Street
Boulder, Colorado 80301

Radio Shack
1600 Tandy Center
Fort Worth, Texas 76102

Smith-Corona
65 Locust Avenue
New Canaan, Connecticut 06840

Software

Aspen Software
P.O. Box 339
Tijeras, New Mexico 87059

Discount Software
6520 Selma Avenue, Suite 309
Los Angeles, California 90028

Individual Educational Plans
Learning Systems, P.O. Box 15
Marblehead, MA 01945

Hartley Courseware, Inc.
P.O. Box 431
Dimondale, Michigan 48821

Lifeboat Associates
1651 3rd Avenue
New York, New York 10028

MicroPro International
1229 Fourth Street
San Rafael, California 94901

Muse Software
330 North Charles Street
Baltimore, Maryland 21202

Oasis Systems
2765 Reynard Way
San Diego, California 92103

Peach Tree Software
3 Corporate Square, Suite 700
Atlanta, Georgia 30329

RETOOL
1920 Association Drive
Reston, VA 22091
Sponsored by The Council for Exceptional
  Children. Programs for teachers to modify
  curriculum and survival strategies for special
  teachers.

Ring King Visibles (diskette storage files)
215 West Second Street
Muscatine, Iowa 52761

Special Administration System
Sysdata International, Inc.
7671 Old Central Avenue NE
Minneapolis, MN 55432

Special Education Computerized Information
  System (CIS)
Dallas Independent School District
2517 S. Ervay
Dallas, TX 75215

Special Educational Retrieval System
Learning Well
200 South Service Road
Roslyn Heights, NY 11577

Special Net (National Association of State
  Directors of Special Education)
2021 K Street NW, Suite 315
Washington, D.C. 20006

CEC Software Search Evaluation Form (CEC,
  1983)
Council for Exceptional Children
1920 Association Drive
Reston, Virginia 22091

Modified MCE Program Evaluation Form
  (Taber, 1983)
MCE, Inc.
157 Kalamazoo Mall
Kalamazoo, MI 49007

Courseware Evaluation Form (Naiman, 1982)
Microcomputer Resource Center
Teacher College, Columbia University
212 Hamilton Hall
New York, NY 10025

MicroSIFT Courseware Evaluation
Northwest Regional Educational Laboratory
300 SW Sixth Avenue
Portland, OR 97204

Magazines

BYTE
P.O. Box 590
Martinsville, New Jersey 08836

Creative Computing
Box 789–M
Morristown, New Jersey 07960

Interface Age
P.O. Box 1234
Cerritos, California 90701

Personal Computing
4 Disk Drive
Box 1408
Riverton, New Jersey 08077

The Computing Teacher
University of Oregon
1787 Agate Street
Eugene, Oregon 97403–1923

Clearinghouses

Computer Assisted Instruction for Handicapped
    Children and Youth
CEC Publication Sales
1920 Association Drive
Reston, Virginia 22091

MECC (Minnesota Educational Computing
    Consortium)
2520 Broadway Drive
St. Paul, MN 55113

Use of Computers in Regular and Special
    Education
Teacher Education
CEC Publication Sales
1920 Association Drive
Reston, Virginia 22091

Apple Computer Clearinghouse for the
    Handicapped
Prentke Romich Company
RD 2, Box 191
Serene, Ohio 44676

Trace Software Registry and Listing of Programs
    Adapted for Rehabilitation
Applications with Microcomputers

Trace Research and Development Center for
    Severely Communicatively Handicapped
University of Wisconsin
1500 Highland Avenue
Madison, Wisconsin 53706

INSTRUCTIONAL RESOURCES AND MATERIALS

Child's Series on Psychologically Relevant Themes

AUTHOR: *Joan Fassler*
PUBLISHER: *Videorecord Corporation of America*
DATE OF PUBLICATION: *1971*
LEVEL: *Preschool and elementary grades*
    Child's Series on Psychologically Relevant Themes is a videorecord program that is based on bibliotherapy (helping children to solve their problems through identification with literary characters who have similar problems). The series contains six video cassettes, ranging in length from six to eight minutes, thus holding the attention of younger children. Each cassette contains a beautifully illustrated story, which is narrated by a child; this aids in the identification process necessary for bibliotherapy to be effective.

The teacher's guide contains a brief synopsis of each story, discussion questions, and relevant activities that correspond to each story. The stories in the videorecord program are described below.

The Man of the House. A little boy, David, takes over his father's role and becomes the protector of his mother while his father is away. He is happy when his father returns because he loves and needs him, but he is a little bit sad because he is no longer "the man of the house."

Don't Worry Dear. Jenny was a little girl who wet her bed, sucked her thumb, stuttered, and cared for her stuffed animal, Barky, as if he were real. The boys from down the street laughed at Jenny when she stuttered. Her mother was upset but said, "Don't worry dear, when you get bigger you won't talk like that." One day Jenny's aunts came to visit and told her mother to put bitter medicine on her thumb, but she disregarded their advice and said, "Don't worry dear, when you get bigger you won't feel like sucking your thumb anymore." And she didn't.

A Boy with a Problem. Johnny had a problem; it upset him so much he could not eat, do his school work, or sleep. He even had a stomachache. Johnny took his problem to the doctor, his teacher, and his mother; they all gave him advice before he told them what his problem was. His problem persisted until his friend Peter came to call. Peter was a good listener and allowed Johnny to tell him his whole problem. Johnny slept that night and felt much better.

All Alone with Daddy. Ellen is enjoying her stay with her father while her mother is away visiting. When her mother returns, she becomes jealous and resentful of her. Later she realizes that if she grows up to be just like her mother she may marry a man like her father. And she did.

One Little Girl. Laurie, a little girl, is "slow in school," and she has problems with reading and mathematics. Laurie is unhappy because people refer to her as a "slow child." She discovers that if she concentrates on what she does well instead of complaining about the things she does not do well, she will be happy.

Grandpa Died Today. David's grandfather died. They had been very close; they had talked about special things and played ball together. The story deals with David's struggle to understand his grandfather's death, and his reactions to this sad situation.

Videorecords express the psychodynamic viewpoint; many of the stories provide excellent introductory material for discussing relevant topics (death, accepting one's deficits, coping with a problem). Strong emphasis is placed on the Oedipus and Electra complexes (in *All Alone with Daddy* and *The Man of the House*).

First Things

AUTHOR: *Joseph C. Grannis (concept development and curriculum design) and Virginia Schone (script for filmstrips)*

PUBLISHER: *Guidance Associates of Pleasantville, New York*

DATE OF PUBLICATION: *1970*

LEVEL: *Primary grades*

First Things is designed to introduce the primary grade child to the basic concepts in both the physical and social environment. The program aims at helping the child to understand himself or herself better as an individual and as a member of a group. It helps the child to identify with and recognize the various interactions that occur within groups. *First Things* increases the child's awareness of the effect of these interactions on the individual and helps the child to see how expectations influence interactions. The program deals with five themes: (1) *Who do you think you are?* (2) *Guess who's in a group!* (3) *What happens between people?* (4) *You got mad: Are you glad?* and (5) *What do you expect of others?* Each theme is accompanied by two or three sound filmstrips, which are designed to be motivational. The manual suggests activities to follow each filmstrip that are designed to get the child involved with the theme, to interest the child in collecting and examining data about himself or herself and his or her relationships with others. The activities revolve around observation, classification, sociodrama, and experimentation. The manual states the objectives of each theme, the concepts discussed, and the generalizations that can be drawn from each theme. Suggestions for facilitating discussion are also given to aid the teacher.

The themes of the *First Things* program are interrelated. *Who do you think you are?* deals with the idea that an individual is a combination of facts and figures, actions, and feelings. *Guess who's in a group!* deals with what a group is, the different types of groups, how being part of a group affects people, and the norms of different groups. The concepts dealt with in *What happens between people?* are interactions (both physical and symbolic), goals, and conflicts. *You got mad: Are you glad?* explores the causes, effects, and ways in which hostility is expressed, as well as the ways that conflict can be handled and resolved. *What do you expect of others?* considers the ideas of expectation and prejudgments, how things live up to people's expectations, and the need to be open to people who are different before making prejudgments.

First Things fosters conceptual thinking and can serve to increase the child's listening vocabulary. Ideas and concepts are presented clearly, and the incidents used to present the themes on the filmstrips are easy for the young child to identify with, for example, moving, meeting new friends, or being excluded from a group.

DUSO D–1 (Developing Understanding of Self and Others—Revised)

AUTHOR: *Don Dinkmeyer and Don Dinkmeyer, Jr.*

PUBLISHER: *American Guidance Service*

DATE OF PUBLICATION: *1982*

LEVEL: *Kindergarten and lower primary grades*

The *DUSO–I Revised* program is designed to be used by the teacher or elementary school counselor to help the primary grade child understand social and emotional behavior. The DUSO–I Revised activities "make extensive use of a listening-inquiry, experi-ential, and discussion approach to learning." Listening activities rarely extend for more than five minutes, reflecting the consideration given to the short attention span of the young child. The program helps the child to build a vocabulary; strong focus is put on teaching the child words that can be used to express feelings. The program also focuses on the dynamic relationship between feelings, goals, and behaviors, and helps the child learn how to express herself freely.

The DUSO–I Revised program revolves around eight unit themes, each containing four or five cycle themes. The program is designed for use over a full academic year. The eight unit themes follow:

Understanding and Accepting Self is introduced by presenting the following rules of group discussion: (1) raise your hand, (2) listen carefully, (3) don't clam up, (4) stick to the point, and (5) think together. The major emphasis of this unit is to help the child to develop a realistic self-concept, to be aware of his strengths and liabilities, and to build on his strengths.

Understanding Feelings focuses on helping the child to understand and express both positive and negative feelings. Activities evolve around the ideas of sharing, being sensitive to the feelings of others, and building friendships.

Understanding Others emphasizes helping the child understand what working in a group entails (cooperation and responsibility), and the benefits inherent in working together.

Understanding Independence focuses on helping the child see the benefits of doing things for himself, on doing the best he can, and on the importance of evaluating the consequences of one's actions.

Understanding Goals and Purposeful Behavior helps the child to devise a systematic, appropriate, realistic approach to work. Emphasis is placed on evaluating the whole job, seeing its component parts, establishing an appropriate plan of action, and proceeding efficiently.

Understanding Mastery, Competence, and Resourcefulness focuses on helping the child realistically understand his capacities. The idea that competency and achievement are results of both desire and ability is stressed.

Understanding Emotional Maturity helps the child to investigate both effective and ineffective ways of dealing with stress and change. The activities focus on the ineffectiveness of worrying, crying, throwing temper tantrums, impatience, anger, etc.

Understanding Choice and Consequences helps the child to understand that feelings, values, and behaviors are interrelated. It stresses the need to make value judgments, to hold to beliefs under group pressure, and to accept the consequences of his choice.

The *DUSO D–1* program is packaged in a convenient metal carrying case, and all the components are bound or packaged in vinyl folders. The kit contains the following:

1. A manual, which includes the rationale and objectives of the program, the stated purpose of each activity, and clear directions for conducting the program. Discussion activities, supplementary activities, and reading are also included.
2. Two storybooks, which contain 41 stories and 200 beautiful colored illustrations. The stories are designed to introduce each cycle theme and to motivate discussion.
3. Thirty-three full-colored posters, which state the main idea of each cycle story.
4. Thirty-three puppet and 33 role-playing cards to provide the child with opportunities to dramatize real-life situations connected with the cycle themes.
5. Seven puppets.
6. Puppet props, which help the children to create the desired setting for their puppet shows.
7. Group discussion cards, which present the five rules for group discussion.

The *DUSO D–1* program is excellent. Most characters are animals or Duso's underwater friends, which adds to the delight of the children. The discussion, role playing,

and puppet activities allow the children to become involved with the topics and allow their creativity to be expressed.

Focus on Self-Development, Stage Two: Responding

AUTHORS: *Judith L. Anderson and Patricia Miner*

PUBLISHER: *Science Research Associates, Inc.*

DATE OF PUBLICATION: *1971*

LEVEL: *Elementary grades*

Focus on Self-Development is an audiovisual guidance program for the elementary grades. The program is designed to be used by the classroom teacher. Its purpose is to get the child to think and act about himself or herself, others, and his or her environment in an intelligent fashion. The program is based on 19 units: three on environmental influences, six on the personal self, eight on the social self, and an introductory and summary unit. The units and their objectives are as follows:

1. Self-concept: helps the child to realize he responds differently in different situations
2. Interests: the child becomes aware of social, emotional, and intellectual aspects of himself
3. Abilities: helps the child to explore his interests
4. Limitations: the child comes to understand his abilities and limitations
5. Goals: helps the child to find his goals and to understand how he may approach them
6. Concerns: discusses the death of a dog and how to deal with such problems
7. Responsibility: describes what responsibility is and what it entails
8. Physical environment: the child becomes aware of how his environment affects him
9. Cultural differences: the child learns to accept and understand people with different backgrounds
10. Social influences: provides awareness of how attitudes toward others affect personal interaction with the individual

11. Communication: discusses what it means to communicate

12. Honesty: child becomes aware of the effects honesty and dishonesty have on others

13. Companionship: discusses the concepts of friendship

14. Acceptance and rejection: helps the child to deal with rejection

15. Respect: discusses respect and the lack of it and how it affects others

16. Trust: discusses the effects of trust or the lack of it on others

17. Loyalty: the child explores what it means to be loyal

18. Competition and cooperation: discusses winning and losing in relation to the competitive spirit

19. Summary: the child is asked to reflect on the year's work and to determine how his behavior has changed

The materials included in the program are as follows:

1. The teacher's guide, which presents the purposes, content, and components of the program. Suggestions are given to help the teacher introduce the various units. Questions for discussion and a list of supplementary materials are enclosed. The appendix of the teacher's guide gives suggestions on group techniques, including principles of guidance, how to set up a role-playing activity, role of the teacher, and working with feelings.

2. A workbook, *The Me I Know*, that allows the child to express his personal feelings about the concepts presented in the units. (The workbook is regarded as the child's property; the child should not be required to show his or her work or lack of it to the teacher.)

3. Filmstrips. Six of the themes' activities revolve around filmstrips with accompanying sound tracks.

4. Story records. All themes not introduced

by a filmstrip utilize story records to present the themes.

5. Photoboards. Twenty two-sided photoboards and a displaying easel to stimulate discussions and role-playing activities are included.

Focus on Self-Development is a total counseling program that will produce desirable results when used by the creative teacher.

Bill Martin's Freedom Books

AUTHOR: *Bill Martin, Jr.*
PUBLISHER: *Bowmar Publishing Corp.*
DATE OF PUBLICATION: *1970*
LEVEL: *Fifth to twelfth grades*

The *Freedom Books* are designed to be used with fifth- through twelfth-grade children as a social studies program. (However, they appear to be usable with fifth- through ninth-graders because of the simplicity of the text and the nature of many of the recommended activities.) The *Freedom Books* depart from the usual textbook format, which stresses reading ability, memorization, and the development of study habits, and emphasize the building of conceptual abilities. The themes of these books revolve around the author's desire to "help children keep faith in the American Dream." The subject matter is mostly nationalistic, and the program is designed to inspire creative, analytical thinking about the problems that confront people. The author describes the purpose of the books as follows: "The first purpose of the *Freedom Books* is delight." The second is creative involvement, the third is analytical investigation, and the fourth is to help the child organize personal and social meaning.

The books are beautifully illustrated, with a multiplicity of techniques. The story lines are short and written in poetic verse. In most of the books, the story line is contained in the illustrations, and in some of the books it departs from the left-right progression across the page. This style can make reading more joyous but also limits the use of this program. Children who have learning problems in reading, figure-ground discrimination problems, or visual perceptual problems might have a difficult time using these books as readers. The program, in addition to the books and teacher's manual, includes a tape or record for each book. On the tape the author reads or sings the story line, provides musical accompaniment for the children to read by, discusses his ideas about the theme of the story, has a discussion with the illustrator of the book, and in some instances sings songs or reads poems and/or stories related to the theme of the book. The use of these tapes creates a language model for the children and helps them to see how effectively words can be used to express thoughts and feelings. As a result of the repetitive nature of verse, many words become part of the child's vocabulary almost unconsciously. Many new words are introduced in a nonchalant manner in the tape discussions as well.

The entire program is designed and presented in a delightful fashion. Even the teacher's manual is designed creatively. It includes the purposes of the program, the stories, and suggestions for creative involvement and discussions. Dance and dramatization make up a large part of the program, the stories, and suggestions for interaction with the themes of these books. The creative presentation of this material and its focus on creative, analytical thinking aid in motivating the uninterested child.

Each book deals with a specific theme. *I Am Freedom's Child* emphasizes the need for a positive self-concept and the acceptance and appreciation of differences among people. *Gentle, Gentle Thursday* points out that everyone needs time for themselves, a gentle Thursday, to be a contributing member of society. It stresses the need for people to be in touch with their personal feelings and

desires and to reflect on the demands others are putting on them. *I Reach Out to the Morning* deals with the individual's reactions to things and people that are strange and different and stresses the need for the individual to accept and not be frightened by the differences encountered. *Freedom's Apple Tree* evolves around the idea that every individual is an important component in the make-up of a free society. *America, I Know You* deals with the idea that "America is a collection of beliefs, happenings and circumstances of times conflicting that need to be understood." *Poor Old Uncle Sam* stresses the importance of believing in the value system of America. *It's America for Me* points out that protest is part of America and that the diversity of opinions contributes to making America a land of personal freedom. *Once There Were Bluebirds* focuses on the beauty of nature and on the fact that this beauty is being threatened by pollution. *Spoiled Tomatoes* also deals with the theme of pollution, showing how pollution can shift the balance of nature. The last book in the series, *Adam's Balm*, is concerned with the threat of the atomic bomb and deals with the ideas behind nuclear disarmament.

The Adventures of the Lollipop Dragon

PUBLISHER: *Society for Visual Education, Inc.*
DATE OF PUBLICATION: *1970*
LEVEL: *Primary grades*

The Adventures of the Lollipop Dragon is a sound filmstrip program for the primary grade child. Six filmstrips portray stories that focus on the concepts of sharing, working together, littering, caring for personal property, taking turns, and being kind to animals. The first filmstrip introduces the Lollipop Dragon, who is the main character of the program. The program is designed to motivate discussion and interest in the concepts that are presented, and it can be utilized in the classroom media center or for individualized instruction.

The kit contains (1) a teacher's guide, which states the objectives of the program and scripts that correspond to the cassette recordings of the stories; (2) a coloring book that is analogous to the first filmstrip, *How the Lollipop Dragon Got His Name*; (3) filmstrips; and (4) cassettes or records.

The Lollipop Dragon appears to have great appeal for young children. The filmstrips are beautiful illustrations of a small kingdom where lollipops are made. The morals of the stories often appear to be overemphasized, but this does not detract from the child's enjoyment of the program.

DUSO D–2 (Developing Understanding of Self and Others—Revised)

AUTHOR: *Don Dinkmeyer and Don Dinkmeyer, Jr.*
PUBLISHER: *American Guidance Service*
DATE OF PUBLICATION: *1982*
LEVEL: *Upper primary and fourth grades (ages 7 to 10 years)*

The *DUSO–2 Revised* program is designed to help children meet the challenge of personal development and social growth through sets of activities that address specific affective goals. These activities include appealing stories, songs, discussion, career activities, problem situation and guided fantasies. The *DUSO–2 Revised* program employs the inquiry method of learning to facilitate eight skill areas. The eight major themes follow:

Towards Self-Identity: Developing Self-Awareness and a Positive Self-Concept
Towards Friendship: Understanding Peers
Towards Responsible Interdependence: Understanding Growth from Self-Centeredness to Social Interest
Towards Self-Reliance: Understanding Personal Responsibility
Towards Resourcefulness and Purposefulness: Understanding Personal Motivation
Towards Competence: Understanding Accomplishments
Towards Emotional Stability: Understanding Stress
Towards Responsible Choice Making: Understanding Values

The general objectives around which these themes revolve are developing understanding about the value of a good self-concept and of interpersonal relationships; the teleological aspects of human behavior (in both cognitive and affective domains); the dynamic interrelationship of ideas, feelings, beliefs, and behaviors that enable people to express feelings accurately; and understanding the components of achievement.

The *DUSO D–2* materials are well organized and are contained in a convenient metal carrying case. They include the following:

1. The manual, which presents the general format for the *DUSO D–2* program. Each cycle includes a story, a problem situation, a role-playing activity, a discussion picture, a career awareness activity, and supplementary activities and readings. Guidelines for the presentation of these activities are in the manual.

2. Eight self and social development activity cards that are designed to be used early in the program and are aimed at helping children become better informed about themselves and others through involvement and activities that stress communication.

3. Seventeen records or five cassettes that contain dramatizations of stories and songs that correspond to the cycles. These are designed for high motivation.

4. Thirty-three colored posters that review the themes of each story and which are included in a vinyl folder that can be used as a display easel.

5. Thirty-three role-playing activity cards.

6. Thirty-three puppet activity cards, designed to give children the opportunity to dramatize situations that are related to the cycle themes.
7. Eight puppets for role playing.
8. Thirty-three career awareness cards, designed to relate cycle themes to career awareness and exploration.
9. Thirty-three discussion pictures (and an introduction card) that are related to cycles and themes are designed to stimulate discussion about feelings, attitudes, values, and purposes the child perceives and interprets.
10. Six discussion guide cards, which are presented in the introductory lesson. They are designed to stimulate discussion and are recommended for use throughout the program. The activity cards are packaged in vinyl folders, and each day's activity is printed on a separate card. This makes the kit more manageable during use.

The instructions for use of the various components of the program are very explicit; however, because of the expressive, open nature of the activities, the teacher must be adept in carrying on discussions and motivating productive participation. The *DUSO D-2* program is an excellent tool for helping children to understand themselves and others better and, if used by a skilled teacher, can be of great benefit to the child in conflict.

Dimensions of Personality

AUTHOR: *Walter Limbacher*
PUBLISHER: *George A. Pflaum Publisher, Inc., and Standard Reference Works Publishing Co.*
DATE OF PUBLICATION: *1969*
LEVEL: *Fourth to sixth grades*
    Dimensions of Personality is a graded program in affective education. It is intended for use in the elementary grades, junior high

school, and high school. Materials for fourth-, fifth-, and sixth-grade students were written by Walter Limbacher. The publisher has expanded the program to include the primary, junior high, and senior high levels.

Dimensions of Personality considers the whole child—his or her emotional and intellectual capacities. It is hoped that through this program children will come to understand their physical, intellectual, and emotional growth better. The program fosters interaction. Pictures, cartoons, text, "What's your opinion?" questions, activities—all seek to involve the children by provoking lively discussion and individual insight.

Special editions have been designed to provide teachers with classroom activities that they can use to initiate goal-oriented group responses. These activities are devised to open communication so that children can identify with the message of the text.

A brief review of the fourth-grade text gives an indication of the total thrust of the program. It is titled *Here I Am*. Individual topics include the following:

1. Are there two different kinds of "feeling awful"?
2. Are being awake and aware the same?
3. The five senses and what consciousness means
4. Recognizing and accepting differences in others

One activity at this level is especially fun for the children. They are asked to trace each other's body outlines on large sheets of butcher-type paper. Each child then fills in his or her own image with paint, crayon, and so forth. If possible, the finished products are hung where all can view them. Such an activity could well spark a unit entitled, *The Body I've Inherited*.

Teachers who have used these materials report that the enthusiasm of the children was high. Their enjoyment served as a challenge to consider additional ways to make their education a satisfying and rewarding experience.

Developing Basic Values

AUTHOR: *Rebecca Barnhart*
PUBLISHER: *Society for Visual Education, Inc.*
LEVEL: *Elementary*

Developing Basic Values has three major themes: (1) consideration of others, (2) respect for property, and (3) recognition of responsibilities. Each of the areas has a cassette audio tape, video slide tape, and teacher's guide and reading script. The material is best suited to general classroom use for the affective area.

(Contact) Maturity: Growing Up Strong

AUTHOR: *Editors of* Scholastic Scope
PUBLISHER: *Scholastic Book Services*
DATE OF PUBLICATION: *Copyright 1968; updated printing July, 1972*
LEVEL: *Eighth to tenth grades reading on a fourth- to sixth-grade level*

This program is designed to stimulate student interest in learning, reading, thinking, and expressing thoughts and feelings and to help the student read, speak, and write better. The program is designed primarily for use in a student-centered classroom in which the teacher functions as a catalyst. The program provides means for involving inattentive, passive, withdrawn children. It allows children to reflect on themselves and their social interactions with others while enhancing their expressive skills. Teaching materials include the following:

1. A teacher's guide containing suggestions for activities and presentation of the materials
2. An anthology containing short stories, poems, plays, letters, comments, and questions that are intended to motivate the reader to investigate his or her own feelings about what was read
3. A logbook of activities corresponding to the readings and providing an opportunity for subjective expression
4. Posters corresponding to the chapters in the anthology and logbook activities

This program can be used as a language arts program for the unmotivated child. It offers useful guidelines in the promotion of self-evaluative skills by way of role playing, discussion, and drawing and writing activities. The subject matter in the anthology deals primarily with the affective domain while interest in reading and learning is nurtured. The creative teacher will find this program an effective and productive tool.

Target Behavior

AUTHOR: *Roger Krothe*
PUBLISHER: *Select-Ed, Inc.*
DATE OF PUBLICATION: *1973*
LEVEL: *Can be adapted for use at all ages*

The *Target Behavior* kit is a diagnostic tool; it aims at selecting behavioral objectives that will improve the child's self-concept. This is accomplished by recording data of how the child perceives himself or herself (real self) and how the child would like to see himself or herself (ideal self). The kit includes two sets of 25 behavior cards; one set corresponds to classroom behavior and the other to home behavior. The child is presented with one set of cards and is asked to arrange them on the target behavior board under the column that best describes him or her (the real sort). The board is divided into the following nine columns: (1) most like me, (2) very much like me, (3) like me, (4) a little like me, (5) undecided, (6) a little unlike me, (7) unlike me, (8) very much unlike me, and (9) most unlike me. The columns are arranged in a normal distribution; allowing for just one response at either end of the distribution, the median response (undecided) allows for the placement of five behavior cards. This arrangement forces the child to be discreet in placement of the cards. When the child has completed this task, the number of the column in which each behavior card was placed is recorded. The cards are then removed from the board, and the child is asked to arrange them to show how he or she would like to be (the ideal sort). These responses are recorded, and the differences between the real sort and the ideal sort are calculated. These differences are then squared. Any squared difference of 16 points or more constitutes a significant discrepancy. These discrepancies are treated as target behaviors for modification. A formula is provided to show the correlation between the real and the ideal sortings. The higher the correlation, the better will be the child's adjustment. The manual also suggests administering a posttest to check the effectiveness of the behavior modification program.

Teachers can adapt *Target Behaviors* to any grade level by designing their own behavior cards that are appropriate for their students. This kit is a useful synthesis of the behavioral and self-concept theories. Its simple design makes administration easy for the teacher or parent. The behavioral objectives are those aspects that the child would like to obtain, thus making modification both motivating and relevant to the child.

The Coping with Series

AUTHORS: *Shirley Schwartzrock and C. Gilbert Wrenn*

PUBLISHER: *American Guidance Service, Inc.*

DATE OF PUBLICATION: *1973*

LEVEL: *Junior high and high school*

The Coping with Series comprises a set of informative, nonjudgmental books that focus on the interest, concerns, and frustrations of today's adolescents. The books are designed to stimulate thought and discussion on the related themes covered in the books. The set consists of 23 books and a teacher's manual. The teacher's manual contains objective procedures and activities for the presentation of the books, and it also contains a teacher and student bibliography.

The books are:

Facts and Fantasies about Drugs, which is a report of laws, uses, abuses, and effects of stimulants, glue, marijuana, LSD, heroin, and other hard drugs

Facts and Fantasies about Alcohol, which deals with how young people become acquainted with alcohol, its effects, and misconceptions about it

Facts and Fantasies about Smoking, which presents motivational factors concerning the risk and effects of smoking

The Mind Benders, which discusses the motivational determinants of drug abuse, an actual account of an ex-addict, and the problems of people who use drugs

Some Common Crutches, which examines the dynamics involved in the use of crutches in alleviating emotional problems

Food as a Crutch, which examines the dynamics involved in the use of food crutches in alleviating emotional problems

Alcohol as a Crutch, which conveys the physical, emotional, and social effect of alcohol dependency

Living with Differences, which deals with understanding and accepting differences in religion, age, nationality, and race

You Always Communicate Something, which examines the conscious and unconscious effects on communication and how to communicate effectively

Understanding the Law of Our Land, which describes what laws are, how they are changed, civil disobedience, and the arrest of a drug pusher

Easing the Scene, which examines the effect of one's self-concept on social interaction with others

In Front of the Table and Behind It, which describes the function, rules, participation, and leadership of group dynamics

Can You Talk with Someone Else? which discusses the need, importance, and method of effective communication with others

To Like and Be Liked, which conveys the importance, problems, and suggestions for improving relationships with others

My Life, What Shall I Do with It? which pertains to the importance of making well-thought-out decisions in planning for the future

Do I Know the "Me" Others See? which examines the importance of realizing self-worth and objectively assessing one's strong and weak points

Crises Youth Face Today, which explores problems that arise out of an inability to adapt to a rapidly changing world

Changing Roles of Men and Women, which takes the position that society's attitudes toward members of the opposite sex are changing as the entire social order of society changes

Coping with Cliques, which discusses the various types of cliques and the problems associated with being excluded from and being a member of a clique

I'd Rather Do It Myself If You Don't Mind, which deals with considerations one contemplates when making decisions

Living with Loneliness, which illustrates the feelings of loneliness and ways to deal with them

Parents Can Be a Problem, which discusses conflicting values of parents and teen-agers, problems with communication, and special problems that parents may have (alcoholism, divorce, being overly permissive or overly restrictive)

Grades, What's So Important about Them Anyway? which examines the importance of grades and their effects on the child

Each book contains illustrations, stories, and factual information to develop further understanding of its theme. The great variety of themes presented in *The Coping with Series* makes the series extremely adaptable to the needs of the pupil; these books can be of great value in stimulating thought and discussion in the classroom.

Additional materials are presented in the companion methods text by Swanson and Reinert (1979). Two recent publications of the National Information Center for Special Education Materials (NICSEM) are available to teachers. These are the index to mentally retarded, specific learning disabled, and emotionally disturbed, which includes over 10,000 media and material items, and the master catalog of special education information. The NICSEM materials are available form the University of Southern California, Los Angeles, California.

ADAPTED MATERIALS

Since formal materials for children in conflict are in short supply, teachers must call on their own ability to adapt standard materials for use with individual children. A few of the materials that have been adapted by teachers are described briefly. These are presented with the hope of stimulating teachers to use similar materials and to develop others.

Punching Bag. Children sometimes need to express themselves with inanimate objects. An old tackling dummy or other soft but durable object can be used for this purpose. The bag should be constructed so as to take abuse without breaking, even when kicked. The bag should remain stationary so that it will not "return" blows dealt by the child, which might cause more frustration.

Dartboard. A dartboard can provide a great deal of tension release. The child can put a picture of the teacher, a parent, or another child on the board as a target.

Soft Bats. Several varieties of soft bats are available for use with children (Fig. 10–1). These provide a safe tool for swinging, throwing, or even striking another person. An angry, aggressive child can express hostility in an acceptable manner with these soft bats, whereas the withdrawn child is provided with a safe outlet for expression of feelings.

Tape Recorder. The teacher of children in conflict must rely on a variety of educational

FIGURE 10–1. These boys are taking turns releasing their aggression on each other with soft bats. This is a fun way to release frustration in an acceptable manner.

techniques for delivery of information (Fig. 10–2). The tape recorder is one of the most useful. It can provide a nonthreatening tool for individualizing instruction, self-expression, and reinforcement. Recorders should be simple to operate and durable so that children can handle them.

Mats. Soft mats are useful in the classroom for protection of children during games, in self-expression activites, and in physical activities such as tumbling and wrestling.

Individualized Materials. Academic materials that are available in a variety of delivery formats and at several levels are essential for children who have emotional problems. These might include programed materials, materials that utilize more than one sense simultaneously, or materials that appeal to a wide variety of interests.

Materials for Therapeutic Play. A variety of materials are needed to develop individual skills. These might include rackets for lawn tennis, table-tennis paddles and balls, fly rods, basketball goals, handball equipment, and a place to swim, ice-skate, hike, and fish. Much of this equipment can be rented when ownership is impossible.

Quiet Areas for Study. Children in conflict often need a quiet area in which to work (Fig. 10–3). This area can provide children with the security they need when they feel out-of-sorts with the world or with a place relatively free of external stimuli when things become too much for the child to tolerate. A quiet area or office can be constructed from dividers that extend from the floor to above eye level. Generally these carrels should be individual, but some teachers have placed two carrels facing one another to save material and space.

Large Shatter-Proof Mirror. Many activities can center around a mirror: building self-image, getting a realistic view of the image one is presenting to others, and practical activities such as grooming.

Individual Diaries for Children. The keeping of individual diaries by children (if they wish to do so) can be a cathartic activity. Children must be free to say whatever they want to say without fear of teacher snooping and/or reprisals.

In addition to these adapted materials, the teacher should have ready access to the following teaching essentials:

Art supplies
Bulletin boards for displays
Chalkboards

FIGURE 10–2. Teaching machines are available to teachers in a variety of types and price ranges. These machines can help a teacher to individualize instruction so that he or she can interact on a one-to-one basis with children.

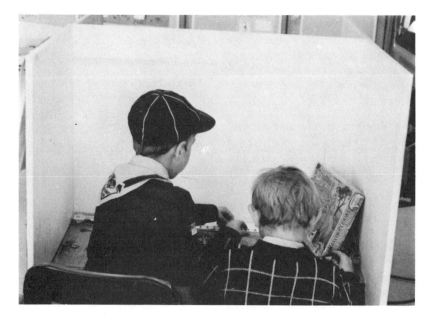

FIGURE 10–3. Large desks with plenty of space for one or sometimes two active children provide a roomy atmosphere for work. Enclosing these areas provides a measure of privacy.

Pencil sharpener

Shades to darken room

Lounge area for quiet reading (can be used in reinforcement)

Clock and 30-minute kitchen timers

Carpeting, at least in one section of the classroom

Telephone or other intercommunication system

Storage cabinets for materials, at least one drawer with a lock

Typewriter

Book shelves

Small conference tables for group work

Sink and running water, bathroom in primary classrooms

Time-out facility that can be shared with one other classroom

Large student desks with elbow room

Audiovisual materials including 16-millimeter projector, overhead projector, slide projector, phonograph, and cassette tape recorder and player

Portable chalkboard to use with small groups

Adequate lighting and ventilation

Stapler and other teacher desk supplies

Social Skills and Me

AUTHORS: *Crave and Reynolds*
PUBLISHER: *Crave and Reynolds*
DATE OF PUBLICATION: *1983*
LEVEL: *First through sixth grades*

The *Social Skills and Me* program is a curriculum guide consisting of 100 lessons to be used for individual and/or group instruction, in the classroom setting, for one hour each day. This program encompasses four skill areas:

1. Communication—the messages one sends to other people with one's voice and body.
2. Responsibility—acting appropriately and accepting responsibility for one's own behavior.
3. Assertiveness—polite ways of expressing opinions and standing up for one's rights.
4. Problem-solving—solving problems in ways that please oneself without hurting others.

Many activities, such as relaxation exercises, keeping a scrapbook, reinforcement time, "I Like Me," and individual student conferences are sugggested in the program. This program appears to be very helpful to teachers.

The Coping Series

AUTHORS: *Wrenn and Schwarzroch*
PUBLISHER: *American Guidance Service*
DATE OF PUBLICATION: *1984*
LEVEL: *Upper elementary through early senior high school grades*

The *Coping Series* program is designed to provide students with basic understanding and competencies to deal with the problems in the real world. The program consists of four major themes on coping, including:

1. personal identification
2. human relationships
3. facts and fantasies
4. teenage problems

TEACHER-MADE MATERIALS

In order for the teacher to meet the needs of the individual student, many materials will need to be teacher-made. Several important guidelines for this development have been suggested by Marcie Haloin, former director of the Learning Resource Center at the University of Northern Colorado in Greeley, Colorado.

1. *Objective.* Consider first and foremost the instructional needs of the students. After determining the objective, develop the material.
2. *Attention.* Make materials attractive in color, shape, or another factor to capture interest. Try to be neat since children do notice.
3. *Simplicity.* Keep materials relatively simple; avoid meaningless abstractions

and other extraneous elements, which can confuse or sidetrack the learner from the essential purpose of the materials.

4. *Progression.* Materials should be sequenced in short incremental steps.

5. *Repetition.* Through motivated repetition, learning is reinforced. Whenever possible, use a variety of methods to reinforce skills. Materials don't teach, teachers teach—materials reinforce.

6. *Completion.* Try to develop activities the children can complete or at least achieve some level of success at within a reasonable time period.

7. *Durability and reusability.* Whenever economically practical, laminate or cover materials with contact paper. Cover both sides when the materials will be picked up or held by students, as in card games.

8. *Student directions.* Include directions or rules on the activity or in the storage box. Even if students cannot read the directions, you may forget how to play the game and the rules will be there to remind you.

9. *Self-correction.* Materials should, wherever possible, be self-correcting. This will often save a great deal of time, as well as allow the students immediate reinforcement for correct responses.

10. *Storage.* Design materials with storage in mind. Often file folder games are easy to store and keep track of by skill. Keep a file with cross references of games you have developed and the skills they reinforce.

SOURCES FOR TEACHER-MADE MATERIALS AND ACTIVITIES*

Stik-a-Letter

These letters are paper and gummed to stick on games and so on. All letters come in black,

white, yellow, red, blue, and green. Each box contains up to 1,800 letters depending on the size and style of the letters. There are more of the higher usage letters and more vowels than consonants.
PUBLISHER:
ARBEC, Inc
3909 GN. I.H. 35
Austin, Texas 78722

Suction Cup Spinners

These sturdy plastic spinners are attached to a rubber suction cup base. They spin easily and are excellent to use on game boards, on the floor, on the wall, or on the chalkboard.
PUBLISHER:
Mafex Associates Inc.
111 Barron Avenue
Johnstown, Pa. 15906

Word Making Stickers

The Word Making Stickers come in a booklet containing 420 phonic-oriented picture stickers. They are a timesaver for the teacher who makes games and activities. Also available are Language Action Stickers. The stickers can be either self-sticking or gummed backed.
PUBLISHER:
Word Making Productions
60 West 400 South
Salt Lake City, Utah 84101

Creative Place Markers

Creative Place Markers are excellent for game use and are unique in that they adhere to the game board.
PUBLISHER:
Marie's Educational Materials
P. O. Box 60694
Sunnyvale, Calif. 94086

Vinyl Stick-On Letters

Excellent and easy to use, these stick-on letters are available in a variety of colors and

---

*Developed by Marcie Haloin, University of Northern Colorado Learning Resource Center.

-styles. They are a little more expensive than the Stik-a-letters.

AVAILABLE FROM:
Bachman's, Inc.
1303 8th Ave.
Greeley, Colo. 80631

UNC Bookstore
University of Northern Colorado
Greeley, Colo. 80639

Pencil Grips

These triangular pencil grips are made of a soft plastic and slip onto a standard-sized pencil. They are good to use in handwriting and lessons requiring much writing.

PUBLISHER:
DLM
3505 North Ashland Ave.
Chicago, Ill. 60657

Colored Cubes

The one-inch cubes are made of wood and can be used for building designs or for making dice.

PUBLISHER:
DLM
3505 North Ashland Ave.
Chicago, Ill. 60657

Plain Cubes

The plain cubes are made of wood and can be used for building designs or for making dice.

PUBLISHER:
Stephenson School Supply
3014 Logan Ave.
Loveland, Colo. 80537

AVAILABLE FROM:
P. O. Box 81207
Lincoln, Neb. 68501

Self-Adhesive Labels

Avery Stickers come in a variety of colors and shapes. They can be ordered in boxes of 500 to 1,000 depending on style. Ideal Stickers are gummed circles. Each package contains 500 in a variety of colors.

PUBLISHER:
Ideal School Supply Co.
Oak Lawn, Ill. 60453

AVAILABLE FROM:
Bratton's Office Equipment, Inc.
1303 8th Ave.
Greeley, Colo. 80631

UNC Bookstore
University of Northern Colorado
Greeley, Colo. 80639

Spinners

Plastic or metal spinners for make-your-own games.

PUBLISHER:
Creative Publications
3977 East Bayshore Rd.
P. O. Box 10328
Palo Alto, Calif. 94303

Dice

Standard dice in red, green, or white; blank dice with gummed labels; or numeral dice with numerals 1 to 6.

PUBLISHER:
Creative Publications
3977 East Bayshore Rd.
P. O. Box 10328
Palo Alto, Calif. 94303

SUMMARY

Programming for children in conflict is taking on a new look because of the remarkable advances in microcomputers and the associated software. While materials have always played an important role in the education of these special youngsters, the development of this valuable new technology has set the stage for dramatic new advances in the next decade.

In addition to the computer, there are a number of materials appropriate for use with various age groups. They are identified in this chapter. The number and quality of professionally prepared materials are increasing steadily; however, the affective domain is still in need of useful materials.

Chapter 10 concludes with a discussion of teacher-adapted and teacher-made materials that are effective with children in conflict.

BIBLIOGRAPHY AND MATERIALS REFERENCES

Aspen Software
P.O. Box 339
Tijeras, New Mexico 87059

Discount Software
6520 Selma Avenue, Suite 309
Los Angeles, California 90028

Hartley Courseware, Inc.
P.O. Box 431
Dimondale, Michigan 48821

Learning Systems
P.O. Box 15
Marblehead, MA 01945

Learning Well
200 South Service Road
Roslyn Heights, NY 11577

Lifeboat Associates
1651 3rd Avenue
New York, New York 10028

MicroPro International
1229 Fourth Street
San Rafael, California 94901

Muse Software
330 North Charles Street
Baltimore, Maryland 21202

Oasis Systems
2765 Reynard Way
San Diego, California 92103

Peach Tree Software
3 Corporate Square, Suite 700
Atlanta, Georgia 30329

RETOOL
1920 Association Drive
Reston, VA 22091

Sponsored by The Council for Exceptional Children; developing programs for teachers to modify curriculum and survival strategies for special teachers.

Ring King Visibles (diskette storage files)
215 West Second Street
Muscatine, Iowa 52761

Special Education Computerized Information System (CIS)
Department of Research and Evaluation
Dallas Independent School District
2517 S. Ervay
Dallas, Texas 75215

Special Net (National Association of State Directors of Special Education)
Offers a comprehensive system of personnel development (CSPD) bulletin board—a potpourri of information about personnel development efforts, resources and practices from around the country.

Swanson, H.L., & Reinert, H.R. (1984). *Teaching strategies for children in conflict.* St. Louis, MO: Times Mirror/Mosby College Publishing.

Sysdata International, Inc.
7671 Old Central Avenue NE
Minneapolis, MN 55432

INTERAGENCY COLLABORATION BIBLIOGRAPHY

Audette, R. H. (1978). *Primer on interagency agreements.* Chelmsford, MA: Audette and Gerry.

Baxter, J. M. (1982). Solving problems through cooperation. *Exceptional Children, 48,* 400–407.

Bennett, R. E. (1982). Applications of microcomputer technology to special education. *Exceptional Children, 49*(2), 106–113.

Elder, J. O., & Magrab, P. R. (Eds.). (1981). *Coordinating services to handicapped children: A handbook for interagency collaboration.* Baltimore, MD: Paul H. Brooks.

Ferrini, P., et al. (1980). Use of an unobtrusive measure for the evaluation of interagency coordination. *Evaluation Quarterly, 2.*

Flaherty, E. W., et al. (1978). Use of an unobtrusive measure for the evaluation of interagency coordination. *Evaluation Quarterly, 2.*

Greeman, J. P. (Ed.). (1980). *Interagency cooperation and agreements* (policy paper series: Document #4). Washington, DC: Office of Special Education (BBB18510).

Gromada, H. T., et al. (1975). *Working together for children: A neighborhood advocacy system.* Washington, DC: Bureau of Education for the Handicapped, Social and Rehabilitation Service, Department of HEW.

Guzman, T., & Wahrman, M. L. (1979, January). *Interagency cooperation: A process model for establishing interagency cooperative services agreements to serve secondary school students.* Washington, DC: Mid-East Regional Resource Center.

Helge, D. (1984). *A report regarding interagency collaboration to facilitate services for rural handicapped students.* Washington, DC: Office of Special Education (ED).

Johnson, H. W., et al. (1982). Interagency collaboration: Driving and restraining forces. *Exceptional Children, 48,* 395–399.

Regional Resource Center Task Force. (1979, August). *Interagency collaboration on full services for handicapped children and youth* (6 vols.). Washington, DC: Office of Special Education, Learning Resource Branch.

Schwann, J. (1980). Educating children with special needs: An interorganizational perspective on policy implementation. *Children and Youth Services Review, 2,* 387–402.

Semmel, D. S. & Morrissey, P. A. (1981). Serving the unserved and underserved: Can the mandate be extended in an era of limitations. *Exceptional Education Quarterly, 2,* 17–25.

Sheare, J. B. & Larson, C. C. (1978). The odd couple: Effective public schools/mental health joint programming to provide educational/therapeutic services to emotionally disturbed students and their families. *Psychology in Schools, 15,* 541–544.

BIBLIOGRAPHY

Adler, A. (1962). *The neurotic constitution: Outlines of a comparative individualistic psychology and psychotherapy.* New York: Dodd, Mead.

Beery, K. (1972). *Models for mainstreaming.* San Rafael, CA: Dimensions Publishing.

Beery, K. (1973). *Catalyst profiles and faces (experimental edition).* San Rafael, CA: Dimensions Publishing.

Bennett, R. E. (1982). Applications of microcomputer technology to special education. *Exceptional Children, 49*(2), 106–113.

Birnbrauer, J., & Lawler, J. (1964). Token reinforcement for learning. *Mental Retardation, 2,* 275–279.

Blanco, R. (1972). *Prescriptions for children with learning and adjustive problems.* Springfield, IL: Charles C Thomas.

Christopols, F., & Renz, P. (1969). A critical examination of special education programs. *Journal of Special Education, 3,* 379.

Coleman, J. (1966). *Equality of educational opportunity.* Washington, DC: U.S. Government Printing Office.

Council for Exceptional Children. (1983). *Software search evaluation form.* Unpublished manuscript. Reston, VA: Council for Exceptional Children.

Deno, E. (1970). Special education as developmental capital. *Exceptional Children, 37,* 229–237.

Despert, L. (1985). *The emotionally disturbed child: An inquiry into family patterns.* Garden City, NY: Anchor Books.

Dunn, L. (1968). Special education for the mildly retarded–Is much of it justifiable? *Exceptional Children, 35,* 5–22.

Glasser, W. (1965). *Reality therapy.* New York: Harper & Row.

Glavin, J., Quay, H., Annesley, F., & Werry, J. (1971). An experimental resource room for behavior problem children. *Exceptional Children, 38,* 131–137.

Glidewell, J. (1961). *Parental attitudes and child behavior.* Springfield, IL: Charles C Thomas.

Gluek, S., & Gluek, E. (1950). *Unraveling juvenile delinquency.* New York: The Commonwealth Fund.

Gresham, F. (1982). Misguided mainstreaming: The case for social skills training with handicapped children. *Exceptional Children, 48,* 422–433.

Gulotta, T. (1974). Teacher attitudes toward the moderately disturbed child. *Exceptional Children, 41,* 49–50.

Haloin, M. (1978). *Teacher-made materials.* Greely, CO: University of Northern Colorado.

Haring, N., & Phillips, E. (1962). *Educating emotionally disturbed children.* New York: McGraw-Hill.

Hewett, F. (1968). *The emotionally disturbed child in the classroom.* Boston: Allyn & Bacon.

Hofmeister, A. M. (1982). Microcomputer in perspective. *Exceptional Children, 49,* 15–121.

Jones, R. (1972). Labels and stigma in special education. *Exceptional Children, 38,* 553–564.

Jones, R. (1974). Student views of special placement and their own special classes: A clarification. *Exceptional Children, 41,* 31–33.

Karnes, M., Zehrbach, R., & Teska, J. (1974). Involving families of handicapped children. In T. Kelly, L. Lyndall, & M. Dykes (Eds.), *School and community resources for the behaviorally handicapped.* New York: MSS Information Corp.

Kirk, S., & Weiner, B. (Eds.). (1963). *Behavioral research on exceptional children.* Washington, DC: Council on Exceptional Children.

Leneway, R., & Montegomery, B. (1981). Rehabilitation and the handicapped programmer. *Computer, 14*(1), 49–53.

Levin, G., & Simmons, J. (1962). Response to praise by emotionally disturbed boys. *Psychological Reports, 11,* 10.

Levy, D. (1943). *Maternal overprotection.* New York: Columbia University Press.

Long, N., & Newman, R. (1971). The teacher and his mental health. In N. Long, W. Morse, & R. Newman (Eds.), *Conflict in the classroom.* Belmont, CA: Wadsworth. Mackie, R., Kvaraceus, W., & Williams, H. (1957). *Teachers of children who are socially and emotionally handicapped.* Washington, DC: U.S. Government Printing Office.

MacMillan, D. (1973). *Behavior modification in education.* New York: Macmillan.

Martin, E. (1972). Individualism and behaviorism as future trends in educating handicapped children. *Exceptional Children, 38,* 514–517.

Martin, E. (1974). Some thoughts on mainstreaming. *Exceptional Children, 41,* 150–153.

Menninger Clinic Children's Division Staff. (1969). *Disturbed children.* San Francisco: Jossey-Bass.

Meyerowtiz, J. (1967). Peer groups and special classes. *Mental Retardation, 5,* 23–26.

MicroSIFT. (1982). *Evaluator's guide for microcomputer-based instruction packages.* Eugene, OR: International Council for Computers in Education.

Morse, W., Cutter, R., & Fink, A. (1964). *Public school classes for the emotionally handicapped: A research analysis.* Washington, DC: Council for Exceptional Children.

Naiman, A. (1982). *Microcomputers in education: An introduction.* Cambridge, MA: Technical Education Research Center.

Noshpitz, J. (Ed.). (1973). Report of the Committee on Clinical Issues. In S. Lustman, *The mental health of children: Services, research, and manpower.* New York: Harper & Row.

Payne, R., & Murray, C. (1974). Principals' attitudes toward integration of the handicapped. *Exceptional Children, 41,* 123–125.

Peter, L. (1965). *Prescriptive teaching.* New York: McGraw-Hill.

Pfeiffer, S. (1982). The superiority of team decision making. *Exceptional Children, 49,* 68–69.

Powers, C. (1982). Mainstreaming the inservice education of teachers. *Exceptional Children, 49,* 432–439.

Rank, B. (1949). Adaptation of the psychoanalytic technique for the treatment of young children wtih atypical development. *American Journal of Orthopsychiatry, 19,* 130–139.

Reinert, H. (1968). *Decision making in the educationally handicapped and normal child: A comparative study.* Unpublished doctoral dissertation, Colorado State College, Greeley.

Shotel, J., Iano, R., & McGettigan, J. (1972). Teacher attitudes associated with the integration of handicapped children. *Exceptional Children, 38,* 677–683.

Smith, J. & Arkans, J. (1974). Now more than ever: A case for the special class. *Exceptional Children, 40,* 497–502.

Swanson, H. L., & Reinert, H. R. (1979). *Teaching strategies for children in conflict.* St. Louis, MO: C. V. Mosby.

Swanson, H. L., & Reinert, H. R. (1984). *Teaching strategies for children in conflict.* St. Louis, MO: Times Mirror/Mosby College Publishing.

Taber, F. M. (1983). *Microcomputers in special education: Selection and decision making process.* Reston, VA: Council for Exceptional Children.

Ullman, L., & Krasner, L. (1965). *Case studies in behavior modification.* New York: Holt, Rinehart & Winston.

Valletutti, P. (1969). Integration vs. segregation: A useless dialectic. *Journal of Special Education, 3,* 405–408.

Wallace, G., & Kaufman, J. (1973). *Teaching children with learning problems.* Columbus, OH: Merrill.

Weinberg, B. (1980). The Kurzweil Machine: Half a miracle. *American Libraries, 11,* 603–604.

Whelan, R., & Haring, N. (1966). Modification and maintenance of behavior through systematic application of consequences. *Exceptional Children, 32,* 281–289.

Woody, R. (1969). *Behavioral problem children in the school.* New York: Appleton-Century Crofts.

11

The Future

Several years ago I was debating the merits of investing in some rental property. Before going too far with my ideas, I contacted a professor of business who had a long, successful history of buying and selling real estate for rental. This man told me to consider three factors:

1. Location of the property.
2. Location of the property.
3. Location of the property.

It seems to us that it is the same perspective with which we must view the future of programs for children in conflict—that we can bet on economics, economics, and economics as the main determinants. Money is now the major driving force in developing and maintaining programs and will likely continue to be the crucial element.

THEORETICAL APPROACHES: FUTURE TRENDS

Biophysical Approach

The biophysical approach is the oldest of all current theoretical approaches. While many people do not accept the plausibility of biophysical forces, others, such as Barnard Rimland, have a strong belief that this theory will become the major force in the future study, identification, and treatment of those suffering from emotional disturbance. As technology in medicine continues to escalate there is the possibility of dramatic breakthroughs in this area. Particularly in the areas of evaluation and treatment, the biophysical approach will hold its own or possibly increase in popularity.

Psychodynamic Theory

Psychodynamic theory, known through the efforts of Sigmund Freud, began early in the 20th century and did not lessen in appeal until the mid-1970s when behavior modification surged into the vocabulary and practice of most special education teachers. Many psychologists, social workers, and teachers practicing today were trained with a major emphasis in this philosophy. Therefore, the psychodynamic technique is likely to continue to be used and may even increase in popularity as teachers begin to interface psychodynamic theory with behaviorism. Its use in the junior and senior high schools seems to be on the increase, particularly the techniques of catharsis and gaining insight through verbal interaction with teachers and other helping professionals.

Behavioral Theory

The behavioral approach became a dominant force in the education of children in conflict during the mid-1970s and reached its zenith within five years. Since that time, because of its usefulness, it has continued at a high level of popularity among teachers and support personnel working with emotionally disturbed children. No longer did the teacher have to rely on the word of the medical doctor or psychiatrist (as in the biophysical approach). Neither did the teacher have to follow the direct leadership of psychologists or social workers (as in the psychodynamic approach). The futures of youngsters helped with this technique appear bright, especially when we speak of the most severely disturbed and young children.

This method's popularity with those who teach adolescents and the more mildly handicapped seems to be waning; it will probably continue to be used with these groups, but only for purposes of observation and record keeping. It will likely be used with older students in conjunction with psychodynamic theory and biophysical theory. Behavior modification will become a standard method that is the teacher's option during any given situation.

Social Theory

Social theory came on the educational scene rather rapidly during the early part of the 20th century. In response to this theory, disturbed populations were isolated, segregated, and labeled. This strategy brought to these youngsters funding and specially trained teachers.

Social workers now have become an integral part of the team that supervises programs for the disturbed. Many school districts have social workers as part of the classroom staff. Their expertise in dealing with the social issues that surround the disturbed population has become readily recognizable. The future may bring classrooms staffed with the number of social workers proportional to teachers; perhaps 1 to 1.

Social workers are concerned with social issues within and outside the school. They work intensively with parents and significant persons in the child's environment outside of school. They help not only in the classroom with the staff, but also with parents and other helping professionals.

Ecological Theory

Of all the theoretical approaches, ecological thought offers the most promising future for disturbed children. As program planners become more sophisticated in working with disturbed populations, it is inevitable that a holistic approach will evolve to unravel the complicated problems of children in conflict. In the future we are unlikely to see classrooms of emotionally and behaviorally disordered youngsters being taught by a single teacher and a classroom aide. Collaboration will be commonplace with teachers, parents, social workers, psychologists, and a variety of other professionals working to provide a program for the child.

TEACHERS OF THE FUTURE

The heart of any program is the teacher. Current trends suggest that teachers will be expected to teach children who exhibit a wide variety of emotional difficulties, from mild to severe. Often these children will have additional handicapping conditions. In addition, certification is changing in many states, changes which will require more sophisticated training in shorter periods of time. These two factors could result in teacher burnout and cause even heavier loads to be placed on regular classroom teachers. Mainstreaming, particularly at the secondary level, will continue to be problematic for regular classroom teachers as more and more of them refuse to teach the moderately disturbed youngster. The future will require a larger number of special teachers who are trained more extensively in psychology and special education. And surely in these chaotic times we will continue to see many children identified as "in conflict."

Certification

Over the past two decades most states have developed certification requirements for all teachers of the emotionally disturbed. As the economy of various states has tightened, the tendency has been to "do more with less" or to broaden the certification base to include certification to work with more handicapping conditions. This trend will likely continue for at least the next decade.

Concurrent with this change in certification, many states are modifying general teacher education requirements. This change has come about largely because of the low grades given education by various educational commissions over the past three years. The typical response to the criticism that teacher trainees are inferior to other professions has been to limit or, in some cases, eliminate hiring those with merely undergraduate teaching degrees. Thus teachers of the future may have their initial degrees in one of the liberal arts areas, with some coursework in education. Additional master's degree requirements for specialized areas such as special education will force the student to take courses at the graduate level. Thus beginning teachers may be older and more mature than in recent years. Whatever the future brings, it appears that a shortage of well-prepared teachers of the emotionally disturbed will be a continued trend.

Support Personnel

The future of support personnel appears to be headed in two directions. Exemplary programs will continue to provide the necessary support staff to be effective with children. But those schools that are satisfied with providing just a classroom placement for disturbed children will not bother to any large extent with support personnel, primarily because of funding. As the economy continues to tighten, such poor programs will likely deteriorate to a very low level of effectiveness.

PARENTS

The parents of emotionally disturbed children are crucial to the education of their children. While teachers have always known and believed in the importance of parents' involvement in the education of their children, we have generally not had successful parent/school interactions. It is believed that future parent involvement will be less extensive but more effective. Rather than superficial involvement, parents want to help evaluate, select the curriculum, and assess the various techniques used. Parents are tired of their role as party giver, classroom aide, and bake salesperson.

ADOLESCENTS

Programs for disturbed adolescents have not developed in the number or quality we an-

ticipated at the time of passage of P.L. 94–142. There are several reasons for this disparity. First, we overestimated the readiness of educational programs to work with emotionally disturbed adolescents; second, administrators have been reluctant to commit resources over extended periods of time. P.L. 94–142 has the potential to require providing adolescents with service up to age 21. Administrators might prefer an option allowing them to program for teenagers only up to age 16.

It is a likely prediction that the most successful programs will be isolated rather than integrated into the regular classroom program. This is because teachers and other staff members at the secondary level are often oriented in a way toward performance that doesn't fit well with the needs of troubled adolescents. Successful programs will have strong support staffs, committed to working with this age group, using a variety of curriculum approaches: behavior modification, various psychodynamic techniques, biophysical interventions, and holistic interventions. Use of these techniques will require effective and continuing communication among staff members; adolescents are masters at dividing the staff into factions that make them ineffective in coping with these youngsters. Leadership will continue to come from *within* the programs, with school administrators generally keeping an arm's length from the special program. Work components of programs will become increasingly important; teachers will have a definite role in this work experience. Finally, we view the number of students served as remaining constant, with no large increases expected.

EARLY INTERVENTION

Early childhood education can minimize the effects of risk and lead to fewer manifestations of handicap in later years (McNulty, Smith, & Soper, 1983; Thurman & Widerstrom, 1985; Bailey & Wolery, 1984; Peterson, 1987). Since the inception of the Early Childhood Assistance Program of the Bureau of the Handicapped in 1968, many model programs for young children with special needs, including children in conflict, have been developed throughout the country. Those programs are the Infant, Toddler, and Preschool Research and Intervention Program in Nashville, Tennessee (Bricker & Bricker, 1976); the Down's Syndrome Program in Seattle, Washington (Hayden & Dmitriev, 1975); the Milwaukee Project in Wisconsin (Heber & Garber, 1975); the Ypsilanti High Scope Program in Michigan (Weikkart et al., 1971); and the UCLA Infant Studies Program (Bromwich & Parmelee, 1979).

With the passage of P.L. 94–142 in 1975 and P.L. 98–199 (the Education of the Handicapped Act Amendment of 1983), preschool incentive funds to local school districts can be utilized to support programs for handicapped preschoolers from birth to age 5. Furthermore, in October of 1986, President Reagan signed into effect P.L. 99–457 (the Education of the Handicapped Act Amendment of 1986). Under this amendment, Congress appropriated more incentive monies to local educational agencies with the expectation that all states will establish preschool intervention services for all eligible 3- to 5-year-old handicapped children by the 1990–1991 school year. In addition, Congress provided specific guidelines and new funds directed to services for handicapped infants and toddlers from birth through age 2 and their families, encouraging states to establish a system of coordinated, comprehensive, multidisciplinary, interagency programs. From the above-mentioned current movements, it is anticipated that early intervention for children with affective needs will flourish in the near future.

CURRICULUM

No drastic changes in day-to-day curriculum activities are anticipated, but there likely will be slight increases in emphasis on work/study and career development.

The late 1980s and early 1990s promise to be challenging times for those who teach emotionally disturbed children. The byword of programming, however, will be consolidation rather than expansion.

BIBLIOGRAPHY

Bailey, D., & Wolery, M. (1984). *Teaching infants and preschoolers with handicaps.* Columbus, OH: Merrill Publishing Co.

Bricker, W. A., & Bricker, D. D. (1976). The infant, toddler, and preschool research and intervention project. In T. D. Tjossen (Ed.), *Intervention strategies with high risk infants and young children.* Baltimore: University Park Press.

Bromwich, R. M., & Parmelee, A. H. (1979). An intervention program for pre-term infants. In T. M. Field (Ed.), *Infants born at risk: Behavior and development.* New York: Spectrum Publications.

Hayden, A. H., & Dmitriev, V. (1975). The multidisciplinary preschool program for Down's syndrome children at University of Washington Model Preschool Center. In B. Z. Friedlander, G. M. Sterritt, & G. E. Kirk (Eds.), *Exceptional infants: Assessment and intervention.* Vol. 3. New York: Brunner/Mazel.

Heber, R., & Garber, H. (1975). The Milwaukee Project: A study of the use of family intervention to prevent cultural-familial mental retardation. In B. Z. Friedlander, G. M. Sterritt, & G. E. Kirk (Eds.), *Exceptional infants: Assessment and intervention.* Vol. 3. New York: Brunner/Mazel.

McNulty, B. A., Smith, D. B., & Soper, E. W. (1983). *Effectiveness of early special education for handicapped children.* Denver: Colorado Department of Education.

Peterson, N. L. (1987). *Early intervention for handicapped and at-risk children.* Denver: Love Publishing Company.

Thurman, S. K., & Widestrom, A. H. (1985). *Young children with special needs.* Newton, MA: Allyn & Bacon.

Weikkart, D. P., Rogers, L., Adcock, C., & McClelland, D. (1971). *Cognitively oriented curriculum: A framework for preschool teachers.* Washington, DC: National Association for the Education of Young Children.

Glossary

Accountability. Making a person answerable to that for which he or she is responsible.

Adjustive resources. Resources of an individual child that can be used in solving various problems.

Acting-out behavior. Inappropriate behavior of an aggressive type.

Aggressive. Exhibiting an outgoing manner, either physically or verbally.

Anal-expulsive substage. A substage of the anal stage of psychosexual development in which the child derives gratification from the expelling of feces.

Anal-retentive substage. A substage of the anal stage of psychosexual development in which the child derives gratification from the holding back of feces.

Anal stage. The stage in psychosexual development lasting from approximately 2 to 4 years of age in which gratification is centered around the anal area of the body and the process of defecation.

Anomie. The conflict that arises between the approved goals of a society and the means provided by that society to reach those goals.

Ancillary personnel. Supportive personnel to the professional who holds the major responsibility for a given child.

Anticathexis. The process by which the ego uses its psychic energy to control the id.

Art therapy. A therapeutic process using the various visual arts as a vehicle of intervention.

Asocial. Not social; avoiding contacts and interaction with others.

Atypical child. Child who varies from a given norm to a significant degree.

Autism. Extreme withdrawal from reality and particularly from human relationships.

Baseline data. The data that are collected before behavioral intervention begins.

Behavioral theory. A theory that is concerned with outward, observable behavior.

Behavior modeling. The imitation of others rather than trial and error for behavior and attitude formation; can be used to learn behavior or to induce new behaviors to take the place of undesirable behaviors.

Bibliotherapy. Use of stories to help children overcome conflicts in their lives.

Biochemical diseases. Disorders of the body related to its chemical make-up.

Biochemical factor. An element relating to the chemical make-up of the body.

Biogenetic disorder. A severe behavior disorder that results from the physical-chemical environment.

Biophysical theory. A theory concerned with the constitutional, genetic, and chemical factors that affect the life of the individual.

Catalyst. The name of a particular democratic method used for developing a cooperative effort among administrators, teachers, and children to meet the educational needs of exceptional children.

Cathexis. Use of mental energy to further the needs of the individual.

Castration anxiety. In Freudian theory an unconscious fear of losing the genital organs, usually as a punishment for sexual desires.

Cathartic form of therapy. A form of therapy in which the individual talks out problems.

Child in conflict. The child who manifests behavior that has a deleterious effect on personal or educational development and/or the personal or educational development of peers. Negative effects may vary considerably from one child to another in terms of severity and prognosis.

Classical conditioning. The process by which a specific stimulus is given the power to elicit a response that it does not normally elicit; see *respondent conditioning*.

Classroom teacher. A teacher whose main responsibility is to teach basic educational skills.

Clinical exploitation of Life Events. The process of dealing with a crisis and the events surrounding it in a methodical way, taking as much time as necessary, so that the individual can see the relationships between the beginning, development, and resolution of the conflict.

Clinical psychologist. One who has studied behavior and the mental processes and who subsequently works in the evaluation and treatment of mental illness.

Conformists. Those who follow rules.

Conformity. As used by Merton, the acceptance of cultural goals and the institutional means to reach these goals.

Conscience. In Freudian theory the part of the superego that is morally critical of the behavior, actions, and values of the self.

Contiguity theorists. A branch of behaviorists who hold that the essential element in learning is the closeness in time and space of stimulus and response.

Contingency management. Manipulation of the environmental consequences of a behavior to achieve control.

Counterconditioning. Reinforcement of behaviors that are in conflict with undesirable behaviors.

Counter theories. Those theories that seek to change established procedures; they do not necessarily have common bonds among themselves.

Counter theorist. One who utilizes parts of the theories of more established approaches such as the psychoanalytical or behavioral theories but who adds components that change the original theory to a significant degree.

Crisis intervention. Intervention during a crisis in a child's behavior with emphasis placed on the crisis situation.

Crisis teacher. A teacher who is trained in the process of intervening in crisis situations with a child.

Defensive behavior. A term used by Carl Rogers to designate behavior that is traditionally labeled *neurosis*.

Delinquent. A child over the age of 10 years old who is legally guilty of breaking the law.

Deviant. An individual who breaks rules.

Diagnosis. A careful investigation of the facts in a situation with the purpose of deciding what the difficulty is so that it can be remedied.

Diathesis. An inherited predisposition.

Diathesis stress. An inherited predisposition coupled with environmental stimulation.

Discipline. To control behavior by teaching.

Disorganized behavior. A term used by Carl Rogers to designate behavior that is traditionally labeled *psychotic*.

Dizygotic twins. Fraternal twins, coming from two separate ova in the mother but at the same time.

Director of special education. The administrator of a special education program in a school district, usually working directly under the superintendent.

Dominant genes. Those genes that are expressed in the make-up of an individual even though paired with another gene that would have been expressed in a different way.

Due process. To follow a fair and equitable procedure.

Ecological theory. A theory that emphasizes the interaction between an individual and the environment.

Educational team. Unofficial team designed to help individual children.

Ego. A system within the individual that mediates between the demands of the id and the constraints of the world in which the individual lives.

Ego-ideal. In Freudian theory the part of the superego that comprises the aims and goals of the individual with emphasis on what the individual should be and do.

Ego pathology. Difficulty with language development and relating to people.

Electra complex. A stage in the development of a girl in which she attaches to her father and shows aggression toward her mother; this is usually an unconscious process.

Eliciting stimulus. When used by Merton, a stimulus that precedes behavior, and means the acceptance of cultural goals but not of the institutional means to reach these goals.

Emotional disintegration. A breakdown in the functioning of an individual's feelings or emotions so that he or she functions inadequately or erratically.

Emotional first-aid-on-the-spot. The process of dealing with a crisis and the events surrounding it as quickly as possible to facilitate immediate return to the reality situation.

Emotionally disturbed. Having severe disturbance of emotional processes.

Endocrine development. The development and functioning of the endocrine glands, mainly the thyroid, adrenal, and pituitary glands; these glands produce chemical substances that help to regulate body functioning.

Enuresis. Involuntary discharge of urine during sleep.

Erotic zones. Parts of the individual's body that are vested with sexual feelings.

Exhibitionism. Extravagant or unusual behavior designed to attract attention.

Fixation. The halting of psychosexual maturation at a particular point in development.

Genetic counseling. The process of studying the inherited characteristics of an individual and providing advice concerning probabilities of passing on particular characteristics or genes.

Genital stage. The stage of psychosexual development from adolescence in which a person achieves a mature sexual relationship.

Gestalt. The perceiving of a total object while at the same time observing its component parts and their relationship to each other.

High probability behaviors. Behaviors that the individual frequently chooses to do and that can be used as natural reinforcers, especially for low probability behaviors.

Holistic approach. An approach to children in conflict that emphasizes a variety of techniques.

Humanistic psychologist. A psychologist who has added a component of social theory to psychological models.

Hyperactive behavior. An excessive amount of physical activity and movement.

Id. The inherited system of instinctual energy that supplies power for the entire personality.

Incidence. Number identified.

Infantile autism. The inability of an infant to relate to people or things outside himself or herself.

Institutionalized personality. Personality type of an individual who has spent considerable time in an institution and consequently develops mannerisms and ways of relating to the environment that are artificial and strange to other people.

Intrapsychic conflicts. Conflicts that take place within the individual, arising from desires and demands of the various impulses and drives within the individual.

Interval reinforcement. Scheduling reinforcers at intervals, for example, one reinforcer for every three minutes.

Latency stage. The stage of psychosexual development from approximately 6 or 7 years of age to adolescence in which there is a slowing up of or resting from active psychosexual development.

Learning disability.   One or more significant deficits in the essential learning process that require special educational techniques for their remediation.

Learning disabled.   An individual who demonstrates a discrepancy between expected achievement and actual achievement that is not due to a sensory, intellectual, motor, or emotional handicap or to the lack of opportunity to learn.

Learning theory.   A system of basic beliefs concerning what causes learning to take place and by what process it takes place.

Legislative mandates.   Laws that require a definite action.

Libido.   Psychic energy supplied by the id that allows the total personality system to function; this energy is sexual, fluid, and displaceable.

Life space interview.   A cathartic technique used in crisis intervention in which the teacher talks through the crisis or problem with the child at the time it occurs.

Low probability behaviors.   Behaviors that will tend to disappear if not reinforced; they are behaviors seldom chosen by the individual.

Mainstreaming.   The inclusion of handicapped children in regular classrooms with nonhandicapped children.

Maladaptive.   Exhibiting an inability to adjust to the environment.

Medical model.   A method of approaching questions or problems that seek out causes.

Mentally ill.   General term that describes a variety of emotional problems.

Mentally retarded.   Describes a person who has subnormal mental development and functioning.

Mental health professionals.   Those professionals who help individuals to integrate themselves satisfactorily both within themselves and in relationship to their environment.

Mental hygiene.   Prevention of mental problems through various techniques designed to preserve mental health.

Microcommunity.   The smaller portion of a community that is the immediate environment of the individual.

Milieu therapy.   Of French derivation, a term used to mean the treatment by environment, generally treatment in an institutional or hospital setting.

Modified Z therapy.   Z therapy without holding or tickling.

Monozygotic twins.   Identical twins; those coming from one ovum in the mother.

Music therapy.   Using music to bring out feelings that would otherwise fail to surface.

Negative reinforcement.   The maintenance or increase of a particular behavior caused by a particular stimulus being removed.

Neo-Freudian theorists.   Freudian theorists who offer a newer view of the original theory established by Sigmund Freud.

Neurological impairment.   Damage to or some deficiency in the nervous system of the body.

Neurosis.   A partial disorganization of the personality.

Object cathexis.   The process of investing psychic energy to satisfy an instinct.

Occupational therapy.   A therapeutic process that uses manual activities to treat emotional problems.

Oedipus phase.   A stage in the development of a boy in which he attaches to his mother and shows aggression toward his father; this is usually an unconscious process.

Operant conditioning.   The process of reinforcing desired behavior with reinforcers that will cause the child to repeat the desired behavior again.

Oral aggressive stage.   A substage of the oral stage of psychosexual development in which the child experiences pleasure in biting activities; also known as the *oral sadistic stage*.

Oral dependent stage.   A substage of the oral stage of psychosexual development in which the child experiences pleasure in sucking activities; also known as the oral erotic stage.

Oral stage of development.   The earliest stage of psychosexual development lasting from birth to about 2 years of age in which gratification is centered around the mouth and mouth functions, such as sucking and biting.

Organic brain pathology.   A physical disorder of

the brain resulting in a disorder in normal functioning.

Overinhibited. Holding back normal self-expression in words, behavior, or emotions.

Pathology. Abnormal condition in behavior that stems from medical causation.

Pediatrician. A physician who has specialized training in the development, care, and diseases of children.

Peer counseling. Students counseling other students under supervision.

Perceptual causation. Caused by the way in which the individual perceives and interprets the stimuli that are present to him or her.

Perceptually impaired. Difficulty in perceiving objects or events as they really are; inability to interpret correctly what is seen, heard, or experienced.

Permissiveness. The practice of allowing the child to be free to express feelings completely.

Phallic stage. The stage of psychosexual development from approximately 4 to 6 years of age in which the child is preoccupied with sexual matters, centering around the penis or clitoris; it is in this stage that the child is working out sexual identity.

Phenylketonuria (PKU). A metabolic disorder found in infants who are lacking an enzyme that is needed to properly assimilate phenylalanine, an amino acid formed in foods containing protein. If untreated, it results in mental retardation.

Phobia. Uncontrollable fear of a pathological nature.

Play therapy. Making use of the child's natural world of play for therapeutic purposes.

Pleasure principle. The reduction or elimination of tension from the individual by the avoidance of pain and striving for gratification.

Positive reinforcement. The maintenance or increase of a behavior because a particular stimulus is applied.

Prelatency stages. The oral, anal, and phallic stages of psychosexual development.

Prescriptive educational programming. Educational programming based on individual educational needs, both psychological and academic.

Primary deviance. The initial rule breaking by an individual.

Primary socializing system. System comprising groups of people in the immediate environment and functioning closest to the individual.

Project Re-Ed. A project for the reeducation of emotionally disturbed children in which children are placed in a residential care unit that focuses on the educative process.

Projective tests. Psychological tests used diagnostically in which the material is so unstructured that the subject's responses will reveal something of his or her personality and conflicts.

Psychiatrist. A physician who has specialized training in the diagnosis and treatment of mental illness.

Psychic energy. Energy supplied by the id that allows the total personality system to function; this energy is sexual, fluid, and displaceable.

Psychoanalysis. A form of psychotherapy originated by Sigmund Freud in which a patient delves into the unconscious to become aware of the existence of and reasons for deep conflicts. Free association and dream analysis are used.

Psychodynamic theory. The study of the human person, recognizing the role of the unconscious.

Psychogenesis. Having originated and developed in the psyche or mind.

Psychopathic personality. The personality make-up of an individual who is unable to learn from experiences and does not experience normal feelings such as love or guilt.

Psychopathology. The study of mental illness with its causes, symptoms, and development.

Psychosexual stages of development. In Freudian theory the stages of libidinal maturation from birth to adulthood.

Psychosis. Severely disorganized behavior and personality.

Psychotherapy. The treatment of emotional disorders by psychodynamic methods.

Pull-out program. Taking children out of the regular classroom.

Punishment. In behavioral theory the removal of a positive reinforcer and the presentation of a negative reinforcer to decrease a specific behavior.

Puppetry. In this book refers to the use of

puppets to encourage communication that might not otherwise develop.

Ratio reinforcement.   Reinforcers scheduled according to a ratio of acts to reinforcers, for example, one reinforcer for every three acts.

Reality principle.   The modification of the pleasure principle by the demands of the external world.

Reality Rub-in.   The process of making a child aware of what happened immediately after a crisis situation and what the child's part is in the crisis situation.

Rebellion.   As used by Merton, the rejection of both cultural goals and the institutional means to reach these goals, with the substitution of new goals and new means.

Recessive genes.   Those genes that are only expressed in the make-up of an individual if they are paired with genes similar to themselves.

Reinforcement.   A method by which a stimulus increases or maintains a specific behavior.

Reinforcement theorists.   A branch of behaviorists who hold that the most important element in learning is what happens immediately after the learning.

Reinforcer.   A stimulus that results in the maintenance or increase of a behavior.

Reinforcing stimulus.   A stimulus that follows a behavior.

Resource room.   A classroom where children with special needs go for a part of the school day to obtain special help in learning areas or who go at times of the day when they need it; the amount of time varies from a few minutes to the bulk of the day. The specially trained teacher in this room works cooperatively with the regular classroom teacher.

Resource teacher.   When used in reference to children in conflict, a person who is a change agent to help children to establish more appropriate ways of interacting with those in their environment.

Respondent conditioning.   The process by which a specific stimulus is given the power to elicit a response it does not normally elicit; see *classical conditioning*.

Retreatism.   The rejection of both cultural goals and the institutional means to reach these goals.

Ritualism.   The rejection of cultural goals but the acceptance of the institutional means to reach these goals.

Satiation.   Allowing a behavior to continue until it stops voluntarily.

Schedules of reinforcement.   The rate at which reinforcers are delivered, regardless of the pattern.

Schizophrenia.   A form of psychosis characterized by withdrawal, hallucinations, and avoidance of human relationships.

School psychologist.   A psychologist who has studied the mental processes and behavior and specialized in how these concepts relate to children in a school setting.

Screening.   The process of selecting a small group of children from a much larger group for a specific purpose, such as diagnostic evaluation.

Secondary deviance.   Rule breaking that occurs after an individual is perceived as a rule breaker.

Self-contained classroom.   A classroom where children with special needs are assigned for the entire day and where the specially trained teacher has the responsibility for their educational program as well as for the behavior intervention process.

Snellen chart.   A chart to be hung on a wall that has letters or symbols in graded size and is used to screen out children with visual problems.

Societal reaction theory.   Another term used for labeling theory.

Sociological theory.   A theory of behavior with emphasis on human society, its needs, development, and organization.

Sociometrics.   The measurement of the interaction within a social group.

Sociopathic personality.   The personality make-up of an individual who has an extreme disregard and hostility for society and, in particular, for all organized segments of society.

Socially maladjusted.   Refers to an individual who has difficulty dealing with society and groups of people.

Socially nearsighted behavior.   A term used by Fritz Bedl to mean the inability of individuals to perceive what they have done toward creating their own problems.

Social reinforcers.   Nonmaterial rewards for desired behavior, such as praise or attention.

Social worker.   An individual who is trained in social worker techniques such as case work or group work and who holds an M.S.W. or D.S.W. degree.

Stanford-Binet Individual Intelligence Test.   An individually administered intelligence test that emphasizes verbal ability. It has norms for individuals from age 2 years through adult.

Subconscious.   Refers to both the preconscious and the unconscious.

Superego.   The norms and values of society that are taught to the child by the parents and significant others and are taken into the child's personality.

Symbiotic infantile psychosis.   The psychosis of an infant in which the parent figure and the infant are both disturbed and dependent on each other and who mutually reinforce the disturbance and dependence in each other.

Symptom estrangement.   The process of letting go of inappropriate behaviors.

Tangible reinforcers.   Material rewards for desired behavior, such as candy or tokens.

Teacher counselor.   A teacher who has specialized training in the teaching of emotionally disturbed children and whose emphasis is shared between educational tasks and dealing with behavior.

Therapeutic play.   Play activities that are structured so that maximum therapeutic benefits can be gained.

Therapeutic team.   A team of individuals who work together cooperatively to plan for and service an individual child who has special needs. The make-up of the team is varied and might include classroom teacher, school psychologist, school nurse, social worker, speech therapist, special education teacher, and psychiatrist.

Therapist teacher.   A teacher who is trained to work with the behaviors of children in conflict while maintaining an educational program for their continued learning.

Time-out room.   A room away from the regular classroom where no reinforcement is likely and where a child can go to recoup strengths.

Token.   A small gift that is a symbol of having accomplished something; also used as a symbol to be exchanged for some tangible object.

Total care facility.   An institution where individuals spend 24 hours a day because they cannot be maintained in their home or a home substitute and that attempts to meet basic needs for food, shelter, play, and education, as well as social and emotional needs.

Touch control.   The method of physically touching a child to affect the child's behavior and mental outlook.

Toxic psychosis.   A psychosis that results from the effect of chemicals and drugs on the individual. These might be produced by the body or taken into it.

Transference.   The process of transferring feelings and attitudes that an individual has toward important people in his or her life onto someone else, such as a therapist.

Tunnel vision.   Seeing only the part of the world in the individual's immediate area or interest area without being able to see the wider world surrounding it.

Uninhibited.   Without normal restraints.

Unsocialized.   Being unable to deal adequately with groups of people.

Variable reinforcement.   Random reinforcement after various numbers of acts or varying amounts of time.

Visiting teacher.   A teacher who gives school instruction to students who are unable to attend school for medical reasons.

Author Index

Subject Index